Michael Dues, Ph.D.

Senior Lecturer in Communication
University of Arizona

Professor Michael Dues, a veteran teacher and scholar as well as an experienced organizational consultant, teaches courses in conflict management, argumentation, and organizational communication. He has served as head of the Department of Communication at the University of Arizona; as chair of the Department of Communication Studies at California State University, Sacramento; and as president of the Arizona Communication Association.

Professor Dues received his B.A. in History from Bellarmine College (now Bellarmine University) in Louisville, Kentucky; his M.A. in American History from the University of Louisville; and his Ph.D. in Communication and American Studies from Indiana University. Midway through his 40-year career, he spent a decade serving as a successful full-time consultant, working with both public and private organizations on the human aspects of management. Professor Dues also served seven years as an ombudsman for the University of Arizona. In his work on conflict, he draws not only on academic studies but also on his broad experience as an administrator, consultant, and practitioner.

Professor Dues has been honored by the University of Arizona and Cal State, Sacramento, for consistently excellent teaching. He has also written for academic and trade publications. His books include *Boxing Plato's Shadow: An Introduction to the Study of Human Communication* (McGraw-Hill, 2001) and *The Practice of Organizational Communication* (McGraw-Hill Primus, 1999), both coauthored with his spouse, Mary Brown; and *The Pursuit of Probable Truth: A Primer on Argument* (Pearson Custom, 2009). ∎

D1625491

i

Table of Contents

Table of Contents

Table of Contents

LECTURE 24

SUPPLEMENTAL MATERIAL

The Art of Conflict Management:
Achieving Solutions for Life, Work, and Beyond

Scope:

Conflict occurs in all human relationships. Handled badly, it harms individuals, relationships, organizations, communities, and nations. Handled well, it helps identify and solve problems and build stronger, deeper relationships. Throughout human history, cultures, governments, tribes, organizations, and families have developed mores and rules for handling conflict with the intention of limiting the harm conflict can do and securing the benefits of stable and productive relationships. Why, then, are so many human conflicts handled badly? Can't we do better? Many of the rules and mores developed over time have been helpful, yet hardly anyone would claim that humans in general are good at managing conflicts.

Shortly after World War II, scholars and professional practitioners (mediators, counselors, ombudsmen, consultants, and attorneys) began a concerted effort to better understand conflict and develop better ways to manage it. In recent decades, social scientists have joined this effort. From Morton Deutsch's concept of "win-win," to Roger Fisher and William Ury's "principled negotiation," to John Gottman's study of conflict in intimate relationships, we will explore insights into the nature of conflict provided by these researchers.

In the first part of this course, we'll focus on understanding the nature of conflict, including the roles of perspective, emotions, goals, and power. We will study different conflict styles, some much more effective than others, and describe specific ways to manage conflict and negotiate agreements more successfully—with less damage and more gain.

We'll then focus on the two most common relational contexts in which conflict occurs and where it matters most—our close personal relationships and our work relationships. We'll look at the pivotal role of managers in dealing with conflict in the workplace and devote time to understanding how and where to get and give help in managing conflicts.

After considering the daunting challenges involved in confronting major moral and cultural conflicts, we will look at ways to better manage conflict's aftermath—after a "resolution" has been achieved—and at how to teach our children about constructive conflict management.

The primary aim of this course is to offer new insights into the nature of conflict and the challenges and opportunities conflicts present, including an appreciation of the serious scholarly efforts to find more effective ways to manage conflict. As you move through the course, you'll learn practical tips, tools, and techniques to better handle conflict in your personal and professional lives. ■

Why Conflict Management Matters
Lecture 1

Conflict is going to happen; it's going to do damage. We surely have reason to handle it as well as we can in order to minimize the damage that we do.

Scholars and professionals have been studying **conflict management** intensely since about the mid-20th century, and they've generated some new thoughts based on research that can help us understand what's going on in a conflict, elements that we may be juggling as we deal with conflict, and what specific things we can do to get better results from conflicts. Note, however, that there is no easy recipe for managing conflict.

We begin with some dramatizations that help us define the term "conflict." **William Wilmot** and Joyce Hocker give us a long version of this definition in their textbook *Interpersonal Conflict*: "an expressed struggle between at least two interdependent parties who perceive incompatible goals, scarce resources, and interference from others in achieving their goals." A shorter definition of conflict might be that it is a "discomforting difference." The Wilmot and Hocker definition has most of the five elements that are always present in a conflict: (1) interdependence (meaning that the behavior of one party has an effect on the other), (2) difference, (3) opposition, (4) expression, and (5) emotion.

Why do we need to handle conflict better than we do? First, we want to avoid the harms that can come from conflict, and second, we want to reach the benefits that can come from it. To avoid the harms that stem from conflict, we have to face the "Four Awful Truths": (1) Conflict will occur; it is inherent in human interaction; (2) conflict always involves some risks and costs; (3) the damage that occurs in conflict results not so much from the conflict itself but from the dysfunctional strategies that we use to deal with it; and (4) some of the damage that occurs in conflict is irreversible.

Of course, there is also a positive side to conflict. It brings to the surface problems that we didn't see before, which can be especially useful in organizations. Going through conflict deepens our understanding of one another and enables us to improve our relationships.

Later in the course, we'll talk about examples of successes in resolving major conflicts, such as the Camp David Accords that led to the 1979 peace treaty between Egypt and Israel. Another way we have achieved success in handling conflict is through research. In fact, conflict management is a major area of research in psychology, sociology, communication, and organizational management. Some of the questions that have been explored include the following: In order for one party to win in a conflict, does the other party have to lose, or do the two parties have to compromise to keep one from losing? What are we really after when we engage in conflict? If we want to reach a good resolution, what should we focus on in negotiating?

Keep in mind that there is also a positive side to conflict. It brings to the surface problems that we didn't see before, which can be especially useful in organizations.

It's important to note that when we try to change the way we think about or behave in a conflict, we're not writing on a blank slate. The fact is that we started learning to manage conflict early, and those lessons do not just go away because we've done some research or listened to a lecture. We learn to deal with conflict from our culture, from our families, and from organizations. Probably your first lesson in managing conflict came from your family, when you were in your "terrible twos" and you decided to try out saying "no" for the first time. You've been learning to manage conflict ever since.

Some of what we have learned from our families, our culture, and our organizations works well, but some of our ideas about conflict and the ways we deal with it are misguided. For example, it's not true that if you're in a love relationship, you shouldn't have conflict, or that the person you're having a conflict with is your enemy; conflict most commonly occurs among couples, family members, friends, or colleagues. Some people think that "winning" a conflict requires having more power than the other party. But the only power two parties need in a conflict is a sufficient degree of interdependence to make it worth each person's while to work things out. Finally, it's not true that conflicts are just communication problems. Communication is almost always essential in resolving conflicts, but it's rarely a solution in itself. ■

Name to Know

Wilmot, William: Author of *Artful Mediation* and co-author of *Interpersonal Conflict* and *Innovation: The Five Disciplines for Creating What Customers Want*. Wilmot serves as a teacher, consultant, facilitator, and coach.

Important Term

conflict management: Any and all actions people use in dealing (or not dealing) with a conflict, including resolution.

Suggested Reading

Lakoff and Johnson, *Metaphors We Live By*.

Wilmot and Hocker, *Interpersonal Conflict*.

Assignments

1. Identify where, when, and how you learned your most compelling early lesson about dealing with conflict. What was that lesson?

2. Think of two or three examples of conflicts you have experienced.

Why Conflict Management Matters

Lecture 1—Transcript

I'm Michael Dues. I teach in the Department of Communication at the University of Arizona, and I've been studying conflict and working with it professionally for about 35 years. As a teacher and a scholar at the University, I study it, I teach a course in it. I also spent a little over a decade as a fulltime management consultant working with organizations mostly dealing with their conflict issues. So I come at it from those two angles, both as a scholar and as a professional, and of course I've been living for a long time, so all of us deal with conflict. Over time everybody encounters conflict, and we learn lessons about managing it as we go along.

Scholars and professionals have been studying the management of conflict very intensely since about the mid 20th century, and they're still working at it. What they've generated are some new thoughts, some new understanding, and they've really based that on some good, credible research. So we've got stuff to build on as we think about how we might handle conflict better.

What we can do through this course is help you understand what's going on in a conflict better, help you understand the elements that are involved with it that you may be managing and trying to juggle as you deal with the conflict, and also giving you very specific things that you can do to get better results managing it. I do want to suggest that managing conflict is not the kind of thing that we can just give you an easy recipe. This is not a "gee whiz" course; this is not here's five quick ideas that I can use, and if I follow this formula I will always get a good result.

Conflict is really a fine art. It's among the most challenging and difficult things that humans do, and it involves a lot of subtleties, and every single situation is different. So we can get better at it. We can understand it better, and each of us has to do it within our own personality in an authentic way as being who we are. But we're not going to give you simple recipes in this course. We are going to give you insights, and we're going to give you lots of suggestions of things you can do, and we'll give you some specific processes that you can follow as kind of outlines that will tend to get better results as we go through. In the end I think you'll understand better, and I think if you go with us through this course that you'll be able to handle your conflicts better.

One other thing about this course that I want to tell you right in front here is that it's not just a lecture course. When we're talking about conflict and ways not to handle it and ways to handle it, we have to think about how people would do and talk in conflict situations, so it really helps here to add some dramatizations to use as examples to show you what conflicts look like in practice that you can test your own self against, familiar scenes, common things that happen in conflicts, things not to do, things to do. We can show you tools and illustrate them with dramatizations so that you can have tools and techniques for ways to talk about it in language for handling conflict better.

That's what we're going to be doing in this course. Let's begin here with some definitions and getting ourselves clear on what a conflict really is. The best way to begin actually is not with the definition itself, but with some of those examples, which we can do as dramatizations. Let's start with one here. Let's think about a person named Rebecca who is in graduate school. She's studying in her room. She has a roommate in an apartment that she's staying in in this graduate school, with Jane as a roommate. Jane is a working person, and Jane has had friends over. They've been watching TV with her while Rebecca has been studying in her room.

[Video start.]

> **Jane**: Okay, pizza's on me next week. See you guys!

> **Rebecca**: Hey Jane, I'm trying to study for a test tomorrow! I can't even hear myself think!

> **Jane**: I'm Sorry, I thought you had classes on Wednesdays. I didn't even know you were here. Why didn't you say anything?

Rebecca: I shouldn't have to say anything! How many times do I have to tell you I've got class on *Tuesday* and *Thursday* nights?! Maybe you're just going to have to check with me before you bring anybody over.

Jane: Are you my mother now?

[Video end.]

Classic example, two good people, Jane and Rebecca are probably friends. They see this thing differently. Jane has her interests and needs. Rebecca has hers, there's a clash about this. Two good people, ordinary, everyday, classic, common conflict. All right let's look at another example.

Let's go to a married couple for this one. We'll call them Ken and Kate. Ken is thinking he'd like to take a job in another city, perhaps out west. How does that conflict develop?

[Video start.]

Ken: Honey, take a look at this.

Kate: Sounds like a great job—but it's in Denver!

Ken: Yeah—You know how much I want to get out west. And I think it's the perfect next step for me. I've already applied for it.

Kate: You have to be kidding! You didn't even ask me about this before applying?! I can't leave Chicago right now, I have a real career here! Why should I go somewhere else and start over? Go to Denver if that's what you want, but it won't be with me.

[Video end.]

Ken and Kate love each other. They're married to each other. He's got a longing to get somewhere else that's emerging through this thing and she's got a career here that she's very tied to and stressed about at times, and it's not something she's ready to give up. That's a very classic conflict and in these days of two-career couples that's not the least bit uncommon. So that's the second example of a conflict.

Now let's go to a third. Where could we go for a third? Let's go to work. Don is a salesman. He doesn't like the boundaries of his sales territory. He's driving too long in one direction, spending too much time in the car. He's a little unhappy about that so he's got a conflict with his manager who assigned him this territory. So he's going to talk to his manager.

[Video start.]

> **Dale** [on phone]: I'm sure we can rework those numbers and get those to you by close of business. Promise. All right, no problem, thanks.

> **Don**: Hey, Dale. Look, we need to talk about the new territory you've assigned me. It's just not working for me.

> **Dale**: What's the problem?

> **Don**: You've got me driving all over the place. I'm spending all my time in the car and not enough time with customers. Pat's got way less driving and more potential customers. It's just not fair.

> **Dale**: Look, Don, there are good reasons for the decisions I make. The last thing I need is you questioning whether I'm fair or not.

[Video end.]

Dale is feeling a little unpleasantly challenged here, isn't he? He knows he can't please everybody, and he's feeling challenged because he knows that Don has a bit of a reasonable complaint, but Don has kind of gone over the top challenging him. That's not a terribly uncommon conflict that could happen at work in a variety of situations.

If you think about these examples, think about them in your own life. Do these look or do things like this look familiar to you? They certainly do to me and they certainly do to many of my students. They're just common conflicts that occur. If we can recognize those conflicts, now the definition when we lay out a specific definition will make pretty clear sense to us.

Let's do two definitions. We'll do the long version and the short version. For the long version, let's go and look at Wilmot and Hocker's definition. William Wilmot and Joyce Hocker do a textbook called *Interpersonal Conflict,* and I've used that textbook for years and years and years. I rely on them a lot, and I always rely on this definition of theirs for a conflict. But it's the long form. They say a conflict is "an expressed struggle between at least two interdependent parties who perceive incompatible goals, scarce resources, and interference from others in achieving their goals." That's a long definition. We'll unpack it here in just a few seconds.

Let's get a shorter definition first. The short definition is my own, and the only thing I'm proud of about it is it's so nicely short. I can reduce it to two words. It's a "discomforting difference." We can say that a conflict is a discomforting difference. That is a difference that bothers one party or the other. For the person it bothers, that conflict, that difference constitutes a conflict. Mine is easier for in the moment, in the heat of the situation. Theirs is better for doing the research that we need to do to understand fully what's in a conflict.

The Wilmot and Hocker definition is very good about having most of the elements that are always present. In mine they're just sort of clearly implied. So let's add a little description here. Let's talk about the five elements that are always present when there's a conflict no matter what definition we use. First element was there and it was present. It was present in the definition of the words that Wilmot and Hocker used. They called the parties "interdependent." The parties in a conflict need to be interdependent or there will not be a conflict. Interdependence is factor number one.

By interdependent what we mean is that the behavior of one has an effect on the other. Rebecca and Jane are interdependent with one another. How they behave in that apartment, how each behaves affects the other. How the territory is assigned affects Don. Whether Ken applies for a job out west and takes a job certainly affects Kate and whether she refuses to go affects him. All these parties are interdependent. You don't have conflicts with people that you're not interdependent with.

Second one, difference. There's got to be a difference, at least in Wilmot and Hocker's terms a perceived difference, that really is going to bother somebody. So that element is always there. There's some difference that the parties are going to be unhappy over, at least one of them will be unhappy.

Third element, there will always be some sense of opposition. Wilmot and Hocker in their definition phrased it as "frustration of the goals." The other person seems to be impeding them. Other writers describe it in a slightly different way, but it's always some sense of opposition that's present that one party at least has when that party is feeling a conflict.

There's a fourth element here. The thing has to be expressed. At least the researchers are very careful about this. We don't mean to be talking about, and this course is not about, just the internal conflicts that I feel, I'm drawn this way and that and so I'm having trouble making up my mind. It's conflicts between people, and we can't see that conflict. We can't look at it, we can't deal with it between people until it gets expressed in some fashion. Somebody has got to act in a way; some psychologists call it a behavioral manifestation. I'm in the communication field so I like the term it needs to be expressed. Expression is the fourth of those five basic elements.

There's a fifth basic element and that's emotion. There's always some level of feeling, and it's a negative emotion that's involved whenever there's a conflict. It's most typically some level of anger. It may be extreme, it may be not, but there's always some level of emotion involved, negative emotion, and that's one of the things we'll have to deal with and one of the things that makes it hard to deal with conflict and manage it.

There are two other terms I want to define for you really quickly here as we get started. We use the term "conflict resolution" a lot and we also use the term "conflict management." It's kind of interesting in the first years that I was studying this subject all the way through the `60s and `70s and into the

'80s. The 1980s researchers talked about studying conflict resolution, and we titled our courses "Conflict Resolution." We don't call it "resolution" so much anymore. We're more happy with the term "conflict management" because there's a difference in what these mean.

If it's "conflict resolution" it means we resolved the conflict, but the truth is that many, many conflicts are never going to be resolved, and they're still going to have to be managed. So the term "conflict management" is a broader term. It refers to the whole business of what we do to deal with the conflict. Ideally we resolve it, that is a mainstream part of it, but it's not the whole story of conflict management.

Why do we need to handle conflict better than we do? There's two ways to look at this. One is how to avoid the harms and reduce them, and the other is how to reach the good things that can come from it. When I talk about avoiding the harms, I like to talk about what I call the "Four Awful Truths" about conflict. The four awful truths go this way. Number one, conflict will occur. Conflict is inherent in human interaction. We're all alike in many ways, but we're all different in ways. We have different perceptions; we have a lot of common needs, but we also have different needs. Our timing is different. If we're interacting with somebody else over time, there's bound to be some conflict. So conflict is going to occur.

Second awful truth: Whenever it occurs, conflict always involves some risks and some costs. Consider those examples that we ran there. Jane and Rebecca can end up being hostile to each other and have a hostile living situation, or one might have to move out and have her life disrupted. Costs and risks: Don going to the boss could get in trouble. Ken and Kate could split up over this. There's risk involved and there's cost, there's pain and struggle thinking it through and time and energy taken. So there's always cost and there's always a risk whenever a conflict comes up.

Third major awful truth about conflict is that the damage that happens when there are costs, when there is damage done, the damage that happens results not so much from the conflict itself, the difference itself, but from what I call the dysfunctional strategies that we use to try to deal with it. By "dysfunctional" what I mean is it may get us a result that we wanted, but it will also get us a side effect that we didn't want. Dysfunctional strategies do most of the harm when we're involved in a conflict, not the conflict itself.

And the fourth awful truth is that some of that damage, some of it, is irreversible. Consider the examples again. Kate said if you move out there you're going out there alone. Ken might think boy she values this career more than I, and that could hurt him for a long time. Some of that damage might be irreversible; it often is. So we have to be careful in a conflict situation. Conflict is going to happen; it's going to do damage. We surely have reason to handle it as well as we can in order to minimize the damage that we do.

I want you to note that there's another reason here. There's the positive side. Conflict is also very, very useful. Conflict surfaces problems that we didn't see before. That's especially useful in organizations coming across problems when they arise, because conflict triggers our ability to recognize them. Going through conflict deepens our understanding of one another and enables us to improve our relationships and actually get them to a much deeper, more honest level than they were before. There are actually wonderful breakthroughs in honesty in closeness in relationships that happen as a result of working through a conflict well.

So conflict maybe painful. It's risky; it can do damage, but it can also be our friend in relationships including work relationships because it can also do us all a lot of good. So what we're looking for in terms of handling conflict better, being successful at it, is what we want to do is minimize any damage, even if we can't eliminate it and lower the costs, and we want to gain the gains that can come from it as best we can. Handling it better would mean some of both of those things.

I want to call it a success story the management of conflict and I mean that in a couple of different ways. One is we can have more successes with managing conflict if we do that. The other is we've had a lot of success in understanding it better. Let me just preview some examples. Later in the course we'll talk about examples of some successes in resolving major conflicts. Those three that we'll talk about later are one will be the Camp David Accords reached in 1978 that led to the 1979 peace treaty between

Egypt and Israel. That was negotiated by Anwar Sadat and Menachem Begin with the help of President Carter in the United States.

That treaty has never been broken between Israel and Egypt, the only successful negotiation that we really know of in the Middle East, a marvelous success story.

A second great success story was the Start 1 treaty—later had Start 2 and we've recently extended that—but negotiating that first Start 1 treaty between the United States and the Soviet Union in which they agreed to limit and reduce the number of nuclear weapons and missiles that they had and means of delivering weapons was a marvelous advance in the safety of the world. This was at the end of a Cold War or still in the middle of a Cold War between the United States and the Soviet Union.

The third one that I want to talk about is a solution that came between two governors in the United States of two different states, one of whom was very recognized as a liberal environmentalist and the other was very recognized as a staunch conservative, and the two of them sat down and worked out a set of principles for managing issues and conflicts when they come up for handling issues of environment. So that was a marvelous success story. We'll tell those. So there are successes and you probably have some in your own life. There are successes with the handling of conflict, even the big seemingly intractable conflicts.

There's another way in which we have success with handling conflict, and that's doing the research. I said since the mid 20th century there has been plenty of research. Scholars and practitioners have really worked at this. How can we get better? It's a major area of research in psychology, in sociology, in communication, and in organizational management, all scholars looking in all those areas trying to find better ways.

Here are some of the questions that they've gotten better answers to. Here's one: In order for me to win in a conflict, does the other party have to lose or do we have to compromise in order to keep somebody from losing? It turns out, and we'll talk about this in Lecture 3, but most of the time no we don't have to compromise and no, no nobody has to lose. We can actually both win. That's where the term win-win comes from, and we'll describe that in Lecture 3.

Here's another question: What are we really after when we engage in conflict, and how do we understand that? Why is it in connection with that that we sometimes get what we think we fought for, but we do damage to the relationship in the process so that our victory turns out to be a net loss? We have a lot better understanding of our multiple and complex goals in conflicts now, and we'll talk about that in Lecture 6. Good scholars have produced good answers that help us with that.

Here's another question: If we want to reach a good resolution in terms of all of the goals that we might have, what should we focus on in negotiating, how should we go about that, how should we proceed? We begin to deal with that in Lecture 10. We have some very good answers to that kind of a question.

So we've got successes. We got examples of success. We've got success that's in our own life, large scale, small scale, we've got good research that's successful in getting us better answers. So we have some. We can learn new and better ways to handle conflict.

But I want us to stop and be careful here a little bit because it's not as easy as just oh yeah let's do it differently now and we'll do it better, because we're not writing on a blank slate when we try to change the way we think about or understand or behave in a conflict. The fact is we started learning to manage conflict early, and those lessons are not just going to go away because we've researched this or listened to a lecture or done some reading.

We've been learning to deal with conflict from our culture. We learn in our organizations, and certainly we learn in our families starting very early in our lives. Just think of some examples of that just briefly here. There's a difference in how cultures approach conflict. One obvious one that gets cited very often is the difference between Asian cultures and Western cultures in these terms. What the Asian cultures do is they're much more concerned with the overall context, with protecting one another's face, and they can be very slow to deal with things, and they're not very direct in coming at you with a conflict. You're supposed to understand the context.

In Western cultures, and especially in the United States and in Australia and to a somewhat lesser extent in Canada, we tend to be much more about getting in your face. We want to talk about it right away and we want to get this resolved, and those are cultures that formed with people who migrated from somewhere else. They were getting started in a new land. They were transient; they were newly getting together, and they needed to get this resolved now. So you can see why the cultures would be different. But the cultures teach us things about how to handle conflict.

Yet to a somewhat more specific level, all of our organizations that we belong in and we live so much of our lives in, organizations are like families too, all of us who work live much of our lives there. Each organization develops cultures about how to handle conflict and so do professions. The example that comes to mind for me with that is kind of my own university settings where you have faculty. When faculty get in a conflict, we tend to be fairly dysfunctional about that. We're all trained and acculturated to be individual thinkers, to make our case, to put our stance out there. So we tend to argue, and we're not very good at thinking in terms of what the other person sees. We want to argue everything out. It's just what faculty do.

Another example would be the kind of organization where you've got to be tougher than we are, and there are some where people say things like around here like we don't get mad we just get even. There are organizations where that's the culture and that's the way they think.

Deeper than all of that, deeper than that, is the family structure. We all learned early in life about conflict and how to handle conflict and what it means and what happens if we handle it in a given way. We learned it in our families starting when we were very young as toddlers. That age that parents tend to call the terrible twos. There was that first moment when you as the little toddler tried out saying no for yourself. You'd heard your mom and dad say it, and at one point you looked up and tried it and you looked up to one of those people and you said no. How that person reacted was probably your first lesson in managing conflict, and you've been learning it ever since.

So we learned in the family. And what we did learn, the lessons we learned, led to behaviors that we adopted and we got habitual at it and we got skilled at it. So our early learning drives an awful lot of the way we deal with conflict. Then we go choose organizations where we can apply those skills; it all fits within the culture, so we're not people who come to conflict like it's a new subject. We're people who come to the subject of conflict management having learned it early; we've got built-in ideas. Some of that learning really works well. We're getting along; we're not killing each other; it still amazes me that humans do as well as we do with managing conflict, although we could do a lot better. But some of the ideas we've got and some of the ways we're dealing with conflict turned out to be wrong ideas.

Let's just think briefly of some examples of wrong ideas for handling conflict. Here's one, pretty common. Conflict should not be occurring; we're not supposed to have conflict with each other if we're a good team and we work together, or we're a couple and we love each other or whatever, we shouldn't be having a conflict. It's not supposed to happen; that's wrong. The truth is that conflict will occur in every one of those situations. Conflict is going to occur with people we're interdependent with. So it's going to happen.

Here's another wrong idea: When conflict does occur, the person I'm having a conflict with is my enemy. Wrong, we know now that that's just not the case. Conflict occurs most commonly among couples, among family members, among friends, among work colleagues, the people we happen to be interdependent with, and they're very likely to be the people we should least want to think of as our enemies and people we think we shouldn't be having conflict with.

Here's another wrong idea about conflict: Some people think that winning requires having more power than the other party. That one especially comes up in work settings. Supervisors would often say to me you know I can't deal with him I don't have the power to fire him. You don't need that kind of power over somebody. The only power we need in a conflict to have good odds at getting resolution is enough interdependence from the other party, enough influence on outcomes for the other party so that it's sort of worth their while to take the time to work the thing out with us. There doesn't have to be more power or even equal power with them.

One more wrong idea; this one I hate the most. It's the one that says if we could just communicate better we could resolve all our conflicts. Conflicts are just communication problems. Wrong, it's not true. Communication is essential to resolving conflicts almost always. But it's rarely a solution in itself. Just communicating better might just make it clearer that we had more difference than we thought that we had. So that's a wrong idea. Communication we need, but it's not a solution to every conflict, and it wouldn't avoid other conflicts that are going to occur.

So those are wrong ideas. Those wrong ideas get built into the language we use to talk about conflict, the metaphors with which we think about conflict. If we use a metaphor like battle, "we had a clash over that," if we're thinking in that way about conflict and using that language, it's driving us in a direction that's going to make it harder for us to actually resolve the conflicts that we have. We're burdened with some wrong ideas along with the good lessons we learned for handling conflict, and we'll try to get that better in this course.

What have we learned then? Just here in Lecture 1, we've got a definition of conflict. The short one is that conflict is a discomforting difference. It's a difference that bothers one party or the other. We learned that there are key elements that are in that conflict, in every conflict, interdependence of the conflicting parties with one another; a sense of opposition between the parties, some kind of expression of the conflict has to take place. There are negative emotions always present in the conflict. Those factors are always present.

We learned how to deal with conflict early in life, and that gets reinforced in our organizations and throughout our whole culture so we're not writing on a blank slate. Still we can learn to think about conflict differently; we can understand it and ourselves in a conflict better, and we can learn better ways to manage it.

So let me give you an assignment before we get to Lecture 2. Here's what I'd like to ask you to do, and I'm going to give you an assignment at the end of each lecture and ask you to try it because I think it'll help build in the learning. Here's the one for Lecture 1. Try to identify where, when, and how you learned what you think of as your most compelling lesson about conflict. It's probably an early lesson; the most compelling early lesson you learned for how to deal with conflict, and then try to describe for yourself what that lesson is and what it leads you to do typically when you're handling conflict. That's part one of the assignment.

Then I'd like you to do this: I'd like you to dream up some examples of conflict in your own life that you're familiar with that you can sort of test what we say throughout the course again. Think of two or three examples of conflict in your own experience that you're familiar with, so that as we go along and give insights and suggest ways of handling, you can test those and think how that might've worked in those conflicts. That's you assignment.

Where do we go from here? I've given you the idea in this lecture that we've only been talking about since the mid 20th century and what we know about conflict, but we're actually going to need to start earlier than that. So here's what's going to happen. We'll skip to Lectures 3 through 14 what we're going to do is look at the nature of conflict, the roles that we have in it, perspectives in conflict, the emotions and goals, and we'll look at ways to handle conflict in general better. Then we'll do several lectures, 15 through 18, in which we'll talk about the most important relational contexts in which we have conflict, our close personal relationships and our organizational work relationships, and talk about conflict in those particular situations.

Finally we'll do several lectures where we talk about things like where to get help, how to manage the aftermath after dealing with the conflict is over, how to teach our children about conflict, management of where we go from here in the future. That'll pull the course together. But you notice I started that with Lecture 3 through 14. That's that problem of the mid 20th century. Before we can come to our modern times and research on conflict, we have to go back and we have to think about the most important single discovery in the management of conflict in human history. Arguably the most important discovery that was made, and that was a discovery made by the ancient Greeks about 2,500 years ago and it's called the adversary system. That's what we'll do in Lecture 2.

The Adversary System
Lecture 2

You're not going to escape the adversary system unless you're a very rare individual in the developed world. We can all be expecting to be involved with it sooner or later, in the court as a plaintiff or a defendant or, certainly, as a juror.

We need to understand the **adversary system** for two main reasons. First, we can't escape it. Across the developed world, we engage in processes to resolve disputes, legal proceedings to settle court cases, and so on. If we want to be effective in getting some of our own disputes resolved, we must be able to use the adversary system. Second, there is a downside to the adversary system that we have to pay attention to, that is, the assumption that a conflict is a competitive event, that in order to have a winner, we must also have a loser.

In the cultures of the Greek city-states of the 6th century B.C., it was normal to go to war every spring and summer. Because the cost of such fighting was high in terms of lives, money, and property, the Greeks ultimately learned to substitute verbal combat for physical combat; some disputes were aired before a judge, who then made an award. Over time, this process was systematized. The citizens of Athens, having suffered the rule of several tyrants, decided that they would bring the adversary system into governmental decision-making; this was the beginning of democracy.

The Greeks placed a great deal of emphasis on human reasoning, and a cornerstone of the reasoning process used by the Greeks is known as the **principle of noncontradiction**. According to Aristotle, this is the idea that "a thing cannot be and not be at the same time." This principle bears with it a sense of reducing things to black and white. It's useful, but there's a limit to this kind of thinking.

As the use of the adversary system grew, **Sophists** emerged, who were originally teachers of **rhetoric** and debate. The Sophists believed that it is a good idea to test truth by having both sides argue against each other.

Plato and Socrates objected to this approach on the grounds that it seemed to privilege winning over finding the truth. Aristotle, however, said that it should be easier to argue a case if you're on the side of truth. The evidence should be better, and the reasoning should be clearer.

Portrait of Ancient Greek philosopher Socrates.

Over time, the adversary system has been refined and improved. We have professionals who are trained in using the system. We have standards for practice, for arguments, and for evidence. We use the system in courts, organizations, and the political arena. For all these reasons, we need to develop skills in argument.

One of the skills to master for effective argument is to understand **forensic reasoning**. This is the process of comparing the facts of a case against an established general principle, such as a law. Next, you need to learn to recognize the **issue** and, with it, the starting point for the argument. To find the starting point, think of what would happen if nobody brought up the argument. Richard Whately, a theorist of argument in the 19th century, articulated this idea as a "presumption in favor of the status quo." We presume that the status quo is acceptable unless someone persuades us differently by argument. For this reason, we assume that someone accused of a crime is innocent, and it falls to the government to prove the accused's guilt.

Portrait of Plato.

Another tip for effective **argumentation** is to consider the credibility of your evidence. Always ask: What is the source of the evidence? Do you have reason to accept the testimony of some person or institution as an expert on the issue? Is it possible that this expert is biased or has a conflict of interest?

Also, check your own logic; make sure the conclusions you draw flow solidly from the evidence. Of course, you also need to examine your opponent's logic; think about the possible arguments your opponent might bring up and how he or she might respond to your arguments. Finally, in some situations, you may need to get the help of a professional, such as an attorney.

Earlier, we said that the adversary system has a downside: It sometimes privileges winning at the expense of truth. The underlying assumption of the adversary system is that it's competitive, that in order to have a winner, we must have a loser. This assumption is costly, often in terms of relationships; for organizations, it may result in material costs. For this reason, disputants frequently try to settle matters out of court and legislative bodies try to work out a compromise before putting an issue to a vote. ■

Important Terms

adversary system: System of dispute resolution originating in ancient Greece, in which each disputant presents his or her claims and supporting evidence to a neutral third party, who then judges how the dispute should be settled.

argumentation: The study and practice of how people reach conclusions through logical reasoning, that is, making claims based on premises.

forensic reasoning: Observing and documenting the facts in a given case and deciding how the facts relate to an established standard or rule.

issue: A matter of concern that is unsettled or in dispute between two parties.

principle of noncontradiction: Aristotle's law stating that two contradictory statements cannot both be true at the same time; one of the two must be false.

rhetoric: The art of using language to communicate effectively. Aristotle defined rhetoric as the art of finding all the means of persuasion in any given situation.

Sophist: In ancient Greece, a member of a class of roving teachers of philosophy and rhetoric who taught their students to persuade or convince others.

Suggested Reading

Dues, *The Pursuit of Probable Truth: A Primer on Argument.*

Dues and Brown, *Boxing Plato's Shadow: An Introduction to the Study of Human Communication.*

Jacoby, *The Age of American Unreason.*

Assignment

1. Think about your own level of skill in argument. If you don't think you're very good at, take a course in argumentation or do some reading about it. Set an objective for yourself to strengthen your ability to argue rationally and follow through on it.

The Adversary System
Lecture 2—Transcript

Before talking about conflict management in the 20th century and 21st century, we need to go back about 2,500 years and talk about the invention of the adversary system by the Greeks in the 6th century B.C. That's this lecture, the adversary system. In it we'll explain what it is. We'll talk about the objections to it raised by Socrates and Plato that are pretty fundamental, and they're still with us today.

We'll talk about how Aristotle championed the idea that we should use the adversary system, that we should test what's most probably true by arguing back and forth in order to settle dispute and differences. We'll explain how that was the greatest single advance in conflict management in human history probably, how it vastly reduced the amount of violence, how it gave us great possibilities for democracy in court systems, but it also brought with it a downside that we're going to need to understand because it limits the way we handle conflict today.

I want you to think in terms of two main reasons why we need to understand conflict management. One, you can't escape it. It's still here today. We use it all over the developed world. We engage in adversary systems, processes in order to resolve disputes, settle cases in court, handle minor disputes, make democracy work. We're still using it, and so if you want to be a full participant and you want to be effective at getting some of your own disputes handled, you've got to be able to use the adversary system. That's one reason.

There's a second reason, and that second reason is that there's a downside to it, and the downside, which was sort of pointed to in those objections raised by Plato way back 2,500 years ago is that there is within it the assumption that a conflict is a competitive kind of event; that in order to get a winner, you have to get a loser, and that brings us some downsides we'll have to pay attention to.

We'll end the lecture by offering you some serious tips on winning arguments in an adversarial process. We won't go through a whole course on argument, but we'll give you some tips on how to do that. So let's begin. Go back now, let's go back to that 6th century B.C. and let's talk about how the ancient Greeks invented the adversary system.

The Greeks fought with each other a lot. It was normal in the cultures of the city-states to go to war every spring and in the summer, and then nurse their wounds and settle up who won what over the course of the winter. They fought with each other a lot, and it was damaging. It cost lives, it costs money, it destroyed things, and somewhere in there they began to realize that all this fighting is terribly costly, and somebody began to think there must be a better way.

We have no idea who actually thought of it first, but it began to be used in Athens and in some other city-states fairly early on in the 6th century B.C. and certainly once you got well into the 5th century B.C. What they started doing was substituting arguing with one another and then having someone judge who won, substituting verbal combat in a sense for physical combat. Here's what they're doing. They pick somebody that they trust to serve as judge, and then if you and I have a dispute, I argue my side, you argue your side, we present our cases to the judge, and the judge says based on those arguments here's who I think wins and makes an award, and they agreed that that was better than having us fight it out. It really was.

Of course over time, they systemized this. They began to do some very different things. Instead of taking cases to the oracle or dunking people in water to decide if they were guilty, they began to use presenting arguments and defending themselves to decide guilt or innocence. Then in ancient Athens they came up with Democracy using the adversary system.

Having been through a period where they had several really nasty tyrants in a row, one of those died, who was going to be in charge now. How were we going to do the government became a question, and instead of just having someone else rule absolutely, they decided for the citizens of Athens to meet in assembly, argue back and forth, and decide policies by vote. They brought the adversary system into decision making in government and in doing, invented democracy.

As they went about this the Greeks placed a great deal of trust and emphasis on human reasoning. They understood emotions as powerful human forces, stuff that originated among the gods that needed to be respected, but it needed to be dominated and controlled by reason. They really placed great stock in reasoning. A cornerstone of the reasoning process the Greeks used and gave to us is what we call the principle of non-contradiction.

As Aristotle put it the principle of non-contradiction says that "a thing cannot be, and not be, at the same time." If I'm a this I can't be a that. If it's here it can't be there. They sorted things into categories, and if something was in one category, then it was not in another, the principle of non-contradiction. If it's in this category, it's a contradiction to say it's also in that category. So we have to decide which it is. It kind of has a sense of reducing things to black and white, yes or no thinking. It's very, very useful, but there's a limit built into that, and that's going to be tied to this idea of competition that was involved.

As the Greeks began to do this, using the adversary process and developing it, they had their ways of going about it. Disputants in ancient Greece didn't have attorneys; they were required to present their own case. And you know what that did? It created a market. There were advantages in the wealth you could gain settling disputes, in the status you would have being persuasive in your arguments in the assembly. If you were skillful at arguing, if you could succeed at it as an adversary over someone else and get your way, there were advantages to that. So there was a market for this knowledge and skill.

There were teachers in ancient Greece who taught a lot of things. They were called sophists, and that translates roughly into professor or teacher in general, and sophists began to respond to the market by teaching rhetoric and debate. One of them Protagoras became known as the "father of debate" because he clearly articulated it's a good idea to test truth by having both sides argue one against the other to see what happens.

Plato and Socrates really objected to this approach. Articulated by Plato, this approach seemed to privilege winning over getting at the truth. So Plato objected. He took the position that this was wrong; we shouldn't do it this way. We shouldn't have people deciding this way, and we shouldn't be teaching people this because it privileged winning over truth, and truth was a more important value.

Aristotle, Plato's leading student, came along and said you know what I don't agree with that. It should be easier to argue the case if I'm on the side of truth. The evidence should be better. The reasoning should be clearer. It should be easier to make the case for truth, so yes we should go ahead and do this. Aristotle won that argument. Athens kept its adversary system.

Then the Romans, when they came along, bought into the adversary system and they built it into their teaching system. They built a system of education which built on what was called the "Seven Liberal Arts." One of those seven basic things that you had to know was rhetoric, that's how to argue, to make your case successfully in any adversarial process, so rhetoric was taught as part of basic education and it stayed through the Romans and into medieval times.

But Plato has remained very influential and in part that's because he wasn't just 100 percent wrong. Aristotle was right, but you know what, Plato wasn't absolutely wrong. Sometimes this system does privilege winning over getting at the truth. So in civilization today we still have our doubts about rhetoric in the adversary system and we have those doubts for good reasons.

We may have doubts, but given that we still employ, it we need to know something about how to argue because we're going to be likely to be involved in it. That influence of Plato and that suspicion is still around because that underlying flaw in the adversary system is still going to be present.

The adversary system has been developed and improved. What do we mean developed and improved? If you look around all over the world we have developed professions that can help and be trained and learn a lot about it. We've refined it and evolved it. We have standards for practice. We have standards for arguments, standards for being more sure.

We license and ensure the professionals who help us out. We've expanded it in terms of we just don't use it in court, but organizations use it. We have procedures that are quasi formal where we resolve things in grievance procedures and disciplinary procedures. So it has been expanded and it has been refined. You're not going to escape the adversary system unless you're a very rare individual in the developed world. We can all be expecting to be involved with it sooner or later in the court as a plaintiff or a defendant, or certainly as a juror. We're going to get there one day most probably.

In our organizations we're going to have to make cases, and all of us who live in democracies have got to listen to the politicians make their case and decide who's right, and we've got to make it a pretty good basis. Democracies can be pretty muddled. There are a lot of special interests; there's a lot of money. There's a lot of media.

We worry about our democracy these days, but politicians still have to make their case, and we still have to judge. I'm often comforted by what Winston Churchill said about democracy which went something like, "Nobody pretends that democracy is perfect … in fact democracy is the worst form of government ever invented except for all the others that have been tried." So that was democracy; that's what Churchill though, and that made very, very good sense.

We need to know about argument. We've got to evaluate arguments as a citizen, and then of course in business, we need to make accountable decisions and we need to make pitches for them. We need to know about argument for that. We're going to be involved. So you've got to develop some skill in argument.

As I said this is not a course in argumentation; this is a course in conflict management. There's a wonderful course in argumentation offered by The Teaching Company that's done by Professor David Zarefsky, but here I want to give you some tips. I can't leave this lecture without giving you some tips on argument, and there are six big ones as far as I'm concerned that if you could get those right, you're a long way down the road toward being pretty good at argument.

So let's start with tip number one. There's a process called forensic reasoning; that's a way that we think, and tip number one is understand forensic reasoning. You're going to have to use it to define terms, and you're going to have to use it to build and evaluate the arguments as you go. Here's how forensic reasoning works. There's always some general principle. In the case of court it's the law. The law says do not kill somebody. The law says don't go over this speed in a given traffic area. There's a law or a rule that's stated. It could also be in a more general sense outside of court as some stated general principle. So you've got to have a general principle that you're concerned with for forensic reasoning.

The other thing you have to have is facts, a set of facts about what actually happened. So what we're going to do in forensic reasoning is compare how the facts fit against the general principle. In criminal trials which is where most of us would be most familiar with that because we've at least seen it in fiction if we've never been accused of anything or even served on a jury, in a criminal trial what happens is there's a law which establishes that general rule, and what the prosecutor then needs to do is to go and prove, to document that certain facts took place. This individual did these things, those are facts, and then what we need to do is compare those documented facts to what the law says and decide whether they fit within the law or whether that action was outside the law. If we decide the action was outside the law, the jury decides the person was guilty in that instance.

So forensic reasoning, general rule, specific facts. How do the facts fit against that general rule? If I get the idea forensic reasoning, then I've got a nice start down the way toward being able to argue effectively. That's tip number one.

Let's go to tip number two. Second tip and it's kind of got a couple of pieces in it and I need to put them together. The basic tip is recognize the issue and with it recognize the starting point for the argument. We not only need to figure out what it is we're arguing about, but we also need to figure out who needs to make the case. So recognize the issue and the starting point.

Here's how that works. The issue is the thing that we have a difference over, the thing that's going to be decided. If it's a court case it's is John Doe here guilty of committing this crime. That's the issue that's being decided. If it's a policy issue, should we adopt this new law, pass this new law, the issue decided is should we pass this new law. That's the issue that's being decided.

But there is the question of the starting point, and I want to talk to you a little bit about that.

The starting point is really, if you think of it as what would go ahead and happen if nobody brings this argument up, if nothing is said, what is the case now? If the question of guilt in a court is being decided, the starting point is the person is innocent, if he's not arrested, if he's not accused, if the prosecutor doesn't prove the case, we'll still assume that the person is innocent. Well that's what we would've assumed if nothing ever came up. How do we recognize that starting point? I like to go back because I've studied this some and think in terms of the writings of Richard Whately who was the classic theorist of argument in the 19th century, and much of his thinking carries right through into our own time.

The way Whately put it was there is a "presumption in favor of the status quo." Status quo is just Latin for what we have now. We're going to presume that what we have now is okay unless somebody persuades us differently to argument. Presumption in favor of the status quo, the classic example in court of innocent until proven guilty really fits this. We choose to assume that a person in this society is innocent until the government proves that that person is guilty, because we really value not locking up somebody who might be innocent. So we say the defense doesn't have to prove innocence, doesn't even have to establish probable innocence. Defense just has to keep the prosecutor from proving the person is guilty.

The starting point in the argument in court is a person is innocent, okay. But that same starting point issue applies in any kind of an argument anywhere. Let's think of another example. Remember the example of the salesman back in Lecture 1 who had this territory that he wasn't happy with because he was driving these 40 mile stretches and he thought he was spending too much time in the car? The starting point of that issue is what the salesman's territory is now. There's a presumption in favor in Whately's terms of the status quo. What's the status quo? It's the territory he's got now.

If he wants to use an adversarial process, go make the case, make the pitch through argument for a change in his territory, it's on him to make the case, to show the boss with reasons and evidence why it would be better for the company to change that territory. So the burden is on him. In the court system we talk about it being a burden of proof. The burden of proof is on the prosecution because the prosecutor has got to prove a person is guilty.

Argument theorists these days instead of saying burden of proof, which is actually the term Whately used for all kinds of issues, what we more often say now is the "burden of persuasion." The burden of persuasion is on that salesman to make the pitch for making the change that he seeks in his own example in the territory. So that's tip number two.

Let's go to tip number three. I want to suggest that you make a very careful effort to consider the credibility of whatever serves as evidence when you identify what are the facts or even what's the principle you're trying to consider. This one we miss a lot today and it concerns me more and more in the age of the Internet when there's nobody really screening for us what's the probability that this person who is saying this on the Internet even knows what he or she is talking about, let alone is not biased. It's harder to evaluate the credibility of what passes for information.

But in the argument sense we really do need to evaluate the credibility of the evidence we're getting. What's the source of that evidence? That is a serious question I've got to ask. I've got to go back and say what is the source of this evidence? My first question about that source of evaluating credibility is do I have reason to believe this person or this institution knows what they're talking about. I might find that out by looking what's their expertise; what are their credentials; was that person an eye witness? But if I'm going to accept the testimony of a human being or an institution about a fact that's being contested, I can't just run that off of "they say so." I've got to decide do I have reason to believe what they're saying when they say so.

The first aspect of that is do I have reason to think they know what they're talking about. There's another aspect. I better stop and think should I suspect this person is biased on this? How objective would they be? Might they have a conflict of interest? What I'm looking for is someone who has got plenty of expertise, knowledge about a subject when they testify, and it could be an institution for that matter or that the information has been screened so that we know that it's somebody who knows and then it's reasonably objective.

That's an impossible standard in any absolute sense. Any human who knows much about a subject has got a bias about it. In reality as our knowledge of any given subject goes up, so does our interest in it, our bias, our connections with parts of it, or even attachment to things we might've said in public before, so as we become more expert so does our bias go up. They tend to go together. We really still need to have evaluated the credibility of the evidence presented in any argument, and that runs on expertise and degree of objectivity, and we want as much expertise and objectivity as we can get.

It's never perfect, but I ought to be able to make a judgment that yes this person or this institution can be trusted to make this claim that I'm taking as evidence. So that's tip number three.

Let's go to tip number four. Check your logic. We've all been learning to reason since we were little bitty kids. We can get much better at logic; we need to work on it always to get better at it, but here I don't want to suggest a whole set of technical things about logic. What I want to suggest is in this tip is that you check your own reasoning. What we tend to do when we're in an adversarial situation is we get all wound up about the point we're making; we believe our side. We've got some intensity behind that so we don't notice the little leaps that we're taking that don't really make sense.

We don't notice when we're going from two examples to a generalization about a whole category of things for instance, which would be called a hasty generalization. We don't notice that the conclusions we're drawing don't really solidly flow from the evidence that we've got. So what I want to suggest is, always check my logic, back up, get skeptical about my own thinking as I'm working out an argument. Don't just think hey wow that's a good argument because I'm excited about it. Back up, doubt it, check my own logic, and really try to see for myself if the reasoning that I'm following here really leads to the conclusion I'm drawing. That's tip number four.

Let's go to tip number five. It sort of flows off of checking my own logic. Let's consider what the opponent's logic might be. Tip number five is: Consider the arguments that my opponent, whoever is on the other side, might bring up. Those arguments would occur in two forms. One is it just might be their original argument about the case. I say here's my reasons for. They may say here's my reasons against. So their original arguments in whatever goes back and forth. I better consider what are all the possible arguments an opponent may bring up, and think about how I might answer those arguments. I need to have good answers to their arguments to win in an adversarial process, not just my own good argument.

I also need to think about what the opponent might say in response to my arguments. What might their answers be to what I'm saying, and I have to think about how I'm going to answer their answers, and get back to the conclusion that my argument was right to begin with. So I really have to do some work in advance, getting into an adversarial interaction and process, thinking about what the opponent's arguments are, and how I might respond to them, and how the opponent might respond to me, and how I might answer that to get us back to the conclusion that I gave you good arguments to begin with. So that's tip number five, consider what the opponent might say and how I'm going to answer it.

There's one more tip. Tip number six. No matter how good we might or might not get at this, there are times when we're going to need help, when we're going to need to get help. So tip number six is, when it's appropriate get the help of a professional. Use professionals when they're needed. Sometimes even when I'm dealing with someone on the other side that I may not see as a total enemy or whatever, I really want to consult and get the help from an attorney. There are other times when I want to get an advocate who really knows about a particular subject area.

So tip number six is just use professionals when it's appropriate. Don't hesitate. But with number six I say use professionals, be careful here, just like you're checking the credibility of what the evidence is. There's an enormous difference in quality between professionals. Pay attention and make sure you get a good one. Don't just get any professional, really try to get a good one. Paying attention to that and give that some attention, and maybe spend some extra money on it usually it's well worth it. So when appropriate get the help of a good professional.

Those are my six tips. We've talked about the adversary system. We've talked about how we need to learn it and use it, and we've got some tips for doing that. The adversary system was a great leap forward. That's clear, we've already said that; we've made that clear and we still need to use it.

What we haven't talked about yet in this lecture is the downside, and there is a really significant downside. Let's turn to that at this point. Plato and Socrates remember said that the adversary system privileges winning at the expense of truth. Why did it do that? It's not that they articulated it that way, but the way I would talk about it is there is this underlying big thing that is the adversary system is competitive. It assumes that it's always competitive, which did that.

We've noted that there's more to this downside, some attorneys are better than others; some actually *do* value winning over the truth, and courts do sometimes miscarry justice even when they're doing their best. So citizens have good reason to have doubts and suspicions about judicial processes and about politicians.

The deepest flaw though, the deepest flaw when it comes to managing conflict in the adversary system is the assumption that went right along with substituting verbal combat for physical combat. It's the assumption that it was combat; that it's competitive; that in order to get a winner, I'm going to have to have a loser. We inherited that assumption and we inherited it right along with the ability it gave us to resolve issues, and that assumption it turns out is costly.

When we resort to the adversary system, it's going to hurt us anyway. It may cost less than doing physical violence, but we can do a lot of harm to individuals and relationships. There's a lot of evidence these days about how much children of divorcing couples are scarred and damaged when that couple fights the divorce out in court and they're being fought over. Adversary process is very damaging. There's bystanders getting hurt in addition to whatever is being done to the couples.

The personal, the relational, and the material costs to organizations can be huge. It's striking to me that large organizations, and for that matter even insurance companies, will often write enormous checks, hundreds of thousands of dollars just to avoid having to go into court.

More things, way more things get settled out of court than in court, and it isn't always because that's just better, it's just very expensive to go fight it out. So they write checks and pay it off. Having recognized the problem, their efforts to mitigate it, attorneys and even prosecutors now will negotiate settlements without going to court to avoid it. Judges will very frequently order disputants to seek a mediated negotiation before actually litigating something in court, and that includes couples trying to get divorced.

In legislative bodies, instead of just arguing it out, debating, and then voting, lots of times they'll find it's more useful and constructive to sit down at a table across from one another and work something out informally together, and then go back and vote that in. It can have a downside too, but they're getting away from the cost of arguing it out. It's just too expensive. So that assumption of competitive brings upon this expensive, can be damaging sort of thing. That's an enormous downside we're going to have to get past.

So what have we learned about the adversary system then? Number one, we learned that the adversary system substituted verbal combat for physical combat. Number two, we learned that is the greatest single improvement in conflict management in human history. At least that's my judgment concerning that. It was just absolutely huge. We still need it 2,500 years later. If it has held up exactly that well, so we're going to be called upon to use it so you better understand the adversary system and you better have at least some skill in it in order to do well in society these days.

We gave you six important tips for doing that. One was understand forensic reasoning; two, recognize the issue; three, consider the credibility of the evidence carefully; four, check your own logic; five, look out for the opponent's argument and how you're going to respond to that; six, get good professional help when you need it. Those are the six initial tips.

We paid attention to the downsides. It does sometimes privilege winning over being right. It can be terribly expensive. It keeps us trapped in that assumption that it's competitive. That's what we learned about the adversary system.

Here's an assignment for you at the end of that one. Understanding and skill of argumentation really are essential. So here's what I want you to do. Think about your own level of skill in argument. If you don't think you're very good at it don't sell yourself short, don't get stuck in that idea that I can't think logically. All of us can and do, but every one of us can get better at it. So here's your assignment. If you're not really satisfied with your ability to argue, go take a course in it, read a book about it, do something to build that up. Set an objective for yourself to strengthen your ability to argue rationally in an adversarial process, and then follow through on that. That's the adversary system.

Where are we going to go from there? We're going to come back up 2,500 years. That assumption stayed unchallenged about competitiveness for 2,500 years until the mid 20th century when in 1948, a doctoral student raised the question: Does it have to be competitive? That graduate student was a guy named Morton Deutsch, and we're going to talk about Morton Deutsch and the concept of "win-win" in Lecture 3.

Morton Deutsch and the Concept of Win-Win
Lecture 3

One of the major goals of this course is to help us identify when conflicts are pure and to seek resolutions that are win-win solutions—true win-win solutions, not just compromises.

Over the course of history, the adversary system became less harmful, although it still rested on the assumption that conflict involves a winner and a loser. In the 17th century, for example, the Thirty Years' War taught Europeans the idea of religious tolerance. The 18th century—known as the Age of Reason—resulted in increased **negotiations** between nations rather than total destruction of one nation by another. But the assumption of competition in conflict wasn't seriously challenged until the mid-20th century with the work of **Kurt Lewin** and his student **Morton Deutsch**.

Lewin, a psychologist, developed a conceptualization of human motivation and behavior in groups called **field theory**, which works as follows: We see ourselves as being in a kind of field, or "lifespace." Other people are also in that field. Our motivation is our movement across the field to reach a destination on the other side. Other people in the field can either help or hinder us in that effort, and the way we interact with these people depends on whether we see them as allies or obstacles.

In the course of studying conflict among group members in the context of field theory, Deutsch defined conflict as: "a condition that exists when Person A makes a move that makes it harder for Person B to reach his goal." However, Deutsch noticed that in task-oriented groups with shared goals, most conflict arose over how to achieve the goals, not from the fact that one individual was blocking another's way in reaching an individual goal. Deutsch realized that conflict might be beneficial to groups in finding better ways to reach their shared goals. Findings from a related field, **game theory**, also showed that people tend to compete rather than cooperate in conflict situations.

Deutsch defined two kinds of conflict: competitive conflict, a situation that requires one party to lose in order for the other to win, and pure conflict, a situation in which both parties can fully win. An argument between the head coach and the offensive coordinator over what play to call in order to win a football game is a classic pure conflict. They both have the same goal; they're either going to win or lose together.

> **It's also a mistake to immediately resort to figuring out a compromise. You shouldn't chase "no win-no lose" when you could be chasing "win-win."**

The possible outcomes in conflicts are: (1) win-lose (competitive), (2) no win-no lose (that's a compromise or a tie, which is still competitive), (3) lose-lose, and (4) win-win. Deutsch found that most conflicts are pure conflicts, which means that we can pursue a win-win solution; both parties can negotiate, and neither has to lose. This idea has been the cornerstone of research in conflict management.

What are the practical lessons we can learn from Deutsch? First, whenever you encounter a conflict with someone with whom you have shared goals, try to identify the shared goals and see how you can help each other to reach them. Second, try to treat conflicts as problems or challenges that you can work on together with the other party to achieve a solution for both. Unless you really don't care about the other party, it's a mistake to engage in verbal combat, as if you're trying to win the game at the other party's expense. As we'll see in a later lecture, it's also a mistake to immediately resort to figuring out a compromise. You shouldn't chase "no win-no lose" when you could be chasing "win-win."

More than half a century since Deutsch's breakthrough, the idea of win-win still hasn't penetrated society to any great extent. Research has shown that humans are much more complicated than Lewin's field theory or Deutsch's concept of win-win fully recognized. You might try for a win-win solution and find that your views about what's going on in a conflict differ considerably from those of the other party. Further, in any given situation, we don't have just one shared goal; each of us has multiple complex goals, some of which we're not even conscious of and some of which may be in conflict themselves. Perhaps our greatest limitation in working toward win-win solutions is that each of us comes to the table with deep-seated ideas about conflict and powerfully ingrained strategies. Writing over the lessons we've learned since early childhood is an exceptionally difficult task for human beings. Throughout this course, we'll look at important research findings that will help us push back against those early lessons and reach new understanding about conflict. ∎

Names to Know

Deutsch, Morton: Considered the founder of modern conflict management theory and practice.

Lewin, Kurt: One of the pioneers of modern social psychology and applied psychology.

Important Terms

field theory: Theory developed by Kurt Lewin, which holds that human behavior is a function of both an individual's psychological field, or "lifespace," and the social environment at the time the behavior occurs.

game theory: A mathematical method for analyzing how people make decisions in situations involving competition and conflict. Involves choices in which each party may gain or lose, depending on the others' choices.

negotiation: A process of achieving agreement or resolving disputes through discussion.

win-win solution: A conflict solution in which the outcome is favorable for both parties.

Suggested Reading

Deutsch, *The Resolution of Conflict: Constructive and Destructive Processes.*

1. Work on getting past the *slogan* "win-win." Try to remember the last two or three times you heard or used the term. Consider whether the person using it understood the meaning of the term and used it accurately. If the term was used at less than full strength, what would have been the difference if both parties really understood the concept and sought to accomplish it together?

Morton Deutsch and the Concept of Win-Win
Lecture 3—Transcript

As we saw in Lecture 2, the adversary system invented by the ancient Greeks really did mark an enormous advance in human's ability to deal with conflict. It substituted verbal combat for physical combat, made it a lot less costly, and a lot less dangerous. But we also saw that that underlying assumption, that conflict is a competitive situation in which in order for somebody to win somebody else has to lose, that assumption stood for 2-1/2 millennia. It stood until it was seriously questioned in 1948 by a graduate student named Morton Deutsch, and Deutsch went ahead to seriously study that question, and he's the person who gave us the concept of win-win. The idea that in a conflict, yes most of the time we really can both win.

What we want to do in this lecture is to discuss Morton Deutsch's research and that great discovery of win-win, because that leads the way for the rest of what we're going to talk about in this course. So much research from there forward was about helping understand better how we can communicate and how we can do what we need to do in order to achieve true win-win solutions when we're in conflict.

Let's talk about Morton Deutsch's great discovery. First we need to go back and think a little bit about how they advanced the adversary system and made it less harmful without necessarily getting at that underlying assumption. There were a lot of these, but I just want to give you several kinds of examples from history.

In Western civilization, which is the civilization that I know best, so these examples come from the west, there are a number of interesting ones. One that's fascinating to me is that as a matter of this 30 Years War that occurred in the 17th century, Europeans sort of figured out that it might be better to tolerate religious differences, difference over matters of theology, than to fight and kill each over them. So they developed and began to understand the idea of tolerating difference, but that didn't really question the underlying assumption of competitiveness in the conflict.

There's another one a century later which was called The Age of Reason in the west, the 18th century. It's interesting to watch how nations fought wars with one another. They weren't so much into fighting wars to the death, to the destruction of the other nation. What they did was sort of rationally do a serious fight to the point where they had tested one another's strength and they could pretty well project how this was going to come out and who had the advantage. That was enough destruction, and once they had done that amount of fighting they sat down and did the verbal discussion and negotiated a solution based on the outcomes of those initial fights, without having to destroy one nation or the other, much better than mutual destruction or one trying to destroy the other.

But that assumption that conflict is competitive just stuck. That didn't challenge the assumption of competitiveness. It was only in the mid 20th century when that assumption got seriously challenged. So let's talk about that.

What happened was this. The discovery actually arose in the context of a number of social scientists trying to study how humans interact in groups. The lead scholar in that work was a very important psychologist named Kurt Lewin. Kurt Lewin is the person who developed for us a theory of human motivation that really has served as a foundation for a whole lot of understanding of human motivation in general and human behavior in conflict very specifically. The key concept there, the idea of interdependence really flows from this idea that Lewin had about how people behave and why they behave.

He called it "Field Theory," and Field Theory leads us to see the *interdependence* that's there in humans in the way we operate. Remember that term "interdependence" was right in our definition of conflict from the beginning. The way Field Theory works is this. We just conceptualize human motivation as follows. We see ourselves as being in a kind of field, or what Lewin called a space, some have called it a light space together. Other people are also in that field. Our motivation can be thought of as we're moved to get across the field to a destination on the other side, and the other people there can either help us and be allies in that effort or serve as obstacles in that effort.

The way we interact with other people depends on whether we see them as allies or obstacles in the pursuit of our goal which is to get across. That's a nice basic way to think about human motivation and how humans operate when we're functioning in groups. So that's the basic theory that was in play, that people were doing a number of scientific studies to try and figure out better how things worked. That's the context.

One graduate student working with Lewin was Morton Deutsch. Deutsch, when it came to the point where he was going to his doctoral dissertation, really wanted to zero in on conflict among group members. As he worked with it, his initial definition of a conflict was this. He said a conflict is "a condition that exists when Person A makes a move that makes it harder for Person B to reach his goal." That notion of goals and tying it to what we're doing in conflict gets carried through a great many, most researchers in conflict management since have done the same kind of thing. They draw upon that basic sense of Field Theory, getting through, the notion of being motivated by goals and think of conflict in terms of we might be getting in the way of one another's goals.

So that was there. It was there in the Hocker and Wilmot definition that we provided for conflict in Lecture 1. So he's doing that. Then Deutsch began to look a little more seriously at what is going on here and he noticed this aspect of goals and opposition in conflict in groups. He noticed that what appeared to be going on was that these group members would become obstacles to one another not so much in reaching separate goals, because the groups they were studying were what you call task-oriented groups, they had shared goals. Deutsch noticed that they seemed to have a lot, maybe even most conflict, over how to achieve their shared goals rather than conflict that arises from being in each other's way in reaching individual's goals.

It's a basic insight into how we're operating in groups. In that sense he was even thinking that maybe conflict could be beneficial. It could be an aid to these groups, to the group as a whole, in finding better ways to reach their shared goals. That led him to think more carefully about the nature of conflict. Now here he is working with this. In these studies that they were doing under Lewin, for the most part they were working and building their experiments using what's called "Game Theory." There is, by the way, a wonderful course offered by The Teaching Company by Professor Scott Stevens that's really a course on Game Theory. So they were working with that.

In Game Theory what happens is we treat life situations as if they're games in which individuals are trying to win. Then we set up these games and we see how that's going to work out. The classic game in game theory is a game called the "Prisoners' Dilemma" in which the players in the game are being interrogated, the prisoners are being interrogated, and they have to decide whether they want to cooperate with the interrogator or confess to having escaped. They can cooperate or they can cheat.

Points get awarded, and what happens is you get the most points if you cheat and the other person cooperates and the least points if you cooperate and the other person cheats. But if both of you cooperate, the two of you together end up getting more points. That's the basic pattern. So people are always assuming that they're competing with the other. The highest reward comes if you cheat and the opponent cooperates, but there's a lesser reward the way the game is set up if we both cooperate.

You might think about people in conflict and we tend to say well sure I'm a cooperative person, I try to do that. But if you translate our conflict situations and think about our real life situations, the fact is that we usually tend to compete. That's the first impulse and it goes with that assumption that was there. If you think back to Lecture number 1 and we have our married couple Ken and Kate in an argument over Ken's idea of taking a job out west, or the roommates who are at odds over noise in the apartment in another example, in those situations the tendency would be to compete first. It's that sense of opposition that I talked about when I talked about those basic elements that are present in a conflict.

What Deutsch noticed was that this assumption of competitive seemed to be an assumption. It may not be so competitive, and he wondered whether it always applied or how often, what percentage of the time it really applied. How many occasions might it be that the assumption should be the other way around, that we should work cooperatively. So he moved forward in his thinking that way.

Then he defined two kinds of conflict. He defined what he called competitive conflict as a competition, a competition in which it requires someone to lose in order for the other to win. It's a situation in which you can have nobody wins and nobody loses, such as a tie, but a situation that in order to get a winner requires a loser. Then he defined what he called "pure conflict" and in a pure conflict, he said that would be a situation in which both parties could actually fully win.

Let me give you an example of a pure conflict, what that would look like. Let's think about football. Let's do American football in this instance, and if you picture a scene and a situation in a game where there are only two seconds left on the clock, the home team in this game is behind by one point, and the home team has the ball on the opponent's 30 yard line. They are in range to score and there are two ways to score. They might kick a field goal or they might throw a pass to the end zone and try to score on that. It's a close call at the 30 yard line. It's long for a field goal; it's also long for a pass.

In this situation let's suppose that the head coach and the offensive coordinator, the coach who coaches the offense and usually calls the plays, have a disagreement over what kind of play to call. Should we try a field goal here or should we try a pass, and they're arguing on the side line. They've called time out and they're arguing on that. We have a conflict between these two coaches. That, in Deutsch's terms, is absolutely a "pure conflict." These guys both have the same goal; the goal is to win the game. Each of these two, if they're sensible coaches at all, would much rather be wrong and win the game than right and lose the game. They've each got the same goal; they're either going to win together or they're going to lose together.

That is what Deutsch would call a classic pure conflict. The possible outcomes in conflicts might be viewed as "win-lose," that's competitive; "no win-no lose," that's compromise or a tie, that's still competitive. I want you to see that. Compromise is still assuming it's competitive. You could have a "lose-lose." That happens in conflicts where nobody wins whether it's competitive or not, and then you have the possibility of a "win-win," what Deutsch called pure conflict, both parties truly winning. It's Morton Deutsch who's going to give us this term.

What Deutsch found when he set up his own studies and began to see how this worked in groups when they had conflict is that most of the time the conflict really was a pure conflict, hence the pursuit of "win-win." It's Morton Deutsch who gives us this term. What he means is not just we can negotiate and nobody has to lose. He means that most of the time both parties in a conflict can actually, actually win.

Let's take a moment to think about any conflict you've witnessed or engaged in recently. Do you think the parties involved in that conflict automatically saw it as purely competitive or even basically competitive or did they at first see it as a pure conflict, the way Deutsch showed us was actually possible; most of the time we think competitive first. We go with that impulse that it's an oppositional situation. One of the major goals of this course is to help us identify when conflicts are pure and to seek resolutions that are win-win solutions, true win-win solutions, not just compromises, and not to compete and require somebody to lose when we have to, because that's where the research has driven us, and we really do have better ways to do that.

So building on this concept where did Deutsch go in his career, you know what, that was a wonderful discovery initially, a very important doctoral dissertation that he did. He spent the rest of his academic career doing research on conflict management and helping us understand better how and when we can achieve win-win solutions. As I said, that's going to be our focus in this course as well, and that was the focus of most of the research that followed. So that's why we call Morton Deutsch the father of the modern study of conflict management because he gave us this basic concept, and the rest of us looking at it had been following that path of trying to better understand and better show how we can get win-win resolutions, the preferred outcome in most conflicts. It's the cornerstone idea for this course that we're going to follow because it's the cornerstone idea of the research that has followed Morton Deutsch.

That breakthrough of his was arguably the greatest single advance in conflict management since the adversary system 2,500 years earlier. That term "win-win" really did enter common parlance, you hear it all over the place, and it's often used by persons who don't have any understanding of what it means or whose understanding is vague and really not clear. I'm going to try to make sure in this course that you really do understand it and that you see it repeatedly as we go along, and that you can apply it to get the gains that can come from doing that.

What are the practical lessons we can learn directly from Morton Deutsch even before we get to the additional research that comes? The first one is this. Whenever we encounter a conflict with someone we care about, have to work with, might have shared goals with, what it might be a very good idea to do is really try to communicate and understand one another in terms of those goals so we can identify the shared goals and what we have in common or the goals that each has that we could help each other with. That's drawing on that basic understanding of interdependence, Field Theory that comes from Kurt Lewin, and the idea of win-win that's coming from Morton Deutsch.

Secondly, it suggests that what we ought to be doing is learning to treat conflicts as a problems or challenges that we can work on together with the person we feel we're in conflict with and trying to achieve a solution for both parties; that that's the way we ought to frame what's going on in our minds and work to achieve a true win-win resolution. I'm going to offer you a lot of advice and specific steps and suggestions over the rest of this course on how to do that, but Deutsch shows us that that's what we ought to be trying to do.

Unless we really don't care about the other party, don't mind risking losing, it would be a mistake to do combat verbally on a game that we're really trying to win at the other party's expense, at least as a first option that's not where we should go. It would equally be a mistake to immediately resort to trying to figure out compromise where I'm going to give up something and you're going to give up something. We shouldn't be chasing "no win-no lose" when we could be chasing a "win-win."

That's a direct lesson that we can draw right away from what Deutsch taught us all those years ago and compromise is *not* a win-win resolution. We'll discuss compromise in some later lectures, especially in Lecture 9 when we talk about it as a strategy.

As we all know, that old assumption of competitiveness really does still linger. Here we are in a course talking about it. There it is in books, even though Deutsch learned it a long time ago. We often see potential win-win situations the same way those Game theorists saw them. Maybe we have chances for moderate shared gains versus the greater individual gains. But what Deutsch showed us that breaks through that assumption in Game theory is that what we often have is the possibility for greater gains for both of us, not just moderate gains versus greater gains for the one individual.

Why haven't we gotten this? Some of it is just that it takes time to learn, for information for new knowledge to disseminate through a culture. But we're also up against some things. There's the weight of the existing culture. There are the mass media portrayals of conflict and how they work out that give us the narratives that we all learn from and that reinforce them. There's the powerful early learning that moves us toward how we're seeing conflict. Remember we learn conflict starting when we're very, very young. So our learning about it comes very, very early.

Over the years since Deutsch made this discovery, we've been very slow in picking up on the idea what a true win-win means. I remember seeing the term a great deal as we studied these things in the 1970s when I began to do my own work looking at conflict management. At the same time, as time went on, you would see things like self help books and others that really carried through and presented advice on the assumption that the conflict was really competitive. One of the ones that I used to cite very often back then, carrying this through in the `80s, was a book by George Robert Bach called the *Intimate Enemy: How to Fight Fair in Love and Marriage.*

Notice what's in that title and it was resonant. That book sold very well. It resonated with people. Seeing the person up close as an enemy. The idea of fighting fair is still the idea of fighting; so that assumption of competitiveness is still there. There was some good advice in Bach's book about not doing damage to one another, and even some notion of win-win, but not the real notion of win-win, because it was still fighting. It was about fighting fair; it wasn't about collaborating, working together to get a true win-win.

So here we are today. It's more than half a century later, Deutsch's discovery of "win-win" was made all that time ago and to a great extent it hasn't penetrated society. But it also was limited in what it could do. What are some caches with this that we've learned in the research sense? One thing is that humans are much more complicated than Lewin's Theory or Deutsch's concept of win-win really fully recognized back then. We're complicated beings. What happens often is we might try for a win-win and find that we're just not on the same page with one another; that our views about what's going on in this conflict really may differ considerably. We're just not on the same page. You think you're fighting one conflict, I think I'm fighting another, and this thing isn't working out even if we think we're trying to work together.

We're going to actually spend a lot of time in this course unpacking how those differences happen and how we can do better with getting on the same page. There's a lot to sort through to get at the root of conflict and the way this stuff works. We don't just go through life pursuing conscious goals, and this is another area where we've discovered difference from what Deutsch found. It turns out that the goals we have are not just one goal, one shared goal, but each of us in any given situation has multiple complex goals, some of which we're fully conscious of and some we're not conscious of.

These goals may even be in conflict with one another as we proceed. We might, on the one hand in a relationship, have goals that involve wanting to receive affection and feel included in belonging, and on the other hand we might have a goal to feel independence and want to know ourselves. So there's a challenge here, we can have goals even that are in conflict with one another. How are we going to sort that out? It's not just as simple as oh well you have this goal and I have this goal, let's pursue them together. We're just more complex than that.

The result of these kinds of things, the greater complexity is that we can be making good efforts to follow Deutsch's advice and pursue a win-win. The efforts can easily go awry because of the complexities if we're not really aware of them and we haven't got them well sorted out.

There's one last—perhaps greatest—limitation. This one works this way. I've mentioned already that we learn about conflict management early in life. We come to the table now, all of us, you with this course, I still as I study it and learn it, we come to the place where we're trying to learn better ways to handle conflict management. Not a blank slate to write on, open mind I just don't know this subject so teach me, we come to it already set of lessons well in place, they're powerfully drilled in, we learned them as little kids, we learned them as toddlers, we strengthened them as we grew up, and those are the lessons we've already learned and we've got them built in like default strategies. It's how we go about resolving conflict and it's what we think conflict is, and we don't even think anymore that okay this is a conflict, my concept of conflict is this. It's built in. We think that's just the way it is because this is the stuff we learned early.

So we're not writing on a blank slate. We're trying to write over that early learning, and that's an exceptionally difficult thing for humans to do. We're not learning something that's just new. What we have to do here is unlearn those old lessons. So most of us are familiar with the term win-win, sure, but we don't necessarily get what win-win is all about. The term is known the world over.

It struck me that when the new extension of this START Treaty was negotiated between the American President Obama and the Russian President Medvedev; Medvedev said this is a "win-win" and I wondered I don't know it's possible that the man really understands this concept fully. It's in all of our lexicons, but I watched him say that and listened and mused I wonder if he understands what he really said there. So it's world over, but it's really not fully penetrated.

One indication of that lack of full penetration came to me in some research done by a wonderful sociologist named Calvin Morrill who's at the University of California at Berkeley these days. Cal Morrill got himself a grant to study how top executives in large organizations handle conflict when it comes up. He was able to spend a whole year just shadowing, there were seven different ones in seven different large organizations, different kinds of organizations, and he spent a whole year literally with permission just going with them and shadowing what they did and how they handled things and writing things down, and at times he was able to interview them. So he just tracked how these seven executives handled conflict when it came up.

The result was a very interesting book entitled *The Executive Way.* What he found was that these guys understood the term was a nice idea for "win-win;" they would talk about achieving win-win resolutions. They could all use the term, but in fact when conflict came up, the predominant almost exclusive strategy that all these top executives used involved getting into and competing with one another. The kinds of competition differed. Sometimes it was hostile competition; sometimes they went after it with joy and gusto like it was a competitive game being played. Sometimes it was played with a great deal of respect for the other party that was mutual, but it was still a competitive game being played to win or lose.

They may have been what they learned and what worked coming up. It may be how you get to be a top executive. But losing isn't any fun; winning is more fun; success is better than losing. It turns out that these guys, *The Executive Way* as he called it, was to go ahead and compete. These are six figure and more salaried people, and what they're doing is competing. So it hasn't really penetrated. There are costs to that, which we'll find out, to themselves and the organization.

One other thing I want to point out here. I'm going to emphasize the research aspect. I've talked about that talking about Morton Deutsch and this discovery. It's something we want to do in these lectures and in this course steadily. It relates to that problem of really getting this knowledge disseminated and getting us to accept these new ideas and understand that they really carry weight.

I want you to know where the ideas came from and I want to do that not just to credit people who gave us important insights and new knowledge, which we really ought to do anyway, but I want you to understand that these are not just glib, somebody's new ideas here, resolve conflict this way, as you might find in an easy self-help book. But what we'll talk about in this course are the results of serious research on how to handle conflict better; that grows from that discovery that Morton Deutsch made about the possibility of win-

win. We're going to build on Deutsch's breakthrough all the way through the rest of this course in order to get to better ways to resolve conflict.

Let's summarize then. What have we learned here about Morton Deutsch? The first thing we need to note and repeat, Deutsch is the father of modern conflict resolution research, modern conflict management research because he's the guy who showed us that conflict need not be treated as competitive, that both sides can really have a win-win.

Secondly, that understanding constituted a fundamental breakthrough and it opens up a whole new world of possibilities for how we can get better at resolving conflict. Third, by itself this discovery helps us deal better with a lot of conflicts. It's an insight that helps all by itself, but its utility is limited unless we can learn a whole lot more.

Then we're going to move to subsequent research that's going to begin to fill in those useful details that we need in order to get better and better and better at finding win-win resolutions. We're each going to need to work. I still do after years and years and years of teaching and working with this. We're each going to have to work as we do this with replacing those old lessons, those early lessons that we learned about conflict and new understanding. We're going to keep pushing back against those. That's not going to be an easy thing to do, but it really does help, as I say, to have some sense of the depth of the research and the important scholarship that really points us in these directions. So that's our lecture about Morton Deutsch and win-win.

I've got an assignment for you coming out of that lecture. What I want to strongly suggest that you do is to try to work past that slogan idea of "win-win" and get to where you can think and act in terms of what that concept really means. I want you to get started doing this by going back and trying to remember the last two or three times you heard that term used, the term "win-win." When you do that I want you to consider whether the person using it probably really understood what it meant and used it accurately or just used it goodly as a phrase tossed off the cuff. If the term was used at less than full strength, what would've been the difference—ask yourself that— what would've been the difference if both parties really fully understood the concept and sought to accomplish it. Could they have achieved a better win-win resolution? That's your assignment.

Where are we going to go from here? Well, Deutsch's breakthrough as I say launched the modern study of conflict management. We're going to proceed into that modern study of conflict management. What we're going to do is we're going to have to focus next on the insights that those researchers following up on Deutsch's discovery began to learn about the nature of conflict and what's going on in a conflict.

An important place to start with that, which will be the subject of our next lecture, is with the perceptions that people have with the understanding that conflict results not directly from the difference that I may have with another person, but from the perception of difference that I have with that other person, the recognition that those perceptions can differ greatly depending on where we stand, the perspective from which we look at it. The perception in conflict is the subject of Lecture 4.

Perception, Perspective, and Punctuation
Lecture 4

> We need to understand one another's perceptions and consider what it would look like from their perspective in order to get somewhere.

One of the most important insights that has emerged in research since Morton Deutsch's development of the concept of win-win relates to the role of perception and perspective in conflict. Conflict does not arise so much from a difference itself but from the perception we have of that difference.

Perception is a cognitive activity in which we assign meaning to the things people say or do or the things we see. In a conflict, the parties usually have differing perceptions about what's going on. One may perceive a difference where there's no real difference, and the other may perceive a *different* difference than the one the first party saw. People get off track in attempting to deal with conflict because they're working with different perceptions of what's really going on. Consider the example of the proposal team at an engineering firm. The team has eight days to prepare a proposal, but half that time is wasted because the team members have different perceptions about their assignments.

We need to develop two skills to help us understand the other person's perceptions in any conflict: **empathy** and **perspective-taking**. Empathy is a communication skill; it involves an awareness of one's own perspective and the ability to see things from the other person's point of view. Psychologists call this ability perspective-taking; it requires adopting the other person's psychological viewpoint.

A concept that's closely related to perspective-taking is **punctuation**. In communication research, this term refers to the timing that parties assign to events. Our understanding of the beginning and end of a certain episode affects the way we perceive the situation. In the example of the proposal team, Pete thinks the conflict started with Ellen; she asks him for the list of resources, which he can't deliver until he has her project design. Ellen thinks the conflict started with Pete; from her perspective, he hasn't been getting anything done. In reality, the conflict probably started in the team meeting, when assignments were handed out but the sequence of who would pass completed work to whom wasn't specified.

Wilmot and Hocker, in their text *Interpersonal Conflict*, describe the **lens model of conflict interaction**, a tool for understanding perceptions. In a conflict, parties view each other as if they're each looking through a camera lens, and the meaning of the conflict varies a great deal depending on the angle, the direction, and the distance you have from what's really going on. Using the metaphor of the camera lens helps us to look at ourselves and the situation from the other person's point of view.

One problem that we have to be aware of, even using the lens model, is the **fundamental attribution error**. Almost all of us tend to attribute mistakes or failings on our part to external events, but we also tend to attribute the behavior of others to their own character or emotions. Obviously, this can be a significant problem in dealing with a conflict: I'm unhappy with something you did, and I attribute your behavior to your personality, but you attribute it to outside factors that you couldn't help. My perspective will push you into being defensive, because it will feel like I'm attacking your character.

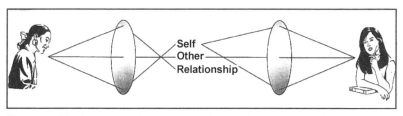

Figure 4.1. The lens model helps us to understand the meaning of conflict, which varies depending on the angle, direction, and distance between you and the object.

We can get beyond the attribution error with person-centered communication, as opposed to position-centered or rule-centered communication. Rule-centered communication, often used in bureaucratic or legal settings, focuses on asserting the facts and their relationship to the rules. Position-centered communication is based on taking a stand and defending it. Neither of these approaches helps the parties arrive at a win-win solution. With person-centered communication, however, the parties are willing to understand the other side, to take into account what the other person is thinking and feeling. This approach requires the ability to question your own perceptions and punctuation of events and to listen to the other party's perspective.

> **In a conflict, parties view each other as if they're each looking through a camera lens, and the meaning of the conflict varies a great deal depending on the angle, the direction, and the distance you have from what's really going on.**

Person-centered communicating does not mean, however, that the objective facts and rules are irrelevant. In fact, in their own way, perceptions are their own set of facts that need to be accounted for, just as rules, deadlines, and standards need to be taken into account. The skills of argumentation we discussed earlier should still be applied. It's also important to note that it takes courage to engage in person-centered communication, to look at a situation and be willing to admit that you may be contributing to the problem. ■

Important Terms

empathy: The skill of being able to understand what another person is experiencing from his or her perspective; the ability to put oneself in another's shoes.

fundamental attribution error: The common tendency to assume that the behavior of others stems primarily from personal character traits rather than the situation at hand.

lens model of conflict interaction: A model illustrating that each party in a conflict has a particular view of himself or herself, the other person, and the relationship; all of these combine to form one's perception of the conflict.

perception: The process of observing and assigning meaning to the things we see.

perspective-taking: Adopting a viewpoint that considers how events might look and feel to the other person.

punctuation: The way each party perceives and defines the chain of events in a conflict.

Suggested Reading

Folger, Poole, and Stutman, *Working through Conflict: Strategies for Relationships, Groups, and Organizations*.

Wilmot and Hocker, *Interpersonal Conflict*.

Assignments

1. Think of a conflict in which you were involved. Apply the lens model to see more clearly how your perspective and, therefore, your perception differed from that of the other party.

2. Identify differences in punctuation of events (what caused a certain event and who initiated it) and notice how changing your punctuation of events in a conflict can fundamentally change your perceptions about that conflict.

Perception, Perspective, and Punctuation
Lecture 4—Transcript

In our last lecture, we talked about Morton Deutsch's great breakthrough in the discovery of the concept of win-win. We noted how that concept really was not only helpful in itself, but that it also launched a great deal of research by himself and other scholars. And that research over the years from about 1950 until now has produced a number of really useful insights that help us understand what's going on in a conflict and therefore help us manage conflicts better. So in this and the next several lectures we're going to look at some of those additional insights that are produced.

One of the most important of those that I want to talk about in this lecture is the role of perception and the role of perspective, the perspective from which we look at a conflict that we have when conflict occurs. You see conflict arises not so much from a difference itself, but from the perception that we have of that difference. In this lecture what we're going to do is explain how understanding perception and how that's related to the perspective from which we look at a conflict, how those understandings can help us deal with the conflict itself and do a job of managing it better.

We're going to explain the process of attributing meaning that happens when we do perception. We attribute meaning when somebody does something or says something, we're not only listening to what they say and taking in the direct meaning, we're thinking why did he or she do that; why did they say that? We're assigning meaning to it. We're going to look at that part because that happens as part of our perception and we're going to explain something called the fundamental attribution error.

We'll also describe how you can develop the skills of taking the other person's perspective to see things and listening with empathy as we pay attention to what the other person has to say. So that's the point of this lecture, perception and perspective.

Here we go. Let's begin by noting that conflict exists not so much when a difference itself exists, but when one party perceives a difference and that perception of difference causes the person to be uncomfortable with it.

We're responding to what we perceive to be the case which may be closely resembling what's the case, but it may not necessarily be the case.

What's perception? Well a definition by Lulofs and Cahn who do a wonderful textbook on conflict management goes like this. They say perception is a cognitive activity; that it's the process of assigning meaning to the things that people say or do or the things that we see. It's assigning meaning to what we hear or see from other people.

In a conflict what happens is that the parties usually have differing perceptions about what's going on. One may perceive a difference where there's no real difference or another may perceive a different difference from the one the first party saw. So they're going to have differences about perception, and conflict not only arises around that, but we can get off track in attempting to deal with it because we're working with different perceptions of what's really going on.

Here's a really common kind of example. Let's suppose for instance that I and my spouse are getting ready to take a nice trip. I'm very excited about the trip; I tend to be excited about upcoming trips. I say something expressing my excitement. My spouse nicely says, but with some stress in her voice, but that's going to be awfully expensive. I listen to that stress and I perceive a difference, and I tune into the stress maybe and perceive more difference than she intended. I think she doesn't want to go. Now I'm having a conflict. You really don't want to go. The perceptions are different. She may not perceive any lack of interest on her part in going, but I do, so we're having conflict about that.

There may be some truth in my perception. She might not be as excited about this trip as I am. She may not really want to go all that much, but notice that in either case it's what the two of us are each feeling as a result of what we perceive to be the case that's driving the conflict. We may not be sure whether there's a real conflict here or exactly what it is. So we have to pay attention to perception about what's going on, because it's how we respond to those and what we do with them that really matters most. So there's a real difference, but it's the perceived difference that's really going to matter.

Let's look at some examples. We're going to use some dramatizations to show you some examples of how things can go wrong when we have perceived difference or maybe that we failed to perceive a difference that's there. So let's go for a drama here to a team meeting of an engineering firm. Al is the boss and he's summing up the tasks that everybody has got to do. There's not much time for this team to get a job done here. They're going to have to work closely together.

[Video start.]

> **Al**: Okay, we only have eight days to deliver this proposal, but I think we can make it. Just to review: Pete's nailing down personnel and resources, Ellen's drafting the project design, and Jayne's on the budget. I'll put the numbers together once I get your pieces—give it a quick edit, and get it out the door. Any questions? No? Okay, let's get started.

[Video end.]

No perceived conflict here. We all seem to be on the same page. At least the perception is that we don't have a conflict. But let's go look a little bit further, let's go back to our dramatization, only pick it up about four days later at which point we're going to discover that Ellen seems to have a problem with Pete.

[Video start.]

> **Ellen**: Hey Pete, where's that resource list for me to use on the proposal? It's been four days. I haven't seen a thing from you yet!

> **Pete**: What?! You mean you haven't done anything in four days? That's just crazy! I can't give you resources until you give me your plans for the design! Al should have given me the design plan; I'd have it done by now.

[Video end.]

Evidently Pete and Ellen perceive differently. Each of them is feeling indignant at this point and we've got a conflict here and it's a problem. They're both stuck waiting for the other to do something that isn't getting done yet. So now it has become evident we've got a problem, but it may not be evident that the problem is a function of the perceptions. Let's see where it goes from here. Let's follow this conflict a little bit further. Let's go to the break room where Ellen is going to share her perspective on this with Jane.

[Video start.]

> **Ellen**: Boy, Jayne, I can't believe Pete! He can't follow through on a simple assignment. You know it's been four days and he hasn't lifted a finger to get me the list of resources for the project?!
>
> **Jayne**: You're kidding me! I've still got to get the budget together.
>
> **Ellen**: Seriously! If we don't get this proposal done in time, it'll be his fault, not ours.
>
> **Jayne**: Wow. Well, I've got another meeting I've got to get to, so I'll see you later.

[Video end.]

Everything was fine after that first meeting. Now we're seeing some very different perspectives, and this conflict is spreading because now Jane is worried too. We're thinking that people didn't do their jobs, and everybody is thinking somebody else didn't do his or her job. So we do have a growing problem with this conflict as we proceed, and nobody has noticed yet that it's about perceptions. Let's follow it one step further. Let's go back to the boss's office where Pete is going to step in to tell Al about his own perspective on the problem. I guess it's a complaint when Pete gets to Al.

[Video start.]

> **Pete**: Hey Al, got a minute?

Al: Sure, what's up?

Pete: Listen, we're in trouble on this proposal. It's been four days and Ellen still hasn't gotten started on the project design.

Al: How come?

Pete: Says she's waiting for *me* to deliver a list of personnel and resources before she can start. She's got the process backwards and she's holding it up. If I were heading up this design, we'd be done by now.

[Video end.]

Where are we now? The fact is Pete is right in one thing at least, we are in trouble at this point. This team is in trouble. Half the time for getting this thing done and out the door is gone. Everybody has got hard feelings. These people are not interacting closely with one another and talking well at all at this point. They've got a serious conflict to resolve and I want you to notice that none of them yet has figured out that the problem is their perception, and it's not just their perception of the conflict which is different, it's their perceptions of what the assignments were to begin with. None of them were as clear on that as they thought they were, although it seemed reasonably clear at the time.

That's very, very human. These are not bad people. These are all good professionals trying to do a job together, and generally speaking they probably know each other well and respect one another. But they've gotten themselves in trouble on this one with a conflict arising from different perceptions, different perceptions of the assignments that weren't perfectly clear to begin with, and now different perceptions of who's doing what and what's going wrong in the conflict.

So the thing's gone awry and the culprit here is perception. So let's talk about how to do better with perception as we go. We need to understand one another's perceptions and consider what it would look like from their perspective in order to get somewhere. How are we going to do that?

There are two skills that people talk about a lot, that scholars talk about that really help with this. They're empathy and then what's called perspective taking. It's interesting when I say empathy, not everybody wants to think of that as a skill you know. But in the communication business we very much talk about empathy as a skill. It is literally a communication skill. It's the skill of being able to see things from the other person's point of view. It involves an awareness that I'm looking from a perspective myself, that I have a point of view and I'm looking at it from my direction, and then it involves the skill of being able to get over to the other person's side and seeing it from their position.

So in the psychology field, psychologists tend to view that as what they call the skill of perspective taking. That really requires, as they say it, adopting the other person's psychological viewpoint. How would this feel and look to me from the other person's position. Ellen might do well to be thinking how does this feel to Pete who must have reasons for what's going on with him when I come to him and just complain that I don't have those numbers yet.

Pete would do well to think about how Ellen feels in this situation and how it would look from her perspective, and then you know what, if they could do that, they might sit down and talk and work something out. So that's empathy and perspective taking.

Now I want to talk about a piece that's closely related to that, a concept called punctuation. Punctuation, interesting, interesting piece that we deal with in the field of communication a lot. Most of us think who had English grammar well I know what punctuation is. It's putting periods on the end of a sentence and putting a comma in the right place. Well this concept that we label "punctuation" in communication research is closely related to that. It refers to the timing that parties assign to events when they notice what's happening. When did that event begin and when does another event end, when I think about where something started, where this conflict started. That's punctuation from my marking the beginning and where a certain episode ends is punctuation for the ending.

That affects the way I'm going to perceive what's going on in it. We all understood this as three and four year olds when we got in scraps with our siblings or our little playmates and we got in a scrap and then we pointed at each other and said he started it, no she started it. Who started it depends on when we think it began. So punctuation, where did it start, where does it end, that's really going to affect how we perceive what happens in a conflict.

In the example we did in the dramatizations, Pete thinks it starts with Ellen getting unreasonable with him and making demands when he couldn't have delivered what she wanted without having what she was supposed to give him first. He thinks the conflict starts with Ellen being unreasonable. Ellen thinks the conflict starts with Pete sitting in his office, maybe not getting anything done, and the fact is the conflict probably started in the meeting earlier when it wasn't clear about the sequence of how things were going to get passed between people, except for everybody getting this stuff to Al for him to finish it at the end.

So how we punctuate, when we think this thing starts, is really going to be a matter that makes a great deal of difference. Starting points matter a whole lot. If we're thinking that it started at a certain point and the other person's thinking it started at a different point, we're going to have conflict over what's going on in this conflict.

Let's look at a tool for giving us a way to work with understanding perceptions better that'll include punctuation. For this we're going to go to William Wilmot and Joyce Hocker who present this in a wonderful text called *Interpersonal Conflict*. We cited their definition of conflict in Lecture 1. It's a great tool for looking at this and they call it the Lens Model.

Here's how the Lens Model works. If you can picture this, and we do the picture in the guidebook, but picture this in your mind as we do it here. Parties are viewing each other in a conflict as if they're each looking through a camera lens. You know when you look at things through a camera lens several things happen. One is the lens flips things over to upside down. It turns them the other way. The other thing is if you think about looking through a camera lens at something, if you're closer it's closer. If you back away, it takes in a larger framework and if you look at something through a camera lens from different angles, you get a very different picture, even moving a little bit you get a very different picture.

It's a nice metaphor for viewing each other in a conflict that Wilmot and Hocker offer us. So if you think of Pete and Ellen's views of the conflict that they were having and looking at it through a lens model, each party if they look at themselves, they got a view of themselves, which is straight up and it's right there, but the view of the other party looks very different. It depends on where they're standing and how far back, how wide the frame is, which is kind of like punctuation in the timeframe that you give it.

Each of them has a lens to look at each other through and to look at the conflict through. It's just like a picture being shot through a camera lens. The meaning is going to vary a great deal depending on the angle and the direction and the distance that you have from what's really going on in that conflict. It's the Lens Model for seeing.

So, a nice tool for thinking about how perception could be different on the other person's side is this Lens Model. If I think of it that way, just picture it in my mind, put myself around on that person's side of the camera, look at this conflict and look back at myself through the lens that I think they see through, how does it look? And what's the punctuation they may be given and how large is it and how do I look to them in this situation? That would help me; using that metaphor helps me go and look at things from the other person's point of view. It enables me to get some empathy. It's literally a tool for doing what psychologists call perspective taking. So think about the Lens Model and it's a wonderfully useful tool that we could apply.

Now let's go to one additional point that we have to consider here that's a problem area we've got to look out for even using the lens model. And that's this business of attributions of meaning and what we call the fundamental attribution error. This is near universal among human beings. This is something that has been very well studied. Here's how that error works. What we do when we view ourselves through our own lens and we see things, if we do something wrong or fail at something looking at ourselves, we're going to explain that, we're going to attribute the meaning of what we did not to the way I am, but most of us are going to attribute meaning to external events that happen.

Well that's a concern because this happened and this happened and this happened. In that example that I started with where I'm all excited about a trip and my spouse is worried about the cost, I would, I might attribute her statement to lack of interest in the trip, but she might be attributing her statement to well I was looking at the budget and I know where we are with this, and this external thing is causing me to be that way.

But the error side of this is that when I look at the other person's behavior and I'm not satisfied with it, I will tend almost always to attribute it not to external causes that made them be that way, but to their own character, their own personality, or their own emotions. And that would be in the way I perceived that as she doesn't really want to go. I'm attributing her statement about the cost to her emotions. That's that fundamental attribution error to do that automatically when that may not be the case at all.

When it's ourselves and our own behavior when we fall short, it's like excuses. We think of it in terms of external events that happened that pressed us or caused us to behave in that way. If you notice what a problem this would be in dealing with a conflict, if when I'm unhappy with something you did and I'm attributing that to just the way you are and you're attributing it to external factors that you couldn't help, we're not going to have an easy time resolving that, and I'm going to push you into being much more defensive because it'll feel like an attack when I say it as though that's just the way you are.

Conversely if you have that attribution error toward me, then you're doing the same thing, Michael doesn't care as much, Michael is just a hostile kind of a guy, whatever. So that attribution error that's fundamental really gets in our way and it's a basic mistake we almost always make when we're attributing meaning to one another when we're not really doing a good job of taking into account the other person's perspective in terms of what's going on.

How do we get beyond that? How do we get beyond it? Let's talk about that a little bit. This approach is what communication scholars call person-centered communication as opposed to position-centered or rule-centered communication. Let's talk about these three, rule-centered, position-centered, and person-centered communication.

Rule centered communication focuses on asserting the facts and their relationship to the rules. It's just like the forensic reasoning we talked about in Lecture 2. What's the rule and what are the facts relative to the rules? In our example with Pete and Ellen, if the specs for the proposal that Pete and Ellen were working on required say a complete, detailed budget to be provided, and they provided numbers that were fairly general and served that up, whoever was reviewing that proposal when it went in might review the thing and say, "This doesn't meet specifications. We don't have a detailed budget here," and reject the proposal for that reason.

It's yes or no, it's rule centered, do the facts match the rule. You need that in bureaucratic thinking, and you need it in the law, and you need it in certain places. I don't mean there might not be perception involved; that reviewer's perception of what's complete and detailed might be different from what Pete's and Ellen's or Al's perceptions were. But still it might make sense in that kind of a process that the communication be about what the rule, what does the rule mean, what does the rule require. That would be rule-centered thinking. It's appropriate. It's necessary in places like the court, like bureaucracies, various places, but it's not what's going to help Pete and Ellen solve their conflict here.

What about position-centered communication as it comes along? Suppose Pete takes a position relative to his conflict with Ellen. What might Pete say? Pete might say, "Look you know you were supposed to do this," and he's going to defend that position. That's position-centered communication as if he's negotiating. He might negotiate later, "Well I can back down a little bit," but he's taken a position on it and he's trying to establish that he has the correct position.

Ellen on the other hand takes the position that Pete is wrong and that she has got the correct position, and if the communication back and forth is about whose position is correct, that's going to be in the way of dealing with a win-win. It's not going to help us get to a win-win, very much the same way that rule-centered communication isn't going to. Those two kind of dance together. They're both necessary at times, but they're not what's going to help this group sit down together and work out a win-win resolution. Now they're down to four days if they want to talk about it.

They're going to have to work out a win-win and figure out how to work together quickly and get the whole thing done. So if they want to do that, if they want a win-win, they have to get to this third kind that communication scholars talk about which we call person-centered communication. In person-centered communication I'm willing to understand the other side. I want to take into account what the other party is thinking and feeling. I want to try to see it from their point of view. It's not thinking from the standpoint of what is the rule required here or what does the assignment say, but what did Pete get as his assignment in his mind, what did Ellen think her assignment was, how can we make these mesh and work out so that we can work the thing together.

It's concern about Pete's perception, concern about Ellen's perception, and how can we make them match. That's person centered-communication. It requires listening. It requires checking my own perceptions and it requires willingness to adjust that I may not have perceived correctly or at least that I perceived differently from the other person and what we want to do is get our perceptions on the same page with one another. It takes a conscious effort to let go of being rule centered or position centered, which a lot of us are used to being.

So person-centered communication can be very challenging. It does require me to be able to check my own punctuation of events, the timing, when did it start, how far does it go back. It might be that the other person isn't being problematic at all except in response to something I did or said, which he took to indicate that he should behave that way. So it requires questioning my own punctuation and my own perspective. It requires asking about and really listening to the other party's perspective and what factors might be contributing to that perspective.

It requires moving together to achieve one another's goals so like really constantly trying to pursue a win-win, working on it together. So if we think about that and take it back to our example of the co-workers, we're not going to act this one out for you, but just go back and imagine what if at the initial meeting they had stopped and checked their perceptions, wait a minute I'm going to do this, and thought through how they were going to do it, I know they were in a hurry. They had to get on with the work, but if they had checked and found out the different perceptions, they might've discovered the sequencing problem and worked out better how to proceed from there.

They could actually do this now four days in. They could go and look and check with one another and see how it's supposed to work. I will talk about ways that they could negotiate that in Lectures 10, 11, 12, and 13. So we're going to get there. We're going to talk about what they could've done instead if they were doing person-centered communicating and actually working out negotiations.

I do want to emphasize though that when we're doing person-centered communicating that does not mean that the reality, the facts, what the rules are, what the specs are, what the objective facts are, it doesn't mean those are irrelevant. Perceptions in their own way are their own set of facts that need to be taken into account. But the objective facts in any given instance still matter. Rules are still rules. Deadlines are still deadlines. Standards are standards. What happened really might have happened and needs to be taken into account. So reality doesn't go away when we get person centered and we do have to take that into account. So it's really a good idea as well to be checking both party's claims about facts.

Those skills we talked about in Lecture 2 in argumentation matter at this point. What are the facts of the situation and how does that work here? A last thing to say about this in addition to the facts still matter is, I want to note that it takes courage to really listen to the other party and to look at the fact that I might be wrong in a given situation. I don't know about you, but I hate most having to look at a situation and figure out that I might be wrong, and when it turns out that I am, admit it and be willing to change opinions. That's pretty daunting stuff, and I think it takes courage to open ourselves up to that consideration of the other person's perspective, to open up to punctuating differently and that the other person may not be wrong so I may share some of the wrong. That takes courage so be gentle with yourself if you try to do this. It's a courageous thing to do taking the other person's perspective.

What have we learned in this lecture? Several things are really key here. First is that conflict arises not directly from the differences, but indirectly from our perceptions of differences that exist between us.

Secondly we learned that we need to interact on a personal, psychological, and full human level without abandoning the objective realities that we face in a given situation. We need to be person centered, but that doesn't mean we can abandon the facts.

Three, we learned that in order to achieve win-win resolutions, we need to avoid thinking in terms of what's correct and who's right, and we need to just think in terms of what did you think, what did I think, and how can we put this together and work something out.

Fourth we learned that we need to try to understand our own and the other party's perceptions of any given situation. We need to understand those well if we're going to work out a good resolution.

Five we learned that each person's perception, each person's perception, is influenced by his or her perspective. Six we learned that that perception is influenced by the punctuation, the point in time at which that person took notice of the situation, the way they think it works depends on a point in time. Seventh, we need to especially be careful to avoid that fundamental attribution error that most of us make most of the time, which leads us to excuse ourselves and to blame the other person when it wasn't necessary.

If we do the work of speaking and listening honestly and openly to each other, understand the other person's perceptions in pursuit of real win-win resolutions, doing that with person-centered communication we've got a much better shot at resolving our conflicts well.

Perception lecture, let me give you an assignment at the end of this one. I want you to think of a conflict in which you were involved and then use that Lens Model provided by Hocker and Wilmot. Use that as your metaphor to think through your perspective versus their perspective and therefore how your perception might've differed from the other party's.

Try to identify the differences in punctuation that the two of you might've made that I think it began in a different time from the other party and how did that affect each of our perceptions of the event. What I'm asking you to do in this assignment is use the Lens Model and try to do some real perspective taking retroactively on a conflict that occurred and think through how things might've worked out differently had you been able to see things from one another's perspective.

Where are we going in the next lecture? Lecture 5, it's going to work this way. We've now talked about perception and punctuation. We know how that is and we know that they generate our sense of what the conflict is. They also generate how we feel about the conflict. Our emotions are driven by our perceptions of what's going on. Our emotions are tricky to deal with in a conflict. They're multiple, they tend to be mixed, they tend to be complex. In a conflict they tend to be negative, including anger. They stir us to action, actions that we do in a conflict can make things a lot worse, especially if we're angry.

So we'd better look at emotions. We better consider how emotions work and especially how they work in a conflict and how we can deal with them in a conflict, and that's our subject in our next lecture.

Managing Multiple and Conflicting Emotions
Lecture 5

> There's a difference between feeling an emotion—communicating about emotion—and behavior, and you want to distinguish the two.

A rising from our perceptions, our emotions are multiple, complex, and changeable, and negative emotions are one of the elements that are always present in a conflict. As we know, the primary emotion here is anger, and humans can be dangerous when we're angry.

In the Western world, we tend to think of ourselves as beings who live by reason, with emotions as a sometimes troublesome element thrown into the mix. Recent studies in the neurology of consciousness and emotion, however, have shown that the reality may be just the opposite. Rather than reasoning beings with troublesome emotions, we're really emotional beings who have evolved an ability to reason that helps us deal with our emotions.

© Digital Vision/Thinkstock.

Happiness (and sadness) are internal facts that exist neurologically.

Think of emotions as internal facts. If you're feeling love or hurt or anger, those emotions are things that exist neurologically. They correlate with physical reactions occurring in the body. Emotions are relevant to any conflict, and they have to be accommodated in the way we deal with conflict.

Emotions occur in reaction to stimuli, which are the perceptions of events that we talked about in the last lecture. The two central elements of emotions are the feeling itself, which can be either positive or negative, and arousal, that is, the strength of the emotion. Note, however, that emotions are mixed and multiple; we can feel anger, sadness, fear, and guilt all at the same time. Emotions can also mask one another; men, for example, tend to mask fear with anger. If we interact badly during a conflict, we can do damage that may be irreversible or set off an upward spiral of hostility.

To handle emotions in a conflict, start by remembering that an emotion is not a behavior. Being angry is not the same as acting on your anger. Telling someone that you're angry does not require you to scream. Recall, too, that emotion is an internal fact; it's a response to perceptions you are having. You don't need to apologize for or explain away the fact that you feel something. Three interactions between two co-workers demonstrate how emotions can be mishandled: by faking, by hiding, and by acting out. We also see what happens when one of the co-workers honestly and constructively expresses how she feels and offers a suggestion for moving forward.

In terms of reporting, you need to take reasonable risks to ensure that your true feelings are known.

How can you take emotions into account when trying to resolve a conflict? First, you have to report them to the other party. Second, you need to remember that an emotion is not a judgment about the other party. You have to own it. You don't necessarily know what the other party's motivations and concerns are; you know only that you feel a certain way. In terms of reporting, you need to take reasonable risks to ensure that your true feelings are known. When you're telling someone about your emotions, phrase your remarks specifically as "I" statements. If the arousal level is too high to do that, then step away from the situation for a few minutes to calm down and steer your thoughts away from the conflict.

Here are five requisites for deciding when you can usefully express emotion in a conflict situation: (1) access, that is, the ability to cognitively recognize that you're feeling something and gauge the intensity of that feeling; (2) appropriate verbal communication skills to talk about the emotion; (3) self-esteem, that is, the idea that you have a right to feel certain emotions and pursue your own good; (4) an environment in which it's safe to talk about emotions; and (5) a willing partner, someone who is willing to listen and work out the conflict. The first three are skills that belong to you; you can develop those. The last two are factors that you can't control; if you don't have a safe environment or a willing partner, you may need to change the overall situation that you're in.

To be a willing partner yourself requires courage and caring. It's difficult to listen when another party is expressing negative emotions without defending yourself or interrupting with your own responses. At the same time, listening to how the other person feels doesn't mean you have to tolerate verbal abuse. Be aware, too, of keeping the conversation level; don't allow your emotions to spiral upward to hostility. Finally, treat the other party's honest expressive emotion as a privileged communication; don't spread that information or use it to hurt your partner. ■

Suggested Reading

Damasio, *Descartes' Error: Emotion, Reason, and the Human Brain* or *Looking for Spinoza: Joy, Sorrow, and the Feeling Brain.*

Goleman, *Emotional Intelligence: Why It Can Matter More Than IQ.*

Assignment

1. The next time you find yourself in a conflict, remember to treat emotions as internal facts and report them. Consider what emotions you feel. How can you express them using "I" statements? Try it and see what happens.

Managing Multiple and Conflicting Emotions
Lecture 5—Transcript

Arising from our perceptions, our emotions are multiple, they're complex, and they tend to changing as we go along dealing with the conflict. They can be very difficult to recognize and to be really clear on exactly what it is we're feeling in the mix of multiple and complex emotions, and they can be even much more difficult to express when we're involved in a conflict. So here we've got conflict and emotions are in it. When we described the nature of conflict in Lecture 1, remember we listed the elements that are always present, and negative emotions were one of those elements. They're always present. If we handle them well, we've got a pretty good shot at handling the conflict well, but very, very often we don't handle our emotions well in a conflict.

This lecture is about emotions in conflict and what we can do to handle them as well as possible. So let's discuss emotions. What are emotions? They're delightful; they're wonderful at times; they can be horrendously painful. They can be dangerous. You know they're an aspect of human nature. Especially in a conflict emotions can be dangerous because the primary emotion that's most likely to be there is anger, and humans are dangerous animals when we're angry.

So emotions are going to need dealing with. How do we think of ourselves as human beings with emotion? There's a long tradition of this in western civilization that also goes back to the ancient Greeks, to those people we talked about in Lecture 2. It goes back very much to Plato with his thinking, and we tend in the western world to think in that tradition of ourselves as human beings being reasoning beings and that's the highest part of it, of what we are. We're reasoning beings, but we have these emotions which can be nice, but can also be very troublesome, and what we have to do is live by reason and rule by reason. That's a long 2,000 year history of thinking of ourselves as emotional animals.

Recently studies in neurology and the neurology of consciousness and emotion and how that works show us that it may be really the other way around. Rather than being reasoning beings who have these troublesome emotions, what we really are is emotional beings who have evolved this ability to reason that helps us deal with our emotions. The last 30 years especially we've learned an awful lot about emotions and we can apply a lot of that to dealing with emotions in conflict.

How should we think about emotions then? I want us to think about emotions as being internal facts. They're facts about us going on. They're not external facts, they're internal facts. If I'm having an emotion; if I'm feeling love or hurt or anger, anything positive, anything negative, it's an internal factor with me. It's something I'm feeling and it exists neurologically. It exists biologically. There are things happening with my body, there are always physical parts of it, and of course it exists in my mind. It's going on and it's relevant; if it's relevant to the conflict it's going to have to be reported and accommodated in the way we deal with the conflict and in what we do to work the thing out.

Emotions are not something that are going to be something I can just put aside and solve the conflict with reason. Emotions occur in reaction to stimuli. What would those stimuli be? Ah-hah, those perceptions of events that we talked about in our last lecture. Perceptions act as stimuli, and when we assign meaning to them, which may be virtually instant, we get an emotional response to some of those events that happen.

The central elements in emotions are actually two. There's a central element of feeling, which can be either positive or negative, and then there's the other central element which is arousal. How strong is it? I may be angry with you, but it can be slight or it can be very much. So there's the scale of what our researchers call the arousal level and then there's the specific feeling that I'm feeling, the question is how strongly am I feeling it. We've always got those two to deal with as we work with this.

I want you to notice that emotions, they're not going to be simple. If you think about your emotions in any conflict situation, if you tended to yourself at all you sort of get that you're not just feeling one thing. In the same conflict, look at the same person in the face at the same time, we could be feeling anger, we could also be feeling some fear. We could be feeling some sadness or loss and fear about the possibility of loss. We can be feeling guilty about our part in making this thing turn out the way it is. We could be feeling shame. We could also be feeling hope and love and admiration all at the same time or all in quick succession as we go through dealing with someone we care about in a conflict.

Emotions are mixed and multiple. They happen a lot at the same time. They're not an easy, simple thing to sort out and work with. I want you to also notice that emotions can mask one another. It's a very common thing. One of the things they study in men and they've noticed is that men tend to mask fear with anger more than a female, and this is a statistical difference, it's not all or nothing, but more than females, males tend to tune into the anger and let it cover the fear because we're less comfortable feeling fear just sociologically or whatever.

Women on the other hand may be more likely to mask anger with sadness or hurt and tune into that feeling. So really clearly, consciously understanding what we're feeling when we're feeling it is not as easy as it may seem. At the same time we could be feeling it very strongly. As I said, human beings are dangerous animals when we're angry.

If we interact badly during a conflict, what's that going to mean? If I shout at you, if I say something terribly ugly I can't take it back. We talked about the four awful truths about a conflict, remember in Lecture 1. One of those awful truths is that some of the damage is irreversible. All of us can remember things that were said to us at some earlier time which when we remember them again they still hurt. Something that was said by someone in the heat of anger that they didn't really mean still hurts us. You can't take back something that's said. So we can do lasting harm when we're feeling strong emotion, and it's negative emotion. We have to handle these emotions and be careful about that.

We can also set off negative spirals. What we can do is I can get angry and say something that's a little bit ugly and that lifts the arousal level in the conflict. We tend to trigger each other in doing that. The other person that I'm in this conflict with can then rise to my level of arousal and say something back and then I'll rise and it's a spiral. You can think of it, in my mind it often spirals up, more and more angry. Other scholars have talked about it spiraling down like it's setting up a vortex. Either way you think about it, it's a spiral that sets off with triggering each other's emotions and we can make matters a lot worse. So it's important when we're in a conflict not to be doing that.

What we need to do is identify some useful rules for handling conflict, emotions in a conflict. So what would those rules be? Let's start with remembering that an emotion is not a behavior. You don't want to mix these two up. I'm feeling something. Being angry is not the same as acting out on my anger. Telling you that I'm angry does not require that I scream at you. So there's a difference between feeling an emotion, communicating about emotion and behavior, and you want to distinguish the two.

Emotions themselves we want to treat those internal facts and I don't want, none of us should be doing any apologizing for or explaining away the fact that we feel something as though we're not supposed to feel it. Emotion is an internal fact. It exists. I shouldn't be apologizing for it. I shouldn't judge myself poorly for not feeling something I'm supposed to feel. It's just what I'm feeling and it's a response to the perceptions that I'm having. I need to just accept it as an internal fact about me. It's not my behavior; it's not my morals, it's an emotion that I'm having, something that I'm feeling.

Let's look at some examples here. We've got some dramatizations to show you about emotions and how people can handle them, and we're going to start with some how not to and then move to some how to. Let's go to a set up where Carl and Anna are colleagues in an organization, not the same ones as the engineering team we talked about in the last lecture. They work together. Carl has a task that he wants Anna to complete for him so that he can leave and go home early. He's not her boss; he's a work colleague. But if she does this it means she's going to be working late and he's going to be going home. Let's see what happens when someone fakes feelings in response to this request.

[Video start.]

> **Carl**: Anna, I hate to stick you with extra work, but I've got a meeting to run to, and I've got to get home after that. I've got

people coming over for dinner. I e-mailed you a draft of the fund-raising plan, but it's not quite done. Can you finish up my part and send it out before you leave tonight?

Anna: Sure. I'll take care of it. No problem.

Carl: Thanks, you're a team player.

[Video end.]

So did you hear what Anna did with that feeling? She faked it. I don't think Anna really wanted to stay and work late. She's not feeling "sure this is fine." There's a problem here. She thinks she's supposed to feel positive and be cooperative. She may've learned that it's not ladylike or charming to say no. But Anna is thinking she needs to be okay with this and so she's faking it. She's acting as though she's okay when she's not. She may even be fooling herself, but she's faking the emotions, and so what's the result. She's stuck working late, Carl goes home early, has his dinner guests, things are fine at home. He thinks everything is fine at work, but you know what, it's not fine at work.

That's one example. Now let's see what happens if someone stuffs feelings. Stuffing is different from faking it. It's not showing a feeling and trying not to even notice that I'm feeling it. It's stuffing it down, hiding it. All of us have done that at times. Let's pay attention to how Anna reacts this time attempting to stuff her feelings.

[Video start.]

Carl: Can you finish up my part and send it out before you leave tonight?

Anna: All right. But I need to take care of my part first.

Carl: Great, um. Thanks.

[Video end.]

Did you notice that? Anna is not happy. Carl picked it up, but she's saying she'll do it. She's stuffing that feeling so the difference is much less in the words than it is in the way she says it. She's stuffing a feeling. Now things are a little more uncertain. Carl doesn't walk away thinking everything is fine, but we don't have a solution. He's still going home early, Anna is still working late.

What would happen if we went the other direction? Let's see, what else could Anna do? Anna could go off on Carl. She could get angry and act out her anger. That's not a good idea either. Let's take a look and see what happens if Anna does that, she acts out her anger.

[Video start.]

> **Carl**: Can you finish up my part and send it out before you leave tonight?

> **Anna**: Look, Carl, you're not dumping your work on me anymore. I've had it with that!

> **Carl**: Great. Thanks. You're a real team player!

[Video end.]

So that time Anna went too far the other direction. She really pushed it in Carl's face in such a way that she created hostility that maybe wasn't necessary to create. She viewed Carl's behavior as the cause of her problem, but she generalized it a lot and she just kind of went off on him about it. Now what Carl is doing instead of being a little uncertain, Carl is feeling a little defensive and angry himself, and he's wanting to accuse her back. Thanks for being such a team player he says sarcastically. So we get that acting out, going over the top, doesn't help either.

What could we do more positively with this? What if Anna just honestly and constructively expressed how she feels in being asked to do this at this point? I wonder what would happen with that? Let's check it out and see.

[Video start.]

Carl: Can you finish up my part and send it out before you leave tonight?

Anna: Okay, Carl, but I've covered for you at least three times in the last month, and frankly, I get angry when this happens. We have two more fund-raising plans to get out next month, so we need to sit down and talk about how we can stop this from happening.

Carl: You're right. I'm sorry. I need to plan better. Do you have any time next week? We could talk about the plans for next month.

Anna: How about Tuesday at 10?

Carl: That works. And thanks for covering for me *again.*

[Video end.]

Now that's a better outcome. Notice what Anna did specifically in this case. She expressed herself using what we call "I" statements. She spoke for her own feelings. She said when you do this I feel this way. I get angry. She didn't shout at him. She didn't say anything ugly. She just honestly reported her feeling. She did what we call owning that feeling. She just claimed it. When this happens, this is how I feel. Then she talked in terms of where we can go from here, and then Carl got the message. I don't know how many Carls would immediately apologize on the spot, but Carls would consistently get the message if we honestly reported out the feeling that we were having at the time.

What do we do with this then? What we want to say about emotions is we need to take them into account. We've noticed that we shouldn't stuff them; we shouldn't hide them; we shouldn't fake them; we need to honestly report them. Now what we need to do is take them into account when we deal with trying to resolve the conflict. How can we do that?

The first thing in terms of taking them into account in the resolution process would be what Anna just did. It's reporting them to the other party. We've got to get them on the table so they can be taken into account, and both parties will need to say enough of how we're feeling so that we can work with that in terms of the emotion.

The second thing would be that we need to remember that emotion is not a judgment about the other party. Own it yourself. It's what I feel. It's not necessarily that Carl is being a clod in this situation; Anna doesn't really know what all is driving Carl and what his concerns are. What she knows is when he does this she feels this way and she's reporting how she feels. So it's not a judgment. It's not a "you" statement that you say to "you" the other person, it's an "I" statement owning the emotion myself. So we would report it in that way.

I need in terms of reporting to take reasonable risks in order to get my true feelings known and on the table. But I don't want to suggest that we need to let our hearts hang out openly and foolishly when it's not safe to be as vulnerable as it takes to put an emotion out there. If I let you know what my emotions are, there's a certain amount of vulnerability that I take on in your presence by doing that. We're not always in safe company to do that so we don't want to be foolish. We need to make some good judgments and some skill to read situations, when is it okay to do that.

Then we note that when I'm telling someone about emotions I want to phrase it specifically as an I statement. Keep that point very strongly in mind. What if the arousal level is just too high to do that well and clearly in thinking about communicating? The advice there is take some time. I don't mean take weeks, I don't mean take days, but I need to step away from the situation to calm down and get clear. Some of us know to go take a walk around the block and come back and then deal with it. Go to our office for awhile, take some time, do something different, but calm down enough, let myself calm down in order to be able to communicate clearly about an emotion without overstating or without shouting or without being over the top.

I need to be careful while I'm taking that time not to make the mistake of ruminating about the conflict and stirring up my anger more, which some of us are want to do in a conflict situation, why did you do that. Don't think in a way that stirs myself up if I'm taking the time to calm down, steer my thoughts away from that direction, use it to calm down.

Note that conscious thought about how I focus on the communication is behavior itself, how I choose to think about the conflict is mental behavior. I can't control an emotion, but I can control my focus. I can control the way I tend to think about it. So I've got a good shot at handling the conflict better and calming down if I do it well. If Anna had been too angry to speak and she could take some time, that would've helped. Of course you can't even always do that because I think Carl would've been gone before Anna got a chance to walk around the block and come back. Anyway, take some time to calm down. Don't ruminate, focus differently, and that will let you calm down enough to think if we're going to express emotions.

There's one more kind of collection of thoughts I want you to think about here that's important and it's what I call the five requisites for deciding when I can usefully express an emotion in a conflict situation. By "requisites" I mean it's not like prerequisites; they don't have to be there before I talk, but they certainly have to be there when I talk. They're not prerequisites; they're requisites. They're five conditions that have to be present in order for me to safely and constructively describe my emotions in conflict situations.

Here are the five. The first one is access. By access what I mean—and I was fishing for a term for this. The others are easier terms—but by access what I mean is cognitive access, the ability to cognitively recognize that I'm feeling something and roughly how intense it is in what I'm feeling. Not all of us are aware all the time of the emotions we have. The common thing that gets described psychologically as denial is actually a good psychological defense mechanism where I don't let myself know I'm feeling something because I need to get past it at the moment becomes a problem if I am denial too long, but you know what, while I'm in denial I don't have the access to the emotion. I don't know what I'm feeling so I can't describe it. I need to get cognitive understanding, I need to get access to the emotion.

Secondly I'm going to need the verbal communication skill to just describe this. I'm going to have to be able to talk about the emotions, and I need the language to do that and the verbal skill to do that, and some people are more verbally skilled than others. So I want to get my verbal skills up to a state where they can talk about emotions. It's not always easy to do, but it's mine to build. I need enough skill to describe what's going on.

The third one in here is also a skill. It's best thought of as a skill, but you don't usually think of it as that, and the term is self-esteem. By self-esteem what I mean is this. I esteem myself enough to get it that I have a right to feel what I feel and a right to pursue my own good in life. What I am is a being existing with the same rights as everybody else. So I have to get it that I have the right and the ability to take care of myself in this situation. It's a skill, the ability to do that is a skill, and a lot of people don't have it at an adequate level to deal with their emotions very well in a conflict.

So these three I can build up. The other two are not belonging to me, but I've got to assess to see if I've got them present. So let's get to four and five.

The fourth one of these five is a safe environment. I need an environment that's safe to talk about emotions. Not every environment is, not every workplace is, not every social setting is. Sometimes even in a close relationship in a marital setting when other things are going on and there's a lot of fear and trouble around, the environment may not be safe. So I need the ability to assess the environment around me and think through whether it's a good time and place and situation to be able to talk about emotion.

Finally what I'm going to need is a willing partner. That's the fifth one. The other person has got to be willing and able to listen and work with me to work that out. If I don't have a willing partner who's able to listen and work with me expressing emotions well isn't going to be something that works.

So the first three of those, those three skills access, self-esteem, and verbal skill, those three are, they're mine, I can build those. Safe environment, willing partner, I need to be able to assess whether they're okay. If I don't have those others, if I can't get to a safe environment relatively soon, I may want to change the situation I'm in. If the partner I have, either a work partner or a friendship partner or even a romantic partner can't get around to being a willing and safe partner to work with me on conflicts, it may come down to my having to decide to change that. I don't have absolute control of my environment. I don't have absolute control of my partner's behavior. I can work with them to try to improve them, but they're not mine, and the hard truth of this is I may have to think differently if I can't get my conflicts resolved. So those might need changing.

Sometimes it only requires waiting for a better, safer time. So let's try to avoid the pitfall of just avoiding conflict here, but check for that and see if we can do it. Deutsch's point that you can get a win-win 80 percent of the time, if you think back to what we said about his research, the guy was looking at task-oriented groups where we're working together, and it was an experimental situation, not a lot of unsafe environments there. So his research doesn't include unsafe environments. So best solution is, if it's not safe, remove ourselves from the situation if it's not safe long-term.

We need to say a little bit about that fifth one. I can only assess whether the other person is a willing and able partner. We're going to talk about listening after awhile in a later lecture, in Lecture 13, so we'll do it in detail then, but we need to say a little bit about being that willing and able partner in this lecture before we leave that subject entirely. So there are just a few things to point out about it.

The first one is I want it to be recognized that being that partner, really listening when the other party is expressing negative emotions, requires courage, requires caring, and to do it without defending myself and putting in responses, really trying to hear it from their perspective, that's hard to do. If Anna says she's angry, what is that like for Carl who has got to get out the door and his wife is expecting him home. If he really listens and works with her on that, that takes some courage. That's some real effort from him. So recognize that first and credit yourself when you do it.

The second thing is, when you're listening to how the other person feels, don't allow them to do a lot of abusive expression. They can tell you how they feel, but it doesn't mean hang in there and take a verbal beating. It does not mean that. That's a second tip.

The third thing to pay attention to is don't let yourself get triggered into that escalating spiral of hostility. If the other party goes up a notch anger-wise, just don't go with them. Stay level and try to keep the conversation there. Odds are they'll come back down with you. Then you want to develop that skill of empathy that we talked about in the last lecture and try to understand how it feels from their expression.

Finally what I want you to do is treat the other party's honest expressive emotion as a really privileged communication. Treat it as confidential. Be trustworthy with it. Don't spread that information around and don't use it to hurt them. Treat it as a privileged communication and honor that they told you something important about themselves, because an emotion really is something important about any of us. So those are your tips for being that kind of listener.

What have we learned in this lecture then? The first thing is we can change the way we think about the emotions that we're having, and humans as you know are emotional beings with reasoning that can help, so we can do that. Second thing is we can recognize that emotions are present in every single conflict. They're one of those basic elements that's there. They're internal facts. We can't wish them away. We can't simply will ourselves to feel differently. They're internal facts and they're going to need to be taken into account.

Thirdly we can and should report the emotions given the requisites being met. We can and should report those emotions so we can take them into account in managing the conflict. Fourth, when we do that, we want to use I statements. We want to speak for ourselves and own the emotion that we're having, I feel this. Fifth, if necessary and of course when it's possible, take some time away to calm down if that's necessary. Don't try to communicate about them when the arousal level is too high.

Sixth, remember those five requisites for communicating about emotions and doing it accurately: access, verbal communication skill, self-esteem, safe environment, and that willing and able partner. That's what we do to handle emotions.

I've got an assignment for you for the end of this lecture. Next time you find yourself in a conflict, remember to treat the emotions as internal facts and try to report them if the environment is safe and the person will listen. Try to report them without going off on the other person. Consider what emotions you feel and think how can I express them as I statements. Go ahead and express them that way and then sit back and watch and see what happens. See if that doesn't work better then pushing it at you statements or yelling at them or something else. Try it and see what happens.

Where are we going to go in our next lecture? Emotions are complex, multiple, conflicting, we explained all of that. The other thing that's very complex, multiple, and conflicting, and changing as we go along that are basic elements always present in a conflict are our goals. We have goals in every conflict. They're complex, they're multiple, they're sometimes conflicting, and they're changing as we go along. They're going to need to be handled in the conflict, and we'll talk about that in Lecture 6.

Multiple, Complex, and Changing Goals
Lecture 6

> Ideally, although perhaps rarely, the perfect thing that we're looking for is for both parties to really understand their own goals and the other party's goals fully. That's what would give us the ideal, the best chance for a real win-win.

Just like emotions, goals are multiple, complex, and changeable and can be tricky to work with in understanding a conflict. Identifying goals can help us think clearly about the resolution we want to reach and handle the emotions we experience in conflict.

Any particular conflict involves multiple goals, and some of them are more conscious than others. In some cases, goals can be in conflict with one another, or they may overlap. This multiplicity and complexity increases geometrically when we're dealing with two parties, each with his or her own set of goals.

Wilmot and Hocker define a goal as the answer to the question: What do I want? Answers fall into four types. The first is the topic goal, that is, the obvious issue on the surface of the conflict. The second is the relational goal. Conflicts occur between people who are interdependent, and those people have goals relative to that relationship. Relational goals address the question: How do I want to be treated in this relationship? The third type of goal is the identity goal; this refers to how you want to be perceived and how you want to perceive yourself. The last type of goal is the process goal: How do I want to resolve this conflict?

Topic goals are usually what trigger our awareness of a conflict and tend to be readily identifiable. These goals represent the issues that we perceive in terms of the element of frustration in our definition of conflict. Topics goals are also most likely to be perceived as being incompatible with the other party's goals.

The relational goal represents how we want to be perceived and treated in a relationship with another party. It's often pursued indirectly through topic goals. Your spouse may disagree with you on an issue, but you want that person to treat you as an equal and to show that he or she cares about you. The relational goal may be the real driver behind the topic goal of a particular conflict, or it may be in conflict with the topic goal.

The relational goal may be the real driver behind the topic goal of a particular conflict, or it may be in conflict with the topic goal.

The identity goal is often overlooked, but it can be the most important. We're all working out our identities as we go through life on any given day. In every conflict, that identity tends to be challenged. Of course, the identity goal may be pursued through a topic goal or a relational goal, or it may require us to choose between topic and relational goals. Process goals are driven by the other three types and represent multiple options for resolving conflicts.

Identifying and clarifying all these goals is an important first step in any negotiation. Understanding your goals will help you stay on target and ensure that you don't sell yourself short. At the same time, knowing your goals makes it easier to be flexible and adapt to the other party's interests.

When you're in a conflict situation, you first need to determine what you want in terms of the topic goal; try to state a satisfactory outcome of the conflict for yourself. Next, look at the relational goals and repeat the process. Ask: How do I want to be treated in my relationship with the other party? Then consider how that answer relates to the topic goal. Do the two fit or clash? If they clash, which goal is more important? With the identity goal, examine how you want to think of yourself and how you want the other party to perceive you, not only in this situation but in general.

As you're working through this process, keep in mind the perceptions we talked about in Lecture 4. Your goals result in part from your perceptions, so question yourself about that aspect of the conflict. Is your perception based on accurate information? Is your punctuation of the situation correct? Finally, you need to think about the process goal: How can you go about resolving this conflict? We'll talk more about process goals in future lectures; for now, we look at several dramatizations to identify the goals of the various people in conflict.

Identifying goals is a rigorous intellectual effort that necessitates thought and calmness. The kind of thinking required to explore your goals is not necessarily what you usually engage in during a conflict. Instead of thinking about goals, most of us tend to stew about the conflict or rehearse clever things to say. We really need to return to Deutsch's insight that we're looking for a win-win solution and that we can often find it if we can clearly identify our goals. ■

Suggested Reading

Wilmot and Hocker, *Interpersonal Conflict*.

Assignments

1. For one of those conflicts, try to identify the topic, relational, and identity goals of each party. These lead to process goals.

2. Consider whether the lens model might help you see the perspectives and perceptions of each party more clearly. Then look again to see if you can now identify more possibilities for win-win solutions.

Multiple, Complex, and Changing Goals
Lecture 6—Transcript

For success in seeking win-win solutions in conflicts, there are several factors that come into play every time, and we need to understand and manage these if we're going to have a good chance of being successful. We've been working our way through these. In Lecture 4 we looked at the role of perception and how that can best be handled. In Lecture 5 we looked at our emotions and how to handle them in a conflict.

Now here we are at the third of these critical factors, and that's our goals. This lecture is the lecture about goals in conflict. Goals it turns out are multiple and complex and changing just like our emotions are, and they can be very tricky to work with in understanding a conflict. Once again we'll use some examples to show how to identify and clarify goals, and clarify the different types of goals that we're having in a conflict and how to work with them in achieving win-win resolutions.

Here we go on goals. We want to note that each party in a conflict, both parties, are going to have goals, not just me if I'm feeling a conflict with the other person and I want something changed, that other party will have goals too. Some goals will be different. Some will be mutual, and we're going to need to find out what they are in order to move toward a resolution that takes both of us into account.

Scholars, really starting from Morton Deutsch who picked up on Lewin's Field Theory for his definition of conflict and worked with it from there on, scholars have used the notion of goals in defining conflict and with working through how we can deal with conflict all the way through. The notion of goals is very much in the research and it turns out it's a very fruitful avenue for finding ways that we can do things better when we're dealing with a conflict.

If we're clear about our goals, we can be clearer in thinking through where we want to get to, and that's going to make it even easier to handle the emotions we dealt with in our last lecture. So thinking in terms of goals is going to help us look forward, keep us from looking backward. It's going to move us toward what we want to do and help us be rational as we move forward going ahead.

Thinking in terms of goals enables us to help identify what would constitute a win for us, and also if the other person can share his or her goals, enables us to identify what's a win for that person so we can work together to get to a win-win. So working with goals is going to be very valuable.

But as I said goals are complex, and in relationships, which are complex, the goals are even more complex. Goals tend to be multiple and complex and overlapping, and then they change as we go along. So it's nice if we can think oh if we just know what our goals are we can pursue that together, but it's just not going to be quite that simple. It's more complex to deal with goals.

We have several goals in any particular conflict, and some of them we're more conscious of than others. Conflict can be confusing because goals often are in conflict with one another. Sometimes I'm really angry at the other person and I want them to just go along with me on this and get in line, but I really want them to like me and my goals seem to be in conflict with each other in that instance. The goals themselves, any individual goal, may have several facets, it may be a complex thing in and of itself so it's very hard to articulate just what it is I want in this goal because it's sort of a cluster or group of things that's hard to describe.

Goals often overlap so that achieving one helps achieve another, or not getting one undermines achieving of the other. So they're tangled up with each other in that sense.

This multiplicity and complexity increases literally geometrically when we've got our own set of these and the other party has his or her own set of these, and we try to bring them together to look for how we can get a win-win meeting all of all of our goals. It's just an enormously-complex undertaking. It's complex enough that it makes Deutsch's simple concept of win-win, and in fact Lewin's wonderful theory, Field Theory for understanding human behavior, look kind of naively simplistic because humans are much more complicated than that and so are conflicts. Still, goals is a useful idea and we need to be able to sort them out and to work with them.

What I think is the very best explanation for sorting out our goals and thinking of them comes from Wilmot and Hocker in that textbook that I use so often that lays out a typology of different types of goals that we can think of, and it talks about how they relate to one another. They define a goal incidentally in a very operational way. They say a goal is the answer to the question of what do I want. I can ask that question several times and get a number of different answers. So I can have multiple goals.

So what are the types of things that we can want in a conflict? Let's talk about those. There are four types of answers to the question, "What do I want?" They represent what Wilmot and Hocker call four different kinds of goals that we have. Let's list them and then we'll explain them. Of the four they go this way, the first one they call the topic goal. The topic goal addresses the thing that is obvious on the surface that I'm after in this conflict. Rebecca wants something. She wants something from Jane; it's quiet. That's our topic goal. She wants quiet to study.

But there's a second kind of goal that we have that they call the relational goal. In every conflict with someone with whom we're interdependent, we've got a relationship with that person, and we've got goals relative to that relationship. Those goals address the question, "How do I want to be treated in this relationship?" So I've got relationship goals as well.

There's a third kind of goal that I have in a conflict. It may be more important than either the topic or the relational goal. That's what we call identity goal. My identity goal is a little different from my relational goal. It refers to how I want to be thought of, how I want to be perceived and seen by the other person or persons in general, and it includes me, how I want to see myself. My identity goal relates to who do I want to think I am. We all have those. We're working out our identity all the time. So identity goals can be very important and they come into play in virtually every conflict.

In addition to those three and in a sense growing out those three we have a fourth kind of goal, and that's what Wilmot and Hocker call our process goal. The process goals have to do with what kind of process I want to follow to go through in dealing with this conflict. How do I want to go about resolving conflict?

There are four types of goals then. Let's get a little better description of each type. Let's start with topic goals.

Topic goals, they exist on the surface. They're what triggers our awareness of the conflict usually. They tend to be most readily identified, I wanted this. It's noisy, I want it quieter. I've got a sales territory I don't like, I want it changed. That's the topic that this conflict seems to be about, that triggers the thing. So they're on the surface; they're more easily identified. They too, though, can be multiple and they can be complex. I may want more than one thing here even at the topic level.

This is the goal, the topic goal, that's most likely to be perceived by us in terms of one of those definitions we used of conflict as being frustrated or impeded, or threatened by the other party's behavior. It's the thing that brings it to mind. It's what this conflict is about on the surface, and it's not just the surface. It's a real thing that this conflict is about. So this goal is also the one that's most likely to be perceived as being incompatible with the other party's goals. That's the topic goal. It's the one on the surface, easiest to articulate, but still pretty complex.

Let's go to another type. The second type of goal is the relational goal that we described. This is usually more important than the topic goal in almost any instance, not every instance, but it's a pretty rare exception in an important relationship when what I want relative to a particular topic is more important to me than that relationship.

The relationship goal, though, is how I want to be perceived and treated in this relationship. It's often pursued indirectly through topic goals. You disagree with me on this, I want you to show me that you care about me. I want you to treat me as an equal, and that may come up not as in general I want to be treated better, but here's how I'd like you to treat me in this instance. So the relational goal underlies, it may be the important thing, but it may be the real driver of why I want something different on the topic goal and I want to pay attention to that.

It may also be on the opposite side competing with or in conflict with the topic goal. Relationship is very important and it may be that I want you to do this my way on the topic, but I want us to still be close and I want you to still be fond of me and be treating me well. So I don't want to force you to knuckle under on this point. So the relationship goal and the topic goal may be inattention or seem to be in a conflict with one another. On the other hand, the relationship goal may be underlying and the topic goal might be a stand-in for it. So it's important to know what both of those types of goals are and to be able to see the relationship between them.

Let's go to that third type of goal, the identity. The identity goal is often overlooked, but it can be the most important. We've got some serious psychological needs about our identity. We're all working out our identity as we go through life on any given day. One of the nice things about getting older is that the intensity of working out identity at least slows down. Pretty much once we get into our 60s we are who we are, you get what you get, but we're still working identity some, that business of how we think of ourselves and how others think of us. What is our identity to our self and to the people around us and to the world is an important thing to human beings.

In every conflict, that identity tends to be challenged and so what our goals are in terms of the identity issue may be more important than either the relational or the topic. Of course the identity goal may be pursued by pursuing a topic goal or a relational goal. They may be standing in for that; they may be tied together.

On the other hand the identity goal may require us to choose between topic goals and relational goals. It may put us in a position where we've got to choose between them. So the identity goal is important. It's a struggle, makes the situation more complex.

The fourth type that we talked about is process. Process goals are sort of driven by the other three goals and the circumstance, given what I have in those other goals. The question is how do I want to go about trying to resolve this conflict? There's a great deal of difference in the ways that we can resolve conflicts. It would be really nice to treat everything as an equal and sit down as equals and work everything through. You can't, you may not always want to resolve that. It may be that what I want you to do is just do it my way in this instance, because my identity goal is so important I need to feel potent and strong. So our other three goals drive our choices of processes for how we're going to do this.

Now we're going to be short talking about this one here because processes are a subject that we talk about a great deal in Lectures 10, 11, and 12. We'll give you some good processes for negotiating resolutions and expand your repertoire of processes that you can go through. But the process goal, how do I want to go about resolving this, is going to be an important one to think about.

So that's our four types of goals. How do we work with it then? What we've got to do is try to identify and clarify the goals that we've got. This is a thinking process that we want to do as we go along through the goals. To begin with, identifying these, it's very, very useful to carefully consider and then try to clarify. Here's some "how to go about it."

Think in terms of clear goals are going to be necessary to guide me in any negotiating that I do on this. The clearer I am about the goals, what I'm after, the answer to what I want, the clearer I can be about that across all four of those, the better I'm going to do dealing with this conflict. They're going to help me stay on target and they're going to help me ensure that I don't sell myself short in terms of what even may be my most important goal as I go along.

Secondly what they're going to do is they're going to make it easier for me to be flexible and to adapt to the other party's interests. If I'm clear about what my goals are here, then I'm clear also about what I don't need and how I can accommodate the other person's goals and interests without putting mine in jeopardy. So that'll make it easier for me to work with the other person.

Ideally, although perhaps rarely, the perfect thing that we're looking for is for both parties to really understand their own goals and the other party's goals fully. That's what would give us the ideal, the best chance for a real win-win. So if both of us could've clarified and been able to articulate our goals, that's when we're going to have our best shot.

How do you go about doing that? Well that's the question. How do we do it? Start at the top. Start with the topic goal. It's number one. Ask yourself in terms of the topic, this thing that I see this is about, what do I want here? Try to imagine what a really satisfactory outcome of this conflict would look like to you. Answer that question for yourself and try to be able to state those answers explicitly and concretely so that you clearly can articulate what your goal is in terms of the topic.

Then go to the second goal and repeat the process, only this time for the relational goals. It gets more complex now that we've got more goals in play. Relational can be more difficult. What do I want here from this other person in terms of how I want to be treated? What's the relationship I'm looking for? Do I want to be treated as an equal? Do I want closeness? Do I want affection? Do I want smiles? What am I looking for in this relationship? Then once I've got that considered then we stop and think how this relates to that topic goal that's I've got. Does it fit with it? Is the topic goal a stand-in for it? Does it clash in any way with the conflict goal, and if it clashes at all, then I want to stop and think well which of these two is the more important? It's really important to decide what's important between goals so that I know what matters most to me and what I can have most give about.

Having done that what I would want to do is go to my identity goal. This one can be the hardest one to think about. It's really hard to think about who I want to see when I look in the mirror in the morning. But it's important to do. What I want to do is consider who I want to think of myself as and how I want that other person to see me, not only in this situation, but in general, in all situations. What's my identity goal here and how does this conflict relate to that? How does it relate to my relational goals? How does it relate to the topic goal? Among those let me stop and think again which is the most important of these three?

As I'm doing all of this, thinking through these goals, it's a good idea to go and do that checking of perceptions that we talked about in Lecture 4. My goals result in part from my perceptions of what's happening, so let me stop and think now that I'm thinking through and clarifying these things, "Is my perception correct? How clear am I on the information on which they're based, might I need to check this with the other person?" I need to monitor myself doing this. I need to ask how I know what it is that I think I know in this particular instance.

What's going on here? Am I sure? Let me check specifically for things like punctuation. Remember the concept of punctuation from Lecture 4, the timeframe in which we view things, when it started and where it ended? That's important and it really affects the way we set goals in terms of what we're responding to. So let me check my punctuation, the timeframe. Let me back up and try to enlarge the timeframe in which I'm thinking about this. Maybe I want to check this one with an objective third party. Am I perceiving this correctly? Because it's very important to get my perceptions relative to my goals in place as I'm checking them. If that check of perceptions shows me something different, then I want to think through how should I adjust my goals in order to deal with that.

I want to consider what I know about the other party's goals. Sometimes I can check with the other party and make this clear, but even if I can't, I really want to estimate what it is, try using that Lens Model that we talked about in perception, think how this would look for the other person. What would his or her goals be on all of those three types that we've talked about so far, topic, relational, and identity goals? What would be that person's goals in this situation? I think it's a real understanding of where the other person is coming from if I really do this exercise and try to do it, and I've got a much better chance to work through a good conflict resolution if I can do that.

Having done those three, then we go and look, okay now let's talk about process goals. How do we want to do this in terms of process here? As I said we're going to talk a lot more about processes in Lecture 10, 11, and 12, so I won't say a whole lot about it here, but having decided what those other goals, are I can think through how it is that I want to go about trying to resolve this conflict or at least trying to manage this conflict in this particular situation.

Let's consider some examples for how this might work. I'm going to describe one to you and then we'll do some dramatizations as we go along. We can put it all together if we think this through in terms of some specific examples now. Remember Anna from Lecture 5? Carl wanted Anna to stay and finish the work for him while he went home early. Let's think about what Anna's goals might've been.

On the topic what Anna was looking for is, she wanted Carl to stay and finish or at least go do what he had to do and then come back and help her finish. Her topic goal was she didn't want to be left there alone. She wanted help from Carl in finishing. That was what she would've wanted as a topic.

But Anna also had a relational goal. She wanted him to respect her, help her as much as she helps him. She was looking for a relationship where they would be teammates and equals, and she didn't always handle the thing if you remember in a way that would serve that goal very well. She did it last and the last time when she told him what was up and asked him to talk it through with her.

What might've been her identity goal as she worked through that? She wanted to think of herself and be seen as a competent helpful team player, but she did not want to see herself as a chump that could be walked over and dumped on and gotten stuck with other people's work. She had a couple of identity goals. They're "see me as this, but not as that."

Process goals, she identified for it in the last time we looked at her in an example when she said to Carl you know this is how I'm feeling when this happens and I want to get together and talk with you so that we don't have to deal with it in the future and try to get it worked out. How she wanted her process goal for resolving it, she could articulate. She wanted to talk that through with Carl and get a solution.

If she's familiar with her goals going through, she's got a much better shot at resolving this conflict. Let's go to our married couple. Do you remember

Ken and Kate? He wants to take a job out west in another city. What if Ken goes and talks to his sister Melanie and Melanie, let's just say Melanie has taken this course. She understands about this stuff so she's going to help Ken sort out his goals before he confronts Kate to talk about it. How might that conversation go?

[Video start.]

>Ken: So I saw an ad for this really great job out in Denver, and you know how much want to get out west, but I don't know how to bring it up to Kate. She's on a real fast track at her firm; I can't ask her to give that up, can I?

>Melanie: Depends. What's more important, getting to Denver or your relationship with Kate? Even if she says okay and goes with you, don't you risk making her miserable and both of you miserable in the process?

>Ken: You're right. I don't know what I was thinking. Of course Kate matters more.

>Melanie: Maybe you don't have to completely give up on going out west. She won't be at this position in her career forever. Maybe you could talk to her and the two of you could decide where the two of you want to be in five years.

>Ken: Good point, Sis. I'm going to try that. Thanks!

[Video end.]

Ken articulated his topic goal and then Melanie really helped him work through his relational goal relative to Kate and steered him toward looking for a win-win solution, suggesting they go after a long-term solution. And she reminded him that that's possible if you think in a longer term, if you enlarge your scope in the way you punctuate what's going on. There's a possibility for Ken to get a solution over time. So Melanie really helped him sort out his relational goal relative to his topic goal, and that's probably going to be better for working this one out.

Let's look at another example. Let's turn the Ken and Kate conflict around, and let's say Kate talks with a business associate, her friend Bonnie, and if you remember thinking back, remember how harshly Kate reacted when we did that example the first time and she said you can go, but you're going out there without me. She could be struggling with a relationship goal of her own at this point and thinking she might've messed that up. She also could be struggling with an identity goal. What kind of a friend and spouse is she being to Ken and what kind of identity does she have at work? She's got struggles here so how might Bonnie help Kate with that?

[Video start.]

> **Kate**: I can't believe he just laid that on me—Denver!

> **Bonnie**: I know!

> **Kate**: Where did that come from? He knows I'm at a critical point with my work!

> **Bonnie**: Well, it's not like he secretly interviewed and took the job without telling you, right? Maybe it was just an impulse thing.

> **Kate**: No, it was more than an impulse. But still, I guess I should think about his needs instead of just my own. I overreacted, and I don't want to be that kind of wife. You know what I mean?

> **Bonnie**: So what are you going to do?

> **Kate**: I don't know. But I want to do what's right for both of us and be supportive.

> **Bonnie**: Here's what you do: When you go home tonight, try sitting down with Ken; find out what's really going on with this getting out west thing.

Kate: Yeah, maybe.

Bonnie: Yeah, okay. Just listen for awhile. I bet you can find a way to get what you both want.

[Video end.]

Bonnie helped Kate work out a relationship, and the relationship that Kate wants is not one where Ken goes off to Denver or some place and she stays in Chicago. She also began to steer her toward looking at those identity goals. She does have them all, career, spouse, we live complex lives today and Kate is struggling with that one. So sorting out those goals really is going to be helpful.

That's sorting goals. Let's do some final notes. There are some additional things I want to mention relative to goals as we talk about them. We explained the four types. We looked at how could they be used to think through what we want in a conflict and just doing that really helps. Some final notes that I want to say about this though. Identifying goals in this sense is a rigorous intellectual effort. It requires thought and calm. It is not necessarily an easy thing to do. So I want you to pay attention to that. There's a lot of intellectual work involved sometimes with resolving conflict and sorting out our goals is one that's important.

Secondly I want to note that this kind of mental preparation that's required to do this, the kind of thinking we need to do, is not the kind of thinking many of us do in a conflict. If I start thinking about my goals, doing that attempt at rigorous work, I'm tempted to do what most of us want to do, what I still want to do after teaching this for 35 years, stewing about the conflict and rehearsing clever things to say, and all of that. So if we're thinking about it, thinking through our goals, we have to be careful not to do that.

Instead what we have to do is start from Deutsch's discovery that what we're looking for is a win-win. Even understand that that's going to be likely if we can identify our goals clearly enough. We need to be understanding that those goals that we have grow out of our perception of events, and we'd better be checking those perceptions to make sure that the perceptions aren't leading us in a false direction relative to our goals.

As we proceed through the process of managing the conflict, we're also going to need to notice that our goals are going to change as we go along. We're going to discover new things. We're going check perceptions, and we're going to have to change them in and adjust the goals too. It's not static. We're not stuck with just the goals we identified at the beginning. We'll have to adapt and recognize the new goals as we come along.

Fourth, as we've seen identifying and clarifying goals is not for the fainthearted. I want to note again, and I'll note this a bunch of times in this course, it takes strength and courage to deal with conflict, and it takes strength and courage to really identify those goals and do what you've got to do and do it well to identify them and work with them.

That's goals.

So let's summarize where we are in this as we go now. What we learned about goals is this. Goals are what we want to hold on to as we move through. What do we want to hold on to from this lecture? We want to note that goals are multiple and they're changing and they're complex. They change over the process of conflict management. If we want win-win, solutions it pays to think carefully about our goals and the other party's goals, and to make them as clear as possible as we go through.

We want to note that we can identify four types of goals and that helps us, the topic goal, the relational goal, the identity goal, and the process goals as we go along. If we identify the four types, that'll help us get to a clarity about our goals that we might not have otherwise had.

Goals, as Wilmot and Hocker said, are the answers to the question what do I want in each of those instances? Clarifying goals is challenging mental work, you've got to be thinking hard, and you've got to have courage to do it, but it's really going to be well worth the effort.

Here's the assignment from this lecture. I'd like to ask you to go back to the examples of conflict that you thought about after Lecture 1. For one of those conflicts, just pick one, the one that's best for this, and try to identify your topic goal, your relational goal, your identity goal, and your process goals relative to that for yourself and then do it for the other party. Try to identify the goals for both parties. Specifically pull in that Lens Model that we talked about in the lecture on perception, and see if using the Lens Model helps you see what yours and the other party's goals might be. Then look again if you can see more possibilities for win-win resolutions when you've understood something and you have a sense of what all the goals are. That's your assignment from this lecture.

For Lecture 7, where are we going to go from here? We've considered the roles of perception, emotion, and goals in conflict. There's one more critically-important factor that we have to look at before we can start talking about processes for handling conflict well. That's what we're going to do in Lecture 7. That one more factor is the factor of power. Every single conflict is also a power struggle, even a conflict with people we love dearly is a power struggle. So the subject of Lecture 7 is dealing with power in conflict.

Power—How Much We Need and How to Use It
Lecture 7

This distributive way of thinking about power ties to that old concept of win-lose, because if I have more, that means you have less. If you get more, that means I have less, so it's that win-lose idea of power carried through into win-lose in a conflict.

Every conflict, even those with loved ones, involves a power struggle. Power can be defined as the ability to cause or influence an outcome. Notice that it is not the ability to control a situation. Control is always limited and is often an illusion.

Understanding power returns us to the notion of interdependence. In an interdependent relationship, each party has some power over the other in the sense that each of us controls consequences for the other. We can behave in ways that will have effects on the other person.

We can identify three basic kinds of power: (1) personal power, such as talents, skills, or knowledge that we may have; (2) relational power, that is, the power that derives from the nature of the relationship between the parties; and (3) situational power, the conditions in the conflict situation that give power to one party or one issue more than another. Most conflicts involve a mix of these three types of power.

A common mistake in thinking about power is the idea of distributive power, that is, that a set amount of power is available and that more power to one party means less to the other. Other misconceptions are that lack of power is a matter of moral weakness or that lack of power is the same as innocence. The fact is that simple possession and exercise of power is neither right nor wrong; it just is. It's also true that we give away power in many situations— to be liked, to be promoted, and for other reasons.

In the 1950s, John French and Bertram Raven identified five bases of power, or **power currencies**. Reward power is what we get from our ability to give rewards, and coercive power, from the ability to punish. Legitimate power is either explicitly given or assumed to be legitimate based on recognized cultural roles. A supervisor in an organization has legitimate power, as does a parent. Referent power derives from the people we're associated with, and expert power is based on expertise or knowledge. Scholars from other disciplines have put forth variations on this list of power types, but the important point to remember is that both parties have power in any conflict and that power derives from the interdependence between the two parties in general and the particular situation they are in.

In strategic planning, organizations consult their stakeholders because the two entities are, in some sense, interdependent, and thus, stakeholders have power to affect the organization's ability to carry out its plans.

The concept of stakeholders used by large organizations in strategic planning can help clarify interdependence in a conflict. A stakeholder is a person or group that has a stake in what the organization does and has an effect on the organization. In strategic planning, organizations consult their stakeholders because the two entities are, in some sense, interdependent, and thus, stakeholders have power to affect the organization's ability to carry out its plans.

In a conflict, you do not need more power than the other party in order to get your needs met and the conflict resolved. What you need is sufficient interdependence between the two parties, like the organizational stakeholders, such that there is a reason to devote time and energy to working the issue out to a satisfactory solution. The concept of leverage helps to evaluate this aspect of a conflict. Your leverage is the other party's stake in your satisfaction with the solution. Of course, the other party has some leverage with you, as well; to move through a conflict, you need to understand the stakes for both parties.

Research has shown that the most important thing to understand about power in a conflict is this: The more equal the conflicting parties are in power, the better the chances are of working out a win-win resolution. Conversely, the greater the disparity in power between the two parties, the less likely they are to achieve a lasting, satisfactory solution.

How can we equalize power? If you've got more power in a conflict, you should exercise restraint and explicitly recognize the interdependence that's in play. Successful managers understand that they must treat employees as having power and importance of their own. It's also helpful to be aware of the limitations of your power; remember that control is often an illusion and that in any relationship, both parties have power.

If you have less power in a conflict, it's important to stay engaged and keep speaking up. Research shows that if you do that, your power will grow and the other person will begin to listen to you more. You can also gain power by seeking allies or by building your knowledge and increasing your personal skills.

Finally, in either situation, you have to recognize the power you have and be willing to act on it. That willingness often motivates the other person to negotiate toward a win-win resolution. ∎

Important Term

power currencies: Various sources of power that may be used to influence outcomes of social interactions, originally introduced by French and Raven in 1959.

Suggested Reading

Folger, Poole, and Stutman, *Working through Conflict: Strategies for Relationships, Groups, and Organizations*, chap. 5.

Assignments

1. Try using the concept of leverage. Think of a conflict you recently experienced and ask yourself: What was the other party's stake in my satisfaction with the outcome? Notice whether you actually had choices to make about consequences for the other party.

2. Consider whether you could have increased your leverage, and if so, how you could have done that. Get in the habit of assessing and being comfortable with your power in a conflict.

Power—How Much We Need and How to Use It
Lecture 7—Transcript

In the last several lectures we've been discussing some of these key factors that are complex, sometimes difficult to understand and manage, but they really affect how we can deal with a conflict and what's going on in a conflict. We've talked about perception and how these can differ. We've talked about emotions, which are powerful and complex and sometimes contradicting one another, and we talked about our goals, which are also complex and may contradict one another. And we may have always more than one goal at a time. We talked about those factors.

There's one more major factor we really need to consider before we move forward to talking about specific ways to handle conflict and that's the element of power. It turns out that every conflict, every conflict, even conflicts with people we love, it's power struggle. There's power in play. There's a struggle over power in every conflict. So that's our focus in this lecture. We have to talk about power in conflict situations. We have to identify some erroneous ideas about power in conflict situations, and we have to replace them with some correct ideas.

We also have to consider how much power an individual needs when we're in a conflict. How much power do I need to get a resolution that's going to work? We'll introduce the concept of leverage that I use for helping assess power in a conflict, and we'll offer some specific suggestions for how to deal with power in any conflict situation. That's our subject of this lecture. So let's get started.

We need to start with a definition. What is power and then what is power not? Definition first. I would define power as the ability to cause or influence an outcome. Pay attention to the full definition there "cause or influence" and I'm deliberately putting the emphasis on the term influence, and outcome. You know when we think of power we often think of power as control, our ability to control a situation. But most power turns out to be the power we have in the form of influence, which is less clear and less defined, but it's much more present and much more potent.

Control is always limited. Humans have way less control than we think we have at any given time. Often control is an illusion. We just don't have as much. Well we don't need as much either. So I want to get our focus more on the business of influence that we may have.

In understanding what power is I also want to call attention again to that notion of interdependence. It was there in our definition of conflict from Hocker and Wilmot early in the course in Lecture 1, and it was very present when we talked about what Lewin introduced us to in Field Theory, the notion of interdependence in relationships, because interdependence is also a source of power. In an interdependent relationship each party has some power over the other in the sense that each of us controls consequences for the other. We actually can behave in ways that will have affects on the other person.

I also want to note that there are three basic kinds of power that we can have. The first of those would be what you could call personal power. Personal power is what I have as a person regardless of the relationship or the situation that I might be in. Our personal power might be our talents, our skills and abilities that we've developed, our store of knowledge and information that we may have. We hold that. That belongs to us as a person. So that's personal power that gives us the ability to function, physical strength even is personal power, and intelligence is personal power.

But a second kind of power is what gets called relational power. Actually in conflict this is the one that's going to be most obviously in play most of the time. It's the power that derives from the nature of the relationship between myself and the person that I'm having conflict with. It's power that comes from the interdependence that we've cited. So relational power, or perhaps you would even want to call it interdependence power, is the second kind of power that we have.

But there's a third kind of power here and that's power that comes from situations, call it situational power. Every conflict is a situation and it arises in the context of situations. Those situations affect what consequences are going to occur from whom and how that can happen. So every particular situation has conditions involved that give power to one party or the other or more to this and more to that. In most conflicts what you've got is some mix of each individual's personal power, the relational power that's in play, and these are typically affected by the situations in which we're operating when we have a conflict.

Now let's talk about some wrong ideas about power. Like our ideas about conflict, an awful lot of our learning about power and the nature of power came early and so we've got some ideas and some of those ideas are accurate and right. They had to be or we wouldn't be managing to get through, and some of them are problematic, some of them give us some wrong ways of thinking. One of the most common wrong ideas about power that has been widely studied by scholars is what they call distributive power, this idea that power is a single pie kind of thing, and so more power to one party means less power to others. So when we're thinking about power we're distributing a set amount of power. That's why they call it distributive.

What happens here is this distributive way of thinking about power ties to that old concept of win-lose, because if I have more that means you have less. If you get more that means I have less, so it's that win-lose idea of power carried through into win-lose in a conflict. If the conflict itself is a power struggle, that's going to be a problem. So that's one wrong idea.

There are some others. One idea that's wrong about power is that lack of power is a matter of moral weakness, and lack of power isn't weakness. It may be just the state that I've got. A converse wrong idea about power is the idea that lack of power is the same thing as innocence, like if there was nothing I could do about therefore I'm innocent, it's not my fault, I don't have to be accountable. So lack of power could be lack of accountability translate to innocence.

There's that marvelous saying that's so often quoted by Lord Acton which said "Power tends to corrupt, and absolute power corrupts absolutely." We could flip that one over, upside down, and say that lack of power tends to corrupt and absolute lack of power might corrupt absolutely, because it would take away all accountability and all sense of responsibility. It would create irresponsibility. So more power, less power has nothing to do with right or wrong in terms of being innocent or guilty.

Here's some right ideas about power. One is that simply possession and exercise of power is neither right nor wrong, it just is. We all have it. All humans exercise power, consciously or unconsciously. I think we exercise a whole lot more power unconsciously than we do consciously when we're in conflict and at other times as well.

There are some other right ideas that we ought to pay attention to. One of them is that we all give away a lot of the power we have in many, many situations. We give away power to be liked, to be loved, to be hired, to be promoted, to escape responsibility, to avoid making effort. We do a lot of giving away power that we have. It was there in those examples that we had in Lecture 5 if you think back to those. Remember Carl and Anna where Carl is the guy who wants Anna to do some work for him because he needs to get home early and he's leaving asking her to help in that example. Carl wasn't her supervisor, he was asking her to do something confidently expecting that she would do it and Anna gave away power to him. She said okay I'll do it. She just gave it away. He's not her supervisor, they're equal in power status, but Anna just gave him the power that she had.

Where does power come from? That's the next thing we have to consider. There has been a lot of research on this following Deutsch over the years. One of the really classic studies on this that still gets quoted a whole lot was done by two psychologists, John French and Bertram Raven, back in the 1950s and what they did is identify what they called five power bases and that idea of thinking about the bases or some other scholars have called it currencies in which power exists; that idea of thinking of bases of power really gets started by French and Raven and other scholars that followed it through.

French and Raven gave us five what they called bases of power. They said we get power from our ability to give rewards. That's reward power, so ability to give rewards is a power base. Secondly they said well there's coercive power. The ability to punish delivered negative consequences is a form of power. That's a power base and they called that coercive power.

Thirdly they said it's obvious that there's what we might call legitimate power. Legitimate power is either explicitly officially given or soon to be legitimate in the roles that are recognized in a culture. A supervisor in an organization has legitimate power. He or she has the power to order people to do things and to evaluate and withhold or punish assignments. The officer who stops me for going too fast has legitimate power in a given situation. Lots of parents and children, parents have legitimate power. So we expect power to be exercised by this person. That's a base of power.

They also noted that there's what they called referent power. We get power from whom we're associated with or attached to, and that connection gives us an ally or status from which we draw power. They called that referent power. Finally they said there's expert power. If we know a lot, if we have a lot of information and expertise the knowledge itself, the information is a power base, and they called that expert power.

A good many other scholars have studied this business of power using that ideal of power bases and talked about kinds of power. I'm just going to give you a couple of examples and the point with giving you examples by the way is not, I don't want you to have 19 lists, but I want you to see that there are variations in the way you think about this. It's not just the way French and Raven thought about it.

An organizational theorist named Kipnis, D. Kipnis back in the `70s simplified the list. He said well in an organization you've got these power bases. You have threats, you have promises, you have control over information, and you have control over reinforcements, threat, promises, information control, reinforcement control. That was one way to structure. If I'm giving you examples, I'm a communications scholar so I've got to give you one from communications scholars, and there are three of these that do a lot of wonderful research on conflict, Joseph Folger, Scott Poole, and Randall Stutman who gave us a more exhaustive list.

Their list went like this. They said well skills and abilities, a form of personal power, that's a power base. Then they said expertise, knowledge, information, that's a power base. Then they said control over rewards and punishments, that's a power base. Allies just like referent power with French and Raven they said it was a source, and then they also noted possessions, including money, is a power base. That's another list.

The general idea that I want you to get here is that there are a lot of different ways to construct this list. But what happens is that there are a variety of sources we can draw on that give us power, and these are going to vary with the relationship we're in and the interdependence in this situation that we're in and we're going to want to be able to assess these.

In a conflict from whatever collection of sources, however you conceptualize that, both parties have power. If the conflict in part is going to be a power struggle, we're really going to need to be able to assess and understand the power that we have, the power that the other person has, and how these relate to one another. When we're doing this assessment, we've got our personal power, they have theirs. There is this situation, but mostly we have to understand that the power that's in play in a conflict is going to derive from the interdependence between the two parties in general and in this situation that they're in in particular.

So if I'm in a conflict I really do want to ask what power do I have here in this conflict, where does that come from, what are the bases of it. What power does the other person in this conflict have and where does that person's power come from? What are the bases of it? We're going to want to know what these things are, even with someone we love because I can use power to punish, reward, it's responsibility that I have and the other person too, so we need to know this.

Let's think about some examples of these. Remember Ken in earlier lectures, Ken and Kate in that conflict. This is a guy who wants to take a job out west and his wife Kate wants him to stay put because her career is taking off right now. Each of these two has relational power. This is a marriage and we can assume that they love each other and it would be painful to split up. So each has power, each wants the other to be happy. But Kate in this situation also has well some personal power, she's obviously excelling at work, but she has situational power in that now in this particular timeframe those skills and efforts are paying off so her career is taking off.

The situation of her current career trajectory gives her a kind of power that trumps Ken's wishes at the present time. So that situation though is temporary. It's a mix of relational power and situational power that gives Kate the trump at this point.

Let's think about another example. Think about two roommates from Lecture 1, what the problem of noise, one making noise, the other trying to study. Roommates in an apartment will each have the power to greatly affect living conditions of the other. They can make those conditions easier and more pleasant, they can make them more difficult. In this case you've got that general relational basis for power going, but you also have this situation that on this given night one of these people is studying for a difficult test. That should give a situational power base to that person.

If we also go back thinking of examples to our folks Carl and Anna, the work colleagues. In that situation, though she didn't exercise that she gave it away, Anna had a great deal of power in that relationship, it was relational, but in that situation she held the cards. She was the one who could do the work, let Carl go. Carl was sort of stuck. He needed to get home, probably his wife is expecting him, and she gave it away. But in that instance she should've known she actually had more power than Carl, and she didn't have to give it away.

So notice in all of these, all of these examples, the power is derived from the interdependence of the parties, and they're always happening in the context of a situation. So power in each of these cases is a function of the interdependence that's in play.

It's interesting when I think about interdependence, there's a concept employed by large organizations when they do strategic planning that helps make this clear. When an organization wants to do a competent job of strategic planning, what they know they need to do is go consult with what they call stakeholders, and a stakeholder is a person who has a person or for that matter a group or an institution or organization who has a stake in what the organization does. That stake means that what the organization does or how we do it affects that person or that group. Conversely what they may do will have an effect on the organization. It's a two-way relationship.

So when they're going to try to do a strategic plan and figure out where they're going to go from here for the short-term and the long-term, organizations who are doing that confidently know that they need to go consult their stakeholders. Why is that? Because those stakeholders are in some sense interdependent with the organization and so they have power to affect the organization's ability to do what it wants to do. So those relationships work that way, they're interdependent.

How much power then do we need in a conflict is the next question we've got to consider. Remember in Lecture 1, one of the wrong ideas I listed for you was that in a conflict we need more power than the other party in order to succeed, in order to get our needs met, in order to get our conflict resolved well. Well it turns out that the right idea is that we do not. We absolutely do not need more power than the other party. What we need is for there to be enough interdependence there that we affect consequences for the other party enough, just enough, that they have a reason like those stakeholders the organization would consult, they have reason to give us time and energy to work with us because it matters to them that we're satisfied with how this works out.

To evaluate this and view it quickly in a kind of a shorthand, a term that I've used over the years is just to use the word leverage. If I ask what's the leverage that I have in this situation? My leverage can be defined as the other party's stake in my being satisfied with the way we worked this out. Let me say it again. My leverage is equal to the other party's stake in my being satisfied with the way we worked this conflict out. Get the idea. I can ask that question for myself, what's the other party's stake, okay.

Examples her: Ken's leverage with Kate in that Ken and Kate whether he's going to take a job and move. He does have some leverage. Kate is his spouse. She loves him. She doesn't want him to be unhappy. He's got some leverage in this situation. Of course she has leverage and more leverage relative to the situation of her career. Anna in her interaction with Carl where he's asking her to finish the project for him has plenty of leverage here. His stake is that he needs the help that only she can give him at this point. She also has some longer term leverage here that she apparently isn't thinking about much in the sense that this issue of teamwork, he's going to need help over time from her. They need to work together on stuff and for that long term he needs it.

Of course the other party also has some leverage with us too. So it's really useful to understand what's the other party's leverage with me in a conflict. We need to look at what are the stakes for each of us as we move through these things. How much leverage do I need, not more than the other party, just enough that it's worth the time and energy and a bit of risk for the other party to listen to us and try to work this thing out well with us. That's what we need to go pursue a win-win resolution.

In the 20th century research on this issue, the most important point that's come through consistently about power in the number of studies where it just keeps coming back to this point, the most important thing to understand about power in a conflict is this. The more equal the conflicting parties are in power, the better are the chances of working out a good resolution. The more equal, the better the chances in getting a good resolution. Conversely, the greater the disparity in power between the two parties in a conflict, the less likely we are to achieve a lasting, satisfactory resolution.

So we're really interested here in equal power. So we don't have less power if the other party gains some. It would be very nice to move toward making the power more equal, bringing theirs up doesn't bring ours down. Our interest is to work to make power more equal.

How do we go about doing that? Taking together the lessons we've observed so far here tell us that we should be working to equalize the power. Whether or not we have more or less power, that's still going to be true. We should be working to equalize power.

If I've got higher power, what I really want to be doing is moving to exercise restraint and to explicitly recognize the interdependence that's in play so we can add power for the other person. It would help when Carl asks Anna for help here, if instead of just confidently relying that she's going to do it for him, he really acknowledges the power that she has, puts it on the table, helps her be aware of it, because in equalizing the power here they're much more likely to work out something that's going to work well for tonight and work well for the long run.

Similarly Kate and the issue with her husband Ken would really help things, and you can picture this in the marriage, it would really help things if Kate can explicitly acknowledge that Ken's happiness means a lot to her, that that carries weight, and that her ability to succeed at work may be affected by having that strong loving relationship and that she doesn't want him to be unhappy for the long-term. Helping Ken understand how much power he's got in this situation, which makes it more present and equalizes, would really help them for the long term.

Notice in neither of those examples where the person acknowledging the power and moving some to the other person, that person isn't giving up any power at all. They may be giving up the illusion of power or the lack of knowledge of what the other party's power is, but they're not losing any real power. So equalizing, bringing it up, doesn't cost me power.

At the general level doing this, successful leaders in organizations and communities really do understand that leadership works best if we treat others as coworkers and each having power and importance of their own. That doesn't mean it's equal. If I'm the boss and consulting my colleagues and people that work with me and listening to them and granting them the power they have doesn't mean it's just democracy, everything's going to a vote. It can be honest consultation that can really influence me. So I'm acknowledging the power they've got and giving them more power to influence me, but it doesn't give me less. It's going to give me more information with which to function effectively.

Similarly more equality in power, if you think about, it is going to create the power of complicating things a little more. So it may seem more complicated and less simple, but we have to recognize the value of the research which tells us that we're going to get better management of conflicts and better solving of problems if we equalize the power and make things work out.

It also helps to note the limits of the power we have. I said at the beginning of the lecture when I was talking about definition, that control is often an illusion. All relationships are two-way relationships, even ones where we think we have all the power and the other power doesn't have any. Relationships are two-way relationships. Power always belongs to all parties.

Supervisors in organizations which I've worked with a lot have clear, assigned, legitimate power according to French and Raven's terms. They can give assignments, they can set standards, they can enforce standards, they can reward, they can punish, but any good supervisor, any supervisor that's been on the job for awhile knows very well that those powers are extremely limited. A supervisor can work very hard to enforce minimum standards, but when I ask supervisors is that what you wanted, your people to all meet minimum standards, they all say no, I want them to go way beyond that. My power as a supervisor to get my people to go way beyond that has very little to with control and it doesn't have all that much to do with handing out rewards and punishments.

My ability to listen to them, work with them, guide, and encourage really is going to affect how successful I am as a supervisor, and it requires me to recognize the limits of my power. So when I spend time and energy encouraging and listening and influencing by consulting rather than trying to enforce or distribute rewards and punishments, I'll be more successful if I do that, recognizing the limits of my power. And that applies when I'm in a conflict with an employee too.

What if I have less power than the other party in a conflict, what can I do? There really are things that I can do to balance this and to be more effective. One of those and it's very well backed by the research is given to us by Wilmot and Hocker in their book *Interpersonal Conflict*. What they say is stay engaged and keep speaking up, and if you do that it's kind of like high torque rather than one big punch through, if you do that, if you stay engaged and keep speaking up, your power will grow and the other person will begin to listen to you more. The evidence supports that.

If we apply this to our examples, Anna's starting point with Carl in that relationship, the way that example worked doesn't look all that equal, but if she keeps speaking up about her needs and interests and time needing to be taken into account, her influence over Carl in this situation will grow. I suspect that Rebecca, our graduate student, is probably going to need to just stay engaged and do some persistent speaking up with her roommate Jane to keep that noise down, because we're not always thinking about keeping the noise down with the other person, so we may feel we have less power, but staying engaged and speaking up really makes a big difference and can be very effective.

We also can gain power by seeking allies. Any of us whoever survived on a playground if we were smaller than some other people know that getting an ally can help. That's a legitimate thing to do if we need to build our power, but when I mention it, and it'll come up several times later in the course, I want to suggest that we be very careful in doing this because we don't want to set off a spiral of getting more allies and triangulating conflicts and making matters worse. So I'd be careful about it, but we can gain power by getting allies. We can also gain power by getting more knowledge and information building our expertise and increasing our personal skills. That one we can pursue at all times.

Finally I want to note here talking about balancing power that whether you have more or less than the other party, I've got to be willing to recognize the power that I've got and I've got to be willing to act on it. If I'm not willing to act on the power I've got, it'll be the same as giving it away. We've got to be willing and able to impose consequences on the other person.

That willingness and ability often motivates the other person to negotiate with us, helps them think about it might be a good idea to get with us and work on a win-win resolution. So we need to be willing and able to exercise power.

A kind of extreme example of that, thinking in terms of our couple Ken and Kate, might arise if for several years Ken hangs in there and things aren't changing and Kate just wants to stay where she is. What if Ken at some point was to say to Kate, look I need to have a change, I need to get out of here, and we need to talk about that. And if we can't talk about it and work something out, I'm gone anyway. At that point because he was willing to walk away, Ken might have a whole lot more power with Kate because he was willing to exercise what he had. It's kind of paradoxical, it's a dilemma in a way, but we have to be willing to exercise our power sometimes even with loved ones in order to move things to a better place. Ken's power would increase if he did that.

Let's summarize what we've learned about power. What do we know about power in a conflict? First, most important thing here is that power, that definition is that our ability to influence outcomes, influence is the most important word. Secondly, power resides in persons, in relationships, and situations, and it comes from a variety of sources. It's complex and it's always changing and moving, it's in all of those things at once.

Thirdly, we all have some power in every conflict and we need to assess the power we've got and the power the other party has. Fourth, we don't really need more power than the other party, we just need enough to make it worthwhile for that person to work with us. Fifth, the more power one person has does not mean that the other person has less. We can both gain more power together.

Sixth, the more equal the conflicting parties are in terms of power, the more likely they are to actually achieve a satisfactory and lasting resolution. That's the important finding from all the research on this point. Seventh, if I've got more power from the other person resulting from that idea of equal power, I need to exercise restraint, explicitly recognizing interdependence, bring things more equal. On the other hand if I've got less power than the other person, I can do things. I can stay engaged and speak up. I can seek allies, but I want to avoid setting up downward spirals. I can build up my expertise and my personal skills, but I've always got to with more or less power, whatever it is, be willing to recognize and act on the power that I've got. Power in conflict.

Here's your assignment from this lecture. I want you to practice using that concept of leverage and I want to suggest that a good way for you to do that is to think back to a conflict you recently experienced. Try working leverage just for that, how it would've been. Ask yourself what was the other party's stake in my being satisfied with the outcome of that conflict. I want you to notice whether you actually had choices or consequences for that other party that you might or might not have been aware of and might or might not have been willing to exercise.

I want you to ask yourself whether you could've increased your leverage and if so how you might've gone about doing that. I want you to do that as a kind of practice with a past tense thing so you can get used to beginning to assess your leverage, assess your power in any given conflict. That's your assignment for this lecture.

Where are we going to go from here? This is a good moment to kind of sum up where we've been. We've got conflict defined. We're really looked at all these different factors, these key factors that make a difference that we need to understand. We looked at perceptions. We looked at emotions. We looked at goals and we looked at power in conflict. So we've got a lot to work with there.

Now we're going to move forward and begin to focus on strategies for managing conflict, and first we're going to focus on the strategies that most of us acquired early in our life that sort of became our default strategies. These come to be called our conflict styles, and they'll be our subject in Lecture 8.

Conflict Styles
Lecture 8

What I really want—my objective—is to have skill in all five of those modes of conflict management so that I can choose the one that best applies to the situation and the relationship.

In managing conflict, most people appear to operate with a repertoire of one or two default strategies, regardless of the specific situation or whether the strategies result in win-win outcomes. Scholars in the field call these strategies **conflict styles**.

In the mid-1960s, two management theorists, Robert Blake and Jane Mouton, developed a theory of management styles based on a grid. In the 1970s, **Kenneth Thomas** and **Ralph Kilmann** applied the earlier theory of management styles to managing conflict. These researchers identified five conflict strategies and arranged them in a model according to the degree to which each reflected "concern for self" and "concern for the other person" and the degree to which each represented cooperativeness or non-cooperativeness.

The first of Thomas's and Kilmann's conflict styles is avoidance, that is, acting as if the conflict isn't present. This style results in a lose-lose resolution. The second style is competition, one party attempting to get what he or she wants at the other's expense. This is a win-lose strategy. The third style is compromise, a no win-no lose strategy in which both parties give something up. Accommodation is the fourth style; here, one party gives in but doesn't get anything in return, resulting in a lose-win resolution. Finally, the fifth style is collaboration, that is, working together with the other party to achieve a win-win outcome. This is the best strategy, but it's certainly not the most common conflict style in use, and it may not work all the time; it may be impossible to get the other party to cooperate. We should also note that most people don't use a single style; most of us tend to follow a pattern of conflict styles, using one as a primary strategy but falling back on a different style if the first one doesn't work.

This model can help us observe the styles and patterns we use, and once we're aware of these patterns, we can expand our repertoire so that we can respond with strategies that are better suited to specific situations and relationships. The objective here is to develop skill with each style.

More recently, **John Gottman**, a psychologist, has developed a typology of what he calls "bids" and "responses." A bid is one party communicating with another, seeking a response of some sort. If that communication is about a conflict, the bid would be an effort to negotiate a compromise or to collaborate. The three types of responses that the first party might receive are characterized as turning toward, turning away, and turning against. Turning toward acknowledges and validates the bid; it moves toward closeness in the relationship. Turning away is an indifferent response and creates distance between the parties. Turning against acknowledges the bid but rejects its validity. This is a hostile response, and it creates hostility in the receiving party.

Gottman's work is primarily in close personal relationships, but his model can be applied to other types of associations, as well. Our responses to others should make it clear that we want to hear what they are saying and that we're

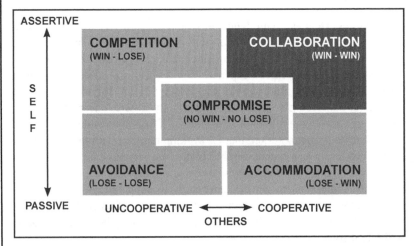

Figure 8.1. Thomas-Kilmann conflict style model.

happy to work together to resolve conflicts. Turning toward is not always easy, but Gottman tells us that it is the best response most of the time.

How can we relate Gottman's work to the five conflict styles of Thomas and Kilmann? Collaboration is clearly turning toward, and compromise is, as well, but compromise sets limits and boundaries. Accommodation might appear to be turning toward, but it's not good for the relationship and it doesn't help to resolve conflicts; in many cases, it's another version of avoidance. Competition is most obviously turning against, but it can also be turning away. Turning away can be a power game, as in not letting the other person in on what's going on. In the same way, avoidance is turning away, but it can also involve competition in that it's a way to show less respect. In conflict management, the most consistently effective strategy is the correlate of collaboration: turning toward. ■

Names to Know

Gottman, John: Well known for his groundbreaking research on marital stability, Gottman is a professor of psychology emeritus at the University of Washington and currently heads the nonprofit Relationship Research Institute.

Kilmann, Ralph: A consultant and author of 15 fifteen books and more than 100 articles on organizational design and conflict management.

Thomas, Kenneth: Has taught as a professor of management at UCLA, Temple University, and the University of Pittsburgh.

Important Term

conflict styles: Default strategies for managing conflicts that people tend to employ across different situations.

Gottman and DeClaire, *The Relationship Cure: A Five-Step Guide to Strengthening Your Marriage, Family, and Friendships*.

Wilmot and Hocker, *Interpersonal Conflict*, pp. 130–177.

Assignments

1. Identify your own default conflict style. How does it limit your ability to resolve conflicts?

2. Discuss with someone with whom you have a close personal relationship how you respond to each other in a conflict; do you turn toward, turn away, or turn against?

Conflict Styles
Lecture 8—Transcript

Morton Deutsch showed us all those years ago that we can have win-win resolutions most of the time. So one would expect that most people would turn first to strategies aimed at getting win-win outcomes. But that's not what happens. Instead most people appear to operate with a repertoire of like one or two "default" strategies for managing conflicts, regardless of the specific situation and most of those don't necessarily have to do with win-win outcomes.

We call default strategies these days "conflict styles" and that's what this lecture is about. It's about recognizing the various conflict styles that people acquired early in life, from their early learning, developed skill in over time, and so they're just sort of default ways that they turn to to resolve conflicts. We want to understand them and understand how to work with that better.

So let's get started. Actually way back in about the mid 1960s, two management theorists, Robert Blake and Jane Mouton, developed a theory of management styles. They referred to it as the management grid and they laid it out in a square shaped thing, and they talked about the styles that seemed to be the default styles that most managers have.

About ten years after that two important social psychologists K. W. Thomas and R. H. Kilmann took that concept of styles and they applied it to managing conflict. Their notion of conflict styles and the work they did, the research they did to support that, became an important area for further research and got lots of general application, and it's held up over time. It's still useful. It's still being used in training and still continues to spawn more research. So we want to talk about the basic concept of conflict styles that Thomas and Kilmann gave us.

What did Thomas and Kilmann do? They identified five general conflict strategies that they said are the default strategies that we tend, not always, not totally exclusively, but that tend to be the default strategies that most of us turn to when we have a conflict. They arranged those five conflict styles into a model according to the degrees to which each style reflected "concern for self" and "concern for the other person" and the degree to which each style represented cooperativeness with the other person or non-cooperativeness.

They laid that conflict description out in a general square diagram with each style representing a place in the big square. Picture this square in your mind if you're not looking at this, and we do have a representation of it in the guidebook.

Here are the five styles. First style, you think of this one, go down to the lower left-hand corner picturing it. Here we have the style of avoidance. Avoidance seems to be a low-risk thing to do. It's the style in which what we do is we simply act as though the conflict isn't there and we hope it will go away. We just don't do anything about it. It's not very cooperative, it doesn't cooperate with the other party, and it's lose-lose. It's low concern for myself, low concern for the other person.

Let's look at an example of what avoidance would look like. Here's a guy named Hank. He's the head of an architectural design team and he's at his desk. And one of his team members George pops his head in to check with Hank about something. Here's the picture.

[Video start.]

> **George**: Hey Hank. Any word on those designs we sent to Barry?
>
> **Hank**: Well, as a matter of fact, I just got an e-mail. Barry and his team seem to have a problem with our designs. They say the designs don't mesh with our other projects.
>
> **George**: Really? What do you think we should do about it?
>
> **Hank**: Well, let's just see if it blows over. I hate haggling with those guys.
>
> **George**: Yeah. Sounds good. Talk to you later.

[Video end.]

Is that you, avoiding a conflict? Hank just doesn't want to deal with it. But it's not going to go away, and if that's Hank's general pattern there are lots of things that are just not going to go away.

So let's look at another kind of a style. This would be the style of competition. That, in the Kilmann and Thomas model, moves up. It's still on the left side, but it's in the top corner. Competition is attempting to get what I want at the other party's expense. It treats this thing like a win-lose situation and goes after getting what I want at the expense of the other party. It's very high concern for myself; it's low concern for the other party. It's mostly not cooperative although some battles involve a certain amount of cooperation. But what this is is a win-lose strategy. I'm looking for an outcome in which I win, the other party loses. Let's look at what would happen if Hank had a style of competition.

[Video start.]

> **George**: Hey Hank. Any word on those designs we sent to Barry?

> **Hank**: Well, as a matter of fact, I just got an e-mail. We have a little challenge here to deal with. Barry and his team seem to have a problem with the designs.

> **George**: A problem?

> **Hank**: They say they don't mesh with our other projects.

> **George**: Really? What do you think we should do about it?

> **Hank**: Our designs are fine; we know what we're doing. Those guys just think they know it all. We need to let Barry know we're not going to give an inch on this one.

> **George**: All right. Sounds good to me. I'll talk to you later.

[Video end.]

Would that be your style, competition? Hank is treating this as a contest now and that may not give us the result either. It's not adaptive to the situation.

Let's go look at a third style. This style would be compromise. Compromise in the model sits right out there in the middle. It just muddles around in the middle of this square. Compromise is giving up something and expecting the other party to do the same thing, kind of meeting in the middle, I give up something, you give up something. And some of that, some of us have that as our automatic response, as our default response.

It assumes that the situation is competitive, but it seeks to minimize the damage by splitting the losses. It has some concern for self, some concern for the other. It's cooperative to an extent, cooperative with boundaries and limits. It's no win, no lose. Here's Hank and George again. Let's see what happened if Hank is a compromiser for his style.

[Video start.]

> **George**: Hey Hank. Any word on those designs we sent to Barry?
>
> **Hank**: Well, as a matter of fact, I just got an e-mail. Barry and his team seem to have a problem with the designs. They say they don't mesh with our other projects.
>
> **George**: Is that so? What do you think we should do about it?
>
> **Hank**: Let's just split the difference. Can you get back to Barry and let him know that we'll tweak a few things here and there. That ought to keep him happy.
>
> **George**: Yeah, I can do that. I'll keep you posted.

[Video end.]

Is that one you, is that your style? Some of us go to compromise pretty automatically, but you notice it really didn't center on getting at what the problem was. Hank is just immediately moving to split the difference. In that situation, it would be the state if Hank were a compromiser in terms of his conflict style.

Let's look at one more. That would be the style of accommodation. Accommodation will be down in the lower right-hand corner of this thing. It's down there where I'm not going to take very good care of myself down there with avoidance, but it takes care of the other person. It's taking care of the other party by giving in, but it's not doing anything to take care of myself. Some of us are accommodators as a style. We're all concerned for the other party and we're not enough concerned for ourselves. It's totally cooperative, but it doesn't require the other party to be cooperative with us. So it's a lose-win, I lose, the other guy wins.

What if Hank were an accommodator, maybe a little unlikely at the head of a design team. What if Hank were an accommodator in this situation, what would that look like?

[Video start.]

>   **George**: Hey Hank. Any word on those designs we sent to Barry?
>
>   **Hank**: Well, as a matter of fact, I just got an e-mail. Barry and his team seem to have a problem with the designs. They say they don't mesh with our other projects.
>
>   **George**: Really? What do you think we should do about it?
>
>   **Hank**: Well, the designs seem fine to me, but we need to keep Barry happy. I hate to waste the time, but can you ask your team to take another pass at the designs?
>
>   **George**: Uh, okay. Yes, we'll take another look.
>
>   **Hank**: Thanks.

[Video end.]

Accommodator, Hank is ready to give away the store here. He might have a perfectly good design going, but he's giving it up too easily. Some of us are accommodators. It doesn't take good care of us, and if we're too much accommodators ,we don't necessarily take good care of the other person either. We don't let them know who we are or we don't surface problems that ought to be surfaced. So accommodation as a default style is its own set of problems, although sometimes we would have to use it.

Fifth style let's turn to. The one that would most suit Morton Deutsch is collaboration. It's in the top right-hand corner of this model. Collaboration is working together with the other party to really achieve a win-win outcome. It treats the conflict like a problem and it tends to engage in creative problem-solving to get what's good for both of us. It's high concern for self, high concern for the other party, and it's cooperative on both parties' terms. It's looking for a win-win. It's the best strategy, but it's certainly not the most common conflict style that we see in use.

What would it look like though if Hank really engaged in collaboration as his style? Let's look at that one.

[Video start.]

> **George**: Hey Hank. Any word on those designs we sent to Barry?
>
> **Hank**: Well, as a matter of fact, I just got an e-mail. Barry and his team seem to have a problem with the designs. They say they don't mesh with our other projects.
>
> **George**: Really? What do you think we should do about it?
>
> **Hank**: Well, I think our designs are solid, but let's hear what he has to say. Can you set up a meeting with Barry for tomorrow?
>
> **George**: Yeah, sounds good. I'll get right on it.

Hank: Thanks.

[Video end.]

Is that one you? I hope so. When we have that as the default style, the one we would go to first, it's easier to back into the others. But we can't do collaboration all the time, it doesn't work all the time. We can't get the other party to cooperate all the time. Collaboration though is the style that we'd like to have as our go-to style more often than not.

I want to say something about the idea of patterns of styles that come along. We don't just have one single style. Most of us are a little more complex than having just one single style. What we do is we tend to have a pattern, it's like I'll do this first, I'll try this, and if that doesn't work and I'm finding that doesn't work, I have a backup, a number two thing that I turn to. People tend to have default patterns of styles.

Some common examples, for instance, suppose I'm into avoidance and I'm going to avoid as long as possible, but some people have that as their first style ,and then their go- to style after that is competition. So I'll do avoidance and then if that doesn't work I'll get angry and compete, avoidance backed up by competing.

Another one is they may start by being hostile and being competitive, and then when that doesn't work go back down. It's patterns that become the styles that we tend to go by. So all of us have these. We learned them early. We've got this set of conflict styles.

How do we put what Kilmann and Thomas taught us to work? The first thing we can do, we can observe the styles and patterns that we have. In fact that's a very common thing that's done in training sessions all over the country with the Kilmann and Thomas work. We can determine what is our default style and what is our default pattern of styles. Once we know what that is we can sort of intervene on that. Aware of it we can consider how we might expand our repertoire so that we can better respond with strategies that are better suited to specific situations and specific relationships.

If I have a wider repertoire and I start thinking in terms of responding in the conflict in a way that best suits that situation and my relationship with the other party, then I'm going to be in better shape. But as I'm trying to expand these, I want to caution you a little bit. It's not like I can try the new thing and I'll be as good at it as I was at this thing that I learned early that has been my default style. I've got a lot more experience with my default style. It may be a less desirable style, but I'm better at it.

I've got to be patient, but I really want to expand my repertoire and get better and more often at using the other strategies listed on that list of styles. So that instead of one style, what I've got is skill in each of them. In fact, Thomas these days calls them not so much styles as he refers to them as modes for conflict management. What I really want, my objective, is to have skill in all five of those modes of conflict management so that I can choose the one that best applies to the situation and the relationship.

That's what I can do making use of it. Thomas and Kilmann's work not only spawned a lot of research, but it has also had this direct, practical application over the years and it holds up well over time. It's still very much in use today, and that's a good dual test of any social science discovery.

I want to talk about one other type of set of styles that takes place although the author didn't call them that. It really fits what we're talking about in this instance. And that's the work that happened more recently when John Gottman, the psychologist, developed a typology of what he called "bids" and "responses." He did this about 2001. It turns out it's very helpful in relationships to get this pattern and to use it to deal with our conflicts and to improve the relationships as we do.

Gottman talked about bids and responses. A bid is what happens when one party communicates with the other seeking a response of some sort. If that communication is about a conflict, that bid would be an effort to either negotiate a compromise or to collaborate, one party brings a conflict to us, wants a response. And what Gottman focuses on that makes a huge difference is how the other party responds. What are the types of responses that I can give when the other party makes a bid in that sense?

There are three types, they're very easy to understand and follow. The three types are these. He calls them turning toward, turning away, and turning against. That one starts on the positive side with turning toward, so let's put the good one up here first.

Turning toward acknowledges and validates the bid, turns toward the person and literally moves closer in the relationship. Let's look at the example of responding to a bid by turning toward. Here's one where we have a guy named David, he's watching a ballgame on television. David has left a mess in the kitchen when he grabbed a snack, and his wife just went in the kitchen and found it. Let's see what happens.

[Video start.]

>**Spouse**: David, you left a mess on the counter.

>**David**: I'm sorry hon. Can I clean it up at half time? It's about two minutes from now.

>**Spouse**: Sure. But please remember to clean up your mess next time, okay?

>**David**: Will do, hon.

[Video end.]

David is really turning toward his wife in that instance. He's acknowledging that she's got a complaint. He's not walking away from the game and jumping up and just totally accommodating, but he's clearly turning toward her and responding in a way that brings them closer. So that's a pretty good response. That's turning toward.

Let's go look at what turning away might look like. What's turning away? Turning away is a response in which you really just don't acknowledge or validate the bid. It's indifferent. It creates distance. It doesn't object; it just doesn't acknowledge and respond in a way that does anything. It's turning away.

What would happen in this same scenario if David used turning away as a response? Let's take a look and see.

[Video start.]

> **Spouse**: David, you left a mess on the counter.
>
> **David**: Honey, the game's on. I'll clean it up at half time.
>
> **Spouse**: Never mind. I'll do it myself.

[Video end.]

What David has done in this instance is just not acknowledged. She's going to do it herself. If I'm David I might be thinking I got by that one and it's no problem, but I'm going to bet in most marriages David is going to pay a price for this. His spouse is not being well served. So there's a conflict here that's not being handled. It'll get under the rug. Turning away is not a very good response in terms of doing anything to resolve the conflict, and it's not good for building and strengthening the relationship, not the kind of response you'd most want to give.

Let's go to that third type. Let's look at what turning against would be like. Turning against acknowledges the bid but rejects its validity. Instead of being indifferent it's hostile and it creates hostility that counters the hostility it gives. So if we go there and we think about turning against, let's consider our example again. What if David instead of turning toward or turning away turns against in this situation?

[Video start.]

> **Spouse**: David, you left a mess on the counter.
>
> **David**: Do you have to complain about every little thing? I'm trying to watch the game.

Spouse: All you do is watch games and make a mess. I'm sick of cleaning up after you. I'm not your maid!

[Video end.]

I hope that's not you. We don't need to be that hostile with each other, and in any ongoing relationship turning against really just makes it be a fight and doesn't move things to resolving your conflict. We did that one with a married couple example and that's actually where Gottman does most of his research. He's focused on building strong, happy marriages and researching how that can happen. But it applies to any kind of relationship, turning toward, turning away, turning against, at work, with friends, romantic relationships, and it applies to any kind of relationship.

In this case, the style that we have, the predominant style that we're looking for, ought to be turning toward. Let's talk about our applications of Gottman.

As I said Gottman's work really is in close personal relationships. He's primarily concerned with marriages and getting them stronger. But this applies to every kind of thing, every kind of relationship we could be in. He makes it clear that what we need to do is respond in ways that say that we really want to hear what our partner is saying and that we're happy to work with that other person to try to get this done. That requires some risk taking on our part and we're going to talk about that more as we go along. Turning toward is not an easy thing to do, but he makes it clear that the best answer most of the time what really ought to be our style is turning toward.

What would we do relating that to the Thomas and Kilmann five styles? Let's look at these and see how they fit together. In the first place, collaboration is clearly turning toward. Carl and Anna, the colleagues working on a fundraising plan, could be in a collaborative mode. If Carl wants something from Anna, Anna can turn toward him and set boundaries. In those examples, you can see how collaboration would be turning toward, compromise can sometimes be turning toward.

Accommodation might appear to be turning toward, that style, but it really is going to involve withholding on just accommodating the person. That's not going to be good for the relationship and it's not going to help resolve the conflicts. So accommodating can kind of be bogus turning toward. What if David jumped up and ran in the kitchen and cleaned the mess up and ran back to the game. I don't know that that would've been a very good response really. So accommodation is not exactly the same as turning toward.

Anna in the accommodation mode, in that example if you think about Anna back then, she was agreeing when she said hmm, yeah I'll do it, but accommodating can be covert. She could be turning away or turning against later in some other way. I might even agree like Anna to go ahead and do something. I might smile when I do it and then resent and resent being asked, and so that doesn't get the conflict resolved.

Accommodating isn't turning toward; it doesn't really get the conflict resolved. It just doesn't get it on the table. It's another version of avoidance. So if I keep this to myself and I don't want the other party to know, I'm making distance, not good for relationships in the long run. So you can where when you lay conflict styles against Gottman's ideas of turning towards some of these don't work.

Compromise is turning toward, but it sets limits and boundaries, and sometimes it's really the right answer to do although it draws boundaries and limits. It might be better to really collaborate.

Competition, how does that play in terms of the thing with Gottman. Competition is most obviously turning against, but there's also some competition in that just turning away and not acknowledging. Turning away can be a power game, not letting the other person have power, like not letting them in on what's going on. So when we lay these together we can see the lean, where we ought to put it. Compromise really isn't as good as collaboration, but it is there.

What about avoidance though? That's the style we started with. Where does that go? Avoidance is by definition turning away. It can also be a way of turning against because it's a way to disengage. It's a way to show less respect. It can be less respectful than turning toward and turning against and fighting. So I remember back an example of Anna, the first time Carl asked her and she said well I can't promise, but I'll give it a shot. What's that, he doesn't know what's happening as he's going away. So it's there in our examples.

Turning away and turning against can create distance, and they don't solve problems. If we want to solve the problem, if we want to get the conflict resolved, the best strategy is consistently going to be turning toward. That's going to be the best mode in Kilmann and Thomas's terms, which is collaboration. And it ought to be, though we said it isn't, it ought to be our style. So we want to get moving in that direction.

What have we learned then in this lecture? We learned we have default styles. We learned that we learn them early; that those styles are our ways of dealing with or not dealing with the conflict and they're what we turn to automatically, and we have them in patterns as well.

What are the styles: avoidance, competition, compromise, accommodation, and collaboration. As Thomas and Kilmann point out, no one style is appropriate for every situation, not even collaboration. But we really can and we really should try to broaden our repertoire so that we can respond to any specific conflict in any specific relationship with what that conflict, that situation, and that relationship demands.

Secondly we learned that we have three options when another party turns to us in a conflict and makes a bid and wants a response in a conflict situation. Those three are turning toward, turning away, and turning against. You know what, not only do conflicts get handled better, but relationships tend to get better and stronger and to do so consistently, it's the predominant style of both parties is turning toward. They tend to get worse if it's turning away or turning against. That's conflict styles.

Let me give you an assignment relative to that one. What I'd like to ask you to do is this and actually it's two. First I want you to really look at and assess your own conflict style. Think back across the conflicts you've engaged in over some time and think about what it is you turn to automatically. Where do I go first and then maybe what's my backup after that. Think about how it limits the way I resolve conflicts and see if I can begin to broaden my repertoire.

Secondly I want you to look at those response types. Sit down with someone with whom you have a close personal relationship and talk to one another about how you respond in terms of turning toward, turning away, or turning against. If it's not mostly turning toward, talk about how you can make that better over time.

In our first eight lectures now we've gotten a good general understanding of what happens in a conflict and what are some general options for handling conflict. In our next several, we're going to get to some more specific strategies, some to try to avoid, and some very specific processes and principles we can use to try to be more successful at negotiating win-win resolutions. In Lecture 9 what we're going to do is start with those strategies to avoid, the strategies I call dysfunctional conflict strategies.

Dysfunctional Conflict Strategies
Lecture 9

Everybody knows revenge feels good. One of the things I love about Aristotle is [that] when he listed what he called his seven causes of human happiness, he put revenge on his list.

In the last lecture, we talked about conflict styles and the fact that we need a full repertoire of strategies we can use depending on the specific situation. In this lecture, we'll look at **dysfunctional conflict strategies**, that is, those that have harmful side effects or excessive costs that may outweigh the desired benefits.

The first of these strategies is avoidance, which we saw in the last lecture. Avoidance can take a number of forms, such as hoping the problem will blow over or changing the subject. Of course, such tactics can result in harmful effects; most of us know that problems not addressed often fester and get worse. Further, avoidance can result in losing one's credibility for dealing with problems. In some cases, however, avoidance may be a useful strategy. For example, if you feel that the other party has more power and will impose an unwanted resolution, it may be wise to avoid the problem if possible.

In withdrawal, one party who has a conflict with another tries to reduce or eliminate interaction to avoid addressing the conflict or to punish the other party. Tactics used for withdrawal include avoiding eye contact and speaking in a flat unemotional tone. The person on the receiving end of withdrawal feels hurt and confused and may become resentful or may reciprocate. The relationship may be damaged, and the original problem remains unsolved. Again, there may be some situations in which withdrawal is useful, specifically, if you need to withdraw temporarily from a conflict to calm down.

The strategy of imposition involves the direct exercise of power; one party unilaterally imposes a resolution. Imposition can be overt or covert; that is, a manager may use his or her authority to end a discussion or an employee may go behind the manager's back and do things a different way. Imposition may cause the other party to counter with a greater exercise of power, escalating the conflict. In an organization, this strategy may cause resentment and decrease morale. Imposition may be the best strategy, however, when immediate action is required or when the goals are important and the other party won't cooperate.

Triangulation is defined as complaining to a third party instead of addressing the conflict directly with the other party involved. This strategy can be used to gain an ally and secure a resolution without the other party's participation or just to vent, which we sometimes think of as a beneficial activity. Research has shown, however, that venting can actually make you madder instead of calming you down. The harmful effects of triangulation tend not to appear immediately but to build up over time. In organizations, cliques develop, morale declines, and teamwork breaks down. Tactics of triangulation include complaining under the guise of asking for advice or presenting oneself as the victim and the other party as the villain. Triangulation might be useful to gain an ally in situations where the other party has more power and won't cooperate to solve the problem.

> **Research has shown, however, that venting can actually make you madder instead of calming you down.**

Manipulation may be more subtle than triangulation, but it's equally dangerous. It's using indirect means to achieve a goal without letting the other party know and without regard to the other's interests and goals. Tactics here include planting information with third parties or masking true motives. This strategy usually damages the other party's interests, as well as the manipulator's credibility. Manipulation is a self-centered, deceptive behavior that should never be used.

Absolute framing sets up the conflict issue in black-and-white terms, stating what absolutely must or must not happen or what the other party must or must not do. The tactic here is basically drawing a line in the sand and daring the other party to cross. This strategy precludes mutual agreement and tends to lead to escalation, but it may be useful in conflicts that require a clear moral and relational stand.

Another dysfunctional strategy is payback or revenge, defined as doing harm to or withholding good from another person in order to balance a sense of wrong one feels. Of course, tactics here can be quite creative, ranging from withdrawal all the way up to murder. A difference in the perception of the harm done tends to cause escalation in conflicts where this strategy is used.

The last dysfunctional strategy on our list may be a surprising one: compromise, that is, negotiating a solution in which each party gives up something. Compromise is often a good strategy, but we should use it only if we have really tried to achieve a win-win resolution and couldn't do so. In most cases, the parties can reach a solution that's better for both of them without having to settle for less. ■

Important Terms

dysfunctional conflict strategy: A conflict strategy that yields unwanted side effects that may exceed its benefits.

triangulation: Drawing a third party into a conflict instead of directly addressing the other conflict party.

Assignments

1. Think through the strategies you used in a recent conflict—and there was probably more than one. Identify the strategies and ask why you used each one and whether it got you the result you hoped it would. What other results—unwanted results, especially to your relationship with the other party—did using certain strategies produce?

2. See if you can document for yourself the harmful effects of a dysfunctional conflict strategy.

Dysfunctional Conflict Strategies
Lecture 9—Transcript

In our last lecture we talked about conflict styles, and a conflict style is a style that you generally revert to as a predominant way of doing things, a kind of default strategy. The whole point of understanding conflict styles really is to understand that we need to have a full repertoire of strategies that we can use depending on the situation rather than one or two styles that we revert to rather automatically.

In this lecture we're going to talk about strategies in a more specific way and we're going to talk about strategies that we ought to avoid if we can. I call these dysfunctional strategies for managing conflict. By "dysfunctional" what I really mean is they have harmful side effects that are worse than necessary and they might even outweigh the desired effects that you were after.

As a matter of fact two of these dysfunctional strategies were also on our conflict styles list. Those would be avoidance and compromise. I want to repeat them here and to talk about them just very specifically in terms of why we really want to avoid them if we can. So we've got dysfunctional strategies to talk about, and I've got a total of eight of them to talk about. So let's go ahead and get started.

Let's begin by being clear about the definition of a dysfunctional strategy. I don't mean they don't get what you want. A dysfunctional strategy is one that while it may get us what we were after, will also get side effects, costs, that were significantly greater than necessary, and they might even outweigh the beneficial effects we were after. So let's talk about those dysfunctional strategies.

Let's begin with one that was on our styles list, that's avoidance. We described avoidance in the last lecture. If you remember our example back then, we had Hank telling George that Barry had a problem with that design team's design. And Hank's reaction if you remember was he didn't want to do anything with it. He just wanted to hope it would blow over. Well it might, but then it probably won't. That was by definition an avoidance strategy. If it was what Hank did all the time predominately it would be a style. But in this instance at least that was just an avoidance strategy.

There are a lot of tactics people use for doing this, more than I can really list. It can be just doing nothing and hoping it will blow over. It could be saying yeah I'll deal with it and then sort of not getting around to it. It could be not responding to a call. It could be changing the subject. There are a lot of ways that we use to avoid dealing with a certain conflict, but it is going to have harmful effects, the first of which is we just don't solve the problem. Problems faced, and you know what, problems not addressed often fester and get worse.

There are additional harmful effects. We can lose our credibility for dealing with things. So avoidance doesn't get it done. It's kind of a lose-lose strategy. It doesn't take care of the other person. It doesn't take care of myself. It just hopes it will go away.

Still, avoidance is something that we're going to have to use some of the time. There are occasions when the other party has more power and will impose an unwanted resolution if this thing comes up, taking care of themselves, but hurting you. And sometimes it's wise to just duck and avoid it if you can.

There are other times when the risk of bringing it up myself is just too great or the occasion is just not one on which it's okay to bring it up. So there are also times when there's no resolution that's possible. So what that means is there are going to be times when we're going to need to use avoidance. We need it in our repertoire of strategies that we can use, but we want to avoid it if possible, avoid avoidance if possible, only use it if I have to.

Let's look at another strategy. Let's turn to withdrawal. Withdrawal is partially avoidance, but it can go further than avoidance. We often use it in conjunction with avoidance. But withdrawal goes a little beyond it. What is it? It might be best on this one to start with an example. So let's do a dramatization here. Picture this scene. We're in an office, Elaine is at her desk working and she looks up and sees her colleague Margie coming toward her, but Elaine kind of averts her eyes and looks down and gets busy working some paper.

Margie walks up smiling and speaks. We're not going to know why Elaine is withdrawing at this point, but we'll probably find that out later in the lecture. Let's listen in.

[Video start.]

> **Margie**: Hi Elaine. Didn't see you at happy hour after work Friday. Did you have a nice weekend?
>
> **Elaine**: It was okay. Look, I'm really busy. I'm pulling some numbers for the boss.
>
> **Margie**: Oh, sure. You okay?
>
> **Elaine**: I'm fine.
>
> **Margie**: Okay. I'll see you later.

[Video end.]

Have you been there? The other person withdraws from communicating and you don't know why they did it. Something is wrong and you don't know why. We've all been where Margie is in this situation. It happens at work; it happens in friendships. It happens in marriages. It happens in a lot of relationships. One person has a conflict and what they do as a strategy is withdraw. The definition of this is reducing or eliminating interaction with the other party to avoid addressing the conflict, avoidance, and/or to punish the other party, and that's very, very common. Don't you suspect Margie is being punished here?

What are the tactics that might be used in this kind of a situation? Well we can avoid encounters with them. We cannot respond to greetings. We cannot return phone calls. We very often do things like avoiding eye contact and averting and turning away and speaking in a flatter tone emotionally, and Elaine did all of that in our example. We don't get very forthcoming answers. We don't know exactly what Elaine is working on. So there are a lot of different ways to withdraw.

What are the harms that come from this? Number one is that tactic is seen and felt as a social slight by the other party. You generally have some punishment in it and they feel the hurt. That party feeling hurt and probably confused as well may get resentful over these perceived slights and they may reciprocate so this can escalate and go on. The relationship can be damaged. Of course the problem in the meantime remains unsolved, and we may compound it and get it worse by making distance in the relationship and not dealing with it.

When would we want to use it regardless? When would that be? Well some occasions I need to avoid and the only way I can manage to avoid is to withdraw and not be there, hmm, ducking, avoiding may require some amount of disappearing, so there are time when I need to withdraw in order to avoid, and if I had to avoid well it's the best option.

There are other occasions when the resulting damage to the relationship is just not as great as the risk of addressing the conflict. So if I'm feeling that okay, this strategy. There's this other occasion. What if I need to withdraw like temporarily, I just need some time to calm down. We talked about that relative to emotions. We'll talk about it again when we talk about the step process to go through to resolve this. If I need some time to think this through and I need to withdraw to do it, that's okay. But the best thing to do is let my other partner know why I'm withdrawing and then make sure I get back to them and let them know what it was about. That's withdrawal.

Let's turn to another one. Let's go next to imposition. Imposition is doing the power trip. The definition of this would be a direct exercise of power. Suppose I unilaterally just impose a resolution and I want to you to notice that this can be done overtly right out front and obvious. It can also be done covertly by doing it secretly and not getting caught.

Let's think of some examples of this one. Let's go back to Hank and our architectural design team. Let's think about Hank sitting at his desk and suppose he's going to be in the imposition mode rather than the avoidance mode. So let's suppose Hank catches Barry and wants to confront him about Barry's problem with the design. Let's look at that.

[Video start.]

> **Hank**: Hey Barry. Can I talk to you for a minute?
>
> **Barry**: Hey, I'm Glad you stopped me. I wanted to talk to you about those designs. You know—
>
> **Hank**: Listen, Barry. I'm going to stop you right there. We're in charge of the designs, and we know what we're doing. Your team takes it from there.
>
> **Barry**: But I just wanted to make—
>
> **Hank**: Look, Barry, don't question our designs. Got it?
>
> **Barry**: Sure. We'll just have to work with what you've sent.

[Video end.]

This is obvious overt imposition. Hank is just imposing on Barry, but it's usually not helpful. Hank may think he's exercising his authority and protecting his turf and he's doing that, but whatever the problem is isn't getting addressed. Remember I mentioned covert imposition? Let's talk about that a second. Hank may have less power here, less control than he actually thinks he had. Barry and his crew are working out in the field. They're actually doing this project that's been designed, and you know what, crews working in the field very often can do things not according to design. Barry can go out and use covert imposition and do what he thinks he needs to fix the design hoping not to get caught.

There's a problem either way, either with Hank's imposition overtly or Barry's imposition covertly. How do we do this kind of thing? It's unilateral action. It's issuing orders or just doing it visibly. If we did it covertly it could be acting surreptitiously and trying to get away with it. It happens all the time including in construction projects.

What would be the harmful effects? It may cause the other party to counter with a greater exercise of power, and then you get an escalation and a power struggle going on. It can create distance and damage in the relationship especially if the deception is caught. It creates resentment if the overt thing is caught and that decreases morale and makes distance. Then the problem that might be exposed by dealing with the conflict isn't going to get solved.

Still, when would we use imposition? There are times when it's the best thing to do. Sometimes immediate action is required and there's no opportunity to consult. In teams that do forest fire fighting they have a concept called an incident commander. There isn't any discussion. They've got to put somebody in command because they're actually fighting a battle with a fire, and decisions have to be made instantly. There are times when imposition, giving orders and expecting them to be followed overtly is absolutely the right answer. There are times, and there are other times when the goals are important and I just can't get the other party to cooperate. I might need to impose in that kind of condition. So imposition sometimes, but only when it's needed. That's three.

Let's talk about a fourth dysfunctional strategy. Let's talk about triangulation. Triangulation is exactly what it sounds like. It's creating triangles. Let's start here with a dramatized example. Remember Elaine doing her little withdrawing from communication with Margie. She's not talking to Margie, who is she talking to. Hmm, she's talking to her coworker, an ally friend about this. Let's listen in on that.

[Video start.]

> **Fred**: Hey, Elaine.
>
> **Elaine**: You hear what Margie pulled on Friday before happy hour? She went to the boss and tried to snag the new Lockhart account. And then she came by my desk all friendly this morning as if nothing had happened. She knows I want that account.

Fred: Did he give it to her?

Elaine: I don't know; he might still be still deciding. Think you could find out what's going on when you meet with him later today?

Fred: Yeah, I can give it a try. I can't promise anything, but I'll try.

Elaine: Thanks.

Fred: All right, I'll see you later.

[Video end.]

Elaine is triangulating here. She's creating a triangle putting Fred in the middle with she and Margie at the other two corners. When you've been put in the middle like Fred is here especially if you're not already an ally with the person bringing it to you, that's very uncomfortable. It creates a problem.

What's the definition of triangulation? The definition is this. It's complaining to a third party instead of addressing the conflict directly with the other party, the other party you actually have the conflict with. Why would we do this? It can be done to gain an ally, secure a resolution without the other party's participation by going over their head. It's also done to just complain or vent or punish the other person.

There are some things I want to make note of about this. An awful lot of people believe and a lot of people even advise venting to a third party to relieve anger thinking we can get it off our chest. But you know what, the studies on this suggest that venting actually can make us madder; that what we do when we wind up and talk about it is we walk away more heated up and more angry rather than calmed down.

There are a couple of other things to note about it. One is that honestly consulting an appropriate third party, somebody that can be trusted about how to address it, help sort it out is not triangulation. The difference here is motivation. If I'm doing that to help myself prepare to talk to the person and that's honest and that's what I'm doing, I'm not doing it instead of talking to them I'm doing it as preparation, that's not triangulation either.

A final note about this and when we talk about the harmful effects is that the harmful effects on triangulation very, very often, in fact more often than not, tend not to appear immediately; they tend to build up over time. They can be devastating though when they actually explode. What happens cliques develop in groups and in organizations and there's a lot of this grousing back and forth around and people get separate and the teamwork breaks down in a lot of different ways and then it explodes at some point. So you really don't want triangulation going on.

Lots of organizations I've worked with could've been described as terrible tangled webs of triangles. So you want to avoid that. The tactics here for this come, well let's see what would the tactics be. Well we could complain, sometimes under the guise of asking for advice, but I'm really doing it instead of talking. One of the tactics is present myself as the victim and the other party as the villain, and that one is really problematic.

Another tactic is sort of looking for an ally when I really just want the other person to feel bad about this character and when you can't really do something about it. So triangulation is really problematic. It can damage or destroy a relationship. That's a harmful effect. Viewing myself as the victim is harmful to me, victims have a hard time valuing themselves and recognizing themselves. A lot of times when we're victimized really we have to go get help to deal with that. So harm to me, and it's unjust to the other person. It often makes unjust solutions that can happen.

So triangulation is a problem, but when would we use it anyhow? Suppose the other party really does have more power and isn't going to work with me to solve it and I really do need an ally in order to deal with the thing. In that instance let me go use triangulation.

Let's go to a fifth dysfunctional strategy. Let's talk about manipulation. This one could be more subtle, but it's at least equally usually more dangerous than triangulation. Let's do this one with an example too. Let's go back to Elaine. I wonder what she was working on in those papers when Margie walked up and tried to chat with her. Maybe she was working on some numbers to support her own effort to do an end run around Margie and get to the boss and get that Lockhart account for herself. Let's follow Elaine into the boss' office and check in.

[Video start.]

> **Elaine**: Hi. You busy?
>
> **Boss**: No, come in.
>
> **Elaine**: I've just reworked some of the numbers on the Jennings account. We can reduce their expenses and keep them a lot happier. Can I show you?
>
> **Boss**: Yeah, let's take a look.
>
> **Elaine**: We reallocate here; we reallocate here; that results in these reductions—total savings.
>
> **Boss**: Pretty good.
>
> **Elaine**: You know, this is exactly the kind of thing we should be doing on the new Lockhart account.
>
> **Boss**: Yeah.

[Video end.]

Elaine is gaming not only Margie here, but she's gaming the boss. She's not honestly making a pitch. She's maneuvering to look good on this. It's not honest. She's working her agenda behind Margie's back and for that matter behind the boss' back. That's manipulation. How would we define it? We'd say it's using indirect means to achieve a goal without letting the other party know and without regard to the other party's interests and goals. I'm taking care of myself; I'm doing it surreptitiously; I'm gaming the thing, and usually when we're doing this kind of a strategy, when we're doing manipulation, we're manipulating more than one person.

So that one is a problem. What are the tactics? Well we can be planning information, suggestions with third parties who don't know they're being used in the process. We can stage events to do things; we can do things with one motive and pretend it's for another motive. We can fain emotions or concerns that we don't really have as a way of bringing up topics. Manipulation, well humans are pretty creative about it.

What are the harmful effects? The other party's interests are typically going to be damaged. If the other party learns of this, you know what, our own interests and our own credibility is going to be damaged and especially if more than one learns about it. There's almost always some real relational damage. There has to be distance when we're gaming somebody, and when that comes out it's pretty rough.

This is self-centered deceptive behavior and the question about when to use it is, just don't. Never use it.

Let's go to a sixth strategy. Let's talk about absolute framing. By framing what I mean is how we conceptualize and define the issue in a conflict, how we think of what it's really about, how would we think of it and say it. Let's do this one with an example too. How would this look and sound in a conflict?

Let's visit our married couple from Lecture 1. Remember Ken and Kate, and Ken wants to take a job in another city and get himself out west. What if Ken tries to deal with this with absolute framing. Let's listen in.

[Video start.]

> **Ken**: Honey, take a look at this.

> **Kate**: Sounds like a great job—but it's in Denver!

Ken: Yeah, I'm going to apply for it. You know how much I want to get out west. And I think this is the perfect next step for me.

Kate: Well that came out of the blue. You know I can't leave Chicago right now. I have a real career here; I can't go somewhere else and start all over.

Ken: And what about me? I might never see a dream job like this again. I've made up my mind—I'm sending them my resume tonight. If I get the job, you can come with me, or stay here. Your choice.

[Video end.]

There's no room for discussion in here. There's no consideration to Kate. There's nothing she can do but say yes or no, because Ken has framed this as a simple yes or no situation. He thinks he's right and she's just to support him in what he thinks. He's got it set up as absolutes, and I'm really not sure Ken is in a strong enough position to be doing this here.

What's the definition of absolute framing? The definition is that we set up the conflict issue in black and white terms, in absolute terms, so that the answers are yes and no or right or wrong. It's stating what absolutely must or must not happen, what the other party must do or not do. It frequently involves making an absolute moral judgment or taking a position. It's what we call black and white thinking.

The tactics, declaring some absolute principle, making some absolute demand, it's like we say drawing a line in the sand and daring the other to step over it. That's absolute framing.

What are the harmful effects of it? Well it precludes mutual agreement. The other party can only surrender or fight, choose to comply or get in and fight. It tends to lead to escalation. It often destroys relationships and leaves long-lasting emotional scars. Still there are times when we want to use absolute framing.

Occasionally conflicts really do require clear, definite, moral, and relational stand. What if it's a real moral issue with me that's deeply held or sometimes even I need to set boundaries for myself just in terms of taking care of myself and I need to take a clear stand. Sometimes I do need to draw a line in the sand, and when that happens what I need to do is go ahead and frame it absolutely. I need to step up to the plate and do that regardless of what it would cost.

Let's go to seven on our list of eight dysfunctional strategies. Let's talk about pay back or revenge. Everybody knows revenge feels good. One of the things I love about Aristotle is when he listed what he called his seven causes of human happiness he put revenge on his list. I thought that was just deliciously honest of him. Recent research into the neurology of this kind of thing really shows that when we feel we've been wronged, humans literally have a craving, literally a craving, for something like revenge. We want to equalize that. We want to get even.

But if we want to resolve a conflict and we don't want to make things worse, even if it feels good in the moment, revenge is a bad idea. It would be kind of remember having poison ivy as a kid and scratching it, what it does, it can work like that. The definition is doing harm or withholding good from another person in order to balance the sense of wrong that one feels. It's getting even.

It's tactics now has many as we can creatively think of, all kinds of ways to get revenge and they range from withholding through triangulation all the way up to things like murder. The term pay back that I use actually comes from prison populations where if you're in a hard prison and somebody does you harm, you've got to pay them back or else it's going to be open season on you. The harmful effects are pay back adds to the harm.

Difference of perception in the harm done really tends to cause escalation as it goes along. I think the harm you did to me is greater than you think it was so I'll escalate and we'll just make it worse and worse and worse.

Let's look at a quick example of that one. Dan had his next door neighbor Barney, he has talked to him numerous times about not letting his kids trample the flowers. They trample them on their way to school. Kids keep doing it, Dan has had enough, what would his over-the-top revenge reaction be like. Let's look at that.

[Video start.]

>**Dan**: That'll teach Barney to let his kids tromp all over my flowers.

>**Sally**: What are you talking about?

>**Dan**: I just accidentally tripped into his tomato and pepper plants. Let's just see him brag about his salsa from the garden again!

>**Sally**: Are you kidding? How old are you? Five?

[Video end.]

That's really not helpful, Dan. This could set off a negative spiral and escalate and things can get ugly in the neighborhood. I'm kind of with Sally, his spouse, on this way who's just mortified and feels awful. It's not a good reaction. Revenge might've felt good stomping those vegetables, but it's not going to do any good in the long run.

When would we use it regardless? Well, if you're stuck in prison in one of those awful places you might need to use it anyhow.

Let's talk about our last dysfunctional strategy on our list. That's compromise. It's one that we actually talked about under conflict styles. So we don't need to lay out a new example of it for you here. We described it in Lecture 8 and as we noted in Lecture 8 what this is, is splitting the difference. If you remember that scene where Hank confronted with Barry's challenge suggested well let's split the difference, we'll make a few tweaks he said in the design and hope that it'll appease Barry's team. He's going right away to splitting the difference. That's compromise.

Why did I put it on my list of dysfunctional strategies? Compromise is often a really good thing to do, but we do it a whole lot more often than we should because there's a downside to it and so we should really only use it if we have to. When would that be? It's when we've really tried to achieve a win-win and couldn't get it. The definition of it is splitting the difference. It's negotiating a solution in which each party gives up something so nobody has to lose, but then nobody wins. If as Morton Deutsch showed us all those years ago we probably could've had a win-win, we're taking a loss we didn't have to take. So we make those offers and we negotiate. Those are the tactics.

What are the harmful effects going to be? Most of the time the parties could achieve a solution that was better for them both, and they settle for less. This also takes energy out of relationships and it helps keep us from getting to the best thing we could get. So I put it on my list of dysfunctional strategies in order to stress that point.

When would I use it? I would use it only if we've tried for a win-win solution and couldn't get it. Once we knew we couldn't get a win-win, it feels okay and it makes good sense to go ahead and compromise. So that's our list of eight dysfunctional strategies, strategies that give us harmful side effects that are worse than they had to be and as a matter of fact might very well outweigh the good effects. We want to avoid them if possible.

Here's our summary. What are they? Avoidance, use it only if the risk of harm for confronting is really too great. Avoid avoidance if you can. Second on the list withdrawal. Use it only if you really need to avoid dealing with the conflict and the only way to avoid is to withdraw, or if the relationship just doesn't matter.

Imposition, use it only if you really need to achieve the outcome, you can't consult with the other party so imposition is the only way to get it. Manipulation, just don't use it at all. It's dishonest. Relationships that matter ought to be built on honesty. Absolute framing, very few matters are matters of absolute principle, but you know what some of them are. So use it, but use it only if you think you really need to fight for it even if fighting means you're going to have to go down fighting. That would be a good measure.

Triangulation, don't create triangles unless you really, really need an ally. In the long run it's really not good for anybody. Seven is pay back, revenge, don't use it unless you're stuck in prison. That's just going to add to the hurt and probably escalate the conflict. And lastly, compromise. Compromise only if you really couldn't get a win-win and you know that because you tried to get a win-win.

Use of these dysfunctional strategies ought to be rare because I said use them only if. They ought to be limited to the conditions when they're really required and they're going to be especially problematic if they're your patterns, if they're the styles of management that you use.

I've got an assignment for you at the end of this one. Think through what strategies you used in a recent conflict. Go back and think through a conflict, think of the strategies you used. There's probably more than one strategy. I want you to go ask yourself, what were the strategies that I used? Why did I use those strategies? Did I get the result I was after? Then what other results, unwanted results, especially to the relationship did it produce? I want you to go check in one of the conflicts that you dealt with recently and see if you can document for yourself the harmful effects of dysfunctional strategy.

Where do we go from here? So far we've given attention to the challenges inherent in human conflict and we've learned about different ways to deal with conflict. Next we want to turn to some principles and processes that really provide you with useful guides when we're really going after seeking a win-win resolution. In Lecture 10, we'll turn to the work of Roger Fisher and William Ury and talk about "Principled Negotiation."

Principled Negotiation
Lecture 10

We shouldn't be laying out one option and just choosing yes or no. That's a mistake. That's an error in decision making.

Roger Fisher and William Ury, two researchers associated with the Harvard Negotiation Project, have developed four principles for win-win negotiations. The first of these is to separate people from the problem. In other words, focus on events or behaviors rather than the parties involved. The second principle is to focus on interests, not positions. The term "**interest**" here refers to the reason behind the stand someone might take. What are you trying to gain, or what are you feeling frustrated about? The term "**position**" refers to someone's stand on an issue. Fisher and Ury tell us not to take a position and defend it or bargain for it but to focus on the interest behind the position. Keep in mind that both parties in a conflict have interests, and if both can articulate those interests, then they have a shot at reaching a win-win solution.

The third of Fisher and Ury's principles is to generate options for mutual gain. In most conflicts, we tend to put forth one or two options, then try to make a choice from those limited alternatives. Instead, we should brainstorm for multiple options, keeping in mind the goal of mutual gain. When we have a list of options, we move to the fourth principle, which is to base the choice on some kind of objective criteria. Try to identify measurable ways to assess the value of the suggestions.

Consider the example of a married couple, Carlos and Barbara, and their conflict over environmental issues. According to the first principle of negotiation, we should separate Barbara and Carlos from the problem. If we do this, we can easily identify each party's interests: Barbara's interests are to use less water and recycle as much as possible, and Carlos's are to enjoy his long showers and not to have to devote too much thought to recycling. The list of options the two could generate might include installing a low-flow shower head, posting a list of recyclables for Carlos, and so on. The objective criteria for choosing among the options might be, for example, how much water they can save using the various options they've come up with. Ultimately, they might choose a combination of the options that fits their lifestyle.

Let's look at an example in business. Imagine a small to mid-size organization with an annual budget of $30 million and about 120 employees. The vice president of operations wants to buy a new billing and accounting system, which she believes will reduce errors and save money in the long run. The accounting department likes the current system and believes that it will take too much time to get up to speed on a new system. We first separate the people from the problem: It's not that the VP is overbearing or insensitive or that the people in accounting are resistant to change because it requires effort. Either of those statements may be true, but it doesn't help to solve the problem if we focus on the people. The issue is: Should the company get a new accounting system and, if so, would it offer gains in efficiency?

> **Keep in mind that both parties in a conflict have interests, and if both can articulate those interests, then they have a shot at reaching a win-win solution.**

The two parties seem to have taken stands on this issue, but recall that Morton Deutsch found that task-oriented groups have shared goals in many more cases than they have different goals. Here, the accounting employees have a legitimate interest in minimizing unnecessary work and avoiding new sources of error, and the VP shares those interests. The parties now need to generate a list of options for accomplishing those goals. The new accounting software proposed by the VP is just one option. Others might include researching other software packages that might require less adjustment or looking at the processes in accounting to see what can be streamlined. Objective criteria for choosing one option or a combination might include person hours, processing time, or startup and training costs for a new system.

Fisher and Ury also developed the concept of **BATNA**, best alternative to a negotiated arrangement. In any negotiation, to identify your bottom line and your power bases relative to the issue, consider what your best alternative would be if you don't negotiate a good arrangement with the other party. If you know what that alternative is, then you know how hard you can push or whether you need to back off in negotiations. These researchers also draw on martial arts with the idea of negotiation jujitsu: In negotiations, don't meet force with force; instead, draw the other party in and use his or her force. Try to discover the other party's interests, then present your own interests and make suggestions for mutual gain. ■

Names to Know

Fisher, Roger: Professor of law emeritus at Harvard Law School and former director of the Harvard Negotiation Project.

Ury, William: A former professor at Harvard Business School and a founder of the Harvard Negotiation Project.

Important Terms

BATNA: In principled negotiation, this term stands for "best alternative to a negotiated agreement." Each negotiator decides ahead of time what solution he or she will opt for if a negotiated agreement is unsatisfactory or fails.

interests: Reasons underlying a participant's stance or position in a negotiation.

position: A statement of what a negotiator wants or needs.

Suggested Reading

Fisher and Ury, with Bruce Patton, *Getting to Yes: Negotiating an Agreement without Giving In*.

Harvard Business School Press, *Harvard Business Review on Negotiation and Conflict Resolution*.

1. Think through what strategies you used in a recent conflict—and there was probably more than one strategy. Ask yourself: What was the strategy? Why did I use it? Did it get me the result I hoped it would? And what other results—unwanted results—especially to the relationship—did it produce?

2. See if you can document for yourself the harmful effects of a dysfunctional strategy.

Principled Negotiation
Lecture 10—Transcript

In our last several lectures we focused on what we tend to do and on what to do and not to do in general in managing conflicts. In this lecture what we want to do is begin to focus on what to do specifically if we're trying to negotiate a win-win resolution. We certainly advocated negotiating win-win resolutions. Now we get to begin to talk about how to go about doing that.

We want to begin in this lecture with the work of Roger Fisher and William Ury who developed four principles for win-win negotiating. We're going to explain each of the four principles and then we're going to walk through applying those principles with a couple of concrete examples.

I want to note as we begin that Fisher and Ury were working at the time with and are still associated with the Harvard Negotiation Project, which is an institute housed at Harvard University, and that institute works diligently with a lot of people works on a worldwide basis looking to discover, teach, and then help individuals, organizations, communities, even countries with better ways to resolve conflict. That's the mission. Roger Fisher and William Ury developed these four principles working with the Harvard Negotiation Project.

Let's talk about the four principles, walk through them one at a time. So here they are. Principle number one: They said what you want to do first is separate people from the problem, separate people from the problem. That means don't focus on what's wrong with certain people, what's wrong with that person or this person, focus on events, focus on behaviors, focus on what's happening, and why that's a problem. Separate people from the problem.

I want you to notice too that they didn't say separate people from the conflict, the people are in the conflict. They said separate people from the problem. It turns out it's much more helpful to talk about the conflict as a problem to resolve, a problem you can resolve together than to talk about it as a conflict. So separate people from the problem.

We've got a really simple example of that using our roommates with the one being the graduate student needing to study and the other working person needing to relax. If I'm Rebecca the roommate who needs to study and the noise is happening, I could say Jane my roommate is terribly inconsiderate. That would be connecting the person with the problem, making the person be the problem.

On the other hand if she separates those out, separates what her problem is from Jane and simply says I need time to study in quiet here this evening, now she's focusing on the problem and she's got it separate from the person who is Jane. So that's going to be number one, separate the person from the problem.

Let's go to principle number two. Second principle is now that you've got those separated, focus on interests, no positions. Let me define the terms here. What do they mean "interests," and what do they mean "positions"? By "interests" what they mean is the reason behind the stand I might take. What am I trying to gain, what am I feeling frustrated about in this conflict, what's the interest behind whatever position I might take? By "position" what they mean is, when people take positions they take a stand on an issue and then they negotiate or bargain trying to defend the position.

So what they're saying is look don't take a position and defend it, don't focus there. Focus on what's the reason I might want to take that position, what's the interest behind it. Interests are really closely related to the goals that we talked about back in an earlier lecture when Wilmot and Hocker gave us that nice list of four different types of goals. What are the interests? If I'm taking a position, a really good way to think about interests is to ask myself why is it that I want to take this position. The answer to that question might really identify my interests. That's what I'm after, and I want to focus on getting my interests met.

I also want to focus not just on my own interests, but I want to focus on the other party's interests. Both parties in a conflict have interests they're trying to achieve, and if both parties can focus on their interests and get those articulated and on the table, then we've got a shot at really looking for win-win. It turns out that's going to work a whole lot better than each taking a position and then defending the position and negotiating or bargaining about it.

So if we take that one to the point where we're talking about our college roommates for instance, Rebecca's interest in needing to get the quiet time, the interest behind that is she wants to know the material well, to learn it, and get a good grade on the exam. Rebecca has got an interest she's trying to achieve, and that can be clearly articulated. Conversely Jane the other roommate who works hard, works all day, wants to have friends over back at her home, which is the apartment at night, would very well want to be able to relax has an interest in being able to use her own environment, her own living room here to relax and have friends over. So she's got an interest.

If both parties can begin to focus on interests and what both of their interests are instead of taking positions and bargaining and instead of connecting the problem to the other, they're going to be able to have a much better chance at getting a win-win. So this would be how we would go forward looking for that kind of a thing. The second principle then is focus on interests not positions.

Let's go to the third principle. Third principle would be this: Generate options for mutual gain. I want to spell this out in some fairly clear particulars for you. Most of the time what we tend to do when we get in a conflict or even when we're trying to solve a problem is we want to put up one or two options and then try to choose between just those one or two.

Fisher and Ury are saying don't do that. They're saying generate multiple options. You really want to come up with more options, several, get a list on the table to work with, and you really ought to keep in mind that you're suggesting options for mutual gain. What this calls for is the classic activity known as brainstorming. What you want to do when you brainstorm is work together, what would get us mutual gain, and put a bunch of ideas out there and you want to be careful, the two of you working together with that or all of you if there are multiple sides here, not to criticize the options that are suggested as they're putting up.

Humans it turns out, we're not very good at being critical and creative at the same time. So the classic idea of brainstorming, which really proves out in the research, is throw the ideas out there, get a bunch of them in front of us so that we can consider them. Once they're out there, then let's get critical and begin to consider how best to operate with them; so we're going to generate a list of options, a broad list, by brainstorming together to get a list we can consider to choose between for a win-win solution if we can.

Once we've got our list together now we can turn to principle number four. Principle number four would be this: We want to base the choice we make on some kind of objective criteria. In looking for the objective criteria we really want to focus on mutual gain; we want to find criteria that reflect the interests that have been identified of both sides in the conflict. We really, really, really want to try to identify measurable objective ways to assess the value of the suggested options.

We're looking now for measurable criteria to do this. This one can be challenging. Sometimes the debate, the argument, the difficulty happens, this can be difficult, finding criteria that you can agree on. There's a little pitfall you can run into here because I might know this criteria would make my interest better reflected and that criteria would make yours. You've got to be a little careful. There's a pitfall here, but you really want to go look for criteria you can use to judge in this instance so that you can choose between the options that are there. You may want to choose between combinations of options. In fact that's more common than not.

Those are our four principles that Fisher and Ury laid out. Those principles have been applied in communities, in organizations, and individuals' personal conflicts. They've been applied lots and lots of times in all kinds of places since the 1970s when Fisher and Ury came up with them. They've really, really, really withstood the test of time and they've done it very, very well.

Now let's go and kind of walk through these applying to them to some typical conflicts and see how they work and describe them in the abstract. Let's try to apply them. Let me walk you through a couple of very different typical kinds of conflicts and see how that would play out. Let's start first with, let's say we've got a couple, let's call them Carlos and Barbara. They're a married couple and they've got a conflict over taking care of the environment. You may think that one's a little trivial or whatever, but I saw an article not long ago that noted couples fighting over how to be more green and who's more green is coming up, rising up on the list of things couples fight over.

Let's take an example like that. Let's say that Barbara just doesn't think Carlos is "green" enough. He thinks what he's doing is fine. He's recycling when he thinks of it. He's avoiding plastic if he can help it without being inconvenienced. He's driving a hybrid car. Carlos thinks that he's nicely green. Barbara on the other hand is just like cringing when he leaves the water running when he's rinsing dishes for instance, or he stays in the shower too long. When she finds something that could've gone in the recyclable bin and it's not in the bin, it's in the trashcan that bothers her.

Barbara is not thinking Carlos is "green" enough. Carlos, of course, thinks Barbara is over the top on this issue, and he doesn't want to be nagged. So what do we do with that? This is that conflict as I said, a recent survey says couples fight over this a lot lately.

Let's walk you through the four principles. Principle one, let's separate Barbara and Carlos from the problem. Let's have it that we're not going to think Carlos doesn't care about the environment or he's just not "green" enough, and let's not just have it that Barbara is a controlling nag. If the two of them are thinking like that, it may be true, but that's not something they're going to negotiate. They can't get anywhere working their way through that one.

What should they be thinking this conflict is about if they want to separate the people from the problem. For Barbara the problem is going to be they're not doing as well with the environment as they could be or should be. That's her point. Carlos' point is well he doesn't want to feel like he's being nagged. He really does like that luxury of the longer shower and he gets confused about what to put where and he doesn't want to have to think too hard about it all the time. He doesn't want to have to struggle with this and he doesn't want to give up the great showers.

If they look at it that way and that's what their concerns are, they've separated themselves from the problem. Now they've got a couple of problems they can put out there and look at and look for ways to resolve. If they're going to go after that, what they need to go is go to principle number two then wherein what they're going to do is focus on interests. It's pretty clear once they've separated people from the problem in this particular example what the interests would be.

Barbara's interest is to use less water and get more stuff in the recycle bin, and that's her interest because she thinks that's more green and she's committed to being more green, an admirable position to take. Carlos really can't quarrel with that. So that's her interest.

Carlos' interest is, he loves his luxury shower. That's a legitimate luxury. He's a hardworking guy. He wants to keep that. He doesn't want to have to struggle thinking about what goes where and he isn't always clear about it. So now we've got his interests.

If Barbara phrases her complaint about the problem being with water conservation and recycling, and Carlos phrases his position as I love that shower I'm not giving it up, I don't want to give it up and I'm not clear on what to put where so I need some help with that, if they phrase it that way they focus it that way, now they've got something they can work on as a problem they can try to solve together. Now we've got it we're focused on their interests, not taking positions, we can go to principle number three, which will be generating options for mutual gain.

What will be the question here if we're going to generate options? Put a question in front of us. How could we reduce water usage and get more recyclables in the bin without Carlos sacrificing his shower or having to check every single item before he puts it in the trash or the bin? That's their problem. They can brainstorm to solve this together. What would be some possible options they could come up with?

Well there are actually a lot of them. You could install a more effective water conservation device in the shower head. You could run the dishwasher less often, like every other day instead of every day and conserve some water. You might change the plants in the yard so they require less water, my wonderful spouse and I did that. We live in Arizona and it really made a difference. You could purchase items that require less packaging or join a co-op. There are all kinds of things you could do. You could post a list of recyclables that Barbara really wants to make sure go in the recycle bin, somewhere close so Carlos doesn't have to think about it.

We could go on with the list here. They could brainstorm for 20 minutes and come up with a bunch, but the point is there are a lot of things that Carlos and Barbara can do that would conserve more water and make more sure that the recyclables get in the recycle bin without Carlos sacrificing his shower and without having him struggle with what he should put where. So there's a lot of ways to think and do that.

So that gets us up to where we can begin to talk about principle number four. Principle number four would be to choose based on objective criteria. They've got some nice criteria built in here, the way they laid out the interests. What's going to save the most water. You could do measurements of what conserves and what uses water and sort that out. What would make it easier for Carlos to notice what should go in the recycle bin. They can measure that kind of thing. We can really get clear criteria there, and then they could combine some of these options and choose a combination that would really fit.

So Carlos and Barbara could work this out. They don't have to nag and push about who's greener. What they can do is combine options and come up with something that's going to work well for both of them and they're both going to feel good about it. So you see how you could work through those four principles that Fisher and Ury give us. Two people working on a very typical conflict and get to a better solution if we just go ahead and apply them. Is that what we're most likely to do? No, that's why we have courses like this. That's why Fisher and Ury did their work, but that is what if we do it will really help. So we've got advice for Carlos and Barbara. Use those four principles.

Let's do one more example. Let's do an example that would be in business. That's another place where we have so many conflicts. Let's create a hypothetical example here. Let's say we've got a small to mid-size organization, give it say a $30 million annual budget; 120 or -30 employees, small to mid-size organization. Let's say we've got a vice-president for Operations and the vice-president wants to by a new billing and accounting system. She's just convinced that's going to be more efficient. It's going to reduce errors. It's going to save money in the long run, even though there's the expense of buying it and installing it and getting up to speed on it. That's what the VP for Operations thinks.

The accounting department on the other hand gets wind of this and they're into resisting it. They're perfectly okay with the system they've got. They like it, they all feel competent on it. They see a big downside in the time it's going to take to learn a new system, get up to speed on it. There are always bugs to work out when you've got a new system and they just think that the net loss is greater than the gain. They're having none of it, so they're resisting. We've got a conflict between the vice-president for Operations and the accounting office. It seems like a waste of time to the accountants, especially their time. It seems like something we can do to really get more efficient from her point of view.

How would we work this conflict out applying the four principles? Let's start again with that first one. Separate the people from the problem. We have to say that it's not that the vice-president is being overbearing or insensitive to the accounting department on this issue; and it's not the accounting department, the people anyway, are a bunch of Luddites who just want to resist change because it requires effort. Mind you, in lots of organizations both of those things could be true. But even if they were true, it wouldn't help to deal with the problem to focus there. We have to separate the people from the problem. It doesn't mean the people are innocent; it's just that we can't go after a win-win if the people are going to seen as the problem.

The problem here, the issue should be whether they should get a new accounting system and if so would that actually help us gain more efficiency. So if they focus on that, what would gain us more efficiency and what would be the role of a new accounting system, a new information system in that, that would separate the people from the problem and enable us to focus on the issue. So then we could go to principle number two.

Principle number two would be to focus on interests, not positions. The way I described that thing for you up front, the VP had already taken a position, we ought to get a new system. The accounting people had already taken a position and said no we want to resist this, this is not a good idea, it's going to be a waste. Now they're at odds with each other. They're not focused on interests. If you go back and remember Lecture 3 when we talked about Morton Deutsch and his research, the focus there and the insight there was that people in task-oriented groups have shared goals much more than they have different goals.

The interests actually of the VP and the accounting people, they have a lot of shared interests in this situation. On the one hand the accounting people really do have a legitimate interest in avoiding unnecessary extra work and avoiding new sources of error that happen when you put in a new system. That's about efficiency, and you know what, the VP has an interest in that as well. The VP has an interest in more efficiency in that that bottom line over the long-term and the accounting people actually share that. So when you really look at their interests, they're looking from two different angles, but they have mutual goals and interests here that they could focus on.

I these guys get together and focus on interests rather than being at each other, focused on people or taking positions, they've got a chance to work things out. That would move them up to principle number three where what they're going to do is generate options for mutual gain.

The question in front of the VP and the accounting people would be this: How can we best maximize efficiency while avoiding new errors and minimizing any unnecessary extra expenses and work. That's the question. Remember they should generate mutual options for mutual gain and it's multiple options that we want to do. The new accounting software proposed by the VP is just one option. We shouldn't be laying out one option and just choosing yes or no. That's a mistake. That's an error in decision making. As a matter of fact Teaching Company has a wonderful course on Critical Decision Making which helps and you don't want to set yourself up with one option, choose yes or no, if you can avoid it. So they ought to be generating multiple options to deal with this. It's just better decision making let alone conflict resolution.

You could think of other things. What would they be? There could be new software other than what the VP is proposing that might be less expensive, require less adjustment, there's bound to be a range of options there. There are any number of suggestions that could made aiming at the process or who's doing what and in what order that could focus on increasing efficiency and holding down errors. Better information about the existing error rates and where they come from and where they happen might be something that would be suggested. There are a lot of things that these guys can go and focus on and suggest to get them to the point where they can begin to combine things and make themselves a decision.

That would get them to principle number four. Principle number four is going to be use objective criteria in order to make the choice between these. Again a clear statement of the interests really helps us focus objectively on what would help. Efficiency is a pretty easy thing to measure. There are a lot of ways to get at it, person hours, processing time, start-up and training costs for any new system. Those things can be projected, person hours and dollars involved, costs and time involved in debugging. You can really lay out a set of objective measures and being to choose based on those things. So you can put a set of things together, a combination, and the VP and accounting department really can work out what's probably the best choice if they go ahead and take some time to do it.

If the parties involved in any kind of conflict walk through those four principles that Fisher and Ury lay out for us and use that as a way to get at resolving their conflict, they can get much better results. So that's the four principles. Since developing those, that was a while back, and neither Fisher nor Ury stopped their work. They've devoted the rest of their careers over time to further research and helping people and organizations, communities, even countries apply those principles to resolving conflicts.

The Harvard Negotiation Project continues to be a thriving program doing lots of research and training and publishing and teaching and interventions and facilitating solutions; that project goes, it's a very thriving concern. There are books that came from this. Fisher and Ury's first book on Principled Negotiation was called *Getting to Yes*, it's one of the most widely read books on conflict management ever developed. It's still used in training programs. They've updated you with several additional editions.

I can remember years ago my wife and I took a trip through the Grand Canyon on the river. It was a marvelous trip and there was a young lawyer on the trip with us on these rafts where we're going down the river through the rapids and stuff and he had a copy of *Getting to Yes* with him. He had taken a new job and before he got to the new job, which was going to start when he got back, he was required to be familiar with this book, *Getting to Yes*. So that principle has been there a long way.

They've done other books and other things since, *Getting Past No* and a number of others. They also generated some really useful additional ideas that I just want mention a couple of and talk about them briefly. Two of them in particular to mention would be these. The first one would be, there's an acronym BATNA, it stands for best alternative to a negotiated arrangement. Here's what Fisher and Ury suggest about BATNA. What they say is you know, should you go ahead and negotiate, a good idea to know where your bottom line is, where your power is relative to that issue of negotiating is to go and think about what would be my best alternative if I don't go negotiate a good arrangement with this other party.

What are the alternatives and what's the best alternative. If I know what that alternative is, then I know how hard I can push, how careful I need to be, whether I need to back off, whether I've got a good alternative really matters. So figure out what your BATNA is, your best alternative to a negotiated arrangement, really good idea if you're going into a negotiation. It helps to be prepared.

My other favorite idea in their book, and there are a lot of them, I'm just giving you my favorites, the ones that seem to work best for me and with the people I work with over time, it's what they call negotiation jujitsu. Here's what they mean by that. It's going to come from martial arts. The concept here is when someone comes at you, you don't want to push back, you don't want to meet force with force. What you want to do is draw them in and use their own force. Make use of it.

So when someone pushes at you with something they say, look for the interests, ask questions, find out what the interest is that they have that's behind their pushing. Once you've discovered that, you can present your interest and make suggestions for mutual gain, how they can get their interests met, helping you get yours. So you're using their push, you're using their own interest to help motivate them to work with you to find a solution. A couple of really nice strategies in negotiating that Fisher and Ury laid out for you, BATNA and negotiation jujitsu.

They did a lot of work after that. Their next book after *Getting to Yes* was *Getting Past No*. Fisher went on to do another book called *Getting Together* that we'll talk about when we talk about close personal relationships in a later lecture. These are principles that we can apply in conflict at any level, personal, organizational, community, even nations. We can apply these at any level wherever they go. When we apply them, we're much more likely to get win-win resolutions, and the relationships in which we apply them are going to get stronger as we go along. So those are our four principles.

Let's summarize. What did we learn then in this lecture on Fisher and Ury's principles for win-win negotiation? The principles are these. Separate people from the problem, that's one. Two is focus on interests not positions. Don't take a position and then defend it. Principle three would be generate options for mutual gain, brainstorm, get creative. Generate enough options that you can combine and choose between. Then principle four, get some objective criteria and agree on them so that you can choose between those options on something that makes sense.

We've got some other great ideas from them here, BATNA and negotiation jujitsu. We learned a lot from Fisher and Ury. I think their work really ranks up there not far behind that of Morton Deutsch and the idea of win-win because they move us a long way toward how to get win-win resolutions. We can use them with friends, loved ones, companions, at work in our communities.

Let me give you an assignment for what to do with this one. Next time you're in a conflict, when you identify what you want, remember our lecture on goals, my goal is the answer to what I want. move that to thinking about positions. If I would take a position about that goal, ask myself what would be the interest behind that position. If I've got my interest identified, that answers the question why would I want to achieve that goal or why would I take that position. With mine identified let me ask the other person what theirs is, see if we can get theirs identified, and then work for getting interests resolved in that conflict.

If you can do that, just give that focus on interest a try, that would be a really good starting point and you're both going to have a good shot at getting win-win resolution. Where do we go from here?

We've learned these four principles for negotiating. Now we're going to move on to a more specific step-by-step process that's going to involve seven steps. My version of a step-by-step, there are a lot of step-by-step processes. This is the way I work it. It's a seven-step process and we'll deal with that in Lecture 11.

Preparing and Arranging to Negotiate
Lecture 11

> The evidence is actually stronger to support our own behavior changing the way we feel than it is to support the way we feel ... driv[ing] our own behavior.

In this lecture and the next, we'll walk through a seven-step process that we can use in applying Fisher and Ury's four principles of negotiation. This lecture covers the steps for preparing to negotiate. The two basic conditions that must be present in order to use this process are as follows: (1) You must be able to define the issue in terms of voluntary behavior from the present moment forward, and (2) the other party must be willing and able to negotiate. You also must be calm enough to do the intellectual work of negotiating.

Step 1 in the negotiation process is to define the conflict issue, that is, state the difference that's bothering you and identify why it's bothering you. Again, the issue must be stated in terms of the other party's voluntary behavior, not in terms of emotions, attitudes, or character, from the present moment forward. Neither emotions nor character are negotiable, although both may be reflected in behavior, which is negotiable. Make sure once you identify the behavior that changing it will fix the problem.

It may be helpful to write the issue down in one of two formats. For personal relationships, John Gottman suggests using the **XYZ formula**: "When you [behave

Without both parties willing and able to negotiate, negotiation is simply not possible.

© JupiterImages/Creatas/Thinkstock.

in a certain way], I feel [negative emotion]." In a professional setting, use this adaptation: "You are [behaving in this way], and that's a problem for me because…."

What if the issue really is a matter of feelings, character, or personality? Remember that these things must be reflected in behavior and try again to identify the objectionable actions. What if the issue relates to past behavior? In that case, ask yourself what you're after. Do you want an apology, a promise not to repeat the behavior, or some kind of compensation? You must bring the discussion into the present. If the issue can't be defined as voluntary behavior, then you can't negotiate. Your options are to accept the current situation, escalate the conflict, impose consequences, get an ally, or exit the relationship.

Step 2 of the negotiation process is to identify and evaluate your goals. Here, you can bring in the earlier types of goals we discussed (topic, relational, identity, and process), as well as Fisher and Ury's focus on interests. Good questions to ask yourself include: Why do I want to resolve this conflict? What is a good resolution for me? How important is it to me that I reach this resolution? How do I want to be viewed by the other party? How does this situation affect the way I view myself? Note that the topic, relational, and identity goals interact with one another.

Step 3 requires you to decide whether or not you want to resolve the issue by negotiating. Consider the degree of interdependence you have with the other party, your leverage, the context of the potential negotiation, the nature of your relationship, the risks of introducing the issue, and BATNA. Once you've looked at all these factors, don't delay the decision. Remember that delaying is one of the most common forms of avoidance. And once you've made the decision, take full responsibility for it. If the negotiation goes well, give yourself credit; if you decide not to negotiate, remind yourself that you chose not to take steps to correct the problem.

You might think that certain conflicts aren't important enough to bother about, but you can use minor conflicts to practice some of the strategies and techniques you've learned in this course. This also establishes a track record for negotiating with others. Be careful, too, not to undervalue your own importance in the situation; you have needs and goals, just like the other party does.

Step 4 in the process is to arrange a meeting with the other party in order to negotiate. Keep in mind that you've done the preparation for negotiation, but the other party hasn't yet. To just launch into a discussion about the issue can take the other person by surprise and cause resentment. In carrying out step 4, approach the other party directly and privately, preferably in person or over the phone. Label the conflict as a problem and state the issue exactly as you defined it in step 1. Tell the other party that you'd like to find a solution to the problem that will satisfy both of you, then ask when would be a good time to meet, providing a specific timeframe. If the other party counters by raising other issues, agree to talk about these after the initial problem has been solved. Step 4 is a commitment, but remember that you can't make progress if you avoid the problem; you have to step up and start negotiations. ∎

> You might think that certain conflicts aren't important enough to bother about, but you can use minor conflicts to practice some of the strategies and techniques you've learned in this course.

Important Term

XYZ formula: John Gottman's useful formula for using "I" statements and avoiding criticism of the other person when communicating during a conflict. Usually stated as: "In situation X, when you do Y, I feel Z."

Suggested Reading

Dues and Brown, *The Practice of Organizational Communication*, chap. 11.

1. Think of three conflicts you experienced in the last year. Consider how the issues were defined by the conflicting parties and how they could best be phrased in terms of someone's voluntary behavior—with a focus on the present and the future.

Preparing and Arranging to Negotiate
Lecture 11—Transcript

Fisher and Ury gave us those four principles for negotiating win-win resolutions and they gave us some nice detailed suggestions for how they could be applied. In this lecture we're going to take that a step further. In this and the next lecture we're actually going to walk through seven steps, a seven-step process that we can use applying Fisher and Ury's suggestions to really work through to win-win resolutions.

Why a step-by-step approach? If you think about it, when you've got a conflict and it's a significant conflict if you start to think well how am I going to resolve this, the question can look overwhelming. That's not the place to start. The place to start is with the question about where do I start. What's my first step in dealing with the conflict? Once I figure out what my first step ought to be then I can go to what do I do next and work through the process step by step if I'm aiming for a win-win outcome.

We break it up into steps. We break it up into seven, and in this lecture and the next we'll get through all seven steps. In this lecture in particular we're going to do the first four. These are the steps we take to really do our own preparation and get ready to negotiate and decide, and then arrange a meeting with the other person to do that negotiation. These are the preparation and negotiation steps that we'll cover in this lecture.

To get started we really ought to talk about the conditions that we need to have in place if we're going to be able to use this process because you can't negotiate just anything. There are two basic conditions that have to be present in order to use this step-by-step negotiation process.

The first one is that we've got to be able to define that issue in terms of somebody's voluntary behavior, and it's got to be voluntary behavior, present tense forward. We're going to find out whether that condition exists right there in step one. The other condition, and it's a fairly obvious one, is that the other party or parties are going to have to be willing and able to negotiate with us, that we're going to have to have access to them, they're going to have to be available, they're going to have to be willing and able to negotiate with us because if they're not, we've got nobody to negotiate with. Two conditions, we'll actually find that one out when we get to step four and we go and try and make the arrangement to meet with them.

We probably also want to note before we start that there's a kind of a step zero that's going to come before step number one. What would step zero be? If you think back to our lecture on emotions and remember that emotions can be painful, complex, multiple, they can even be dangerous, we can be wound up about our emotions when we have them. As Antonio Damasio points out, emotions are really more basic, they come before consciousness. We talked in the emotions lecture about how you need to calm down enough to be able to function.

If you need a step zero, if you're upset enough that you're going to have a hard time thinking clearly, you've got to take a little time; you've got to breathe, you've got to calm down. You've got to focus away from it a little bit. When you're trying to calm down, do not go ruminating a whole lot about why it is I'm angry at this person. Take your mind off of it a little bit, calm down and breathe, and begin to think about the future and where do you want to go with it so that you can get yourself in a mental state that'll allow you to do some real intellectual work and thinking work, because in order to define an issue clearly you're going to have to think.

That would be step zero and it would be there if you need it. You're not always that upset to begin with.

If we're calm enough to think, calm enough to think, we can go to step one. Step one will say define the conflict issue. That is state the difference that's bothering you and identify why it bothers. If you go back to that definition I gave you for conflict in the very first lecture, that simple two-word definition, it's a discomforting difference, just flip it over. What's the difference, what's the behavior that I'm rejecting to, in other words, and why is that a bother for me? That's what I want to be able to do.

This can be a challenging intellectual process. Let me give you some guidelines and then give you a pitfall to avoid here. Guideline number one and it's the preeminent one, you've got to be able to state that issue in terms of somebody's voluntary behavior from the present moment forward. It may've been voluntary in the past, but it can't be changed now. We have to give up all hope of having a better past. So it's not about the past. It's the present forward, and it's got to be stated in terms of behavior.

I can make that clearer. These next two are kind of redundant, but I think very useful to think. That's going to mean that we, guideline number two, do not state the issue in terms of somebody's emotions or attitudes. There's a cycle that's evident in the research between attitudes or emotions and behavior. We know that emotions drive behavior and attitudes drive behavior, and we also know that behavior changes emotions and changes attitudes. It's a cycle. The evidence is actually stronger to support our own behavior changing the way we feel than it is to support the way we feel having to drive our own behavior.

So don't object to emotions. Why not? They're non-negotiable. I've got no control of my emotions. I can turn them down by thinking differently, but I can't negotiate them away. I can't agree to love you tomorrow. I can't agree to just stop being mad and be held accountable for that because I don't have that kind of control over mad. I can agree to try to behave to think differently and focus differently, but I can't agree not to be mad. Don't state the issue in terms of somebody's attitude or somebody's emotion. I can't be objecting to how they feel, how they feel is not negotiable.

If I think I have an objection to how they feel, they must be behaving in some way that's causing me to think that. I'm attributing that behavior to the emotion. So let me not risk the fundamental attribution error, attributing behavior to the feeling. Let me just identify the behavior and be able to explain why that's a problem for me, not objecting to emotions.

Similarly let's don't object to their character. That one comes up a lot. I think this person is lazy. I think this person is sloppy. I think this person is just not an honest person. If I'm objecting to character, if that's the way the person is, character isn't really negotiable. Similarly if I think that person has bad character, that person is behaving in some way and it might be a pattern of behavior, a sequence of things, but there is behavior there that's causing me to think that about their character. So let me identify the behavior and why I object to it rather than a character because we can negotiate behavior, we can't negotiate character or personality. So not emotions, not character, instead identify the voluntary behavior present tense forward.

There's a pitfall to avoid when I'm trying to do this. This is serious intellectual work. I can be working to get it phrased as behavior and when I do that, thinking about it in that way, I'm at a risk of technically get it down to where I'm identifying the behavior, but we could fix that behavior and it really wouldn't solve my problem. So when I think I've got it identified, this is the behavior in why I object, let me double check and ask myself if I solve that behavior, if we get that changed, will that fix my problem. That will give me a check and avoid that pitfall of getting it technically right through step one, but then solving it and still not solving my problem. So make sure that the behavior identified really gets at what my problem is.

To do this I might want to write it down, writing it out gets it out there objectively and makes it clear for me and I can look at it and think with it a bit more clearly. There are a couple of very simple formulas we can cite for actually stating this, two of them. One of them is kind of for close relationships and it's more kind of soft and the other is a little more concrete. Maybe it fits better in a business situation.

The first one, the softer one for closer relationships, comes from John Gottman who does all of that wonderful research on couples. He calls it the XYZ formula, but it really makes use of the "I" statement. And it's a simple formula that works like this. It says when you *fill in the blank with the behavior,* I feel *fill in the blank with the feeling that feels bad.* The softness of that, is that it goes to feeling, probably wouldn't work very well at work, at least not most of the time. So there's another one that I often use especially in professional settings on helping with people.

That one goes like this. You're doing *fill in the blank with the behavior*, and that's a problem for me because *fill in the blank with the explanation*; so you're doing it's a problem for me because.

Let's illustrate this with some examples. Let's go back to the scene with our roommates Rebecca and Jane, grad student and the working person. Jane is in the living room watching TV with some friends and the TV is loud and the laughter is getting louder, and Rebecca is in her room trying to study and she gets more and more angry as the volume and the laughter get louder and louder. Let's see how that one works out in terms of defining the issue.

[Video start.]

> **Rebecca**: Jane is so selfish. Talk about disrespect. I need quiet time to study, but talking to her is a waste of time. I guess I don't blame her for wanting to watch TV and hang out with her friends, and I don't want to lose her as a roommate, but I need quiet time to study. I guess I have to try and talk to her again.

[Video end.]

Rebecca is having trouble defining the issue here. In the first place, she's thinking it's like the fundamental attribution error. It's "she doesn't respect me, she doesn't remember what it's like." That would be the attribution error, but Rebecca is not really stuck there. She's thinking further. She's maybe trying to understand Jane's position and she's thinking she ought to negotiate, but she's still struggling with how to define that issue.

Let's do another example. In this other example let's take it to work. Remember Don and his problem with his sales territory way back from Lecture 1. How might Don define the problem if he wants to negotiate with his boss and work it out? Let's find him sitting in his office thinking that through.

[Video start.]

> **Don**: Dale's got me driving all over the place. I can't make sales if I'm stuck in the car. Pat drives less, and she's got more potential sales leads in her territories. Dale's playing favorites, and if Pat's his favorite, there's not much I can do about it. But what's my real

problem here? It's too much driving and not enough selling, and I need to get a better balance; I can talk to Dale about that.

[Video end.]

Don is a little further along than Rebecca in this case. He gets it that if Pat really is his boss' favorite, there's not much he's going to do about that. You can't go negotiate that with your boss. You might even be creating an attribution error if it's based on that anyway. But he has figured out that he can negotiate about changing that assignment, give him less time in the car. That's real, it's tangible, it's about his boss' behavior in assigning the territory that affects the minutes that it takes him, the time he needs to do the job.

That's a good example of getting toward a better definition. But there are some what ifs we need to consider here about definition. What if it can't honestly be defined in terms of present and future voluntary behavior? That comes up sometimes. What if it really is a matter of feelings, character, or personality? If I'm thinking that remember, that cycle let me try to push to see if I can honestly define it as behavior because there must be behaviors I'm seeing that are causing me to object. But if the person really doesn't care or really doesn't like me or really isn't trustworthy, I'm not going to negotiate those emotions or character away. If I can't get it as behavior, I can't negotiate.

What if it's about a past transgression only and it's not about present? What am I after? Maybe I'm after apology, promise not to do it again, ask the person to make up for what they did. I've got to bring it to the present. The past in this thing might be relevant information, but I've got to be negotiating about what's going to happen now.

So if it can't be defined, if it really can't be defined as voluntary behavior, then I've found out that that first condition can't be met and I can't negotiate. So what would my options be then? I can choose to accept the situation as it is, and a lot of times we do that in important relationships at work, in love and marriage, and all kinds of relationships. We sort of make a decision that's the way it's going to be. It's not a deal breaker for me.

We make a lot of these choices in our lives and remember I can change my mind and negotiate later. I can choose to accept it. I can also choose to escalate. I can impose consequences. I can go get an ally. I can get help. I can escalate. That is an option if I can't negotiate. The third option is I can leave. I can exit the relationship. It's painful, it can involve risks. It requires courage a lot of the times, but sometimes the very best choice for the long run is just to get out of there. That's one we need to be willing to take if we decide we can't negotiate.

Let's suppose though that we made our definition and we got it defined as voluntary behavior, now we can most to step two. What would we do in step two? Step two says identify and evaluate your goals. Remember we did a whole lecture on goals and we've already talked about Fisher and Ury's concept of focus on interests, not positions. So we've got a lot of concepts to work with here in terms of identifying our goals.

I would suggest this. Go to that list of goals that Hocker and Wilmot give us. We want to think first in terms of our topic goals in this instance, and think of trying to get at my interests that would underline a position I might take. Ask myself why is that I want to resolve this? What's the problem here? What's the good in a resolution for me? How important is it to me? Figure that one out. An example of that would be if we go to that conflict we did in the workplace where Anna had the conflict with Carl who wanted her to finish his job for him doing his work as well as hers.

The two of them share an interest in getting the proposal out on time, and that would certainly be her goal, and she has an interest in sharing time and effort fairly and not getting stuck with too much. So she's got goals that she can focus on there in terms of getting something that would work better for her in terms of Carl's behavior. But then go and think about relationship goals? How would that work? How do I want to be viewed by the other party in this? What are my relationship goals?

I want to think about how that relates to my topic goals because I don't want to chase a topic goal in a way that's going to mess up my relationship. An example of that might be if you remember our teams, design team and the other team, the team that did the production with the design team led by Hank, and Barry the other team leader didn't like Hank's design. Barry would have relationship goals for his working relationship with Hank, and Hank would have goals for how he wanted to work with Barry. Before they get into a clash about this it would be well for both of them to think about what are my relationship goals.

I probably also want to think about my identity goals in a given situation. How does this conflict affect the way I'm viewed by the other party and how does this situation seem to be affecting the way I view myself, because we're all working on our identity all the time. If I've got a good sense of all three of those goals, identity, relationship, and topic, I'm going to be in better shape to figure out what I'm after here.

Here's an example of that with Rebecca and Jane, our roommates. Jane, in terms of an identity goal, would not want Rebecca to see her as inconsiderate or a slob, and Rebecca wouldn't want to be seen as a nag, and they both want to have a good relationship to keep a better life together of living together. Anna would not want to be seen by Carl as some kind of a doormat that he can walk over, and she doesn't want to think that's what she's looking at when she looks in the mirror in the morning getting dressed. She wants to feel like a strong, equal, team player. That's an identity goal in addition to having to do with the relationship.

Notice how all these goals, those three types of goals interact with each other. So you want to do some serious thinking this through. Each influences the other as we move along. Some are stand-in for others. Topic goals can influence relationship goals and identity goals and vice versa. We really want to do some thinking here, some critical thinking work and sort out what our goals are in terms of at least those three types of goals.

For the process goal issue we're thinking in terms of a process here that's pursuing a win-win negotiation, so we know where that one is. Sort out, do some thinking, get clear on what my goals are in this particular conflict. Once I'm clear on that, I can move to step three.

Step three requires me to make a decision. I've got to decide whether I want to attempt to resolve this by negotiating with the other party. Nobody has got a sure formula for this. Nobody can make the decision for you. We just know you've got to decide. We do have some suggestions to help consider how to do it, but you're stuck with making the decision if it's your conflict.

Suggestion number one would be to consider how the other party is interdependent with me. The shorthand way of doing this that I talked about back in Lecture 7 when we talked about power is to think about my leverage. What's the other party's interest in my being satisfied with how we work this out? I want to think about what kind of power I've got in this situation, leverage is a good handle to get a hold of that.

The second thing is consider the context. What else is going on right now with you and the other party? Is this a time, a setting, where this thing can be negotiated. Be careful here, don't use this to put it off, but make a realistic consideration. Thirdly consider the relationship, what's the nature of the relationship I have with this other party. Is negotiation appropriate with this person? Are they really able to negotiate responsibly? Consider that.

Fourth, consider the risks. What comes up? What are the risks I take in bringing this up? Once I bring something up, it's on the table, we can't go back to where I hadn't brought it up. It's part of why we're reluctant to bring things up, but consider the risks and know what they are so I can decide to go ahead.

Fifth comes straight from Fisher and Ury. Remember BATNA from the last lecture, the best alternative to a negotiated arrangement? Think that through, what would be my best alternative so I know what my backup is if it doesn't work, and that really lets me better understand how much power I've got and helps me decide whether I want to try to negotiate.

The sixth one is this, go ahead and decide. Actually make the decision. Don't rush it, but don't linger over it. Delaying is one of the most common forms of avoidance. We just have trouble making the decision whether we're going to try to negotiate it and so we don't get in there and get that thing done. So go ahead and make a decision. Don't rush it, but don't delay it.

Seventh, once I make this decision consciously, let me assign myself full responsibility. I made the decision and now I'm going to go ahead and act on it. If this works out well, I'm going to credit myself. If it falls on its face, I made the decision. If I decide not to go ahead and negotiate which I very well might in a lot of instances, I've got to remind myself that I'm deciding not to go try to negotiate with this person to fix it. It's not that they're deciding to keep bothering me. I'm deciding not to take the steps to change it. I want to own the responsibility. It's credit if it works out well. It's mine if it doesn't work out well.

There are some what ifs to talk about with making this decision like, here's a really common one. What if, just what if, what if the conflict doesn't seem important enough to trouble the other party or what if now is not a good time. A lot of things are too small to bother with. I've got a suggestion about that one to deal with. If I don't have a history of working through a lot of conflicts with a person, those small, relatively unimportant conflicts are really good ones to practice on. When you bring it up with them, you can even say this is little, but I'd like to work it out with you, because you don't want to wait until you've got a big conflict that just can't be avoided to try negotiating when you wouldn't have a track record.

It's nice to use those smaller conflicts to do it. If now is not a good time, try to move it on to identifying a specific time when it would be a good time. Now is not a good time might be a way to do it too. Be careful not to undervalue your own importance in the situation. You've got needs and it's easy to sell ourselves short when we're trying to decide this. It's a good idea to take the small steps and practice, get on with it if you can. If now is not a good time, identify a specific later when you're going to get to it.

If context and timing allow you to negotiate, then you're ready to proceed. So where are you? You've got this step done. You've decided to proceed, you've got an agenda, but the other person doesn't have this agenda yet.

Now we're at step four, and what we do in step four is we approach the other person and we try to arrange a meeting in order to negotiate. If I've decided I want to negotiate, that doesn't mean I can just go negotiate the other person and start the negotiation. At that point, I've got an agenda but the other person doesn't have it yet, and the other person hasn't agreed to negotiate with me. So I really want to take this extra step here and arrange a meeting with them to do the negotiation.

If we don't arrange a meeting, we just go start a conversation on it expecting the other party to cooperate, what would that mean? I'd be awfully presumptuous to do that. I'm presuming on that person's time and I also risked wrecking the negotiation before it starts. We've all been in this position, the other person has a complaint with us and they want to negotiate, and here they are in our face starting the negotiation. They may have an agenda to get their problem solved, but if we haven't agreed to negotiate and we're being surprised by this, our agenda as the receiver of that is just to get them out of our face. So the thing can go wrong from the beginning.

This step four is really important. It's important to get right. Taking it by itself if you got nothing else out of the whole course would really help increase the likelihood that you're going to get a lot of conflicts solved better. We're going to approach the other person and we're going to try to arrange, try to set up a meeting for the purpose of negotiating a resolution. We've got some guidelines for this.

The first guideline is this. Approach the other party directly and privately. You'll want to do this face to face if at all possible. Phone is next best. I don't like email for it. Email has a different kind of element to it. It's much better if you can do it with a live conversation. Second guideline, refer to the conflict as a problem. Remember when Fisher and Ury said talk about it as a problem, not a conflict? Do it here. You don't want to go to the person and say I've got a conflict with you, I've got a problem. Label it as a problem to begin with so we can begin to think about it as something we can work on together.

Once you've done that, guideline three says let's state the issue. Let's state it exactly as we defined it in step one. State it clearly. Don't approach it with a fog saying I've got some problem with your behavior I wish to discuss with you. Tell them exactly what it's about. Tell them what the behavior is. Tell them why it's a problem. Then tell them what you'd like to do is find a solution to that problem that's really going to satisfy both parties. So you're telling them the topic of the meeting you want to hold and you tell them the purpose of the meeting is to find a solution that both they and you are going to be happy with.

Having told them that, ask them when is a good time to do it. Ask for a meeting, give them a timeframe to choose. When is a good time today, when is a good time this week? When is the next time in the next couple of days? Give them a little range of timing to choose and ask for that meeting.

Here's an example of doing that. Rebecca, good old Rebecca, she's thought this through a little further. She's going to approach Jane and ask about working something out to control the noise in the apartment. Let's listen.

[Video start.]

> **Rebecca**: Hey, Jane, I'm sorry to interrupt. Listen, I need to set up a time for us to talk about the noise problem. Right now I'm trying to study, and the TV's really loud. Other times I can't concentrate because your friends are here. This happens a lot, so can we set up a time where we can talk about it tonight or tomorrow? We have to agree on something that works for both of us.

> **Jane**: Tonight's not going to work; Rick's picking me up in a couple minutes.

> **Rebecca**: Okay, how about tomorrow night after you get home from work?

> **Jane**: Yeah, that's fine.

> **Rebecca**: Thanks.

[Video end.]

Ahh, now Rebecca is nicely on track. She's focused on voluntary behavior that creates the noise. It's present time forward and she has arranged a meeting to deal with it. She's on track getting this thing going.

Let's look at another example. Here's Don, he's talking to his boss Dale. Remember Don figured out how to define the issue. How would he arrange to meet with Dale to talk about negotiating a change in this territory?

[Video start.]

> **Don**: Hey, Dale, can we talk sometime this week about my new territory? I'm concerned because I've been driving so much lately that I haven't had enough time for my customers. I'm thinking maybe we can adjust it a little—somehow cut back on my driving time and still have it work for you.
>
> **Dale**: Don, I'm always as fair as I can be.
>
> **Don**: I know, I know. But, maybe if we put our heads together we can think of a better layout for my territory. You know, it's all about boosting my sales while still cutting back on travel time. Can we just try to sit down together and figure it out?
>
> **Dale**: This week is so busy for me, Don.
>
> **Don**: How about next Monday then? It will only take a little time, and I'd really appreciate it.
>
> **Dale**: Okay Don. I owe you at least that. Monday morning? 8:30?
>
> **Don**: Thanks. I'll be here.

[Video end.]

Oh good, Don is right on track here. He's got it well defined. He's being persistent, but he's being proper in his relationship with Dale, and he's talking about behavior. He hung in there and he has got a meeting for 8:30 on Monday morning. We at least know he's going to get himself a hearing with this.

Think how you might've responded if you were in Dale's position. You might've tried to put it off, but Dale doesn't have a lot of room to maneuver here. It's pretty obvious that the right thing to do is to sit down with Don and talk this thing through. You might do that even if you didn't particularly want to reconsider the territory, but felt some obligation to do so. That's proper in the relationship you've got with Don, so this works that way.

Let's consider some what ifs in this situation because the other party is involved now. What's the other party going to do? Suppose they claim to be too busy in the timeframe. Ask them to check their schedule and then get back to them. Suppose they want to jump to discussing the issue. Check with them that we ought to discuss it now and make sure that the purpose of the discussion is to resolve it. Suppose they counter by raising some other issues they want to discuss. Treat that as their approach step. Agree to talk about it, volunteer to talk about it, just don't put it ahead of yours on the list. Why, because you asked them first.

One more thing about step four, just to mention here before we get beyond it. It's pretty frightening to confront the other person. This is a place where we might want to chicken out. It's a commitment move. Once you bring it up you can't get back to where you were before. But if it's something you really want to negotiate, go ahead and do it. Don't revert to avoidance at this particular point. You can't make progress unless you step up and go ahead and negotiate the thing. So even you're afraid of it, go ahead and do it.

Let's summarize then. Where are we with this? Here are our steps. We're going to have to mention a step zero for you. You've got to calm down enough to think clearly. Once you've done that, if that was necessary, here are your first four steps. Define that issue in terms of voluntary behavior, not objecting to emotion and not objecting to character. Two, identify and clarify your goals, get clear on what you're after here.

Three, make that decision do I want to go ahead and try to pursue a resolution by negotiating with this person or not. Get a decision made, and then four, the first thing to do acting on it is go make an approach to the other person and arrange to have a meeting in order to negotiate a win-win resolution.

I've got an assignment for you too at the end of this one. Defining a conflict issue in terms of behavior can be challenging, especially if you're in the heat of emotions. So I want you to go back. Think of three conflicts you experienced in the last year and consider how the issues were defined by both parties. Consider how they could've been best phrased in terms of somebody's voluntary behavior with a focus on the present and the future. Think about it. Think through what difference that might've made.

That's where we are. Where're we going from here? We've got the first four steps to find. We've got our meeting arranged. In our next lecture, what we'll do is go ahead and conduct the meeting and push that all the way through to following through. Next lecture, how to do the meeting and get our win-win resolution.

Negotiating Conflict Resolutions
Lecture 12

It's very typical to require more than one meeting and more than one discussion to get an ongoing behavior change and make it stick. You've got to fine-tune things.

In this lecture, we continue with the seven-step process for negotiating conflicts. Step 5 is to conduct the meeting that you arranged in step 4. Come to the meeting prepared to explain your point of view and to offer suggestions for solving the problem, but don't be overly committed to your own solutions. Also come with the mindset that you will listen to the other party's views, feelings, and suggestions. If you asked for the meeting, you should take the lead; begin by thanking the other person for his or her time and willingness to listen. Restate the issue and the purpose of the meeting—to find a solution that works for both parties. Then, ask the other person how he or she wants to proceed. What if the other person attempts to hijack the agenda by raising other issues? As you did in step 4, agree to discuss those issues, but do not put them in front of yours.

As the meeting proceeds, don't allow discussions of feelings or explanations to become repetitive. Stay focused on interests and goals and move forward by pushing in that direction. Of course, it's also important to get suggestions on the table; steer the conversation toward something you can agree on, again, based on objective criteria.

In step 6, you make a **contract**, an agreement between the two parties about what each will do to solve the conflict. The contract must be clear, and it must address voluntary behavior from the present forward because it will hold each party responsible for following through on the agreed-upon terms. It must also be an unequivocal agreement. In your negotiations, verbalize the agreement, then check to make sure that the other party has the same understanding. Ask the other party whether he or she agrees to the contract and confirm your own agreement. In some cases, you may want to specify a time when you will check back to make sure that the agreement is working. A word-of-mouth agreement is generally acceptable in early negotiations. If the other party consistently fails to follow through on agreements, you may need to put them in writing. In reaching an agreement, the other party may offer a statement that does not relate to clear, voluntary behavior; in other words, he or she says, "I'll try." In this case, push through to identify concrete behaviors that stand behind "trying." What if you just can't find a win-win resolution? If that happens, acknowledge it and consider a compromise.

What if you can't find any acceptable solution, not even a compromise? Deutsch showed that most of the time, you can find a win-win resolution, but not always. If that's the case, you may decide to escalate the conflict or end the relationship.

Step 7 in this process can be more difficult than the first six steps combined. This step involves following through on the contract. Obviously, you must do what you agreed to do and stick with it. You also need to pay attention to whether or not the other party complies with the agreement. If the other party is in compliance, you should express your appreciation for his or her behavior. Without positive feedback, the other party will almost invariably revert to the old behavior. If the other party is not following the agreement, you should arrange another meeting and see if you can adjust the original solution to make it work. If the other party fails to follow through repeatedly, you may decide to escalate the conflict, give up, or exit the relationship. If you're making progress with each meeting, stay with the program, but if you're spinning your wheels, you may have to make a more difficult decision.

> **Push through to identify concrete behaviors that stand behind "trying."**

In some cases, unforeseeable difficulties may arise after you've reached an agreement. If that happens, go back to step 4; explain the problem and ask for another meeting. Finally, hurt feelings or broken trust may linger after a conflict has been negotiated. We'll look at the process of forgiving, healing, and rebuilding in a later lecture.

This seven-step process of negotiation is not a recipe to follow that always results in an agreement. Because every conflict and every person is unique, there is no guarantee that going through this process will result in a good resolution every time. You can't control the other party in a conflict, but you can influence outcomes, and you have a chance at reaching better outcomes through this process. ■

Important Term

contract: A concrete, stated agreement between conflicting parties on what each party will do to solve a conflict and for which each party can be held responsible.

Suggested Reading

Kellett and Dalton, *Managing Conflict in a Negotiated World: A Narrative Approach to Achieving Dialogue and Change*.

Assignment

1. Start with a smaller conflict—one that is not extremely emotional or crucial in your life—and try to apply all seven steps of the negotiating process. Then look for other chances to use the process. Build it into your repertoire for managing conflict.

Negotiating Conflict Resolutions
Lecture 12—Transcript

In Lecture 11 we discussed steps one, two, three, and four in our seven-step process. In those steps what we did was get the issue defined in terms of voluntary behavior. We sorted out our goals and got clear on them. We decided we did want to go ahead and negotiate a resolution with the other person, and then we went in step four and arranged a meeting with that person.

Now we're going to talk about steps five, six, and seven, conducting the negotiation will be step five. Contracting a solid resolution agreement that we can make work will be step six, and then following through on what we agreed to will be step seven. These steps very much involve interaction with the other party so we're going to have to consider ways to respond to what the other party does as we go along our way. We'll do those in a context of talking about what ifs.

So here we go. Remember at this point we've done step four. We've arranged to do a meeting so now we're at step five. Step five would be this. We go ahead and conduct that meeting. Do what we agreed to do. Show up and do it. Here are the guidelines for your part in conducting that meeting. First one, come prepared. Be ready to explain your point of view. Have suggestions to offer for solving it, but don't be overly committed. Don't push them to positions that they have to follow, but prepared to make some suggestions. You also ought to prepare yourself to listen to what the other party says. Listen to their views, listen to their feelings. Be open to their suggestions. Getting myself prepared in a frame of mind to listen is an important part of preparing.

So I show up, I'm prepared in those ways. Then what I want to do is take the lead. I asked for this meeting. It's kind of up to me to get it started. How do I start it? I want to begin by thanking the other person. Thank them for agreeing to meet with me for doing this. I owe them thanks. This is my problem. I own it. I need their help to resolve it, and they're willing to take their time and they're willing to risk hearing something they didn't want to hear. So I ought to thank them, besides if they listen to that thank you, take it in and feel good about it, they're a little more committed now to following through with the meeting in a constructive way.

Having them what I want to do is state the issue again, just exactly as I stated back in step four when I asked for this meeting. I also want to state the purpose of the meeting, remind them that what we were looking for here is a solution to that problem that really does work for both of us. Having done that, I've set the agenda. Now I can ask the other person how he or she wants to proceed in the meeting. They may want to talk first. They may want to explain further. They may want to be expressing their own suggestions right away. I want to ask them how they want to proceed because they've probably done some thinking about this and they're ready to talk too.

Let's look at an example of that. Let me set it up for you here. Let's see, let's go to Don and Dale. Let's say they're meeting on Monday morning to discuss—you know that 8:30 meeting that Don got himself with Dale—and they want to discuss altering Don's sales territory. How would that meeting get started?

[Video start.]

>   **Dale**: I'll be right with you in just a second.
>
>   **Don**: First off, Dale, thanks for agreeing to talk. So here's what I'm thinking: I'm hoping we can figure out a way to reduce my travel time while still increasing my face time with customers, and maybe picking up some new sales leads, too. But I want to make sure I'm meeting your needs, and I don't want to cause any problems for Pat and her customers. So, where do you want to begin?
>
>   **Dale**: Look, Don, I don't have a lot of options here. Let me go over what I was thinking when I split up the territory, and then you can break down how that affects you. Pat's out of town this week, and we'll need to loop her in on this, too. If we look at the highway, sort of the main logical dividing line …

[Video end.]

Well that's a good start. The issue is on the table. Dale clearly wants to explain his reasoning. That's where it all starts for him ,so it makes sense for him to get that out first. They're not going to negotiate much until that's already on the table what the territory is and why it's there. But it looks like Don has got a good opportunity to make his case here. Dale is really indicating that he's ready to listen and negotiate. So we've got a good start on this one.

Now we need to think about some what ifs. Suppose it didn't go quite that well. What if the other party wants to talk instead, not about their position on this issue, but they come with a complaint of their own and they say if we're going to talk about your problem I want to talk about this, and they want to try to highjack the agenda and put their problem in front of yours.

If they do that, you nicely respond the way you got them to respond in step four. Volunteer, agree right away to discuss their issue. But do not put it in front of yours. You could even do it in this meeting after you talk about yours, or you could offer a time to negotiate that. If they say why do we have to talk about yours first and they want to get to theirs first, you can smile and say because I asked you first. Any kid that ever survived on a playground already understands how to do that. So just don't let it get in front of yours. Treat it as a step four.

Let's do an example with that. Let's go back to Rebecca and Jane. So they're in their living room. They've agreed to meet at this time to chat about the noise problem and Jane has just returned from work. Let's see how that works.

[Video start.]

>**Rebecca**: Hey Jane!

>**Jane**: Hey.

>**Rebecca**: So how was work?

Jane: It was good. We finished beta testing today, so tomorrow I move on to a new project.

Rebecca: That's great. Listen, thanks for agreeing to talk about the noise. I really want to work it out. Where do you think we should start?

Jane: Well, there's a bunch of stuff that you do that bothers me, and I don't say anything. Like, leaving dirty dishes in the sink and using the last of the detergent. If we're going to talk about stuff that bothers us, we need to talk about all this stuff.

Rebecca: Wow, I didn't realize those things were bothering you. But sure. Let's talk about them. Let's start with the noise, then go down the list. If we don't get to everything tonight, we can talk more this weekend.

Jane: Why do we have to talk about the noise first? It's no worse than your stuff.

Rebecca: Because we agreed to talk about the noise problem tonight. I *do* want to talk about all our issues; Let's just take them one at a time.

Jane: All-right. The noise … the TV … my friends.

[Video end.]

Rebecca did a really good job here. She held her ground very nicely about the negotiation. You can kind of put yourself in Jane's position. You can understand how Jane would feel. She's got a lot of complaints she has been sitting on and here she has got to listen to Rebecca's. But you would feel pretty much required to listen and negotiate about the noise. Why is that? It's because you agreed to. You already agreed to this and Rebecca is very happy to talk about yours, you're just not getting yours in front of hers.

So you'd feel pretty much able to bring up and discuss what was handed to you, but you really feel like you needed to work with her and deal with her issue first. So Rebecca did a good job in that discussion. So now we've got the meeting started. How does it go from there? As the discussion proceeds we're talking about feelings and making explanations. You don't want to get stuck in things that repeat.

As I work with people on these and facilitated a lot of these conversations, it's as if you can watch people get into a cycle of repeating. You don't want to get it going there. What you want to is focus on principles and interest, keep pushing it in that direction. If the feelings and the explanations get repetitive, you can point that out and say can we move forward, what are our interests, what are our goals here. How are we going to do this? Start asking for suggestions once we've started repeating ourselves with explanations. Focus those suggestions on interests, focus them on goals.

Let's see how that would work. Let's go again to Don and Dale, and they're offering ideas for how to handle this in Dale's office about sales territory.

[Video start.]

> **Dale**: Okay, I think we understand where we're each coming from, now. Let's get a little creative and see if we can divvy up the territory in a way that takes better care of you, but also works for Pat and for the company.

> **Don**: I was thinking that I could take east of the river and Pat could take west; that's one possibility.

> **Dale**: Okay, we could do that. Here's another way we could go with it. If we look at the highway as the dividing line, rather than the river ...

[Video end.]

This is progress. If there are really some reasonable alternatives for adjusting the territories, it's hard to imagine that some adjustment at least can't be made to make this a little better for Don. So what we want to do here is we do want to stay on track as we go. We're making these. We've got goals clearly in mind. We're getting suggestions out and we're considering the suggestions that come up. You want to steer this conversation towards something you can agree on, and you want to be choosing these based on some kind of objective criteria. You know that's going to fit with Fisher and Ury told us to do.

Let's look at another example and let's look at Don and Dale and see what progress they made looking at how they can choose the best option.

[Video start.]

> **Dale**: All right, so we've come up with four different options here. How do we decide which one is the best for everyone?

> **Don**: Well, we can look at travel time and total number of miles for both me and Pat, and compare them.

> **Dale**: Okay, good. What about the number of clients and their locations for each option?

> **Don**: Yeah, that matters a lot. And the locations of clients where we already have relationships.

> **Dale**: Okay, let's look at each of the options with three main criteria: Equalizing the distribution of clients, the travel time and miles, and maintaining good relationships with existing clients. The option we want is the one that gives us the best balance of all three.

> **Don**: Okay. I'm good with that.

[Video end.]

Good, this negotiation is going very well. Don and Dale have several ideas on the table, several ways they could deal with the territory, and they've got several very specific, very measurable criteria for choosing between them.

They're doing well in this negotiation. If they're doing that well and they're looking at those, we can get to where we can make a decision. We can do step six. We can begin to contract.

When you do the contract, I want to use that term very deliberately. We're going to agree on what's going to be done, but I want to specify that this is a contract. A contract exists morally and legally under just certain conditions. It exists if it's clear what's being agreed to. It exists if it addresses voluntary behavior from the present tense forward because the contract would hold each other responsible for following through on, and the only thing humans can hold themselves or anybody else responsible for is voluntary behavior.

It also has to be unequivocally agreed to, so it's got to be clear about voluntary behavior and it has to be an unequivocal agreement in order for it to really be a contract. You know that's it legally as the case. You think about written contracts, but the written contract with a signature is a document, it's documentation of the contracting that was done and the signature is there to be an unequivocal, clearly identifiable agreement. It's a contract even if it's just word of mouth.

You've got to state it in simple concrete terms. You've got to state it in a way that addresses voluntary behavior, and you've got to get it clearly agreed to. So the guidelines for this involve making sure that all these conditions are met. Let's look at those guidelines. The first thing you want to do if you're running this meeting, you want to state the agreement very clearly, verbalize it, try to state it clearly, and then check whether the other party has the same understanding. This is a communication thing stated very clearly, and don't be bashful about over clarifying in this case. Don't leave it vague. State it clearly, state it in terms of voluntary behavior. Double check with yourself to make sure that what it's doing is specifying behavior that each other can be held responsible for.

Having stated it, ask clearly whether the other party agrees. Is this what you agree to? Then confirm that you also agree if they say yes. So now you've got a clear statement of a voluntary behavior and you're clearly agreeing to it. Sometimes, not always, but sometimes it's very useful to just specify when and how you're going to check on how that's working and whether it's being followed through. A lot of times it's let's meet again in two weeks and see how this is working. You might want to specify how you're going to do it. It's usually not a good idea, most conflicts, at least the first or second time you talk about it, to go beyond a word of mouth agreement. You don't need to be writing that down. Supervisors in work situations a lot these days think they've got to document everything in the discussion. If I'm an employee who's going to not follow through regularly on what I'm agreeing to, if that's going to be my pattern enough that you can take disciplinary action, you can have a few voluntary agreements that I fail to meet before you start writing things down.

You might want to start putting things in writing after an agreement or two when the other person is not following through, it's proving not to be clear. But that's kind of an escalation when you go to writing. It's fitting after the word of mouth agreement hasn't worked for awhile.

Let's look at some examples of getting an agreement. Let's see, let's go back to Don and Dale and follow them through. They're both confident they've determined the best option. Now they're trying to contract an agreement. Let's see how that works.

[Video start.]

> **Dale**: All right, we're agreed then. I'll talk with Pat next week and see if she has a problem with making a change. If she's okay with it, we go with option two; we give her the near part of your territory west of the river, and we expand your coverage into the Woodland Hills area. If she's not okay with that, we'll meet together—with her included—and see what we can work out. Is that right?

> **Don**: Yes, that's right. Thanks.

> **Dale**: All right, then I'll get back to you after I talk with Pat.

> **Don**: Great! Thanks, I appreciate it, Dale.

[Video end.]

Dale and Don have got a clear agreement going. It's not a final thing because they don't have Pat included yet and she's a party that's involved. But they've got a contract, it's by word of mouth. It's very clear. They can hold each other responsible for it, and they know when they're going to check to see and find out if it's actually working very well. So that's a pretty good agreement that has been reached.

There are some what ifs that we need to talk about relative to those contracts. What if I encounter some problems making the agreement and what might those be? What if the other party offers something but it's not clear, voluntary behavior. One of my favorites among these, it just happens a lot, it shouldn't happen, it's a favorite in the sense that it's interesting to watch and it's not all that hard to fix. The other party says I'll try.

Let me give you a marvelous example of this one occurring that I witnessed some years ago. I was helping a supervisor and supervisee work through some issues. One of the issues was that this supervisor, the young employee, he was a young man. He was in his mid 20s and he had recently become a single father. His marriage had broken up and he was trying to take care of a toddler. He was coming to work late pretty often. His supervisor was trying to work with him to get this worked out.

There was this great moment where he said I'll try. You know I'll try. She, who had raised kids herself understood what his problem was. He just didn't know how to get a toddler ready and off to daycare and still get himself to work on time, and that was a struggle. So she said John you know I see that you try. I see how stressed you are when you come through the door at 20 minutes after 8 three days a week. I know you're trying. Let's talk about what behavior trying is going to be made of.

Then that supervisor who is a mother who had been around for awhile said, let's talk about what you do the night before, and she talked about laying things out. She talked about things with getting the toddler up, having the breakfast ready, making the moves to get the kid ready on time. The young man felt like that would work, and what they agreed to do was a list of things that he would do to get ready the night before, and she said I'm not going to bother you about being 20 minutes late, what I'm going to bother you about is did you do those things.

He agreed to that. I checked back with them several months later. The young man was doing much, much better. He was getting there on time and feeling better about himself. So if it's I'll try you can push it through to what behavior it's made of. Try is a noble thing and humans are great because we do that. But push it to the concrete behavior.

Let's look at another example. Our roommates Rebecca and Jane have come up with a solution, but let's listen to Jane's agreement to it and see how clear that is and look at that as a what if kind of problem that can come up.

[Video start.]

> **Rebecca**: Okay, so we agree that you can have friends over any Tuesday or Thursday night since I'm in class. Monday and Wednesday are quiet nights, so nobody comes over. And you'll turn the TV way down, right? Friday, Saturday, and Sunday are free; we can both have friends over if we want.

> **Jane**: All right. I'll try my best.

> **Rebecca**: Jane, I really appreciate that you'll try, but I don't want us slipping back into the same old routine. I can't afford to let my grades drop. Let's stick with this for a month and see how we do?

[Video end.]

We can't contract on I'll try. Rebecca is really right about that, and notice that Jane really doesn't sound all that confident that she's going to be able to keep the noise down. So if we're Rebecca listening to that, we don't know what we've got from Jane here. Is this an agreement or is it not? It's really not very clear. I think Rebecca handled this one fairly well. She hung in there and she went to pin it down. At least she got a time that we're going to move back to go ahead and check on it. So Rebecca is handling this one pretty well.

Let's think about another what if. What if you just can't find a true win-win resolution? If that's the case, and sometimes it's really true, you can't get there, at a certain point you've got to acknowledge that fact. It looks like we can't make this work for both of us. At that point, you might very well want to consider backing into a compromise. Remember I said compromise is a dysfunctional strategy. Use it only when you've tried to get a win-win and you can't. This is a good time to do that.

Let's do an example here. Let's talk about Don, Dale, and now Pat is in the room, the other sales representative Pat. They're in the conference room and Pat has noticed some problems with option number two that Dale and Don propose. So she didn't want to agree to it right away. Now you've got the three of them comparing options on the same criteria and every option has got tradeoffs. What happens with that?

[Video start.]

>   **Pat**: Listen, I know you two worked hard on this, but it looks to me like we don't have an option that's best on all three counts.
>
>   **Don**: Right. If we equalize the number of miles, we mess up the balance in the number of clients, and all the versions disrupt the customer relationships for at least somebody. Can we compromise a little? Split the difference? I do still need to cut down my driving time, at least some.
>
>   **Pat**: I can understand that. Now, I'd be willing to give up the big Garfield account just east of the city in exchange for the Schuster account further up state.
>
>   **Dale**: Wow, Pat, that's a big concession. What do you think, Don?
>
>   **Don**: Yeah, that would be great.

[Video end.]

They really can't get a full scale win-win. There are tradeoffs with every option so compromise really is in this ongoing working relationship the next best alternative. Pat is going to go ahead and offer compromises and she's doing that. This is the right time to back into a compromise situation. All the parties know because they've really worked on getting at that they can't get a win-win. So now everybody is going to be much more comfortable resorting to compromise. That's the place compromise belongs in our repertoire of conflict management behaviors. That's the kind of contract you can move to negotiating.

Let's look at another what if. What if you just can't find any acceptable solution, not by compromise, not by any means? If that's the case you've got to acknowledge that fact and that is sometimes the case. Deutsch showed us that we can get it most of the time. Sometimes you can get no resolution at all. If that's the case, then I'm stuck with having to decide either to escalate or give up or exit the relationship. I've got to be willing to walk away from it and make that kind of choice. It could come to that, but it usually doesn't.

Let's just assume now that we've gotten ourselves to the point where we have in fact gotten an agreement made and we've got it at a contract level, it's in behavior terms. It's clearly agreed to. We all understand it. We're not finished. We've done most of what we've talked about, but the long run is step seven and it can be harder and longer than any of the first six, or all the six combined.

Step seven is to follow through. I've got to follow through on what I agreed to you and I've got to pay attention to the other party. Here are our guidelines. The first one is obvious. I should go ahead and do what I've agreed to do. I've got to keep doing it and doing it with persistence. That's not easy. I'm going to have to remind myself because those behaviors that we were doing before may have habit to them. They may be existing patterns, but I've got to go ahead and do what I agreed to do.

Secondly I need to pay attention to whether the other party complies with the agreement. Is that person doing what he agreed to do? When I say pay attention, I'm trying to choose my words kind of carefully here. I don't want to be camped on their head like cops and robbers ready to catch them the minute they fail, but neither do I want to be on the other extreme walking away saying you agreed to it. I trust you, I don't have to pay attention. We do have to pay attention, and humans need to hold each other accountable. That's not a disrespect, just blindly trusting is sort of more than we should do for any other human being because most of us are not up to that absolute level of trust. So I've got to pay attention.

This is very important now. If the other party does what he or she has agreed to do, especially if it's repeatedly, what I need to do is take note of that and I've got to let them know I took note of that and I've got to express my appreciation. I've got to give them positive feedback for doing it. This one and there's research to support this one. You know what's almost bound to happen with a normal human being if I get them to change their behavior by an agreement and then I move on and don't pay any attention to the new behavior? They will almost invariably revert to the old behavior. That's what normal humans do. If I want them to keep up that new behavior they agreed to, I've got to talk positively reinforce it over time.

There's not a whole lot left that we're sure about from the very psychologists B. F. Skinner, but that thing about positive reinforcement holds up, it's true, that was his idea and it sticks. So I've got to reinforce it. That's if they do it. What if they don't do what they agreed to? If they fail to do all or part of the agreement, this is actually very, very common. It's very typical to require more than one meeting and more than one discussion to get an ongoing behavior change and make it stick. You've got to fine tune things.

If they're not doing some part of or all of what they agreed to, I want to go back and point out that we agreed on this. It's not happening, let's do another conversation and see if we can work it out in a way that we can make it work. So I want to go and redo that. Then what if I meet a second time and they agree and it doesn't work out and we meet a third time and we agree and it doesn't work out, what do we do with that?

I call it spinning my wheels. If after repeated meetings they're still failing to supply, some people call that you get jailhouse promises. Yeah I agree I'll do it and then they don't do it. If that's what happens, at some point I've got to decide I'm either going to escalate, give up, or exit because negotiating isn't working. Some people will agree, they'll negotiate and agree and then they won't deliver. So then you're going to have to make a decision if repeated agreements don't work. If you're making progress each time you discuss it, I'd hang in. But if we're spinning our wheels and not making progress, I'd stop and make that hard decision.

On the other hand, I've gotten an agreement, I've made an agreement, but I'm having difficulty, something is here that I didn't foresee. I didn't think about this one. I agreed and now I'm having trouble. I can certainly go back and ask for another meeting with the other party. I'm just back to step four. I go to the other party explain the problem that I'm having and ask for another meeting to discuss it. That's not really very hard to do and usually it works out pretty well. There's another point I want to get to here beyond that. Just ask for another meeting and go.

What if this conflict that we've done, we've now got it negotiated and we've got an agreement, but suppose it involves some missteps along the way and so there are still hurt feelings or perceived transgressions or there was some broken trust involved. We're going to talk about that later when we talk about aftermath, but there's going to be some forgiving and healing and rebuilding work that you're going to have to do because sometimes even though we've got an agreement now, the hard feelings can linger. You'll have to work on forgiveness and healing in order to make that work. We'll do a particular lecture on that and that'll be Lecture 22.

Let's do some final notes now on this business of steps five, six, and seven. We've done the whole seven-step process so we've got a sound guide. But any guide, I want to repeat that, any guide is going to have limits. It's not a simple cookie cutter follow this you'll get an agreement every time. Every conflict is unique, every person is unique, and we're all different. So there are no guarantees, you can do it all perfectly and not always get a good resolution worked out even if you're both trying, but the odds are really with you if you do it right, and they're certainly much better than they would be if you did it wrong. Most of the time you're going to get good resolutions.

A whole lot depends on the other person and their actions, and we don't control them. We can influence outcomes, but we can't guarantee it, we can't control our outcomes. So have it that way. You're an influence in the situation, you're one of the actors, but you're not the whole act, so think of it that way. It'll get you better outcomes and won't have you reaching for too much.

Negotiation is an individual art. You've got to personalize this. It has got to fit your own style. The language can be your own, don't be mechanically following someone else's language, but these seven steps really do give you a set of guidelines. If you follow them, if you gave it a good shot and you know you did it pretty darn well, you can congratulate yourself, it helps to know that you did your best, and it's easier to accept the outcome. That's our seven steps.

Let's summarize where we are. We outlined this whole seven step process now over the last two lectures. It gets us win-wins whenever they're possible and it helps us find compromises when it's necessary. Including the preparation steps we described in Lecture 11, the seven steps are, I'm going to walk back through all of them now. First step was define that issue, put it in terms of voluntary behavior. Second step was identify and clarify your goals. The third step was decide whether to pursue a resolution through negotiating.

The fourth step, approach the other party, arrange a meeting, get it set up and make clear what the agenda of the meeting is, the topic and the purpose to get a win-win resolution. Fifth step, go ahead and conduct that meeting. You take the lead, focus it on the issue, focus it on goals and interests, both of yours, and focus it on finding a win-win resolution. When that resolution gets pointed out, you're up to step six, which is get a contract, clear, unequivocal agreement in behavior terms so that you can hold each other responsible.

Finally step seven is to follow through. Remember do what you agreed to do, give positive feedback if the other person does what they agreed to do, and renegotiate if that's necessary. As I said there's no such thing as a perfect formula that will always guarantee you a good outcome, but you've really got good odds if you follow this seven step process.

Let me give you an assignment going from there. I want to suggest that next time you've got a small conflict, start with a small one, one that's not extremely emotional or crucial in your life or in that relationship, a nice little one that is bite-sized is easy to handle. It's best to start and build skill working with a smaller one so pick one out and do it. You can even tell the other person you want to try this with them when it comes up really try to do the seven step process. It's only useful if you give it a try. Start with defining, go through the steps in order, and start to build your repertoire of behavior using the whole seven step process.

Where are we going to go from here? We've got a step process laid out, we've got principles laid out, but we've been focusing all of these things like how to talk to the other person about it. That only works to the extent that both of us are willing to listen so we better stop and do a whole lecture on this challenging matter of listening in a conflict situation. Listening is the most taken for granted communication skill and it's one of the most difficult things to do, and particularly difficult in conflict. So next lecture we'll talk about listening in a conflict.

Listening in Conflict

Lecture 13

> Some of the estimates say we run as high as 75 to 80 percent of our communicating activity involved in listening, but we're still not doing very well.

We spend much more time listening than we do speaking, but most of us are not very good listeners, and conflict situations often make listening more difficult. Even when they're trying to communicate, parties in a conflict may feel that they are not being heard.

Listening is a complex task, and it's not passive; it requires attention, focus, and openness to what is being said. Researchers in communication have identified different kinds of messages or different dimensions of messages that come at us when we're in a discussion. The British scholar I. A. Richards, for example, labeled four kinds of messages we receive in communication: sense, feeling, tone, and intention.

The sense of the message is what's on the surface, the words that are spoken. Feeling, such as hostility or indifference, underlies the sense message. The tone relates to the relationship between the speaker and the listener; they may be equals or one may talk down to the other. If the listener rejects the message about the relationship, he or she will probably not process the sense or feeling of the message. The intention of the message relates to why the speaker is conveying the surface message. These four types of messages come at the listener all at once, and they may complement or contradict one another.

In communication, there is always some difference between the message the speaker sends and the message the listener receives. Two researchers, Claude Shannon and Norbert Weaver, developed a model that helps to illustrate the difficulty experienced in matching up those messages. According to the Shannon and Weaver model, a communication transaction has five steps. The source (the speaker) first gets an idea to communicate, then encodes it into words. The communication then travels through some medium, such as sound waves, to reach the receiver. The receiver (the listener) decodes the communication and holds the idea. We can see that differences arise between the sender and the receiver in communicating even a simple message. In a conflict, psychological "noise" may distort the message to an even greater extent.

What can you do to listen better during a conflict? First, you should appreciate the difficulty of the task and credit yourself and the other party for trying. As a listener, you should assume equal responsibility with the speaker for the transmission. You're working with the other party to try to communicate a message and ensure that the message received matches the intended meaning. You also need to focus fully on the task of listening and attempting to understand; try to disregard psychological noise. It may be helpful to agree with the speaker on a time limit for the communication. As you listen, ask questions to try to draw out meaning and confirm your understanding. Instead of listening for what the words mean, work to understand the meaning that the speaker is trying to convey. A good way to check whether your interpretation matches the speaker's intention is to paraphrase his or her message.

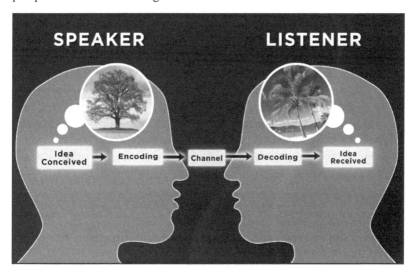

Figure 13.1. The Shannon and Weaver model of communication illustrates how the message that was sent was different from the one received.

As a listener, it's also important that you respond to and reciprocate the message you receive, even if it's painful. Let the speaker know what you intend to do with the information. Communication encompasses a general **rule of reciprocity**. You need to give back information that is equal to what the speaker has given to you.

> **Instead of listening for what the words mean, work to understand the meaning that the speaker is trying to convey.**

In many conflicts, especially heated ones, the speaker may need to help the listener process the intended message. If you're the speaker in this situation, again, acknowledge and appreciate the other party's willingness to listen. Do not challenge or make demands on the listener; confine your message to "I" statements. Then, work with the listener to ensure that your intended meaning gets across. Always remember that saying something is not the same as communicating it. Pay attention to the listener to make sure your message gets through accurately. If the listener doesn't paraphrase your message, invite him or her to do so. If what you have to say may cause pain or fear, try to put the listener at ease first, then be honest. In some situations, such as conflicts in a personal relationship, it may be helpful for the two parties to agree on a signal for times when one or the other needs a brief break from the conversation.

Most people respond to conflicts with one of three fundamental strategies: fight, flight, or communicate. Lower animals can choose the first two, but humans have the option of communication, which often requires taking risks, enduring pain, and persevering to reach a resolution. Listening is a skill that can be learned, but practicing it can bring immediate gains in your relationships. ■

Important Term

rule or norm of reciprocity: The universal social expectation that people will respond to each other in kind—responding to a positive action with another positive action and responding to a negative action with another negative action.

DeVito, *The Interpersonal Communication Book*, Parts 1 and 2, especially chap. 5.

Assignment

1. Think about the most recent argument you engaged in with a friend, loved one, or work colleague. Did you feel that you were really being heard or understood? If not, to what extent might the suggestions in this lecture have helped? You might want to write out your responses to this assignment.

Listening in Conflict
Lecture 13—Transcript

We spend a whole more time listening than we do speaking. It's strange to say then we're not really very good at listening. In fact even in the very best relationships when we start out with the best of intentions to work something out, but we're in a conflict, we find it's very, very difficult to listen. So this lecture is going to be a lecture about listening and especially about listening in a conflict.

We need to talk about why it's really hard to listen, especially in a conflict, and it's a difficult challenge. We need to make some useful suggestions for doing a better job of listening. But we're also going to flip that over. Good listening really begins before somebody speaks, making a safe environment for somebody to talk. But listening is made a whole lot easier if the person speaking can make it a little safer and easier to listen. So we're going to have some suggestions for the speaker too that'll help the listener out. Let's get started.

Why in the world do we need to devote a whole lecture to the subject of listening? Sometimes when we approach a discussion about a conflict we do it with the best of intentions and we get in there and we're really trying to communicate and things go all wrong. What we feel most, what we feel most, is that we're just not being heard and we're terribly frustrated about that. That problem gets illustrated very well in the lyrics of a song that's called *Your Meanings*. Let me just say some of the lyrics for you.

It says:

> You put your meanings in my words
> Till my words don't mean what they say
> I don't mean you hear just what you want to hear
> No, you hear what you think I would say
> And when some of your meanings hurt you
> Then you get angry at me
> And I put my meaning in your bitter tears
> And I hate you for hurting at me

Ooh pretty intense lyrics. They get right to that point of the challenge. We don't feel like we're being heard. We've all been there. You're in this conflict, you're trying to communicate, you think you're talking, and you just don't think you're being heard. Both parties usually are doing that. It's really hard to listen in a conflict, but we're trying to be heard. That song lyric goes on. The song goes on to say:

> But I only wanted you to know me
> To see me and hear me as I feel me inside
> Laughing easy, crying hard, seldom certain,
> always wishing we could fly
> But you put your meaning in my words
> While my meanings stumble and fall
> Our lips are still moving, there's sound in the air
> But I don't think we're talking at all

Not communicating, we're not communicating if we're not being heard. So let's talk about what it takes to really hear one another. To do that principle of negotiating we talked about that we got from Fisher and Ury somebody needs to be listening all the way through and we need to trade that back and forth. Hearing physically is not the same thing as listening. That's just the signals getting in and being received. That kind of hearing, physical hearing is automatic. Listening can be really painful and difficult because we're going to hear things we didn't particularly want to hear. Listening is not passive; it's not just being there. It's an active that we've got to do. It requires focus. It requires attention. It requires openness to hearing what we're going to hear and it requires communicating back with the speaker.

It's a pretty tricky task. It's also a complex task. Let me talk to you about the complexity a little bit. Most researchers in communication talk about different kinds of messages or different dimensions of messages that come at us at the same time when we're talking because no communication between human beings is as simple as one strand of message coming through. The most elegant description of that that I know comes from a British scholar named I. A. Richards and Richards talks about it this way. He talks about it as critical points of view to listen for, but I just call it messages that are in any communication that takes place. And there are four kinds of messages in Richards' terms. The labels he puts on them are sense, feeling, tone, and intention.

Let me explain those to you. The sense of the message, Richards says, is what's on the surface. It's just what the words say. If I say I want you to get this point about listening, the words said I want you to get this point about listening. But the way I say it will give you an additional message, and that's the second one, the feeling. It turns out we can't say anything to anybody about anything without also sending them a message that tells them something about how we feel about the thing that we're saying. So there's a feeling message that underlies that sense message. If I say it intensely, that's more feeling. If I say it hostilely, that's a different feeling. If I say it like I don't care, then it contradicts the sense message. Feeling message is there.

The third one he talks about is the tone message. I love his term for this because it's like don't talk to me in that tone of voice. Social science scholars looking at it these days are more likely to call it the relational message that's involved. You can't say anything to another person without also making a claim in the way you say it about the relationship between you and the other person. You're speaking as equals, you're talking down to them, you're talking up to them. You're talking from a close to a further away position. You give them some message about the relationship.

It turns out if the receiver rejects that message about the relationship, they're probably not going to process the sense and the feeling of the message. So that is one there. You also give them one more message. There's also a message in there that's the intention. Why am I saying this and the receiver gets that? So there are four messages at one time at least in Richards's terms coming at the listener and they match each other pretty well and they may contradict each other. These things have to be juggled and sorted out, so it takes a lot of interpreting.

So here we are trying to listen and get this right. Some of the estimates say we run as high as 75 to 80 percent of our communicating activity involved in listening, but we're still not doing very well. I can appreciate not doing very well when I understand this business of all these messages coming to me at once. But what would good at it me if they say we're still not good at it. What would good at it mean?

Good at it to me would mean that the message we got as the receiver really closely matched the message, the meaning, the intention, the speaker sent. Listening well is difficult and to get that and get it exactly is really going to be difficult especially in a conflict. There's always going to be some difference between the message the speaker sends and the message the listener receives. How hard is it to get them to match? Well one good way to get at that is the scene in a model that was developed by two researchers many years ago named Shannon and Weaver, they were actually working as consultants for the phone company at the time, but that model is still in virtually every basic text about communication that you can find. So it's called the Shannon and Weaver model.

It works like this. There are sort of five steps in a communication transaction. It says there's a source, the person that's the speaker. The first two steps happen with the speaker. The speaker gets an idea, but in order to communicate it, the speaker needs to encode it into words or queues of some sort; so idea, encoding, first two steps.

Then there's a middle step that's between the speaker and the listener. It's got to go out through some channel or some medium. If it's spoken it's through the air in sound waves. Then it's going to get to the senses of the listener where it can be physically heard. It's taken in by the listener and there are two steps on that end. It's decoding and then having the idea and holding the idea in the listener. So if we take that and we think in terms of that model moving across those five steps, we could do it with a very simple idea that can be encoded.

Let's say I get an idea I want to communicate and it's a tree. See I had to encode it even to tell you. Tree is an easy thing to encode. We've all seen thousands of them, I know what they are. So I've got the idea tree, I say tree, it goes through the sound waves, you hear it, you take it in. What you hear physically is the word tree and you decode it and you got the message as sent, just what I sent you, tree.

But what do you think are the odds that your tree is going to look like, be as tall as, be the same kind of tree, be the same tree that I sent you? There's always going to be some variation there. I can say maple tree, you get it better, but yours will be a different size. I can add adjectives and get it closer. We can work together, but they're never going to be the same. That's difficult just with something like a tree.

What happens then if instead of tree we're talking about an idea like that's not fair or that hurts, and it's not one thin message of the meaning of a word going across, but it's all four of those messages in Richards' terms coming at the receiver. There's noise in this channel. Shannon and Weaver talked about the noise in the channel and they were talking about static on phone lines, but there's physical noise, there's also psychological noise between these people. If we're emotionally aroused or emotionally upset as we are in a conflict, there's all of that noise clouding and distorting the message as it comes through.

So getting it the same, really hearing each other, especially in a conflict is going to be really, really tough. So we need to focus too in here on how the speaker is going to be able to help because when this is about feelings and values and abstractions and everybody is upset, it's going to be a problem.

Emotional arousal has us upset. We're getting painful information. The speaker's emotional state and nonverbal messages, may be adding to the negativity. This can be so difficult that some research says you know what it might be impossible to do what we call active listening when we're negotiating about a conflict. It may not work during a conflict because the listener is feeling attacked.

What can we do then? We can make a series of suggestions that'll help us to do this better. The first one is, and I say this a lot, just appreciate the difficulty of the task and credit each other with doing that. If you're doing that I say this a lot because it's hard and I want you to credit yourselves. If that's what you're doing, you're going to be helpful to each other and more understanding. Then from there I want to suggest you do these things. If I'm the listener, I need to assume equal responsibility with the speaker for this transmission.

Notice in that Shannon and Weaver model half the action is on the listener's side. It's active on both of our parts. We're working together to try to get a message across and make it match, think of it that way. Next suggestion is this. Set aside other activities and give your full attention to the speaker. That can be hard to do. You want to focus fully on listening, focus on trying to understand, any noise including psychological things, other things that are on your mind, other activities, try to get them out of your way. Show that speaker that you're listening.

If I'm worried about how long this is going to take, sometimes it really helps to agree with the speaker to set aside a time, like look I can work with you for 20 minutes here, will that be enough to work this out so that you know there's going to be an end to it and you can set a free time. Clear your head and clear the deck so you can focus fully on the speaker to get what they have to say. As you're doing that focus then I want to suggest that instead of listening for what the words mean, be working to get what the speaker is meaning to say with those words. Try to get the speaker's meaning, not just the correct meaning of this thing.

To do that, you're going to have to check perceptions. Ask a lot of questions, try to draw out meaning, and confirm your understanding. Checking for reception is really important. Let's look at an example of that.

Let's go to an office setting. Here we're going to have Denise and Steve. Denise is Steve's boss. Steve has been complaining to her about a new signoff process that she has implemented. Let's listen in.

[Video start.]

> **Denise**: Steve, can you help me understand how this new sign-off process is causing such delays? What's really bothering you? I want to figure out a way to fix the problem.

[Video end.]

Notice what Denise is doing here. She's asking questions and she's really aiming at trying to understand and she's telling Steve she's really trying to understand and you can hear it in her voice. Denise is being a good supervisor. He showed up with a complaint and she's really trying to understand and she appears willing to help. That's going to draw him out and help the communication take place. So that's Denise getting a start.

Now you want to check whether your interpretation matches what the speaker's message was, and a really good way to check that is to paraphrase back. You don't want to feed back the exact same words the person said because if you do, you get what communication scholars call a bypass that can happen. I feed back the same words, then you know I heard the words you said and can repeat them back, but we haven't checked for meaning. We just repeated the words back and forth.

So if you paraphrase it, kick it back in different words, you'll get a better check on the meaning. As you're doing this you want to attend to the nonverbal queues and if the words and the body language don't match, you probably want to check for meaning there. Let's look at another example. Let's go back to Denise and Steve, same setting and see what's happening.

[Video start.]

> **Denise**: I want to see what we can do to fix the problem.
>
> **Steve**: It's just the idea of having to run around the building to get signatures from people all these different people before my team can move on with our piece. It's insulting—like my team isn't trustworthy or dependable.
>
> **Denise**: Okay, I'm getting that we have two problems here. One is the delay aspect. The other, which looks like it might be more important, is that the new process seems to show a lack of management confidence in your team. Am I right on that?

[Video end.]

Denise is checking for meaning now. She's showing receptivity. She has picked up on the fact that Steve feels un-trusted and insulted, the word here, the sense message that he led with led in time, but that feeling message that came along in the way he said it came stronger and Denise has really picked up on that. So what she's doing is listening for, I. A. Richards' four messages, sense, feeling, tone, and intention, and she's working with all of them. If they don't seem to match, it's a good idea to check for meaning and help the speaker sort out what he or she means. So you want to be checking for meaning, paraphrasing back.

Next suggestion, when you've gotten the message from someone, you need to respond and reciprocate. We hate it when we tell somebody something and we don't know what they did with the information. Humans want a response and they want reciprocation, so you need to show understanding and appreciation, especially you need to show understanding when you've heard painful things even if that's hard. You need to let the speaker know what you're going to do with the information.

The speakers need to know that a communication effort mattered. They took a risk talking to you and they need to know what mattered and we need to communicate back given the information about yourself that's kind of equal to what they gave you. There's a rule of reciprocity at work here that is true in psychology generally between human beings. We equalize, you do something for me, I do something for you. It has survival value. In communication you think of it as information. You give me information about you, the rule of reciprocity says I'm going to give you some information back; equalize that.

What would reciprocating sound like? Let's look at an example of that? Here's Denise following up with Steve.

[Video start.]

>**Denise**: You busy? Can I come in?

>**Steve**: Sure. What's up?

Denise: I wanted to get back to you on the new sign-off process. I have an answer on one problem and a proposal on the other.

Steve: Okay, what you got?

Denise: I checked with Ted about why he set that process up. He says it's got nothing to do with dependability. He's just looking for a way to make sure that everybody with responsibility is involved.

Steve: That makes sense.

Denise: He understands, and I do too, that the way he announced this thing could look like a vote of no confidence—but that wasn't his intent. He's sorry about that.

Steve: Okay, what's the proposal?

Denise: Well, Ted realized that having everybody sign off is too time-consuming and cumbersome. But he still needs a way to make sure we're all on the same page. So he wants to meet next week to see if we can all figure out another way to accomplish that, or at least to streamline the new process so it's easier on everybody. Sound good?

Steve: Yeah. We should be able to work something out. Just tell me when and I'll be there.

[Video end.]

Denise has gotten back to Steve promptly and she's got an answer as best she can get at this point. The decision wasn't all hers, so she couldn't just decide what to do with it so she's reciprocating for herself and for her boss. She has come to Steve's office which is a really nice touch. He came to her in hers. She's coming to him to his office. It's a nice touch, expresses equality, and it reciprocates and she has worked this issue. She has done what she could do with it. Steve is okay with this for now. This is going pretty well. Good listening on Denise's part.

We said that listening is really hard, it might be impossible in a really hard conflict. In our examples there, Denise did a great job, but there wasn't a whole lot of heat in that conflict. There were some hard feelings, there wasn't a whole of heat. It gets much harder if the emotions are stronger in a conflict. So if it's going to be that much harder, we better talk some about how the speaker can help the listener. Steve didn't do a lot of work helping Denise and she didn't need it. In a lot of conflicts, though, the speaker is going to need to make it easier for the listener.

Let's talk about guidelines for the speaker. First thing here, as I repeat often remember to appreciate the listener's willingness to listen, give you time, effort, risk, remember when I talked about the seven steps I said thank them to begin with. That's real, you want to feel that, and I'll say that every time it's relevant as we go through the entire course. Then the specific suggestions, the thing to really avoid here is any kind of face challenges, any kind of demands that you make on the other person. Do not make demands. Don't make you statements as in pointing your finger at the other person who's saying you this, that or the other.

I'm not the expert on the other person. I'm the expert on myself. So let me make I statements in the conflict. Begin with I and tell them how you feel and how you see what's going on. Don't trick yourself into an I statement that really is a you statement. I feel that you're being stupid here is a you statement. Don't do that, make genuine I statements. Then work with the listener to ensure that your intended meaning is getting through to him or to her. You've got to work with them. That's a two-way street working this thing back and forth.

Let's revisit that first scene again with Steve and Denise. But let's have Steve do a better job. Let's listen to how differently he might express his view.

[Video start.]

> **Steve**: So, I have two problems with this new sign-off arrangement. One is that getting all those signatures is going to cause delays. You know how hard it is to track people down around this place. But second, when I heard Ted's announcement, I started to worry that

you and he maybe had doubts about my team's ability to get the job done. I'm really concerned.

[Video end.]

That's a much better way for Steve to voice his complaint, notice what he's doing here. He's making it very clear. He's very accurate. He's owning the feeling himself. He's making an I statement and he's saying this is how I feel. If I'm Denise, if I'm the supervisor, that one is a lot easier for me to work with than the complaint the way Steve expressed it initially. It's just easier for the listener to hear and respond so the speaker can do a lot to make that happen.

Let's talk about some more guidelines for the speaker. What I want you to do as a speaker is really remember that just saying something is nothing like the same thing as communicating it. So often we just assume we said it so it got communicated and most of the time it didn't. If I don't make that assumption, what do I do instead. I really need to pay attention to the listener when I'm talking and I need to be watching and listening and paying attention to the listener's nonverbal to see if my message is getting through accurately.

Then I need to work back and forth with the listener checking for meanings. If the listener isn't paraphrasing back to check with me, I might invite the listener to do that if I'm the speaker so that we can check to make sure we got it. I want to treat myself as a partner with the listener especially when the thing is difficult and work it back and forth. I'm also going to want to anticipate when what I say may be about to cause pain or fear, and I want to do what I can to put that listener at ease up front. I need to be honest, but I want to make this conversation as safe as I can make it.

Let's look at an example of that. Let's go back to Denise and Steve, but in this situation it's not Steve's complaint. Denise is reviewing a report that Steve and his team have submitted and there's a little problem with it.

[Video start.]

> **Denise**: Steve, first off, let me put you at ease. You've done an excellent job on this report. Overall, we're really happy with it and impressed with your team's work. And we pretty much buy your conclusions and recommendations.

> **Steve**: Good, I saw all those notes stuck all over it and I thought I might have to defend everything in there. So what's the "but" here? There's always a "but."

> **Denise**: One problem is with the layout of the data, but I know we can figure that out. Then there are some little things we need to go over. Okay?

> **Steve**: Okay. Let's tackle the data layout first.

[Video end.]

Denise has done a nicely effective job here as the supervisor. She has made this as safe as you can. Of course lots of us when that would happen we might know another shoe was going to drop, but she softened that as much as she can. Steve knows she thinks it's a good report and we're talking about minor things, so that's much more comfortable for him to work with. She made it as safe as she could make it.

One thing counselors suggest for this, and I think it's a very useful one, is if you're in a long-going relationship and you have to deal with conflicts that may hurt a lot and difficult things may be said and it may be hard for people to deal with or people may not be able to express themselves, that it's nice to have a signal that asks for a pause or a timeout to stop. I think about that signaling idea a lot the way it works with my dentist. I go to my dentist and when I'm in the chair and he's getting ready to drill or something he'll say well Michael, I want you to know that you can signal me. You won't be able to talk, but you can signal me if it starts to hurt at all or you just need to take a break. He tells me to just raise my hand.

So there I am in the dentist chair lying there and I know that I can just lift my hand up and he'll stop. Even if I don't have to lift it up, which I usually do several times, I know I can lift it and so I've got a break. It's nice to have a way to break it when the thing starts going in a direction that's problematic. That's very helpful for listening and for the speaker.

Then finally long-term, you're going to want to build the kind of trusting relationship where it feels generally safe because you know each other and can predict that the other person is going to respond with listening and respect when you speak up. That's really going to help a whole lot.

Where have we been in this lecture then? Let's go try to summarize. Remember we started out saying that listening and speaking are among the most challenging things that humans can do and that it's especially challenging during conflict. So the listener and the speaker really have to work together with the task of communication in this kind of a situation. There are some critically important things to remember from this lecture.

For both of you, appreciate the risks and the efforts that the other is making and the challenge for doing their part, both for listener and speaker. Then the listener should assume equal responsibility with the speaker. Check perceptions of meaning with the speaker as you go along. Attend to the nonverbal and verbal queues as you go along. As you do this take in those four messages Richards talks about, sense, feeling, tone, and intention, and compare them and check back if you need to on those. Then lastly, if I'm the listener respond. Check back with the speaker, respond and reciprocate.

What about the speaker? What do we recommend for the speaker? Speak in I statements, not you statements, own the thing yourself, speak for yourself. Work with the listener to ensure that the intended meaning is transmitted. Work up front if you have to to minimize any pain or threat that the message may give to the listener. It's going to make it a lot easier to listen.

In a conflict there are three fundamental strategies that are obvious. There's fight, flight, and there's communicate; and those first two, fight and flight, lower animals can do those. We can do those too, but that third one communication when you think about this from the standpoint of speaker and listener together in this situation requires taking some risks, requires time, attention, enduring some pain a lot of times, and hanging in there and getting it through, but you can do it working together. So this is tough, but you can do it.

The last thing that I just kind of want to end with about listening is that this is a skill that's not all that hard to learn. You've got to work at it, you've got to try, but the suggestions I gave you here in this one lecture, if you followed those, if you get about half of them right, you'll experience a gain right away. Listening pays off right away. So it's easy to incorporate into your repertoire of communication behaviors just in general and it can incorporate in the conflict, so it's not all that hard to learn what we suggest in this lecture.

Here's an assignment for you. Think about the most recent argument you engaged in that went back and forth as a real argument with a friend, a loved one, or work colleague that really went back and forth. You might want to write out some of what was said in it so you can think about it. When you've got a description of how that went back and forth, consider this: Did I feel that I was really being heard and understood when I spoke? If not, and the answer for most of us is probably not, but if not, to what extent might the suggestions in this lecture have helped? Which suggestions, how might they have helped? Really try to apply what we said in this lecture to your last conflict and see if we can see how that would've helped.

Where're we going to go from here? Everything we've talked about up till now has been about managing conflict in general and about handling specific episodes of conflict. They would apply everywhere. But every conflict occurs in the context of some kind of a relationship. Some are casual, some are close, some are work, some are personal. Two kinds of relationships are where we have the most conflicts and where they matter most. So the next several lectures are going to focus on how the conditions and dynamics of those relationships affect conflict in conflict management. The two kinds are close relationships and then work relationships. In Lecture 14 and in Lecture 15 we're going to talk about conflict in our close relationships.

Dynamic Patterns in Close Relationships
Lecture 14

> Recognizing the stages is going to help by reducing blaming to start with, but it's also going to help us if we want to go ahead and resolve conflicts and stay in the relationship.

Conflict is inherent in human interaction, and in close personal relationships, it can do the worst damage or the most good. In this lecture and the next one, we'll look at the dynamics of close relationships to see how these affect the way we handle conflict.

A close personal relationship is characterized by significant interdependence and deep emotional involvement. Such relationships are common contexts for conflict because they involve a good deal of interaction; the consequences of conflict in personal relationships also tend to matter more than in other associations.

Relationships are more challenging to maintain now than they were in the past. Humans live longer now than they used to, so relationships last longer. We also have more outside interests that compete for our time and attention and more social supports for pursuing those interests as individuals.

John Gottman identified a list of the top five issues that couples fight about: communication, sex, jealousy, in-laws and stepfamily members, and chores, including financial management. All these issues can be extrapolated

Bonding gives humans a feeling of affection and a sense of belonging.

to other types of relationships. For example, jealousy might appear in sibling relationships or friendships.

It's important to remember that relationships are dynamic, not static. We can think about relationships as an ongoing pattern of interacting with others. In many cases, the patterns are predictable based on the nature of the relationships. Recognizing these patterns and understanding how they work can reduce the threat and the intensity of conflicts.

Leslie Baxter, a researcher in interpersonal relationships, developed a model that illuminates such patterns of interaction. Evidence shows that humans are motivated both to form bonds with one another and to carve out individual space for themselves. We achieve an individual identity and freedom by separating, but we receive affection and a sense of belonging by bonding. According to Baxter, these oppositional motivations create a situation of **relational dialectics**, that is, opposing tensions that result from the conflicting emotional needs of partners. People manage this tension by moving closer and farther away at different times; of course, we're rarely in perfect sync with our partners in this movement, which can result in conflict.

To sustain a close relationship, we need to put it on the line repeatedly with experimentation, then move toward intensification, integration, and bonding again.

Another researcher, Martin Knapp, put forth the idea of relational stages, which expands, in some ways, on Baxter's model. According to Knapp, most relationships are temporary and are characterized by stages of moving in and bonding, then moving away. Knapp's stages of coming together are as follows: (1) initiation, (2) experimentation, (3) intensification, (4) integration, and (5) bonding. Bonding results in a honeymoon kind of feeling, but even in loving, long-term relationships, once this stage is reached, it isn't permanent. Both partners need some space to keep the relationship going. People also go through stages in moving apart, although relationships don't have to reach the final stage. These stages are: (1) differentiation, (2) circumscribing (that is, communicating less), (3) stagnation, (4) avoidance, and (5) termination.

If both parties aren't experiencing these stages at the same time, conflict will arise, but in long-term relationships, those conflicts can serve as triggers to bring partners back together.

In terms of Knapp's stages, when partners identify and negotiate a conflict, they are cycling back to the experimentation stage, which can lead to a deeper, more satisfying relationship. To sustain a close relationship, we need to put it on the line repeatedly with experimentation, then move toward intensification, integration, and bonding again. This is risky and difficult work, but the process results in increased closeness and trust.

John Gottman identified what he called the Four Horsemen of the Apocalypse for relationships, that is, actions that signal the end: (1) complaining and criticizing, (2) showing contempt, (3) becoming defensive, and (4) stonewalling. Gottman has found that most relationships don't survive when these patterns appear.

The ways in which people handle conflict in a given relationship tend to stabilize as conflict styles, such as avoidance or compromise. A more beneficial conflict style for close personal relationships is collaboration. Here, the parties recognize the potential for conflict caused by Baxter's relational dialectics and work together to deal with these tensions. Just being aware that ebb and flow are natural in a relationship removes some of the threat and makes it easier to handle conflict. Knapp's relationship stages can help us see when we're moving toward stagnation and can trigger us to pay more attention to our partners. Recall, too, Gottman's idea of bids and responses from Lecture 8; in a personal relationship, the pattern of response to a bid should be turning toward instead of turning away or turning against.

Maintaining close personal relationships has been shown to have positive effects on physical health, and understanding the dynamics of these relationships can help us reduce conflict and grow even closer with our partners. ■

relational dialectics: Opposing tensions that result from conflicting emotional needs of relational partners; such tensions are constantly in flux and affect couples' communication patterns.

Suggested Reading

Baxter and Montgomery, *Relating: Dialogues and Dialectics*.

Fisher and Brown, *Getting Together: Building Relationships as We Negotiate*.

Gottman and DeClaire, *The Relationship Cure: A Five-Step Guide to Strengthening Your Marriage, Family, and Friendships*.

Assignment

1. Talk with your partner about how the two of you handle conflicts. Ask your partner whether he or she would like to handle your conflicts differently and, if so, how. Then ask what you might do to make the relationship a safer, more inviting place to bring up conflicts, talk about them constructively, and work out win-win resolutions. Create a plan, identifying specific actions you will take and avoid.

Dynamic Patterns in Close Relationships
Lecture 14—Transcript

Conflict is inherent in human interaction so it does occur in all kinds of relationships. But in our close personal relationships, the ones involving deep, strong emotions, in those kind of relationships conflict can do its worst damage or it can do its most good. That's where we've got lots of opportunity for conflict to happen. So in this lecture and in the next lecture we're going to focus on close relationships or close personal relationships and the elements between the nature of the relationships and the way we handle conflict in them.

We're going to talk about how strong relationships promote constructive conflict management and conversely constructive conflict management makes for good long-term relationships, so the two help us handle each other. We're going to take a kind of systems approach here because we need to look at the dynamics of close relationships so that we can see how they really work, how those dynamics affect the way we handle conflict. That'll be useful. We want to look at the value for the relationship of handling the conflicts well so that we can maintain strong relationships. We're going to make some suggestions here in this lecture for ensuring that those close relationships actually support good conflict management.

Let's get going then. What do we mean? Let's define close personal relationship. Researchers who look at this have several key points they use to define it. They say a close, personal relationship is one where there's really significant interdependence, you have a lot of consequences for each other, there's emotional involvement, the parties care, they're emotionally attached. Beyond that there's identity involvement, our identities are involved in our close personal relationships. What I think of myself really is affected by who I'm close friends with and who I'm married to and who my siblings are. So we've got identity attached to those close relationships.

These kind of relationships are contexts where conflict is very likely to occur because there's lots of interaction in them and where the consequences of how we handle that conflict are going to matter for better or worse because the relationships matter more. Most of the research on close personal relationships happens to be on couples. The reasons for that are twofold, one is that we've got a lot of interest in making marriages better, the other is that couples are easy to identify as a kind of close personal relationship and it's easier to get subjects and control for factors, so the researchers tended to steer that way. But really we can extrapolate an awful lot of what we find in those relationships to other kinds.

We do know that relationships are more challenging now to maintain. Let's think about why that might be. We live longer so our relationships last longer. We've got more outside interests and attractions that compete for our attention and our time, so there's more tension between other things and other people and other interests and our close relationships. We have more of those individual interests and we've got a lot of social support for pursuing our interests as individuals. We've also got more alternatives to maintaining real and close relationships. So it's harder now than it used to be.

In this harder era what are the things that we might fight about? Here most of the research comes from couples, and John Gottman whom I've cited several times and has just done lots of wonderful research on couples, has a list of top five things that couples fight about. Communication is number one, then sex, then jealousy, then in-laws and step family members, and then number five is chores, which includes financial management, who should be doing what.

Conflicts about those top three, communication, sex in the couple, and jealousy really spring a lot from the dynamics that are inherent in the nature of these kinds of relationships. So Gottman focuses on couples, but we really can extrapolate. Communication is a major area of conflict in all relationships. Chores, who's going to do what, a major area of conflict in all. Jealousies, that works in sibling relationships, it's there in close friends relationships. So these work very well for us. Tensions about in-laws can also be tensions about other associates and friendships and that sort of thing. So we can extrapolate a lot from that kind of research and focus on communication in close personal relationships.

When I talk about relationships I'm always a little uncomfortable talking about them as though they're things because they're dynamic, they're not static. Relationships are something we do. We ought to be talking about relating rather than having a relationship. But we can also abstract and think about the relationship as something, an ongoing pattern of interacting that we're doing. The patterns there are very predictable based on the nature of the relationships.

It turns out that if we can recognize those patterns, the understanding of how they work and how the dynamics of the relationship works, and how that drives a number of kind of conflicts that we're going to have can really help reduce the threat, reduce the heat, reduce the blaming. Just understanding how conflict arises naturally from the dynamics of relationships really is going to help us deal with conflicts and be less threatened by them.

In this lecture we're really going to focus primarily on getting that better understanding. There are two models that I find most useful when I'm thinking about relationships, I and my students find it useful to sort of understanding what's going on. One of these is developed by Leslie Baxter who studies interpersonal relationships and the other is going to be by Mark Knapp, who is also an interpersonal communications scholar.

Let's talk about Leslie Baxter's first. It really illuminates the patter of how we do these. Baxter notes, and there's plenty of evidence to support, that humans have these two things going at one time. We're drawn together to bond so we're motivated to come together in the bond. Humans are just drawn to do that. It's natural with us. But we're also motivated to separate, to carve out our individual space. So we achieve an individual identity and freedom by separating, but we receive closeness and affection and belonging by bonding, and we're trying to do those at the same time.

As Baxter puts it, these are oppositional motivations that create what she calls a dialectical tension, in and out and in and out, and they set off each other. She calls this relational dialectics. Parties manage this tension by moving closer and then moving away. The only thing is and how that relates to conflict is that you know this would be fine if we could be in perfect sync. I want to be close and bond when you want to be close, and I want to be separate when you want to be separate. But who can manage to be in perfect sync, no matter how close the relationship without coming together and moving away.

We move away by communicating less clearly and creating distance, and then that distance if the other person wasn't in the moving away mode in sync with us can be painful for that person and create jealousies and create cost and create lack of communication which is the top thing that we're going to have conflicts about. So painful conflict is arising naturally from those relational dialectics that are happening because we just can't be in perfect sync when we do them, it's natural. It's part of relating. Leslie Baxter helps us a lot with understanding that point.

Now let's look at Martin Knapp's idea of relational stages because that's going to help us a little further with doing this. What Knapp says is relationships are just not all permanent. Most relationships are going to be temporary. So we ought to be able to understand relationships in terms of moving into them and getting close enough to bond and then moving out and getting beyond where we terminate. So what Martin Knapp developed and then he tested and developed a lot of evidence to support it was this notion that we have these stages of relating that we go through.

There are a set of stages moving in leading up to bonding and then a set of stages moving out, moving away. The moving in stages works like this. The first one he calls the initiation stage. It's like saying hello. We get the other person's attention and we initiate an interaction. That will extend into, and these will overlap some, that will extend into what becomes an experimentation stage. We try out being together, we try out interacting. We might meet for coffee. We might have a first date. We might try out, we experiment with being together and we see how that goes.

If that goes well, if a series of experiments were positive, overlapping with that we'd begin to intensify. We get more involved in this emotionally. We like the person more, we're having more fun. The relationship heats up. It intensifies. If the intensification keeps going well, we integrate. We start working things out so we can spend more time together. We organize.

I love it when my students at school when they get close either in a friendship or a romance that's budding, when it's time to register for courses for next semester they get together and work out so they can take some courses at the same time, maybe to be in the same class, maybe busy on the same evening. They work their schedules out so they can spend time together. That's integrating. If integrating keeps going well we get all the way to where we're bonded. We get to the point where we really feel like an us.

Let's look at some examples of some of these steps. You know what saying hello looks like so let's skip over the first one. Let's say the initiation took place and let's look at an experimentation stage. Here we're going to have a woman and a man talking on the phone about working a project together in the community.

[Video start.]

> **Jim**: This is awesome! I'm so glad you're getting involved!
>
> **Keisha**: Yeah! I'm excited to help with the campaign to save Smith Park. But I do need to tell you, Jim, I'm not ready to make any long term commitment to the project, given my schedule. But let's just talk and see what I can contribute. I'm free tomorrow after work.
>
> **Jim**: Oh, that's great, Keisha. How about if we meet at 5:30 in the community room at the library? We can map out a plan of action.
>
> **Keisha**: Sounds good. I'll see you then.
>
> **Jim**: Okay, great! Thanks. Bye.

[Video end.]

They're not sure how much they're going to want to work together, but they're moving in that direction. They're pointing that way and they're feeling each other out. It's interesting to me in that little dialogue that Keisha is setting a little boundary. She's saying I don't want to make a long-term commitment, we'll see. So she's setting some boundaries and we're experimenting here. That conversation when they get together and talk tomorrow will be a further experiment and it might move toward integration.

Now let's go look at an example of integration. Let's shift the kind of couple for this one. Let's have it be a romantic. They're getting past experimentation, they're still experimenting some, but there's clearly affection happening so we're going to be intensifying and looking at and moving toward integrating. Let's see what happens here.

[Video start.]

>**Jack**: And then he spilled the thing all over himself!

>**Maria**: Oh my gosh. My stomach hurts from laughing so much. Today has been such a great day. I really love hanging out with you.

>**Jack**: I feel the same way. Listen, what would you say to dinner next Sunday at my folks' house? They'd love to meet you.

>**Maria**: Well, I think that's a great idea, Jack. I'd really like that.

>**Jack**: My mom makes amazing desserts. You would not believe her cheesecake.

[Video end.]

We can see in this one they've been experimenting, that's going well. Sunday is going to be in one sense a further experiment meeting the family, but this thing is intensifying, it's heating up, you can feel that in the conversation and we're really looking at moving toward integration when we're talking about meeting the family. So this relationship is moving forward, experimenting and then intensifying and then integrating and moving forward.

If this keeps going we're going to get to bonding. Bonding I don't know if we can show an example of that. You feel that, it's that honeymoon feeling. It's that moment when it's really an us; we really feel good together. We'd all like that to be like the fairytales say, happily ever after. But bonding is never permanent. That feeling doesn't stay, you hate for it to go away, but on the other hand if you were stuck in it you'd feel stuck. You need space and you've got to move. It needs to keep recurring if you want to keep the relationship going and feeling wonderful, but it's not permanent, it's temporary.

Now we get to think about moving out. Here's what happens. Even in loving long-term relationships some of this happens, it just doesn't have to go all the way to termination. Mark Knapp's moving out stages work like this. He says once bonding has occurred, at some point and one will be able get there before the other so we'll be out of sync again. At some point somebody is going to start differentiating, thinking in Leslie Baxter's terms about how am I different, doing that separating out. So I'm differentiating myself, trying to feel different, and in order to do that I'm going to slide into what Knapp calls circumscribing.

What do we mean by circumscribing? Circumscribing is communicating less, carving out more space for myself, more life space for myself, some room to maneuver without the other person knowing what I'm doing or thinking. I've got to sense myself independently, separately and I'm making the space in the way I communicate and the way I behave to do that. If that continues, that's going to move to stagnation, a conversation between you, the intensity is going to go flat if you keep circumscribing and the conversation will stagnate.

If it keeps going in a negative direction, we're going to start avoiding each other. So I'm going to move toward avoidance, one before the other, and that will move, if the relationship is going to end, toward termination. That's the steps moving out. So differentiation is going to occur inside somebody's head, but the outward signs as it moves on are going to slide right into circumscribing pretty quick.

Let's look at an example of circumscribing. Remember our pair, the couple that was volunteering to work together on a project; well what if this relationship is not so perfect, starting to fray a bit, how would circumscribing look?

[Video start.]

    Keisha: Hello, this is Keisha.

    Jim: Hey, this is Jim. Are we still on for 6? We've got to get these flyers posted.

    Keisha: Uh, not sure. Maybe a little later. I still have a lot of work to do here at the office, and I need to run some errands. I'll have to call you.

    Jim: Well, okay. Give me a ring.

    Keisha: Will do. Bye.

[Video end.]

We don't know whether Keisha really has all that other stuff to do. It's probably more likely that she's circumscribing here. She just needs some life space. Either way she's making some space for her to operate independently. So differentiation, circumscribing is going on. This moves to stagnating the conversation. That moves to avoidance, and all of these things that if the other party isn't in sync, if it's not happening for both of you equally in an equal way, all of those elements of moving out, those stages of separating, generate conflict.

If the conversation is stagnating somebody is unhappy. If I don't know why you're not here and you're not seeming to come across to me, I'm unhappy. So they generate conflict. So going through the stages when you're not in perfect sync causes conflict. The dynamics inherently cause conflict.

Let's look at another example. Let's go back to our romantic couple, but make it later in the relationship.

[Video start.]

>**Jack**: Hi Maria, it's Jack. Do you want to hang out? Call me back or, actually maybe I'll just stop by. Okay. Bye.

[Video end.]

Hmm, things don't look too promising. Maria is deliberately choosing not to pick up on that call and we don't know when she's going to call him back. Now we're into the avoidance stage. It would be moving towards separating, but Knapp says most relationships are temporary. He doesn't say they are all temporary, so let's talk about the difference in how we handle conflict now between those temporary relationships that can slide on out with those conflicts and relationships that are going to stick around. What's the difference?

The difference is that members in an ongoing relationship when those conflicts come up, be it at the circumscribing stage, the stagnating stage, or somebody's avoiding, those are triggers they call us back. A conflict arises and it says wait a minute, this relationship is headed south. Let's talk. So in those, when we recognize those, they can cycle back and decide to deal with them as a conflict or decide to let what's happening go, it's not a deal breaker to be all right. So recognizing the stages is going to help by reducing blaming to start with, but it's also going to help us if we want to go ahead and resolve conflicts and stay in the relationship. It's lowered and we know what we've got to do.

Directly addressing the conflict really has risks to it, but it's going to offer rewards. I want us to think about this a little bit. What does it mean in terms of Knapp's stages of relationship to recognize a conflict, put it on the table, and set up to negotiate about it? What it really means in Knapp's terms is we're going to cycle back to the experimentation stage. We're going to do an experimenting again and see if we can work this one out. It puts the relationship literally on the line, but that can bring us breakthroughs to a deeper, more satisfying relationship.

What Knapp shows us here is that to keep a relationship close and make it longstanding and permanent, we're going to need to put it on the line over and over again, cycling back to that experimental stage and get good at that, and develop some trust in each other to cycle back to that, and know we're going to move back toward intensification and integration and bonding once again. So we've got to appreciate the courage it takes. We're putting the whole thing at risk, we risk the relationship itself in order to keep it. That's not stuff for the fainthearted. This is tough stuff to do, but it certainly has its rewards.

When you're doing that tough work, don't chew each other up. You can be gentle, you can do that pretty well. Let's consider what that might sound like. Try this.

[Video start.]

> **Jack**: Maria, I just want to let you know that I really appreciate that you're willing to hang in there with me and work these issues out. I know it's hard.

> — **Maria**: Yeah, it is hard. But I'm glad we're able to be honest with each other. I think we just need a little room to breathe, and some time to think things through. But we'll get there.

> **Jack**: I hope so.

[Video end.]

That doesn't sound like what most couples would say if they'd been having some spats and struggling, but it ought to be more like what most couples would say if they're appreciating each other and struggling in. Maria is needing space, but she's also saying she thinks we'll get there. These two are working it out. We don't know for sure that they will, but they're working through some hard things together. If you get through those hard times together in struggle, you build closeness and trust so there's really value in going through the process and doing this.

Let's talk a little bit about what you should not do, and a good list of what you should not do also comes from John Gottman. He talks about what's going on in relationships and he has observed these closely in his research when things are coming to an end, like it's about to go. He calls it the "Four Horsemen of the Apocalypse" for relationships. It's a list of four things. One is complaining and criticizing. The second one is showing contempt for each other. The third is getting to defensive, and the fourth is stonewalling each other.

Gottman talks about those four and in his research he finds that when couples are in that, this relationship is headed for the dumpster. They're about through. It's very predictable the relationship is not going to survive. So that's what you don't want to do. You don't want to get into a pattern of doing those things. Let's look at an example of that.

Jim has continued to make demands on Keisha let's say and Keisha's not meeting these demands. She either can't or is not willing to do it. This working together relationship has really been affected. It's heading into a downward spiral. I want you to listen to this one and consider would you want to stay in a relationship with somebody who speaks to you like this.

[Video start.]

> **Keisha**: Jim, I just can't do that.

> **Jim**: Just forget it, Keisha. I thought we had this great working relationship. Turns out I'm the only one working.

> **Keisha**: Wait a minute, Jim! I told you before we got started that I only have limited time for this project. Why can't you understand that?

[Video end.]

This relationship is truly headed downhill and you can see it, you can hear it, you can feel it in their words and the way they're talking. They're criticizing. There's contempt in their voices. Jim is criticizing Keisha and

Keisha is responding with defensiveness and criticism for him. The conflict has escalated, this thing is going nowhere but downhill. That's those four horsemen at work that John Gottman is talking about. That's what not to do if you want the relationship to continue.

I want to go back and just connect this thing about relationships and understanding their patterns to some of what we've talked about earlier. The patterns in how people in a given relationship handle conflict can tend to stabilize as patterns. They can become styles. Remember back in Lecture 8 when we talked about conflict styles and we can apply conflict styles not just to an individual, but to a couple, to some business partners, to teammates or close friends in an ongoing relationship. That relationship can have conflict styles.

If the conflict style is avoiding dealing with conflicts as though they weren't there, that's not going to work. In some relationships that's the style. In some relationships, the style is more competitive, battle over everything. That's not pleasant.

In others it's compromise on all kinds of things. That's safe, but it saps the life out of the relationship. It's boring. There are relationships where one party really accommodates the other too much. That party is being oppressed and that relationship isn't really close so that pattern accommodation isn't good.

Talking and collaborating really builds stronger relationships so I want to suggest to you that every close personal relationship ought to have a conflict style and that that conflict style should be collaboration. You may want to have the wider repertoire and you'll need it sometimes, but most of the time in a close relationship you ought to be going to a collaborative approach to try and resolve a conflict. Relationships are like two parties dancing together and it's a combination of the two that makes that dynamic.

The nature of the relationship brings dynamics to it like the nature of the dance they're doing, but you want to try to do it well together. In that as you do it, you've got to understand, as Baxter says, you're going to be moving closer together and moving away and you've got to understand also that you'll be moving in and moving out and those elements will create conflict. If we go back to collaborating to deal with them, if we can maintain and grow the relationship, if we don't do that, what we're going to do is weaken and perhaps destroy the relationship.

When I say destroy a relationship I mean that in two ways, and let me just spell that out a little bit for you. I don't necessarily mean that the people have entirely left each other. There's many a close relationship where there's still something there, but it's empty. It's not tight, it's really not close as a relationship. They could be two people living in the same house together, but living two entirely separate emotional lives, even though they're going through some of the steps together. That's a destroyed relationship too if you really think about it.

How can we use these insights now to help, just the insights that we've got. I'm going to give you more specific recommendations for relationships in the next lecture. But how can we use these. Just recognizing the dynamics of ebb and flow and the tensions they create and knowing, getting that that's natural and normal really helps take the threat out of it and helps us understand what's going on, which makes it easier to handle the conflict.

When those conflicts arise from dynamics that can help us not overreact and help us get to work working through the conflict and get it that that's part of relating. Knapp's stages of relationship in particular can help us when the thing moves towards stagnation and helps us to see that as a trigger to pay more attention, give more information, and move back towards a partner that can yank us back.

This set of recognitions can also help us understand that what we should do is treat each conflict as a new instance of the experimentation stage and get it that it takes some guts to put the relationship on the line. Go back through another experiment and push this thing through, but there can be rewards and there typically are rewards when we do it. We can also observe the persistent patterns that we have when we interact with each other and see what those patterns are and look for changes in how we relate in a conflict when we're looking at the dynamic in that close relationship.

Finally here in terms of applying these, if I go back to Lecture 8 and pick up one more idea, we can pick up the idea from Gottman, the idea of bids and responses, in a close personal relationship the pattern of response to a bid if you remember those terms ought to be turning toward rather than turning away or turning against. Those ought to be the patterns that we follow. How important is this? One way to see how important it is, is to think about the relationship between relationships, our interpersonal interactions and things like even our physical health.

There have been studies going back as far as 1858 when a character named William Farr was the first ever to document what came to be the marriage advantage. What they found was in research since Farr all that time ago has consistently supported this, married people in general are happier, they're less depressed, they're physically healthier. They live longer, they have less pneumonia, they have less cancer, they have less surgery, and advantage.

But recent studies are pretty clearly documenting that that so-called advantage does not apply to what you can call a troubled marriage. If that relationship isn't handling its conflict well, if it's ugly, if they're not close, if they're together but they're not really relating well, that advantage goes away. They are just as poorly handled, their health is as poor as the single person who doesn't have a marriage at all. So if you think about it in close relationships, handling our conflict well is important not just to general happiness, it's important for my psychological and even my physical health, pretty important stuff. We want to handle conflicts well in a close personal relationship.

What have we seen in this lecture then? Let's summarize. Remember, number one we can apply all the basic conflict management strategies we've learned about so far, everything up until now in the course, to help us resolve conflicts in close relationships. But in those close relationships, number two, the stakes are really going to be higher and the dynamics of those close relationships will pose particular challenges because the dynamics themselves are going to create conflicts that we need to manage.

Number three, those conflicts are really generated by the natural ebb and flow that happens in close relationships. That's going to be going on in the relationship. Number four, if I get a better understanding of those dynamics, that ebb and flow, that moving through stages, really can help me because I understand what's going on, reduce the threat level and help me understand the other person's actions, reduces the conflict level, makes it easier to work with.

Number five, if I recognize those patterns, I can more easily see what I need to do and adjust when it's time to adjust. If I'm in the stagnation I may get it that I need to turn the other direction and talk. I probably should be aware too of those end warnings, those four horsemen that Gottman talks about, complaining and criticizing, showing contempt, being defensive, and stonewalling. If we're down there, that's red lights flashing, you should be hitting the alarm button, this relationship is really in big trouble.

Finally this is important because handling conflicts well in a close personal relationship matters to my physical health as well as my psychological health and happiness; pretty important stuff.

Here's an assignment for you. I want to suggest that you sit down with a partner in any close relationship, whatever one works best for you, and I want you to try to have a conversation about how conflicts get handled in that relationship. Ask each other whether and if so how you would like to handle those conflicts differently. It's an important conversation you can have. Then I want you to ask what might you do to make the relationship safer, a more inviting place to bring up conflicts and talk about them constructively and work out win-win resolutions.

What could you do to make it more inviting? Be considerate with each other, don't promise the moon in one shot for this, but try to create a specific plan for what you're going to do to make it a better environment for handling conflicts. There's your assignment.

Where do we go from here? We're going to do another lecture on close personal relationships. What we're going to do in Lecture 15 is we'll talk further and make some more specific recommendations about what you can do to handle conflict better in a close relationship situation now that we understand those dynamics that we've been talking about here. Then secondly in Lecture 15, we're going to talk about disruptions that can occur that change the nature of the relationship and every relationship can have that happen. It's going along in a certain way and then something can happen that really disrupts the whole thing. Those are called critical communication contexts and we'll talk about those in Lecture 15.

Disruptions in Close Relationships
Lecture 15

> If you haven't said anything positive to your partner and now you've got something negative to say, that's not going to feel fair, or it's going to feel more threatening.

A s we saw in the last lecture, conflict in close personal relationships differs from that in temporary or casual relationships. The stakes are much higher in close relationships; a conflict that is not handled well can disrupt your life and undermine your sense of identity. The risks of both speaking up and listening are greater because strong emotions are involved. At the same time, there is greater opportunity to get the conflict resolved. The caring, identity, and investment you have in the relationship increase your motivation and put you in a better position to work through the conflict.

Roger Fisher and Scott Brown, authors of *Getting Together*, offer suggestions for building strong, supportive relationships that make good contexts for **conflict resolution**. First, try to balance emotion with reason, and second, develop an interest in your partner's viewpoints. Always consult before deciding on anything that might affect your partner and listen to his or her feedback. Fisher and Brown also tell us that we need to be wholly trustworthy but not wholly trusting; to be perfectly trustworthy is too heavy a load to add to another human being. Never try to coerce or push your partner; negotiate as equals. Finally, practice acceptance of your partner; then, when you have differences, deal with them seriously.

As we discussed in Lecture 5, strong emotions that are relevant to a conflict should be expressed but not acted out. A safe environment and a willing partner are necessary for emotional expression. As we saw in Lecture 7, it's also important to work for equality in a relationship because the more equal the power is between the two parties, the better the odds are of reaching a win-win resolution. In Lecture 13, we touched on the rule of reciprocity, that is, giving the same level of intimacy as you receive in a relationship. In communication, this translates to trading information equally because, as we saw, information is power. If each partner has equivalent information about the other, the relationship becomes a stronger, safer place for handling conflict.

Another suggestion for building strong relationships is to give at least 80 percent positive feedback to the other party. We learned from the psychologist B. F. Skinner that humans have a need for positive reinforcement to function at an optimal level. If we apply that idea to our handling of conflict, we can see that it's much easier to listen to something negative if you have a general sense that you are appreciated in a relationship. As we said in the last lecture, collaboration is the optimal conflict style in personal relationships. The seven steps of negotiation we described in Lecture 10 can be applied to this collaboration.

> **Stability is achieved through the development of roles and patterns of interacting, but when significant events occur—either positive or negative—they can disrupt these ongoing patterns.**

Counselors often urge their clients to call a **family meeting** or a couples meeting, which serves as a regular opportunity to bring up and respectfully discuss conflicts. Such meetings should be scheduled at least twice a month and can serve a broader purpose of communicating; they don't have to be limited to only dealing with disagreements. The general rule is that each person gets time to talk while the others practice active listening. Questions may be asked, but not to challenge. If time allows, negotiations can take place during the meeting.

We turn now to the topic of **critical communication contexts**; here, a disruptive event creates a situation in which effective communication becomes simultaneously more important and more difficult. Think of close relationships as living systems, which have tendencies toward both stability and adaptation. Stability is achieved through the development of roles and patterns of interacting but, when significant events occur—either positive or negative—they can disrupt these ongoing patterns. Destabilizing events change the self-concepts of the members in a relationship, alter individuals' ability to perform, change the demands of established roles, and threaten the identities of the individuals involved, setting up a perfect storm for relational communication. The parties in the relationship may feel fear, anger, and uncertainty; the need for communication increases—to renegotiate roles— but the stress caused by this emotional overload makes it difficult to communicate directly, especially about conflicts.

To deal with critical communication contexts, keep in mind that you can't prevent them; life brings both pleasant and unpleasant surprises. Even though it may be difficult, talk more, not less, and make sure you get the taboo topics on the table. You may also want to get professional help. Finally, bear in mind that you can achieve a "new normal"; you can't return to your earlier relationship, but you can work through the immediate problem and come out on the other side. Gottman urges us to celebrate the struggle of surviving disruptive events together. ■

Important Terms

conflict resolution: A process leading to a recognized outcome of a conflict—a negotiated agreement or a unilaterally imposed solution.

critical communication context: A situation in which a distressing, destabilizing event creates a "critical context" among relational partners; in this context, effective communication becomes simultaneously much more important and much more difficult.

family meeting: A scheduled time set aside with a structured agenda and ground rules to promote meaningful communication, encouragement, cooperation, joint decision-making, and problem-solving among all family members.

Suggested Reading

Baxter and Montgomery, *Relating: Dialogues and Dialectics.*

Fisher and Brown, *Getting Together: Building Relationships as We Negotiate.*

Gottman and DeClaire, *The Relationship Cure: A Five-Step Guide to Strengthening Your Marriage, Family, and Friendships.*

1. Agree to hold a couple or family meeting for one hour or less at a set time each week for four weeks. In the meeting, try to speak up honestly about what feels good to you and what bothers you. Do your best to listen to one another without arguing.

2. Ask for what you need or would like from the others at the meeting. Treat the issues raised as problems and try to work together to solve them. Then, determine whether such meetings are worthwhile in your relationship.

Disruptions in Close Relationships
Lecture 15—Transcript

In our last lecture, we focused primarily on the natural ongoing dynamics that are there in close personal relationships and how those dynamics create natural conflicts that occur. We tried to get us to where we could understand how seeing those natural dynamics in play can help us handle conflicts more easily and help us build stronger relationships.

What we're going to do in this lecture is talk about two kinds of things. One we're going to further with applying specific suggestions on how we can make use of those insights, and we're even going to reach back to some earlier lectures and talk about how we can apply the insights from those here in close personal relationships especially to get better results handling conflicts. That's the first thing we're going to do.

Then we're going to turn to a second thing, which is going to come up this way. Any close relationship is going along in a given pattern, but life happens, events can happen, major events, that change the nature of the relationship and give us all something major to adapt to. Those are disruptions that occur, and we're going to talk about how to deal with those in what we call critical communication context. Those are two things to talk about then.

So let's move and get started talking about first the suggestions that we can make. What I want to do is begin by considering here and making sure we're clear on the two ways in which conflict in these close personal relationships that are permanent and long-term will differ from what happens in temporary or casual relationships. As we noted in the last lecture, the stakes are going to be a good deal higher. It's going to cost more. A conflict that's not handled well in a really close important relationship can be a major disruption in my life. It can undermine one's self-identity and feelings. So the stakes are very, very high. The risk of speaking up is greater and the risk of listening is greater. So we want to know that about our close personal relationships.

There's greater threat to the listener. We talked about that in Lecture 13. It can be very difficult listening and especially harder listening when the conflict is occurring in a close personal relationship because there are strong emotions involved because we care more. Those strong emotions can lead to overreaction, more emotional involvement, so we've got more emotion involved, the anger can feel greater, the fears can feel greater, so the load, the risk here is a good deal higher. That's the first difference in what is different from casual.

The second way is really more like good news. There's more opportunity here to get the thing resolved and resolved in a way that works. That caring and identity and investment we have in the relationship make us more motivated, give us more knowledge of the other person, and so we're in a better position to work through the conflict. We have some existing levels of trust. We know this other person so we have something to work with building toward a resolution.

Even in long-term relationships they allow us to go back to that experimentation stage and if that doesn't work out, we can try another solution and we can do several rounds of working out solutions. We have much more opportunity to get good resolutions and make them stick in an ongoing relationship. So they're different in those ways. The second way is really helpful. We've got a better shot. It's harder, it's bigger, but we've got a better shot, we've got more opportunity.

Secondly here I want to talk about just what we can do in those relationships in terms of making the relationship a place where it's easier to resolve conflict. Roger Fisher and Scott Brown, that's Roger Fisher who is in the Harvard Negotiation Project, Scott Brown is too as a matter of fact, but it's Fisher of Fisher and Ury. They had a book some years after *Getting to Yes*, which he called *Getting Together* and that's about building the kind of strong relationships that are supportive enough that they made good contexts for good conflict resolution.

Fisher and Brown give us a set of suggestions there that are just extremely useful in the book *Getting Together*. They say first balance emotion with reason. We're two kinds of beings, we're emotional beings who can reason, let's use both and keep them in balance. Let neither one dominate. The second thing they say is get really interested in learning how the other member sees things and feels. Remember the lecture about perspectives, when we talked about the Lens Model? Try to get yourself around to the other partner's lens and see things as they see them a lot so you understand them better. That's their second suggestion.

Third they said always consult before deciding on anything that might affect the other person in the relationship and listen to what you get when you consult. Listen to what they say and work with them.

The next thing they say, and it's a really nice piece of advice, is what you need to do is be wholly trustworthy, but not wholly trusting. Work as hard as you can to be perfectly trustworthy, but don't be wholly trusting, don't add that heavy load to anybody because no human being is really up to being perfectly trustworthy. That would be too much stress. That's a nice piece of advice.

Then they say, never try to coerce, never try to push too hard, persuade, negotiate, and they say as equals. That fits with all that we've seen about managing conflict. Finally they say practice acceptance of the other person. That person is who he or she is. Then when you have differences, take them seriously and deal seriously with them. That's a set of advice on how to operate in general in a relationship that will make it a good place, a good atmosphere, a good context for handling conflict.

Let's go back and pick up some things from some earlier lectures and bring them through to close relationships and talk about what to do with them. Remember our Lecture 5 where we talked about emotion? We can apply what we learned about emotion here in a close personal relationship. Remember in Lecture 5 we said that when you're having feelings, strong emotions that are relevant to a conflict, they need to be not acted out, but they need to be expressed. In order to express them you need a safe environment and a willing partner to do that. Bring that forward to the close relationship, make the relationship itself a safe environment, and try to be the willing and able partner. That's especially important in a close relationship.

Move forward across the lecture to Lecture 7 where we talked about power. Remember the fundamental thing I told you that all the research really points to most significantly about power in conflict, there's always a power struggle no matter how close the relationship. But the more equal the power, the better the odds. So you really want to work for equality in that relationship.

Of course there are some exceptions, parent-child, 8-year-old Johnny wants to bring the snake he caught into the house. Momma can say no and that one can work out. Or 14-year-old Wendy wants to stay out until after midnight. You can say no, the power shouldn't be equal in those instances. But in general, you want to work toward equal power in relationships.

Let's bring it forward from some earlier lectures. I've got some additional suggestions I want to point to here and bring them into this close relationship. One of those is the rule of reciprocity that I mentioned. I talked about it when we talked about listening two lectures back. You want to give back information that's equal to what you're getting, as much personal information as you receive from the other party in a close personal relationship and at the same level of intimacy you want to be giving that back.

You ought to follow the rule of reciprocity in a close relationship in the way you communicate. That helps us keep power relatively equal because information, as you remember when we talked about power, is also an important power base. So it keeps power equal if information is equal. Each of us knows about the same amount about the other. That's going to make a stronger, safer place for handling conflict.

It might be that the other party gives you more information than you're prepared to handle or share at that time. If that's the case, you know what you want to do, you want to tell them I really can't go that far with you now, you want to be real with the person about that and be real about why not because you've got to follow rule of reciprocity and not let it get too far out of line, and then they can begin to withhold. So that's that suggestion.

Here's another really important one. It's extremely, extremely useful. This suggestion says give at least 80 percent positive feedback to the other party in that relationship. Do you have to tell them good things all the time? A lot of people think I don't, you know I love you. You know I feel good about you, why should I have to tell you? The research says we need to keep hearing that. The great psychologist B. F. Skinner, a lot of his research didn't exactly pan out in the long run, but one finding of his, one assertion of his that keeps panning out in his own research and in others following up is this business about the need for positive reinforcement, which is the need for positive feedback.

It translates into a kind of rule of thumb theory that says you need at least 80 percent positive feedback. Humans need that to function at an optimal level. That's what Skinner showed us and certainly at an optimum level in the relationship. But if you take that notion and apply it to our handling of conflict, if I'm hearing plenty of positive things, I know that what I do that's right and it's good is noticed and feels appreciated, then I know that I'm doing well in this relationship and it's going to be a lot easier for me to hear if now you have to say something negative, which sooner or later you will.

If you haven't said anything positive to your partner and now you've got something negative to say, that's not going to feel fair or it's going to feel more threatening. So you don't want that, 80 percent positive feedback. If I can't find 80 percent positive things to say to somebody I'm in a close personal relationship with, there's something wrong here. I don't think I belong in a personal relationship, at least not a close one, with somebody that I can't say at least 80 percent good about. So look for the positive things and go ahead and say them, 80 percent positive reinforcement, that would be really, really useful. That's an important suggestion.

Now let's move and talk about the conflict styles and conflict strategies a little bit, patterns in the relationship. Here what I want to suggest to you is that when conflict occurs we really ought to have, as I said last lecture, a conflict style that's collaboration. It ought to be what we do as the norm and we back into other things. We looked at principle negotiation. We described that in Lecture 10 and there's a useful guide there. You've got the seven step negotiating process, and both of those work for collaboration. They work for getting win-wins. That's what we always ought to be trying to do first if this is a close personal relationship that we value.

If accommodation by one party is required and you can't get to that and you couldn't compromise, you might want to make sure that you take turns accommodating the other and it's not all one person or the other doing the accommodating. We ought to make use of one of the ample opportunities in an ongoing relationship to make sure we follow through, to track whether the other party follows through. They're closer to us, we can see it, and there's plenty of opportunity to give them positive feedback when they do or to renegotiate when they're not or when it's not working out for us. We've got plenty of opportunity to do it. So think collaboration as the dominant way that you're going to handle conflicts in a close relationship.

One thing that you can do to help that, and this is another suggestion, is to create a dependable opportunity that with the social expectation that conflicts will be brought up and they're going to be respectfully discussed and they're going to be resolved. A regularly-timed dependable opportunity to do that, that would be a situation in which you respect the claims that an individual's time and attention has, but you set aside time to do it, okay. The way you do that is you schedule a meeting. Counselors often call this a family meeting if it's the whole family, a couples meeting, it's really suggested by counselors a lot as you do this.

You set that meeting up, whatever you call it, I don't particularly like either of those terms, they sound a little soft. But you set a regular meeting up you give it priority and everybody puts it on their schedule and really try hard to honor it. It should be a regular time. It should be weekly or twice a month, certainly at least that often. These meetings will serve a broader purpose of communicating, they're not limited to just bringing up conflicts so they don't have to feel negative coming. They ought to be about telling each other what's going on with us and how we really feel about what's going on. That way they can prevent unnecessary conflicts and misunderstandings from arising as well as help us have an opportunity to bring up conflicts when they occur.

It's important to communicate in these meetings what's really happening and then how we feel about those events. The general rules in those meetings should be that each person in the meeting gets a time to talk and the rest of us are going to really try to listen and actively listening following what I suggested in Lecture 13. Questions can be asked, but not to challenge. You want to hear and understand, and if we want to response, we ask for it. If we want to negotiate, we can ask for that. We can negotiate there in the meeting if it fits or set a time.

But if you set up a meeting that way that's regularly scheduled, you know you're going to have an opportunity and you can rely on each other to be there. In our busy lives going in a lot of different directions these days, it's a wise thing to get busy and do that so you can ask for solutions, negotiate, and you have a meeting set up in which you can do that, and it's a regular meeting.

Those were suggestions, that's a set of suggestions that you can follow that really help. They bring forward what we've been talking about all along and give you some guidelines for dealing with conflicts in the ongoing aspects of a close personal relationship. Now I want to turn to those disruptions that I said I was going to talk about, what Mary Brown, Mike Peters, and I have called critical communication contexts.

Here's the way these things work and I'll explain as we go along why we call them critical communication contexts. You're going along in a relationship and occasionally things happen, life happens, things happen that can seriously disrupt the relationship and really alter the normal dynamics that are going on. When those things happen they're going to create new conflicts and they're going to make the conflicts you've got harder to resolve. The consequences of potential disruptions here can really be measured.

Why does it work this way? In all close relationships, all of them, including couples and families, you can think of them and understand very well as systems that are going on, as living systems. In a living system, that kind of a thing is characterized by this tendency everything is interacting all the time, but the tendency in a system as it's operating is to seek stability on the one hand, keep it as stable and as long-lasting as we can, and on the other the tendency of systems is to adapt as they have to to solve problems and survive. That's what living systems do, and biological systems and human systems and families and couples and relationships and organizations, that's what living systems do okay. They're looking for stability.

How you get the stability is we develop roles and expectations of each other and patterns of interacting, and we've all got roles and we know our part and we're doing those and we're counting on the other party to do his or hers. We do them without thinking about it. Most of them haven't really been negotiated, they've been worked out over time. They've just fallen into those places; that's what's happening in these relationships.

Then an event can come along that can change all of that and it can surprise us. We don't have to have caused it. Like what? Suppose one member in this couple or this family gets a serious injury or acquires a long-term illness that changes that person's ability to function and participate. It may even require the other members to step up and take care of that person. Mom for instance gets Alzheimer's disease. It could be a positive thing too. Say you have a member, dad, who's an alcoholic and he gets help and becomes sober. Well the family system was running around the way he behaved as an alcoholic, now he's sober, he's got a different role and everybody has got to change. When these things happen they're very disruptive to the ongoing pattern of the relationship.

I was privileged to work with a couple of really fine scholars in working out this concept, Mary Brown and Michael Peters, and the three of us agreed to label these critical communication contexts, and I'll explain them and explain why we call them that. What happens to create a critical communication context is one of these destabilizing events happens. It changes members self-concepts, alters individuals' ability to perform, and changes the demands of roles, really threatens the identities of the individuals involved.

They make demands for performance in a new way on people. All the members get distressed, even if it's a good change all the members are going to get distressed. This tends to magnify any sense of personal consequences and it alters the relationship and it may in fact threaten the relationship that's taking place. That sets up a kind of perfect storm for relational communication.

What do I mean by perfect storm here? On the one hand because of all these new uncertainties and even the doubts about who we are and what we're able to do, everybody is insecure. We're often uncertain even about our identities and our abilities. We're afraid, and some of us are going to be angry about having to change and step up or what we can't do anymore, we could just be mad at the universe about what has happened to us. So there's a lot of stress. There's fear and there's anger and uncertainty all at the same time for all the parties involved.

What that does is make communicating about personal matters on the one hand much more necessary. We've got a lot we need to talk about and a lot we need to renegotiate because we've got this relationship. The old roles are blown up, we've got to negotiate new ones, what're we going to do. So it's much more important that we be able to talk, talk intimately, and conflicts will arise from this sometimes on a daily even an hourly basis and we've got to talk about them and work them out.

But at the same time because of all of that uncertainty and all that emotional overload and all of that stress, it's a whole lot more difficult to communicate directly, especially about conflicts. Everything is more loaded with more dangerous pitfalls. So what you get is this perfect storm. On the one hand it's absolutely much more necessary that we talk constructively and intimately and personally and handle our tough conflicts, and on the other hand it's a whole lot harder to do.

If we can do it well and get through it, then what we have is a relationship that's going in a good direction. We can move to a new normal. If we can't do it well and get through it, the relationship is going to get blown up and destroyed. So we call this context of getting through this change a critical communication context. It's absolutely critical that we communicate well, but it's extremely difficult to do at the same time; tough spot, critical communication context.

What can we do about it? It's not hopeless. What can we do about it? The first thing is just remember that we can't really prevent critical communication context. We can be careful so we don't get injured and that sort of thing, but life happens sometimes. It brings surprises, pleasant or unpleasant, that really change things fundamentally. So we can't prevent them.

We do have to recognize once again we're up against something difficult and appreciate that for each party. I need to appreciate for the other party how difficult it is. That's true if I'm the one who feels like the victim, I'm the one that's sick or if I'm the one who has suffered the injury, the loved ones around you watching you go through that are going through something that can be harder than what you're going through. So appreciate the spot that each other is in, all members.

Here's what you have to try to do. Even though it's hard, go ahead and talk more, not less. Even though it's hard talk more, not less. The second thing I want you to do is when there are taboo topics that emerge, get those topics on the table. They are going to need to be talked about. Some of the kinds of critical communication contexts that have been studied, I know that Michael Peters did some really wonderful work studying the critical context that's created when the woman in a married couple has breast cancer and has to have a breast removed. What does that do?

Boy when she comes home with that, you could have a taboo topic and that couple better get it on the table and talk about it and work through it, not just be quiet about it. That kind of thing can happen. So for couples it can be sex issues, that one might be related to that. How one feels about the other's mother might be an issue; that might be taboo. You might need to get that on the table, or friends or family members, whatever has become taboo, get it on the table and talk about it. You want to be honest and clear, but try to be kind as you're doing that.

The next thing I want to suggest is that this is an occasion where you really, really, really want to get professional help. Counselors really help with this, you're going through a tough spot. Then finally I want to suggest that you ought to trust that a new normal can be achieved.

There's a wonderful friend of mine who contracted multiple sclerosis, he found that he had MS. And he found it not long after he'd retired, had a good life set up for himself in retirement, everything was good, and then the symptoms began to occur. He struggled with MS. He all sorts of wonderful plans for how things were going to go, and my friend with the wonderful spirit said Michael what I'm doing is learning to be comfortable with the new normal.

The relationship you've got when you get through a critical communication context is never going to go back to the way it was. I can't go back to the way it was before I had MS. I can't go back to the way it was before this person had this operation. We can't go back to the way it was before mother contracted Alzheimer's, but we can get to a new normal if we stick with this over time that's really going to work out.

So that's critical communication context. It's something we've got to deal with and the relationship is going to change, but we can get to a normal when we're finished if we do it well. If we don't do it well, a great many relationships are just going to break up over it. One of the things, even with that good change that I mentioned, if you've got an alcoholic in the couple and that alcoholic cleans up and gets sober and you've got a change, the fact is that a great many couples don't make it through that change. They were making it through all the drinking and they had adapted to that, but the change imposes new roles and they don't get through that. So it's a threat, critical communication context, and I want to suggest that you be very careful with it. Do what you've got to do, get help, and you can get through, and press that you can get to a new normal.

What've we seen here? The first thing, I want you to go back to those suggestions and let's remember what we talked about. You want to use constructive conflict management to build and maintain strong personal relationships. And vice versa, you want to build strong personal relationships to help you with constructive conflict management. The first thing is that when a conflict occurs you want to go back, you want to address it through collaborative negotiation, you want to be playing for a win-win.

You want to use everything we've talked about in the lectures up to now, and you've got a better shot at doing that being creative, working together to get win-win solutions, you've got a better shot. Fall back on compromise if that fails or accommodating each other and taking turns to balance it if you don't want to compromise. But you can do that and you've got a much better chance to follow through on your agreements.

Secondly I want you to make sure you notice to create some kind of dependable opportunity, regular opportunities, to discuss conflicts where you know you can rely on the other person to be there in your busy lives. Thirdly, when you're dealing with a critical communication context, and we went over these a few minutes ago but they really need to be repeated now, talk more, not less and get taboo topics on the table.

Secondly, be honest, but be considerate. Get professional help if you need it or maybe even if you think you might need it or could use it. Then the other phrase, John Gottman's phrase, celebrate the struggle of surviving this thing together. Celebrate that you got through something and honor each other for doing that. That's important and then trust that a new normal is going to come about; that that new relationship can be built.

I've got an assignment for you coming from this one. The most helpful thing a couple can do that's concrete right now or the parents in a family can do that's concrete right now that would move you in this direction is to do the thing about setting up a family or a couples meeting. I want to strongly suggest that you try this. Agree to hold a couple meeting or a family meeting or if it's close friends, you could do it in some other relationships too. Agree to do it for one hour or less at a set time, half-hour, 45 minutes, an hour, a time limited time. I would suggest you do it weekly and stick with it for four weeks. Do it, follow through on doing it. Try it for a month, four weeks in a row. Follow those rules that I gave you, those guidelines.

In that meeting speak up honestly about what feels good and what bothers you. Do your best to listen without arguing. Bring up conflicts as they come up and try to work out how to negotiate them as they go. Do the thing about having a regular meeting. When you're doing those, ask for what you need from the other person. Treat issues like problems raised like a fourth step, follow through and do that.

When you've done it for four weeks determine if that's good for you and if you want to continue. I think if you try it you're going to find that it's a useful thing and you'll probably want to continue. But you have to make the commitment and be there to honestly try it.

Where are we going to go from here? We've done close relationships at this point. We looked at the dynamics, we made a bunch of suggestions, a good set of suggestions for handling conflicts in them, and we talked about those disruptions that create critical communication contexts.

Now we're going to turn to the other kind of relationship in which conflicts are most likely to occur and affect us most. That's conflicts in our work relationships, conflicts in organizations. That's going to be the subject of our next two lectures.

How Management Theories Affect Conflict
Lecture 16

Some years ago, the American Management Association commissioned a study on how conflict affects managers. One of the conclusions from that study is the estimate that managers spend about 25 percent of their work time giving attention to conflict in one way or another.

Poorly managed conflict makes work life unpleasant, and it affects how organizations function. Conflict in organizations most often occurs in task-oriented groups, which should enable group members to achieve win-win solutions, but that's not generally what happens. The workplace rivals personal relationships as a setting where conflicts are most likely to occur and most likely to matter.

The costs and consequences of organizational conflict stem from how such conflict is handled. Costs to the individual involved in conflict include wasted time and effort, increased stress, reduced performance and motivation, delayed career development, and even loss of employment. Organizations experience both direct and opportunity costs from conflict. Under these headings fall costs associated with impaired communication and function, damaged relationships and rapport, reduced morale and productivity, increased absenteeism and turnover, and even litigation. The accumulated costs of everyday organizational conflicts seem to cause the most damage. Reducing these costs requires avoiding unnecessary conflict and improving the conflict management behavior of employees.

Organizations are social realities; their existence depends on a shared idea of what the organization is and how it is structured. One of the components of an organization as a shared idea is an underlying management theory, a set of assumptions that establishes rules, controls, and relationships. Over the course of the 20th century, four primary management theories developed that govern how we set up and run organizations: classical management, human relations management, human resources management, and systems management. Each of these has advantages and disadvantages for managing conflict, and each changes the way people go about managing conflict in an organization.

Most organizations still rely heavily on classical management. This theory emerged around the turn of the 20th century with the Industrial Revolution. At the time, the German sociologist Max Weber outlined a structure for factories and other large organizations that he believed would be efficient, productive, and long-lasting. He based his hierarchical, bureaucratic structure on two existing organizations: the Prussian army and the Catholic Church. From these organizations, Weber drew the idea of an ordered chain of command, with communication and decisions flowing from the top down. Although the bureaucratic structure is successful, it embodies power and status differences and communication hierarchies that often impede direct negotiation in conflicts.

The underlying assumption in systems theory is that all organizations are like living organisms, constantly moving, changing, and interacting, and a change in any one element affects the organization as a whole.

The human relations theory of management took hold with organizations around 1930. According to this theory, developed by a social psychologist named Elton Mayo, productivity can be improved by treating employees as individuals and interacting with them on a friendly basis. For Mayo, the correct metaphor for an organization was not a well-oiled machine but a family. Mayo's theory moved organizations in the direction of better conflict management, but most of the inhibiting effects of classical management were still very much in place in his conception of organizations.

The period from the late 1940s until well into the 1980s saw the development of human resources management theory. Here, a key assumption is that the primary resource of any organization is its people; thus, motivation is likely to be vital to increased productivity. Motivation can be achieved by matching the individuals' goals in the organization with the goals of the organization as a whole. The metaphor for this type of organization is a team, with employees participating in decision-making. In organizations with this orientation, communication flows up, down, and across the organization, but again, the classical structure remains in place.

Since the 1980s, systems theory has been applied to organizational management. The underlying assumption in systems theory is that all organizations are like living organisms, constantly moving, changing, and interacting, and a change in any one element affects the organization as a whole. The challenge is to maintain stability while adapting to change and solving problems as they arise. This theory recognizes that some parts of the system operate informally and unofficially; that is, much of the development and maintenance of the real organization occurs through the interactions of its members. With a systems management approach, decisions may be revisited and renegotiated, creating a climate that facilitates effective conflict management.

Managers and supervisors must understand that it is in their best interest to improve conflict management within the organization in order to minimize costs. This goal can be accomplished through understanding the organization from a systems point of view and drawing from the people-oriented approaches of human relations and human resources management theory. ∎

Suggested Reading

Senge, *The Fifth Discipline*.

How Management Theories Affect Conflict
Lecture 16—Transcript

We've looked at the dynamics of close personal relationships and how those dynamics affect conflict and conflict management and how we can do better in those relationships. We've done that. Now in this lecture and the next what we want to do is turn to that other major context where conflicts occur and where they matter most, and that's at work in our organizations. So this lecture and the next we're going to talk about organizational conflict and how it might be managed better.

Poorly managed conflict makes work life unpleasant. We know that. There's terrible cost to the individuals. It just makes life unpleasant, but it also affects how the organization functions. Conflict and how it's managed is going to affect the organization as a whole so we really need to talk about it in both of those contexts.

We want to look at those costs and what the affects are and then we want to look at the way we structure a conflict and think of it and understand it is going to affect the way we handle conflict. That'll be give us a basis for understanding how we can do it better, which we'll get to in Lecture 17.

We've got to make a preliminary comment walking into this. As we discussed earlier, this conflict in organizations and way back in Lecture 3 when we were talking about Morton Deutsch's studies where he made that wonderful discovery about win-win, a critique of what he was doing is while he was studying task-oriented groups where they've got shared goals. Well you know what? In organizations those conflicts really ought to be mostly about task-oriented groups that occur in work units, which are teams, task-oriented groups, the organization as a whole is a task-oriented group. So they really ought to be situations where the members have a lot of shared goals.

You would think you could get a lot of win-wins, but that's not mostly what happens. Deutsch taught us that all those years ago, but it turns out that most organizations don't handle conflict very well that way. They fall very short of that win-win ideal. So let's try to get an understanding of what's going on in organizations, how the organizations affect conflict where the cost to individuals and organizations and get ourselves set up for thinking in Lecture 17 about what we could do better.

Let's begin with this. Conflict at work matters to the individual members, of course, but it also matters to the organization as a whole. That's an important thing to understand about it. It's both the same as and different from conflict in close personal relationships because a lot of these relationships in organizations are close. Some of them are even close personal relationships and the conflicts happen there. But the conflicts and how they're managed there are going to affect the organization as a whole.

That leads us to a definition here. My favorite definition of organizational conflict is very simple. It says an organizational conflict is any conflict that occurs in an organizational setting. How common is conflict in organizations? This context rivals those personal relationships as the places where conflicts are most likely occur and where it's most likely to matter.

The nature it turns out of most conflicts in organizations, most organizational conflicts, is really quite interpersonal. They're conflicts between people, a lot of the same stuff that happens in conflicts in relationships. Some of them are very work related about the project, but a lot of them are very personally related. They still affect the organization as a whole so even the personal ones are organizational conflicts. So we've learned about general principles for handling conflicts and a lot of what we learned about all those principles should apply in organizations.

Let's think a little bit about those effects, the costs and consequences that occur. The consequences for the organization as well as for the individual come from how the conflicts are being handled. The organization is going to affect how conflicts are handled. And we want to note that. We're going to pay close attention to that in this lecture. The organization by the way its structured, by its policies, by the way its managed, by the culture that develops, the relationships it sets up among its members, all of that structuring and context, will have a great influence on how members behave when they're in a conflict. So that's important to recognize.

The costs to these happen to the individual and to the organization as a whole. For the individual what is it? It's time and effort; it's stress, it's pain, it's damaged performance, I don't feel good about my performance if it's not very good. It's reduced motivations. It's hindered career development, sometimes it's job loss. So there are costs to the individuals. But there's cost to the organization and if we're looking at this from a manager's standpoint that cost to the organization is an important thing, a very important thing to attend to.

In the first place there are costs involved. There's time and effort, even when you handle it best. There's a direct cost there and there's opportunity cost. When I'm dealing with the conflict I lose the opportunity to do what else I'd be doing instead of dealing with the conflict. What are some of these costs to the organization that occur in addition to opportunity? There's damaged communication; that damages function. There's damaged relationships; that damages rapport, damages function. There's reduced employee motivation, which reduces productivity.

There's lower morale, which in turn reduces productivity and increases absenteeism. There's greater turnover and there's even litigation that comes. So there's a ton of costs from conflict in an organization.

We can't really measure these costs very well. A number of people have tried and some people claim to be able to measure the cost of conflict in an organization and I'm very skeptical of all of the measurement systems that I've read for that. But what I do know from the research and especially from some years of working with organizations is that the really greatest cost is not that one big conflict that was a blow up, but it's the accumulated costs of those every day conflicts that occur throughout the organization among all the people and how they're handled, because if they're not handled well it may not be visible like one big flare-up, but it's a lot of reduced motivation, a lot of people leaving, a lot of loss, a lot of opportunity costs.

Those things are huge. I think that's the biggest cost. I'm very convinced of that. Some years ago the American Management Association commissioned a study on how conflict affects managers. One of the conclusions from that study is the estimate that managers spend about 25 percent of their work time giving attention to conflict in one way or another. It's an estimate. It could be higher, could be lower, but I think that estimate is pretty nicely in the ballpark. So for managers and supervisors especially, beyond whatever is the personal reason for themselves functioning to getting conflict resolved for the organization, for the responsibility to the organization, they really want to reduce the costs of conflicts that are there.

Reducing costs is going to require reducing any unnecessary conflict, trying to eliminate that, and improving the conflict management behavior of employees, and that's that conflict management behavior that happens every day. If we're going to have a shot at doing that, we need to understand some things first. So that's where we're going to go in this lecture.

What we need to do is we've got two objectives we have to try to accomplish here if we're going to do this. We have to understand the basic nature of organizations and then we want to be able to see how the way we're thinking of organizations and structuring them and defining them sets up relationships and influences the way we handle conflict. So let's work on getting those basic understandings.

That's going to start with getting at that organization's or in fact social realities. What do I mean by social reality? A social reality is a sociologist's term. A social reality is something that actually exists. It's a real thing. It has consequences. It makes a difference, but its existence, the nature of it and the fact that it is that thing really depends on the shared idea that it is and that it is what it is.

My university, the University of Arizona, is a social reality. There are beautiful buildings. It's a beautiful campus. But that's not the university. That it's a university depends on the shared idea of what a university is and how that sets up and what it creates as relationships, and we have to agree on that. And only when we agree on that is it that thing. A state is a social reality. A marriage is a social reality. Any organization is a social reality and exists because we agree that that's what it is and we agree that that's how it is.

If it exists as an idea that's shared then we've got to have ideas about what it is, and that's driven by the sort of management theories that come up from conceptualizing organizations. So we need to understand what those management theories are that we'll use to define and create and structure an organization, and we need to get an idea of how those theories may be affecting the way conflict gets handled. So I want you to bear with me and walk through some understanding theory here so we can get to application in the next lecture.

Any theory about organizations is going to rest on the assumptions that are made at the beginning. It's going to be a response to the conditions that set it up. We develop theory in a certain context, but the theories of what an organization is, the ideas about it, start with those assumptions and conditions and then they establish rules and controls and relationships growing from those theories. They establish and control patterns and rules of communication from what we think is the nature of an organization will control those kind of things.

When you do that you're going to have the intended effects probably, but you're also going to have some unintended effects, and some of those effects, especially the unintended ones may be seriously affecting the way you handle conflict. So now we can look at what theories we rely on to deal with creating organizations. I want to go through a kind of history lesson on that.

We've got theories that serve as foundations. What these theories do is influence the way conflict is going to be managed. We need answers to what those theories are and how that affect is. It turns out that over the course of the 20th century there are four really primary theories of organization, that is general concepts of what an organization is and how it should be structured and how it should function, that really have governed the way we set up and run organizations.

Those are going to be—and we're going to talk about them each—classical management, human relations management, human resources management, and then systems management. Each of these starts from assumptions that were made under certain circumstances responding to conditions and each of them has advantages and disadvantages when it comes to managing conflict. Each changes the way people go about managing conflict in the organization.

Most organizations really these days reflect a kind of mix of these theories, but they're still most heavily reliant because they're structured that way, on the oldest of the theories and that's the one we call classical management. So let's look at that and see how that works.

What are the assumptions that were made and what're the conditions under which classical management was developed? If you go to that era when it was developed you're actually starting in the 1880s and going to the turn of the 20th century, it's that frame into the 19th, early 20th century when this thing was created. What were the conditions people were responding to? Well the industrial revolution had occurred and you had more people, more people you could sell things to, more people to produce for, and the invention of mass production had taken place.

Now instead of small guilds making things we had big factories making things. We had many more large organizations and we needed a way to conceptualize these and figure out how to run them. The German sociologist Max Weber stepped up to the task of figuring that out. He did this mostly in the 1880s and the late 19th century. So he set out to come up with a theory of organization that could be used to structure organizations well. He thought well, what we want is a way to structure this that will be efficient and productive and effective, but at the same time have staying power.

How was he going to do this? He thought about this and he said well what I can do is identify looking around what is the most efficient and effective organization I can see right now among the large organizations, and then find the one that has lasted the longest, has the best staying power and I'll just compare the two and see what they have in common and then I'll base my theory on that. What he got from that were going to be the concept of bureaucracy and hierarchy.

What do you think the two organizations were? Efficient and effective, most efficient and effective in Europe in the 1880s, easy winner for that was the Prussian Army. They were being very efficient, they were well-organized.

They were expanding to create the whole of Germany, the Prussian Army was the most efficient and effective organization so he said okay I'll use that.

What was the organization that lasted the longest that he wanted to look at. He looked around and lo and behold what he saw was the Roman Catholic Church. It had sure been there, had staying power, had taken some big hits in the reformation, but it was still there. So Weber set out to see what these two have in common.

As he studied these he could do, for instance, he looked at the organization of the Prussian Army and that was nicely laid out in a line and box chart, that idea along with idea of chain of command was created by a General von Moltke and Bismark was really thrilled with this when Moltke as really a fiend about order. He really wanted everything ordered. So he created the line and box chart. Weber could sit down and take his descriptions of the Catholic Church and the authorities and how it was structured and draw a line and box chart himself. So he said these we have in common. That's a principle that can be followed.

In naming it he was actually working in a French hotel when he did that and he looked across the room and he saw literally a French bureau, a chest of drawers called a bureau and had big drawers at the top and smaller drawers as it went down. He said ah-hah I'll call it bureaucracy. And you've got the principle of bureaucracy and it carried with it that idea of chain of command. So he did that and some others.

But one other major player in this was Frederick Taylor, who's actually an engineer. He was theorizing about the structural organizations that built things and he really latched on to this Bismark's idea that a large organization should run like a well-oiled machine. That was what Bismark wanted for the Prussian Army. So Taylor added time and motion studies to work with this, and these people developed the classical idea of how to manage and structure an organization.

Well assumptions rode along with that, and what were those assumptions? The Prussian Army and the Catholic Church had certain things in common and these were the boss, who's ever at the top knows what should be done and should rule. Communication should flow downward was the assumption, the rules, the assignments, the instruction, communication was about telling people lower down what to do. Top management, the assumption said, should define everything and set procedures and everybody else should do what they're told. Workers work, decisions are left to managers and supervisors and officers in the army.

Also there was an assumption here that position in the hierarchy moving up carried not just power, but social status. That rode along with it. Classical management with all those assumptions is really still with us even though we've done a lot to improve on things since. It's still effective and efficient. Other means of structuring organizations have been tried, but frankly none of them have really demonstrated the ability to function and be as solid as that line and box chart bureaucratic structure. So we still have all of that.

No theory has been devised that would replace it and we still have all of its negative effects. What are those negative effects? As we saw in Lecture 7 if you remember the results of managing conflict are much better if you have equal power and status among the parties so they can negotiate directly. The bureaucratic structure keeps us from doing that. The power is unequal and we can't talk directly to a lot of people. Communication is slowing down. So you really have these power and status differences and impediments to any direct negotiation. That's a major problem.

Conflict resolution constructively would require that a lot of communication could flow up, down, and across. Classical management still tends to inhibit that so that real communication only flows down. Good conflict management should require that people are treated as individual who really matter as individual persons, not just as members of a category, but classical management inhibits this.

So classical management theory with its wonders of effectiveness and efficiency and stability, really gets in our way when it comes to how we're going to resolve conflicts. So where do we go from there? Theorizing really helped when social scientists got in the business.

We can move on to the next theory that gets developed. In this next theory, we want to talk about what gets called the human resources theory of management. This started really in 1928, it began to take hold around 1930. What it says in general is that productivity in organizations is going to improve if you actually treat employees as individuals and treat them in a friendly manner and interact with them in that way.

How did this one come about? It's kind of an interesting story. Elton Mayo, social psychologist, was hired to try to figure out how to improve the productivity at the Hawthorne Plant of the Western Electric Company in 1928. He was a good social scientist. He was going to do experiments to see what would happen. So he goes and he notices that the lighting is not very good in this plant and he thinks well maybe better lighting would improve productivity. So they went in a separate section of the plant and they set up an experiment in which what they did is improve the lighting and then they measured productivity before and after.

They found that when they improved the lighting productivity went up. Being a good social scientist though Mayo thought well if it's better lighting that makes the difference for the better, than worse lighting should make productivity worse. So he tried making the lighting worse in the second experiment and you know what productivity didn't go down it went up when you made lighting worse.

So he tried some other things, he tried a number of things and everything he tried either making it better or making it worse, whatever he tried, the productivity always got better. So he was trying to figure out what was going on here. What he noticed that the one thing that was constant across all of these experiments was that he and his colleagues working with people to do this had to go into the area where it was happening. They had to talk to the people, they had to interact with them in a friendly way.

He thought maybe it's the friendly interaction that does it and that set him in the direction of developing what becomes human relations theory of management. And what Mayo had discovered was that human relationships here really mattered. You shouldn't treat everybody in an objective way like they're automatons; treat them as individuals. Interact with them in a friendly way and he said you know what we need a really different metaphor for an organization. The metaphor we've been using in classical management is that it's a machine, it should be a well-oiled machine. No the organization metaphor should be family, a good organization that's productive ought to be like a happy family with everybody, employees included, treated like members.

Mayo didn't really question much the basic assumptions of classical management about how to structure. It's just that he moved it to we've got to talk to people and make friendly treatment of them and friendly interaction happen. That's better, it begins to move us in a direction where we can have better conflict management. But most of the inhibiting effects of classical management are still very, very much in place. So Mayo moves us in a nice direction. We move through to human relations.

Let's go talk about the next step. This is what gets called Human Resources theory in management. It's much wider than just one person and it comes into play very much in the late 1940s, after World War II, and the human relations school of research and theorizing in organizations really moves on through from about the late `40s to well into the `80s. What happens here with the number of social scientists working with this is that they make a number of assumptions themselves. Then they seek to apply really rigorous social science methods to test those and see what's going to work best.

Here are the assumptions they articulated. First they said you know what the primary resource in any organization is its people. If that's true they said the next assumption is that motivation is really probably the key to better productivity. Then they theorized that motivation is achieved by matching the individual members' goals with the goals of the organization. Mmm, goal theory, Kurt Lewin, remember that from when we talked about goals and when we talked about Deutsch's research. They're looking at that matching the goals individually in the organization.

Then they said you know what if it's about matching goals we really ought to be thinking differently. It's not just a family, we ought to be thinking that employees at all levels should function as members of a team and participate in decision making, and they entered this idea of what gets called participative decision making. So they advocated, the human resources people, much more open communication and they really began to advocate strongly finding ways to have communication flow up, down, and across in the organization, and these human resources concepts really made for significant improvements in the channels and the environment for addressing conflicts.

Still the classical structure stayed in place primarily. You can't just overrule it with the Human Resources approach.

Let's move forward again to the one that's most urgent now, most helpful now, and that is Systems theory as applied to management. Actually the application of systems theory happened very early and theorists and consultants went to Japan and the Japanese picked it up before American organizations did. It really didn't become strong in the United States until the late 1970s and into the `80s. Key theorists in this, there are a great many of them, but some that especially bear mention. One would be W. Edwards Deming who gave us the idea of total quality management and he did that from a systems approach.

Another whose work I have really admired for years is Peter Senge, who is at MIT, and these people do a wonderful job of applying general systems theory from biology to organizations and how to make organizations better and more productive. What they tell us is really going to help us understand how we can manage conflict better.

The assumptions they start with are that all organizations, they're like living organisms. They're systems, just like living organisms, and they change when any one element changes, that change in an individual element is going to affect all the rest. Everything is moving and changing and interacting all the time, a change in one affects them all. An organization they say is not some stable structure just like a line and box chart, it's like a living organism with everybody moving and changing, and you've got to keep stability, but you've got to adapt and solve problems as you come along.

Along with that they recognized a principle of ecology. They understood that there are stakeholders involved and the organization exists in a larger system and it's got to operate in a larger system and interact with it. They went further and they understood that sharing and understanding its systems are only partially built and structured officially that the system has created also informally and unofficially. But much of that development and maintenance of the real organization and what's happening occurs not with the official things, not even spoken, it occurs by people interacting and working together and changes in the same way.

So each organization, they say, and each unit is its own kind of human climate and culture that's dynamic with things going on in it. In that way of looking at organizations in order to survive and thrive and do better and better, the decisions are going to have to be discussed and re-discussed and things negotiated, and that brings us into a way of thinking that makes it much easier to focus on and talk about managing conflicts because this has got to take into account the needs of all the stakeholders, the external ones in the organization which I mentioned in an earlier lecture, and the internal stakeholders who are the employees.

So the insights here coming from systems theory are really going to help bring us to a point where we can understand what's going on and we've got a much better opportunity to negotiate resolutions. Still, still, most of the systems theorists overlaid this on classical management so as I said at the beginning, you know, our organizations are mixtures of all these things. We're going to need to understand how they work.

What conclusions can we draw from this for managers and supervisors first? First is that it's really in our interest, it's part of our job to try to reduce, try to minimize the cost to my organization that come from conflict and how it's managed. I've really got to focus then on trying to understand the way my people are managing conflict and create the best opportunities for them to manage it well.

If I'm going to do that, I really need to understand how my organization is structured and operating across all those theories, but I've really got to come into the 21st century and understand my organization from a systems point of view if I'm going to make it better. I'm also going to have to make really good use of even the insights from human relations and the insights from human resources because they are nicely people-oriented in terms of how they do this and they really do give us a way to think about organizations with communication going up, down, across. As a manager or a supervisor, those are things that I'm going to need to understand if I want to be doing my job well.

What have we learned so far in this lecture? First the effects of organizational conflict are enormously costly both to the individual and to the organization. That is if the conflicts are not handled well. Secondly reducing these effects, reducing the amount of unnecessary conflict and improving conflict management behavior of all employees is a major interest of managers at all levels and supervisors. Thirdly what I want you to get here is that the nature, the structure, the policies, the way we manage an organization which are all driven by theories, are going to affect the way people handle conflict in the organization. I've got to understand those theories and their effects to understand what's going on.

Fourth I want us to really understand that classical management way of looking at things, which really still provides the fundamental structure of most organizations really has effects as good as it is that inhibit good conflict management in several ways. Then fifth I want you to get at that human relations, human resources, and systems management theories really provide us ways to at least mitigate that damage and make it easier for people to deal up, down, and across, and negotiate as individuals to resolve conflicts.

Finally I want you to note as a summary point here that competent managers and supervisors really need to learn and make use of the opportunities provided by these newer theories if they're going to manage in an optimal way. It's part of my job if I'm the boss.

I've got an assignment for you from this lecture. Number one I want you to stop and think and consider what management theories your organization or you individually are primarily relying on when you structure and run your organization or your work unit. If you're not in charge, whoever structures it, think through how they're handling it. Secondly what I want you to do is consider the extent to which you've operated as though these theories are immutable, if they're just facts the way it has to be because you can change them and think differently. That would be a useful exercise at this point.

Where are we going to go from here? We've created a foundation here, a basic understanding about theories and what they affect, but we haven't said very much about specifically what you can do to improve conflict management. We've really been talking in this lecture about the basic understandings that we want to draw on to improve conflict management.

So in the next lecture we're going to go forward with giving you clear ideas about how management can act in a way to improve conflict management in the organization, to reduce its cost and reap the benefits of good conflict management. That's Lecture 17.

The Manager's Role in Dealing with Conflict
Lecture 17

> Positive feedback doesn't cost anything. It's easy to give, and it really helps with motivation, and it sets up the conditions where you have a safer environment, a more positive environment, to address conflict.

In any organization, pursuit of better conflict management begins at the top; in this lecture, we look at seven key principles that can guide top supervisors and managers. The first of these is to prevent unnecessary conflict, which can be caused by creating competitive situations, failing to clearly define roles and responsibilities, and failing to establish areas and lines of authority. Unnecessary conflict can also arise when managers make decisions without consulting the stakeholders, that is, the employees who will be affected.

The second principle for managers is to be courageous in the face of conflict; step up and deal with conflicts openly and constructively. Third, focus on the general pattern of conflict management in the organization. Practice the art of "management by walking around" to get an idea of how everyday conflicts are handled. Fourth, promote informal resolution of conflict by creating policies that state a preference for resolution by

Managers and supervisors can prevent unnecessary conflict by creating an environment of open communication.

discussion, although with authority still specified for making final decisions. Remember that employees need policy, training, and modeling to manage conflict effectively.

A fifth principle is that along with the emphasis on informal resolution, formal processes need to be in place for conflict management. Organizations need documented procedures for addressing grievances and discipline issues; however, managers should note that these are adversarial processes and should avoid overreliance on them. Sixth, try to assess and, if appropriate, improve on the **organizational culture**. Keep in mind Edgar Shein's method for identifying an organization's culture: It's characterized by whatever follows the phrase "The way it's really done around here is...." Related to culture is **organizational climate**, which is defined as how it feels for employees to work for a given organization. The communication climate is how the organization works to invite or prohibit constructive communication. I sometimes use the term "**conflict climate**" to refer to the collective influence of organizational culture, organizational climate, and communication climate on how individuals manage conflict. Conflict climate factors include relationships among workers, power relationships, communication patterns, flow of information, use of positive feedback and recognition, and conflict management practices. The seventh principle for managers is that they must model the behaviors they desire in conflict management.

> **Remember that employees need policy, training, and modeling to manage conflict effectively.**

One of the most prevalent complaints about supervisors is that they don't deal with conflicts when they arise. In most cases, supervisors should attempt to resolve differences constructively through discussion and mutual agreement. If an employee complains about a supervisor, he or she should listen and negotiate if doing so doesn't require surrendering authority. If an employee wishes to appeal a supervisory decision, the supervisor should support the employee and cooperate with the organization's established procedures for such appeals. Supervisors should also allow time and create conditions for employees to negotiate resolutions themselves rather than interceding for them. This approach gives the supervisor a chance to serve as facilitator and teacher.

To promote effective conflict management, it's important for supervisors to give regular informal feedback to employees, and again, about 80 percent of that feedback should be positive. Getting positive feedback enables employees to handle the negative feedback that comes with conflicts much better. In situations where you must give negative feedback, do so immediately and in private. Do not wait for formal evaluations; nothing said in a formal evaluation should be a surprise to the employee.

The same general principles that apply to managers and supervisors also apply to employees: Deal directly with conflicts and attempt to resolve them by direct mutual discussion. If you're in doubt about whether this approach is acceptable, ask a supervisor or experienced co-worker.

One problem that frequently comes up in organizational conflict management is **workplace bullying**, which refers to repeated mistreatment of a target. Such behavior can corrupt the whole workplace culture and climate. If you're the target of bullying, you need to confront it or report the behavior and ask for help. If you're a supervisor who becomes aware of bullying, you need to resolve the situation immediately or risk damage to your organization.

Better organizational conflict management means better morale, reduced absenteeism and turnover, stronger employee motivation, and higher productivity. Effective conflict management is obviously good for the bottom line, and it's also good for organizations as human environments. ∎

Important Terms

conflict climate: The combination of organizational culture, organizational climate, and organizational policies and procedures that affects the way members manage conflict.

organizational climate: Members' collective perception of how it feels to work and live in a particular organization.

organizational culture: Deep, pervasive, usually unspoken code that governs the way things are done in an organization and its overall atmosphere and determines what ideas and behavior are considered right or wrong, important or unimportant, and acceptable or unacceptable.

workplace bullying: Repeated mistreatment of a targeted individual characterized by disruptive acts that threaten the individual's emotional and/or physical health and career.

Suggested Reading

Cloke, Goldsmith, and Bennis, *Resolving Conflicts at Work: Eight Strategies for Everyone on the Job.*

Assignment

1. How well are everyday conflicts handled in the organization where you work or volunteer? Is the dominant pattern one of discussion and mutual agreement? If so, your assignment is done. If not, ask yourself these hard questions: What is my role in this pattern? Am I helping or hurting? What can I do to improve the handling of everyday conflicts?

The Manager's Role in Dealing with Conflict
Lecture 17—Transcript

In Lecture 16 we considered how concepts of organization and management influence the way organization members manage their conflicts. That's how the organization itself, its structure, its culture influenced the behavior of individuals.

In this our second lecture on conflict management in organizations what we want to do now is look at the roles individuals can play and play better to get better conflict management. We want to look at the roles of managers, supervisors, and the roles of the workers themselves. What can they do to get better conflict management, which will be better for the organization? They could do this of course when they really better understand those concepts that we talked about in our last lecture.

We're assuming we've got them under our belt and we know those as we move into this one. We're going to explain in there that the most important thing all the way through is focus on how ordinary, everyday conflicts get managed, because that's where the biggest cost really is.

Let's get started. Pursuit of better conflict management in every organization, you have to think it begins with top management, and I want you to notice in that just as an aside that even I with all that I'm saying am still struggling with, classical management and the idea that top management is top. That's that hierarchical structure, but these are the folks who need to define what's happening. They need to be guided, and then down the line managers and even supervisors by, what I like to think of as, seven key principles.

As we move into those I want us to think about the fact that while conflict is inherent in any kind of human interaction, there's going to be conflict that can't really be avoided, but by gosh there's also unnecessary conflict in organizations, lots of it that can be avoided. So let's turn to principle number one.

What we see in this first principle is than managers and supervisors can prevent unnecessary conflict. They can do that by stopping doing those things that generate unnecessary conflict. What are some of those things? A big one is that managers cause a lot of conflict by creating inherently competitive situations. They do this by failing to clearly define roles and responsibilities and then set boundaries for areas of authority and lines of authority. So when managers don't define things clearly, that leaves a lot of gray area in which employees down the line need to fight over turf and struggle for who's responsibility is what, and that causes a lot of conflict that didn't have to happen with all the costs that conflict bring.

There's a second area where managers bring about a lot of unnecessary conflict. They do it by making decisions without consulting people who are going to be affected. Now that's huge. I don't like to have to consult people who work for me and the old way of looking at things and the classical way of looking at things, I'm in command and control, I make the decisions, they do it.

But from the standpoint of managing conflict, that's not really very smart because people with a job to do are affected. They're stakeholders. If I can consult them before I make the decision and listen, a, they'll guide me sometimes to better decisions, but b, having been in on it and having things hashed out when they were there that'll prevent a lot of unnecessary conflict from occurring. So that's it, prevent unnecessary conflict.

In addition to causing unnecessary conflict by just not taking care of business up front, managers often compound conflict and help generate even new conflicts by failing to address them promptly and transparently when they come up. That leads us to principle number two.

In this one I want to lead by saying be courageous in the face of conflict, be courageous; step up and deal with conflicts openly and constructively when they come up. Don't sweep them under the rug. There are certain things that have to be dealt with confidentiality, certain personnel issues, but whenever it's not one of those, get it constructively on the table and deal with it up front. That's the second principle.

Let's go to another one, primary concern. As I suggested in the introduction, a manager's primary concern really is going to have to be with that general pattern of the way conflict is managed by all the employees throughout the organization. It's those everyday conflicts. So principle number three, focus primarily on the general pattern of conflict management in the organization.

Handling everyday conflicts affects productivity. It is the biggest cost factor as I said in Lecture 16 in the cost of conflicts. So that should be our primary concern. These tend to be however for managers, especially top managers, not very visible. They're hard to see. In the office upstairs where I'm dealing abstractly with statistics and numbers on paper, I don't have a feel for what's going on and how the employees throughout are handling.

There's a marvelous principle in a book done by Peters and Waterman some years ago called *In Search of Excellence,* and what Peters and Waterman suggested as a principle in there was what they call management by walking around, MBWA. Management by walking around really applies here. If I want to know how conflict is being handled in the everyday situations, I've got to spend some time out there with the troops walking around knowing what's going on, and I've got to do this myself. I can't rely on other people to feed it through to me. So general principle, pay attention to the everyday management of conflict.

Next principle has to do with informal resolution. As much as possible, we've already said resolutions should be informal and arranged by direct mutual discussion between the parties involved. So principle number four is that managers can promote this. Managers can promote informal resolution of conflict by mutual agreement among the parties. Promote it, how do we do that? Well one is I've got to address the problem posed by the hierarchical structure that we're dealing with. There's a power difference here and a status difference. So I want to create policies. I want to create occasions, I want to create ways to get past that. In the human resources approach to management there's a lot of help with that that we can turn to.

This can be done by creating a clear policy stating a preference for resolution by discussion. That policy can really also state that while mutual agreement is preferred, it's not necessarily required and you can clearly specify that the person with the authority will make the decision. It is as I said before consultation, it's not the same as democracy.

But negotiating requires time and effort. It is part of the job as I already said. I've got to allow for it if it's part of everybody's job. Let's think about what that would look like and look at a dramatization to help show us.

Here's a scene in an office. We've got Will who's a clerical worker. He's got an issue with another employee Stacy. He'd like to take some work time to deal with it. Use the conference room to do that, hmm, a couple of clericals time out, go in the conference room. Will is going to check with his supervisor Claire about that and let's see how she handles that.

[Video start.]

>**Will**: Claire, you got a minute?

>**Claire**: Sure. What's up?

>**Will**: Stacy and I have a little problem about which of us should be handling which expense forms. We can talk about it during break time, but I'd rather not wait. Can we use the conference room to work this out?

>**Claire**: Great. Go take care of it. If you need any help, come get me. And by the way, you shouldn't be working these things out during breaks. Breaks are breaks. Sorting out assignments is part of your jobs.

>**Will**: Got it.

[Video end.]

That's an excellent response from Claire. Handling conflicts including the small ones is part of the job so she does give them permission to do that and you know what she not only gave them permission, but did you notice she went beyond that. She took the occasion to reinforce that principle that it's part of the job. So she used it as a teaching moment, nice job on Claire's part.

Employees also are going to need guidance and help to do these kinds of things and there's three ways to do that, we can do it with explicit policy, training, and modeling. To be effective, all of that guidance is going to need to be repeatedly reinforced. So we know that much.

Let's go to another principle. Let's talk about the formal processes that are going to need to be in place. What I mean here with formal processes is this. We've got to have some formal procedures in place with enforcement mechanisms and they've got to be there to handle especially issues of grievance and issues of discipline. There's got to be something to turn to if those informal preferred win-win approaches are not going to work, and I want that in place in my organization.

There are some conflicts that really do preclude win-win resolutions and they require an adversarial process. There are competitions for instance for who's going to get a single promotion. You can't necessarily split that and if someone feels wronged in a decision about that, they may need a formal procedure to try to appeal that and work with it. So I've got to have formal processes in place that we can turn to.

I've got to have procedures for adjudicating disciplinary actions and formal grievances. I need those; it's not that I want to turn to them all the time, but I need to have them in place. If they're in place I want to make sure that they're very clearly described, very explicitly and when they happen, the process needs to be very clearly and fully documented. They have to conform to any applicable laws wherever you are, and they have to conform with any employee-employer contractual agreements. There's a lot they've got to conform with. They've got to be right, they ought to be there.

I want to suggest you not be too careful to over-rely on them because they are adversarial processes. There's a marvelous organizational communications scholar named Linda Putnam, whose work I followed over the years and hearing her speak one time she pointed out that organizations, in their effort to stay out of court, can spend a fortune bringing court inside the organization with elaborate procedures for handling things in adversarial ways. That's a good point Dr. Putnam. So you don't want to overdo that, but you do need to have those procedures.

Let's turn to another principle. Organizations as I suggested in the last lecture are not just the formal structures, but there's that whole set of informal ideas and influences, the organization's culture and climate that have an effect, and these are going to influence the way employees handle their conflicts. Quite beyond whatever we say formally should be done. So I really as a manager want to assess and if appropriate improve whatever those influences are. I don't directly control them, but I can take steps that influence those informal things.

I love a definition of organizational "culture" by a management consultant who has written some wonderful pieces called Edgar Shein. Mr. Shein says that an organization's culture is whatever follows the phrase "the way it's really done around here is *fill in the blank*. What someone says after that points to the organization culture. So as a manager, I've got to recognize the limits of my influence. Management and policy affect culture, but I don't really control it.

There are some other terms and concepts that are closely related here. One of those is organizational "climate." Climate is defined as "how it feels to the employee to work here and be here." There's a term called communication climate that's related to that. It's how this scene, this environment in the organization works to invite or prohibit constructive communication. Management and policy affect all of those, and there's a great deal of overlap in those concepts.

Climate of course may be more affected locally by the conditions in a particular work unit even among a few people than by the organization as a whole and I'd want to know about that too, but that may be more the concern of a specific supervisor.

I've used the term "conflict climate" over the years to refer to that collective influence of the organization culture, the organization climate, and the communication climate, all those elements, the influence of those combined, on how an individual behaves to manage a conflict when one comes up. In that sense, the conflict climate factors include relationships among workers, the power relationships, the communication patterns, the flow of information, whether there's positive feedback and recognition, the conflict management practices that one sees around. What we do when we're in an organization and we think we have a conflict is we do sort of take in how it happens and how it feels here, and that strongly influences how we're going to go about trying to deal with it.

Those factors, lots of those factors, can be specifically identified and assessed and then I can do things as a manager to try to affect those and to try to improve on them. I should note before we leave this thing about culture and climate that organizations go through major periods of change and the change periods themselves create a lot of uncertainty which generate conflicts. So you might need to be patient and get through one of those periods.

Let's look at another principle. This one is fairly obvious. You've got to model the desired behavior in conflict management. People are going to see what you do and they're going to do that. Gandhi said once and it's been an oft quoted thing, "Be the change you wish to see in the world." Well be the conflict manager you wish to see in your employees. That one doesn't require a lot of explanation. It's really, really important. So our employees will follow it.

Now let's go down and think about first line supervisors a bit. That's a nice set of principles, but we need to focus attention on those supervisors. We need to give them particular attention because they have a very pivotal role and they operate where the outcomes are concrete. There's not the kind of wiggle room that you have in the abstractions of the office upstairs. Things either work or they don't. This is where the rubber meets the road. And they often deal with employees who have less in the way of interpersonal communication skills than people higher up.

They in a way have a bigger challenge. It's tempting if I'm a supervisor to just give orders and expect people to follow. It's also tempting to duck managing conflicts. We know the number one complaint about supervisors in conflict management in organizations is that they avoid them and don't deal with them. When they do that, that leads to a lot of discontent. So how should supervisors be handling conflict?

Let's look at another example. Here's a different office setting. Two custodial employees, Ben and Jolene. Let's see how they feel about how their supervisor Sal seems to handle conflict.

[Video start.]

> **Ben**: Just like I said. The night crew has done it again. Left all the trash cans on the 2nd floor for us to empty; and they didn't mop the bathrooms like they were supposed to do. I've talked and talked to Sal about this. He said he'll deal with the night supervisor, and he never does.

> **Jolene**: Sal's not going do anything, you know that. Maybe we should just do them a favor and leave a little dirty work for the night crew.

> **Ben**: Come on, this isn't a joke. We've got to do something.

[Video end.]

Avoidance isn't going to work here. These people need this supervisor's help, the day shift can't talk to the night shift, and they're concerned that his not helping is damaging his credibility and lowering morale. You could flip that over and go to the other extreme, which a lot of other supervisors are known to complain about. In that other extreme supervisors are expected to act kind of in loco parentis and people come to them to arbitrate everything and punish somebody I'm complaining about even though I'm not even willing to let the supervisor say who's complaining. That's a problem too, you want to push that back to the employees, but offer to help them resolve things.

Here's an example of doing that. Let's follow through with Jolene again and now she's complaining to Sal, the supervisor, about Ben.

[Video start.]

> **Jolene**: Hey Sal. Ben's complaining about the night shift again.

Sal: Okay.

Jolene: All he does is grumble about what didn't get finished. We have plenty of time to get things done.

Sal: Right.

Jolene: Can't you just tell him to stop it? I hate working with people who are in a bad mood all the time.

Sal: I get that. I kind of wish you guys would work it out, though. But, I can see what I can do.

Jolene: Okay.

[Video end.]

I'm getting a little suspicious of Jolene here. She's triangulating and we already talked about that as a dysfunctional conflict strategy. She wasn't being honest a while ago with Ben when she was agreeing with him and helping complain about Sal. She really could've told Ben what her complaint was and ask him to stop complaining. And look at the trap Sal would be in if intervenes and tells Ben to quit complaining. That's probably really going to make matters worse. Ben is just going to shut up and go grousing in a different way, but he'll be suspicious of talking to Jolene.

When a supervisee has a conflict with you, what do you do? That's another spot we ought to stop and think about here. What I want to do if I'm the supervisor is I want to listen and negotiate if it doesn't require surrendering authority, and once again it's consultation not democracy. It's hard to listen, but it's useful, so that's something I really, really want to do.

Here's an example with that. Let's look at Ben again, the custodian, and now he's coming and speaking to Sal, the supervisor. Let's see how Sal does listening to Ben.

[Video start.]

Ben: Hey Sal, I've got a complaint and a request I need to talk to you about.

Sal: Okay. What is it?

Ben: Listen, the night crew keeps leaving trash cans for Jolene and me to pick up. I've got a bad back; doctor says I'm not supposed to be lifting and twisting. I want to be exempt from having to pick up those cans. You know, it's a safety issue.

Sal: I've talked to the night supervisor about this. He says they're extremely busy and sometimes has to leave work for us to do. He also said he talked to his people. No change?

Ben: Nope. The 2nd floor cans were all waiting to be picked up again this morning.

Sal: I can talk to their super again. But about your back—you do have a doctor's note, right?

Ben: No, but I can get you one.

Sal: Yeah, I'm going to need to see that.

[Video end.]

That's good, Ben is behaving a lot better than Jolene in this particular example. He can't really negotiate with the crew himself, so he has to go to Sal for that, but he has defined the issue in terms of behavior and consequences. Sal is doing very well here. He's listening. He's offering a response. He's also checking for some evidence that he may need if he's got to do some harder bargaining on Ben's behalf. So Sal has done a good job.

After listening and rethinking and decision you make when an employee complains though, you can go ahead and make your decision and you ought to go ahead and do that. If the employee wishes to appeal that, your decision to a higher place in management, you don't want to suppress that; the best thing to do is just support it and cooperate with it. If we've got formal procedures in place, an employee wants to use them and has the right to use them, fine, let's go with that.

Let's look at an example of that. Let's go back to Sal's office a week later. He has some news to share with Ben.

[Video start.]

> **Sal**: So Ben, I've got an answer for you on the trash can issue.
>
> **Ben**: Great.
>
> **Sal**: I talked to the night crew about this and they said they'll make an extra effort to pick them up, which I think they'll do. However, I can't give make an exemption for the lifting. The doctor's note says that light lifting is okay and our trash cans are light. There's not much I can do. Look, if you come across a heavy can, and Jolene can help you, that's great.
>
> **Ben**: This is not right.
>
> **Sal**: It's the best I can do.
>
> **Ben**: This is a safety issue. I'm going to appeal this. I'm going to file a grievance.
>
> **Sal**: Well, it's within your right to do that, I'm okay with that. And if it's not too excessive, you can use work time file it.

[Video end.]

Sal has handled this really very well. It does kind of begin to look like Ben wants to see himself as a victim here; that's a possibility I may even be beginning to have some sympathy for Jolene at this point. But using formal processes, as a policy if it's appropriate, if it's fitting, he's got a right to it. Don't discourage it. Cooperate and let it play through. I really don't think Ben is going to get anywhere with this one, but if the trashcan is really heavy, that could play out and be settled in an okay way.

That's that piece. I want to strongly suggest with supervisors that we want to make our expectations clear here. We want to attempt to resolve differences constructively and that's the expectation by discussion and mutual agreement. With those employees you want to help them when they need help. Allow time, create conditions for employees to negotiate and renegotiate resolutions. When an employee brings a complaint to the supervisor that could be handled by negotiating, ask if they're willing to try rather than interceding for them with someone else, ask if they're willing to try and offer to help them if they need it. That gives you a chance to be the facilitator and the teacher.

Let's look at an example of that. Let's return to that first dramatization. Stacy, the clerical worker, is now talking to her manager Claire on the phone. Stacy and her other co-worker Will have tried to work this out and they've been unsuccessful on their dispute over the expense report issue. So Stacy is asking Claire to intervene. Let's see what Claire does.

[Video start.]

>Claire: This is Claire.

>Stacy: Hi Claire, it's Stacy and Will. We're just not getting anywhere sorting out this expense report thing. I think you're going to need to come in and settle it for us.

>Claire: Stacy, I'd rather you two figure out a solution if you can. But, I'll be glad to help you try and work through it. I'll be down in a minute.

Stacy: Okay, thanks.

[Video end.]

That's good. Claire did a good job on this. She didn't get sucked into arbitrating, which is always the temptation. But she is going to help. She's going to facilitate and that's going to give her an opportunity to teach Will and Stacy how to negotiate a little better. Claire is being an excellent supervisor in this situation.

Let's talk about the next thing that really comes up a lot for supervisors. Let's talk about feedback. I want to suggest that relative to conflict management, it's very important to give lots of informal feedback to employees and to give it to them regularly. That mostly needs to be positive feedback. You've got to catch employees doing things right and comment on it. About 80 percent of feedback needs to be positive for employees to operate at an optimal level, but that's also important because if they're getting plenty of positive feedback, they're going to be able to handle negative feedback for conflicts much better.

Let's look at an example of that. Here's a good one. Let's go back to the custodial team, Jolene, Ben, and their supervisor Sal.

[Video start.]

> **Sal**: Hey, you two. I love what you did in the break room. It really looks good in there.
>
> **Jolene**: Thanks Sal. We thought so, too.
>
> **Ben**: It feels nice when they notice what you do around here.
>
> **Jolene**: It sure does.

[Video end.]

I really like that example. Even Ben is happy at this moment and he's feeling appreciated and that wasn't that hard to do, and he and Jolene are now feeling like a team. I want you to notice there that that would've been easy to do. Positive feedback doesn't cost anything. It's easy to give and it really helps with motivation and it sets up the conditions where you have a safer environment, a more positive environment to address conflict; so positive feedback 80 percent.

While we're talking feedback I need to talk a little bit about negative feedback. I also need to provide negative feedback when it's due, and that's immediately. It ought to immediate, it ought to be informal and it ought to be private whenever performance falls short. Do not, do not wait for formal evaluations. Nothing said in a formal evaluation ought to be a surprise. Take care of it right then, and if you've got plenty of positive feedback going that's going to be a whole lot easier to do. So work those pieces together.

Let's look at an example with negative feedback. If we go back to Will and Stacy who have come to an agreement now with Claire's help, with her facilitating. Let's look at Claire deftly handling some poor behavior on Will's part and she does it in a timely and a private way.

[Video start.]

> **Stacy**: I'm really glad we got that figured out. Thanks for your help.

> **Will**: Yeah, thanks Claire.

> **Claire**: You're welcome. It's part of my job. Oh, Will. Do you have a sec?

> **Will**: Sure.

> **Claire**: For a while there you were being awfully difficult. It was like you made up your mind and just wouldn't listen. You came around in the end, and I really appreciate that. Next time, though, start trying to listen right from the get-go to what people have to say. I know it'll make the process work better.

Will: Yeah, you're right. Maybe next time I'll do a little more listening first. I think that may have been the problem all along.

[Video end.]

That negative feedback was immediate. It was private, it was measured, it was clear. It acknowledged the context where they ended up with something okay anyhow. So he was feeling pretty nicely regarded, but recognizing that there was a problem with that particular behavior. Nicely on target feedback from the supervisor.

Finally what I want to suggest with supervisors here is that you've got to model the behavior that you want from the employees. I said that for managers, that's true all the way down the line. Be the conflict manager you want your supervisees to be. We need to say a little bit about the employees. We've been talking about managers and we've been talking about supervisors, but in a way we've said what we need to say about employees because we've talked all the way through the course about how conflict ought to be handled. That's what you ought to show up as an employee prepared to do yourself.

The general principle applies: deal directly, attempt to resolve conflicts by direct mutual discussion. Use those seven steps we explained in Lectures 11 and 12; pursue mutual interests, not positions the way we explained it in Lecture 10. That's what you ought to be doing. But if you're at all in doubt about whether that approach is acceptable or is the norm in the organization you're in, you need to ask about that. If you get a yes answer that's official, check out the culture too to see if that's comfortable within a culture because it's not going to be safe to be too far out of line with the way things are done here generally.

If it's not that way and you've been in the organization for awhile and you've built some credibility and you're seen as a valued person, you may have a chance to move conflict management behavior in the same useful direction that I've been talking about with supervisors and managers. If conflicts are handled badly and the handling stays bad and its affecting you negatively, what I want to make to you is a hardnosed suggestion. You might very well if at all possible want to seek another affiliation. You don't need to stay in a place where things aren't handled well.

Speaking of things not being handled well, I want to just briefly mention a problem that's really not within the realm of normal conflict management, but it comes up often whenever I work with people or teach managers and supervisors about conflict management. That's the problem of bullies in the workplace. It's really a very special problem.

The term bullies, bullying means it's repeated mistreatment of someone in particular, someone gets targeted and they're being repeatedly mistreated, that's verbally and in other ways. It's very harmful and it's much more commonplace than one would expect. It causes emotional and physical harm. It can corrupt the whole workplace culture and climate. When that happens, if you're the target of that, you need to confront it, stand up to it if you can, you need to report it, ask for help, get counseling.

If you're a supervisor and a manager and someone is doing that kind of behavior and you find out about it, that's especially a case when you need to be tough, stand up to it, deal with it, and work on getting it resolved even if it means that you have to lose a really valued employee who happened to be the bully. You've got to stand up to that or it will cost the organization a lot more if you don't.

Let's summarize. What do we want to say now about managers and supervisors and employees handling conflict in the organization? One, avoid those inhibiting influences from classical management; think in terms of what the human resources and organizational systems people and all the organizational cultures people taught us.

Two, primary concern of managers and supervisors ought to be to ensure that everyday conflicts are handled constructively by all the employees. Three, establish and communicate clear policies concerning management of conflict and provide training when it's needed. Four, provide for formal procedures for disciplinary actions and grievances as needed. Five, prevent unnecessary conflict by clearly defining roles and responsibilities, and then work with employees to address conflicts promptly when they arise.

Six, managers and supervisors need to model the conflict behavior they wish to see from their employees. Seven, supervisors have a pivotal role. They guide, teach, and help, and they arbitrate only when necessary. That's important to recognize.

Better conflict management means better morale, less absenteeism. It means less turn over. It means stronger employee motivation, better productivity. It's great for the bottom line, ample business reasons for better conflict management, so we've got to work on them.

But organizations are not just places where we work and produce things and make money. They're also human environments where we live, where we spend much of our lives, and so if we manage conflict better there we'll be happier, we'll be more joyful, we'll have better lives in organizations, and I think the fact that they're human environments constitute an even better reason for us to manage our conflicts well.

Let me give you an assignment from this lecture. I want to suggest that you think about the organization where you work or volunteer. Think about how well everyday conflicts, the ordinary ones, are handled there and what might be the dominant pattern, is it really mutual discussion and agreement. If it is, count yourself lucky and the assignment is done. If it's not, here's a couple of hard questions. What do I think is my role in that? Am I helping or hurting? And what can I do to make the management of conflict better there?

Let me give you a preview of Lecture 18 now. If we're looking to improve conflict management in general, or for help in managing any particular conflict, the fact is there's plenty of good professional help available and you want to be able to turn to it. So where are we going to turn from here? In our next lecture is where to get help for couples, families, organizations, relationships, and communities. That's our next lecture.

Getting Professional Help with Conflict
Lecture 18

Most individuals are unable to fully pursue resolution of a dispute through the courts because they just can't afford it. Organizations and insurers even calculate that it's less expensive to write checks—sometimes six- and seven-figure checks—than to take a case to court.

It should be abundantly clear by now that managing conflict is among the most difficult, dangerous, and challenging things humans have to do. One fortunate consequence of all the research and development that has taken place on this subject is that a good deal of competent professional help is available for handling conflict.

A primary reason you might want to get help in a conflict is that the formal adversary system—the legal system—is expensive in terms of money and time. Taking matters to court also often results in collateral damage, such as when children are involved in hostile divorce cases. Further, courts provide only win-lose resolutions.

Studies show that the mere presence of an objective third party can help in achieving conflict resolution; the disputing parties become more cooperative, more reasonable, and less extreme. A general rule is to start by seeking help with a conflict at the lowest and least formal level possible, where the risks are lowest and it's easiest to achieve a win-win. In this lecture, however, we'll start at the highest level and work our way downward.

The highest level of assistance below the courts is arbitration or mediation, solutions that are often promoted by attorneys, state and local governments, and counselors. According to the American Arbitration Association, arbitration is "a legal technique for resolution of disputes outside the courts, wherein the parties to a dispute refer it to one or more persons who are arbitrators, by whose decision they agree in advance to be bound." Many **arbitrators** are attorneys and, in most areas, they must be licensed to practice arbitration. They must be impartial in any dispute, and they must conduct investigations and hearings according to specified rules, including rules of evidence. Attorneys or advocates can participate on both sides, but arbitrators themselves can question the disputants and the advocates; witnesses can also be presented and questioned. Arbitration proceedings may have legal status and the decisions may carry legal weight. Arbitration is generally much less expensive than court proceedings and brings quicker results, but it does not offer win-win resolutions.

According to the National Association of Community Mediation, the definition of mediation is as follows: "a process of dispute resolution in which one or more impartial third parties intervenes in a conflict or dispute with the consent of the participants and assists them in negotiating a consensual and informed agreement." The task of **mediators** is broader than that of arbitrators; these professionals intervene and help with the consent of both participants. Mediation is often suggested for marital disputes or family conflicts, and it may be provided for in labor contracts. Like arbitrators, mediators undergo specialized training and must pass a certification test. Notice that mediation is not an adversarial process; it allows disputants to reach a win-win resolution. In general, these five characteristics define the mediation process: (1) voluntary, (2) collaborative, (3) confidential, (4) informed, and (5) neutral and balanced.

Studies show that the mere presence of an objective third party can help in achieving conflict resolution; the disputing parties become more cooperative, more reasonable, and less extreme.

The next step down the ladder is the **ombudsman**, who assists with problem-solving on behalf of a community or an organization. Many organizational ombudsmen are members of the International Ombudsman Association and adhere to certain standards of practice. Ombudsmen must have independence in structure, function, and appearance; in other words, they shouldn't be part of the classical management chain of command. Like mediators, they are neutral and impartial, and they hold all communications in confidence. They do not participate in formal adjudication, such as arbitration or court proceedings. Many organizations find that retaining an ombudsman is a cost-effective way to resolve conflicts. In some organizations, an informal ombudsman, referred to as a "priest," may emerge. This is an individual who has been with the organization for a long time and has built a reputation as being wise, trustworthy, and willing to listen to and help others.

Finally, we arrive at counselors, who may specialize in marriage and family issues, employee assistance, community problems, or education. Counselors have varying education requirements and training, depending on their specialty and location. In seeking the help of a counselor, it's important for all the parties involved to agree in advance to counseling. In family or marriage counseling, both parents or spouses should participate in identifying and selecting the counselor.

It's a good idea to know what kinds of professionals are available to help before you need them in the midst of a stressful situation. As we said, first seek the lowest level of help, then work your way up the ladder if the conflict requires it. ■

Important Terms

arbitrator: A person with designated authority to hear and evaluate cases and render a binding or nonbinding decision on an issue between parties engaged in a dispute.

mediator: A person who is trained to act as a neutral third party and who helps disputants, with their consent, negotiate a mutual agreement among themselves, seeking win-win solutions whenever possible.

ombudsman: A person appointed to act as an informal, neutral, independent, and confidential intermediary to help solve problems or manage conflicts.

Suggested Reading

Cloke, *Mediating Dangerously: The Frontiers of Conflict Resolution*.

1. Find out what counseling, ombudsman, mediation, and arbitration services are available to you and under what circumstances. Inquire by phone or via the Web sites listed below about specific services offered. Find out what help is offered in your workplace. Ask friends, family, and colleagues for recommendations and keep the contact information you gain on hand.

Resources

Association for Conflict Resolution
12100 Sunset Hills Rd., Suite 130
Reston, VA 20190
http://www.acrnet.org/

National Academy of Arbitrators
NAA Operations Center, Suite 412
1 North Main St.
Cortland, NY 13045
http://www.naarb.org/

American Arbitration Association, Washington, DC, Regional Office
1776 Eye St. NW, Suite 850
Washington, DC 20006
http://www.adr.org/

International Ombudsman Association
390 Amwell Rd., Suite 403
Hillsborough, NJ 08844
http://www.ombudsassociation.org/

United States Ombudsman Association
5619 86th St. NW, Suite 600
Johnston, IA 50131-2955
http://www.usombudsman.org/

The Ombudsman Association
5521 Greenville Ave., Suite 104-265
Dallas, TX 75206
http://web.mit.edu/negotiation/toa/TOAintro.html

National Association for Community Mediation
P.O. Box 44578
Madison, WI 53744
http://www.nafcm.org/pg89.cfm

American Counseling Association
5999 Stevenson Ave.
Alexandria, VA 22304
http://www.counseling.org/

Getting Professional Help with Conflict
Lecture 18—Transcript

It should be abundantly clear by now that managing conflict is among the most difficult and dangerous and challenging things humans have to do. Especially that's true when we have to learn new ways to deal with conflict, which increase the challenge, new ways overall of that early learning that we're trying to overcome. It turns out that even the most skilled among us find that there are occasions when we could really use some help managing conflict. One really fortunate consequence of all that research and development that has taken place on this subject is that these days there are lots of competent professional help that's available. So that's what we're going to talk about in this lecture.

We're going to talk about where to get help. We're going to talk specifically about the roles of the professional arbitrators, mediators, ombudsmen, and counselors. We'll throw in a little short discussion of an informal role by organizational role called priests in organizational cultures. We'll note the role each of these plays and how they're different and talk about when to choose and what kind of help you get from each kind of helper that's available.

Let's get started right away. Let's start with why you really would want to do that. Why is it important to go get help? One way to think about that is that the existing ways to get formal help are awfully expensive. The adversary system, the courts, that's expensive and it's slow and it has bad side effects. Judges and courtroom staff and juries, the buildings those are all very costly. Court calendars get clogged. It can take months or years to get a hearing. Resolving things through the courts may cost more and require more time than disputants can actually afford.

Most individuals are unable to fully pursue resolution of a dispute through the courts because they just can't afford it. Organizations and insurers even calculate that it's less expensive to write checks, sometimes six and seven figure checks, than to take a case to court. Taxpayers of course resist increasing public expenditures for courts because taxes are high enough. Taking matters to court often creates serious collateral damage. I think about this often with of children of couples who take an ugly divorce to court and the damage to those kids. Then there's the lingering hostility that occurs with people after a judge renders a decision, and often when things are fought out in court reputations are permanently damaged.

So courts, they have a necessary function, but it's often not necessary to take things to court. As Deutsch told us back in Lecture 3, win-wins are often possible and courts don't provide win-wins. Courts only provide win-lose. You think back to the bible case of King Solomon trying to arbitrate the dispute between the disputing mothers and there's no compromise possible or win-win when it's one baby and two pretending mothers.

It turns out though that the mere presence of an objective third party, somebody who's seen by both sides as objective really can help in getting a conflict resolved. Studies show that that fact alone helps cause the disputing parties to become more cooperative, more reasonable, and less extreme. So there's value in resolving disputes in win-win ways, but we still may need help to do it.

So we've got some clear guidelines to follow when it comes to that. One thing is just go ahead and recognize there's a virtual army of trained, skilled helpers out there that are available. There are different kinds of help for different situations. It's going to be a good idea and we'll suggest this again at the end of the lecture to know what kind of help is available for you and to know what's available locally to you for seeking help and to know that before you get in trouble and really need it badly.

Then there's a sort of general principle that I want to follow. I'll do the lecture backwards from the principle, but I want to get it enunciated here at the beginning. In general you want to seek help at the lowest level possible and the least formal level possible. The risks are least at that level. It's easiest to get to win-win.

For this lecture we need to start at the highest level below the courts and work our way down to that most desirable kind of help. So let's start here. There are plenty of trained practitioners that are available for help. Many of them are actually attorneys and they've added this kind of competence.

Help for this kind of thing, win-win solutions, has actually been very much promoted by the American Bar Association here in this country really seeing that courts are too expensive and that resolutions without taking it to court and fighting it out are very useful. So even the Bar Association has been promoting arbitration and mediation, and it's exercised the leadership in promoting this kind of thing.

I remember very well a young attorney that I think I talked about in another lecture when I was talking about win-win and the young attorney on the boat having to read *How to Get to Yes* because he was expected to have this kind of competence when he went to work for an organization. Your attorney, if he's a good one, is likely to recommend if possible staying out of court and working out a win-win if possible. Even the attorneys have moved in that direction. State and local governments have pushed for not having to go to court, sometimes requiring that certain kinds of disputes, especially marital disputes be attempted for resolution by mediation or something before you actually take the case to court.

The help for this has sort of evolved in two directions, the pushing down from the formal procedures by the Bar Association and the people who work from an adversarial approach, and then pushing it in the other direction through clinical psychology and counseling and moving toward win-win resolutions, the social scientists. Out of all of that you've got this cadre of professional approaches, several different ones adapted to certain situations and there's a broad array of them. We're going to talk about four in particular.

We're going to talk about arbitrators. We're going to talk about mediators, about ombudsmen, and counselors. Each of these professions has its own body of knowledge, although they overlap, a clear body of knowledge and standards of practice, and schooling requirements they have to meet in order to practice. So let's talk about them one at a time. Let's start with arbitrators.

Arbitrators hear and evaluate disputants' cases and then render judgments. Let me give you a definition, I want to read it to make sure I get it right. This is the definition that comes from the American Arbitration Association. They say that arbitration is "a legal technique for resolution of disputes outside the courts, wherein the parties to a dispute refer it to one or more persons who are arbitrators, by whose decision they agree in advance to be bound."

I read it because it's a long sentence and it's tricky to make sure you get it right. But there's the point, and when you read it and listen to it what does it sound like. You know what it sounds like to me? It sounds exactly like those ancient Greeks 2,500 years ago. Let's get a third person we trust and present our case to that person and let that person decide and agree to be bound by the decision. That's the concept of arbitration and it doesn't have to go all the way to court if we can identify someone that can do that.

In most areas arbitrators have to be licensed in order to practice and they're typically licensed attorneys before they get into arbitration. They need to complete a set of training in order to do that and they're tested and certified when they complete that training. In some places they're required to complete additional training the same way doctors and nurses and other professionals are in order to keep up and maintain their certificate.

They have standards of practice and the keys to those standards are this. They not only have to be, but they have to clearly appear to be impartial in a dispute and then they have to conduct any investigation and hearing according to specified rules that are provided for in that locale or in that organization. There's a set of specified rules and they have to conduct the investigation and in a hearing according to those.

Like the courts, arbitration is an adversarial process. We're not down to win-win yet. The disputants are fighting it out, but it's a lower level, it's less costly, and less hostile than the courts normally. This is a quasi-legal process, arbitration. Disputants do present cases orally or in writing depending on the circumstance. There are rules of evidence required for arbitration, but they're less stringent than the courts. Attorneys or advocates can participate on both sides, but arbitrators themselves can question the disputants and the advocates so they can try to get at the answers themselves. They can ask questions and pursue. Witnesses, of course, can be presented and they can be questioned.

After hearing the cases, gathering the information and listening to both sides, the arbitrator then within a specified time renders a decision. Records are kept in an arbitration process. These proceedings may have legal status and the decision may have legal weight. Arbitration is generally much less expensive than court procedures and usually gets a resolution more quickly, so it's more useful for that reason. So it may be the best alternative.

When would it be the best alternative? If I need a clear and documented resolution to a dispute that I couldn't get a win-win on, and there's no method that's non-adversarial, no way to get to a win-win resolution that would do it. Sometimes arbitration in that instance is going to be the best answer. It's nice to know that it's there and to be able to appeal to it if we need to.

Now let's talk about mediators. What mediators do is assist disputants in negotiating resolutions. Let me give you the definition of mediation and this one comes from the National Association of Community Mediation. They say "mediation is a process of dispute resolution in which one or more impartial third parties intervenes in a conflict or dispute with the consent of the participants and assists them in negotiating a consensual and informed agreement." That a nice definition carefully including all the aspects. What mediators do is broader than arbitrators. They intervene and help with the consent of both participants.

Mediation is widely available to help with such things as marital disputes and frequently courts require an attempt at mediation before granting a divorce. You can be pushed to mediation there. Mediations is available for family conflicts and that really helps often. Mediations is often available in organizational disputes and it's often provided for in the contracts, in the labor contracts. It's interesting to me that way back in 1934, the National Mediation Board for Labor/Management disputes in railroads was established. So it goes all the way back that far. Mediation is available for disputes in the community as well.

So mediators are around. There are a great many of them and many of them do excellent, excellent work. How do they qualify for what they do? Well, they need to complete mediation training and it varies with where you're going to be licensed, anywhere from a minimum of about 40 hour to about

100 hours of training that mediators go through to prepare. Then they complete a specified number of hours doing mediation under the supervision of a licensed mediator, usually around 500 hours.

So if you've got a licensed mediator that's a person who has been trained and done a lot of mediating under supervision already, so that's an experienced person with this. Of course then they have to pass a certification test and be certified to function as a mediator. So you get trained mediators.

What's the mediator's role? As I said it's broader than arbitration. But notice mediation is not an adversarial process; now we've moved over into the win-win category so we're down at a less formal level and we've got a much better shot at a win-win. The mediator's job is "assist" in a variety of ways to try to get that win-win to happen. They can assist in almost any way useful as long as they remain impartial. Many effective mediators work at this profession and it has evolved in that direction from something else.

My favorite example of a mediator that I admire a great deal is a gentleman named Kenneth Cloke. I first encountered Mr. Cloke when he spoke at an International Ombudsmen Association Conference that I was attending several years ago. Mr. Cloke started out as an attorney and he was very effective that way; he then became an arbitrator and he was constrained by the problem of arbitrating and really saw the value of win-win and so he then became a mediator. He evolved in that direction just the way our learning about conflict management has evolved. He helps resolve conflicts literally everything from couples and individuals and families up through organizations, all the way up through major international disputes. He literally travels worldwide mediating conflicts.

He directs an organization called the Center for Dispute Resolution out in California. That's just one example. There are thousands of effective mediators.

What do mediations processes look like? Mediation process ought to have about five defining characteristics. Number one, a mediation process ought to be voluntary. Sometimes they are exceptions because of court ordered.

You have to do this before you can get a divorce, but generally speaking mediation should occur with the consent of all the disputants involved.

Secondly it ought to be collaborative. We ought to be looking for a collaborative solution. That ought to be the style, the conflict resolution style with mediations occurring and the mediator works to get all the disputants to work together with him or her to produce a win-win agreement. Thirdly, mediation processes, unless they're otherwise specified should be confidential. These are not matters of any public record normally. There are exceptions, but normally they're not.

Fourth, mediation processes should be informed, and I love the way the mediators talk about it. Mediators understand that one of their jobs is to ensure that all the parties in this dispute have a full set of information that they need to make decisions. They don't withhold information from everybody. They make sure everybody knows everything they need to know; that the process and all they're working with, their decisions are transparent. Then finally that process ought to be neutral and balanced. I've never been fully comfortable with the word "neutral" myself; I like to tell clients that I work with that I'm equally on both sides. Neutral might suggest that I'm disengaged.

But that's really what mediators mean when they say neutral. Neutral and balanced, the mediator really strives to have all the parties equally helped by his or her service. Mediators do some great work.

Mediation is a good alternative when it is important for the sake of the relationship to resolve a dispute. If it's necessary and you're not getting there yourself, it's very helpful to get a mediator. Secondly when conflicting parties are expressing strong emotions that intervene with what's going on, when you're feeling a lot of emotions and you're having a hard time handling it yourself, it's really helpful to have an effective third party who's neutral in that sense, on both of your sides, help you work through something. Mediators are very good with that, even when you're in a conflict with someone you love.

Mediators are also especially useful when there may be third parties like children in a family or other members in the community or in the organizations who might be harmed if the thing is not settled in a harmonious way. Mediators are helpful for that. Of course there needs to be a reasonable chance for resolution by this means before you would move it to something that would more confirm, a documented resolution like arbitration, you've got to have a shot at getting it resolved. So that's when you would want to use mediations.

Let's turn now to our third profession and let's talk about ombudsmen. What ombudsmen do is provide an informal, confidential service to solve problems and resolve conflicts. The ombudsmen's role is wider even than the mediators because ombudsmen field all kinds of problems that are brought to them. Ombudsmen are appointed to serve as avenues through which these problems can be identified and understood. Any of us who've worked as ombuds persons, and I've done a good deal of ombudsing over time, know that a good percentage of the problems that come to us, a clear majority, involve conflicts of some sort. So they're very much involved with helping solve conflicts.

The term ombudsmen began in Scandinavia and it's an appointed problem solver for a community or an organization. The service of an ombudsmen is provided to the individual who brings the problem to that person. An ombudsmen is set up to respond to someone who brings him or her a problem and help them out, not as an individual benefit, but organizations and communities who appoint ombudsmen and fund that kind of work benefit by having this avenue of redress available for individuals. It really helps getting conflicts resolved in a non-costly way.

So, let me talk just about one set of ombudsmen that's sort of most defined and there's a consistency about. It's a growing area and that's the area of what are called the organizational ombudsman. These are people who are appointed by an organization and have a role of ombudsmen in an organization. Most of the members of the association called the International Ombudsman Association are actually that kind of ombuds person.

Ombudsmen in this sense have standards of practice that are clearly delineated. First they have independence in structure, function, and appearance. If you think about that for second, an independence within the organization in structure, function, and appearance. They don't want to be down the line somewhere and reporting up the chain of command because then anybody coming to them can't fully trust what's going to happen. So the ombudsmen's role really should have kind of a dotted line on that organization chart that we had from classical management that goes, at best, to the president, the top person in the organization, ought to be very high up and ought to be clearly disconnected so that they can be separate and impartial.

Second standard of practice is that like the mediator, they've got to be neutral and impartial. Here again neutral means equally on everybody's side. That when somebody brings the ombuds person a problem, they go am I going to be neutral, yeah, I'm not going to be a triangulation avenue here where I'm going to jump in and advocate for you. I'm going to help you with your problem, but I'm on everybody's side if I'm an ombudsmen.

Third standard is confidentiality. An ombudsmen is required to hold all communication in confidence and divulge that information only if clearly authorized to do so. Ombudsmen often, if they keep records at all, they destroy them at the end of dealing with that person. Sometimes you have to take notes just so you can remember, but get rid of them as quickly as you can. Ombudsmen often like to avoid communications on email that might go somewhere else because they're very concerned with confidentiality. That's important in organizations where there are power struggles and people are afraid of things coming to them.

The only time you can divulge is when there's imminent risk of serious harm unless you've got permission. That's generally supported legally. That's the claim they make. They have a legal right to it and it's been tested in the courts some, but it's generally holding up and being supported.

Fourth standard of practice is informality. What this means is that the ombuds person is not going to participate in any formal adjudication, not in arbitration, not in court, won't go testify, it connects with the business of confidentiality. Why is that? It turns out that a great many conflicts you're going to have people be able to be free and open and work for a win-win if it's not going on the record, if it can be kept off the record and kept confidential. It requires much more willingness of the parties to handle, but it's nice to keep it off the record.

These organizational ombudsmen really constitute a rapidly-growing profession. Lots of organizations are finding that it's much more cost effective to have an ombudsmen on board doing that job than not. They are a cost effective way to solve problems and resolve conflicts. Most of what they do is coaching the individual who comes to them, but they also facilitate. They do many of the same kinds of things that mediators do. So ombudsmen are very useful and particularly available in organizations.

They have their own standards of practice clearly delineated. This is a more recent organization in terms of being defined as a clear profession. Their training is getting standardized and it's somewhat standardized already and certification is now available through the International Ombudsmen Association. So that profession is growing and developing and many organizations are finding it really useful.

When would you want to use it? It's best to use an ombuds person when? You are not certain how to define a felt problem or proceed in a conflict or not knowing, have the information, especially if you need some coaching, that's a person you can go to and get it; and get it without risking triangulation or making trouble. That's a very useful function for the ombudsmen and that's a time when you want to use it. Suppose you wish to keep a problem or a conflict confidential and keep the resolution efforts off the record. Hmm, ombuds person is very useful for that.

Then too if you think you may want to escalate later if you can't get this and you don't want to create a messy piece of record by what you might concede or discuss when you talk about it, that's a really good use of an ombuds person. So these are people that are available and they can help and there're a really valuable times to use them. So you would want to seek the help of an ombudsmen if you don't want it to become part of the official record, if this approach can be done without jeopardizing, or it can be done without jeopardizing a formal proceeding later, and you may want to go that direction, so do that. Seek the help of an ombudsman if possible and if in doubt go seek the help of an ombuds person because it's confidential and you're only investing a little time and you may find it very helpful. It's excellent help in most organizations.

Before we leave that ombuds role I want to talk about the informal ombuds role played by people that could be called priests in an organization. Some years ago two wonderful management theorists in Deal and Kennedy, they had a book called *Corporate Cultures*. They really helped us understand the informal cultures that organizations developed in their work and they laid our roles that different people acquire in organizations in an informal way. The role that's of interest to us in this case is the role of what they called priests.

A priest according to Deal and Kennedy in an organization is someone who has just emerged in the organization, having been there a long time, and has built a reputation among others as being wise and trustworthy and willing to listen and help and to give balanced even advice. The priest is someone people really go to often when they're having a conflict and they don't know what to do. Priests are most typically not in the line of supervisory authority although they're often people who were in that role before and once had more supervisory authority.

Priests are people that people often go to for coaching and help. They over time build a lot of skill in this way and a reputation for handling informal roles well. I know several ombudsmen myself who are officially ombudsmen now and trained as that who had emerged as priests in their organization so they were asked to become the ombudsmen. They get a lot of the same skills, they build it over time. You can trust them very often, but they don't have the official level of confidentiality that the official ombudsmen provides. So you might have some concern there. Some organizations have excellent priests who can advise and help you.

One more profession to talk about and this one varies widely. There are a number of different kinds. This is the profession of counselors. They come in a variety of specializations. There are primary specialties like family and marriage counseling. There are organizational counselors usually attached to employee assistance programs. They're called EAP programs. At the community level there are community counselors, and communities provide them. At varying levels of education there are counselors provided for people to help with counselors at the university to help students when they have problems for instance and employees through the Employee Assistance Program.

Counselors have varying education requirements and training depending on what kind of counselor you are and what state you're going to be licensed in. When would you want to go to a counselor? You do that if a problem appears to be particularly difficult to address. If it's a conflict that appears to be significantly able to damage a relationship and you're not sure that you can handle it, a counselor can often help you with that. Marriage and family counselors do a whole lot of that and some of them do just wonderful work.

In seeking the help of a counselor though to manage a conflict, here are some useful guidelines. It's very important that both of the parties, or if it's more than two, all of the parties in the conflict agree in advance to work with the counselors. Then both of those parties ought to participate in identifying and selecting counselors. It's a good idea to go together and interview several and then discuss and agree between you before you start working with a counselor on which one the two of you agree is best to work with. So that's a really good idea with counselors.

There are four different professions then: arbitrators, mediators, ombuds, and counselors. There is lots of help available.

Let's summarize. As I say we've got a virtual army of help out there that's available and it can be available when you need it. Arbitrators, you want to seek their help if you really need a documented resolution of a dispute and there's no less adversarial way to get it. Mediators, seek their help when a relationship is at stake or when the conflicting parties are really experiencing very strong emotions about an issue and can't seem to get through it on their own, a mediator can really help you a lot.

Ombudsmen, seek their help with a broad variety of problems including conflicts, but especially for seeing when you really want to keep that conflict off the record or when you're considering escalating to a formal effort later and you want to be free to really try a win-win before you do that without damaging the case you might present in a formal case. Counselors, seek their help especially with couples and family and community conflicts. They're very much available to help you and they are of course in organizations, those organizational priests. If you know a good one, that might be the right person you can go to. Don't be afraid to ask for help.

It's a very good idea to know, as I said at the beginning of this lecture, what help is available before you need it because when you need it it's going to be a little stressful to go looking. In general you want to seek the lowest level, the least formal means of help available so counselor, ombuds, mediation, up to arbitration only if you need it. Be very careful in your choice of a helper. Some are actually better than others, so seek the best person available, interview people, advance, check, get advice on who to get, but there's plenty of excellent help out there.

Let's give you an assignment for this time and there's a very obvious assignment that comes from this lecture with what I've been saying. I want to suggest that you find out what counseling, ombudsman, and mediation, and arbitration services are available to you in your community and organization. Know what's available. You might inquire by phone, go on Web sites, do a good job of looking to see what help is available, know what it is and have that list. It's nice to have that before you get in trouble and really need the help. You would ask friends, look for recommendations. Get yourself a good set of advice and have yourself a list of who you'd go to for help.

Where are we going from here? Sometimes it's not a matter of my going to look for help, other times informally as inadequate as we may feel we are, others will come to us and ask for help. When they do that there's always a risk of triangulation when we're asked. But still there are times when we could actually help others resolve a conflict and do it constructively and play a useful role in helping other family members, work colleagues, friends, whoever, helping others resolve conflict. So we need to do a lecture on that and that's what we will do next.

Helping Others Manage Conflict
Lecture 19

That victim/rescuer setup is a terrible temptation into a triangulation role. It may feel noble riding to the rescue and helping someone who feels weak, but being the victim is damaging to the victim.

There may be times when you're asked to serve as a neutral third party for others who are in conflict. One of the most important ways you can help is through coaching, that is, prompting the disputants to identify their goals, recognize each other's perspectives, and decide whether and how to proceed with a resolution effort. You might also serve as an informal mediator or facilitator. In this role, you sit down with the disputants and guide them through a constructive conversation.

Intervening as a third party in a conflict should not be undertaken lightly. You should first ask whether you have clear authorization from both parties to intervene. You should also ascertain whether or not the conflicting parties are truly interested in finding a mutually satisfactory solution. If one or both parties are unwilling to commit to working toward a real resolution, you may want to refrain from engaging.

Before you step in to help, ask yourself whether you have the necessary communication skills. Are you good at listening? Do you have the ability to empathize with people? Can you analyze issues and ask helpful questions? You also have to be honest and trustworthy and have the right motives for wanting to help; avoid self-centered reasons for getting involved in a conflict.

Determine your specific role and get agreement from all parties involved about what assistance you will give. Make it clear that you're not interested in taking sides; you must be neutral and impartial, just like the professional mediators and ombudsmen.

If only one person comes to you for help, you can serve as a coach, but remember that you're hearing only one side of the conflict. Validate the disputant's feelings and express your understanding, but don't jump in and take sides. Try to be a calming and empowering influence. Encourage the person who has come to you to think about a mutually satisfactory resolution. You may want to walk through the beginning of the seven-step negotiation process, as we discussed in Lecture 11.

If you're asked to serve as a mediator or facilitator, spell out your role and the roles of the disputants, along with the process that all parties will follow. The disputants must own the content of their negotiations and agreements; your job is to promote open communication and to guide them in a fair process of resolution.

If you arrange a meeting between the parties, begin by thanking them for their willingness to trust you and encourage them to seek a resolution that will serve everyone involved. To create a safe environment, you may need to set some ground rules, such as prohibiting personal attacks. Guide the discussion using the steps for negotiation we covered in Lecture 12. Ask questions as the discussion progresses and check perceptions, but make sure the parties address their remarks to each other, not you. Observe carefully to ensure that verbal and nonverbal messages match. Keep the parties focused on the current conflict; if other issues arise, you may want to keep a list of these to negotiate at a later time. Once the parties have described their perceptions of the conflict, ask for suggestions to resolve it. If the conflict appears complex and resistant to solution, suggest **fractionation**, that is, breaking the problem into parts and working on one issue at a time. Throughout this process, honor and validate expressions of the parties' emotions, but don't allow them to get out of hand. Keep your own tone level and discourage emotional escalation.

When an agreement is reached, make sure that its content is clear and focused on behavior. At this point, you may also need to clarify what your role will be in following up with the parties on the agreement.

As you work through this process, you may be able to help disputing parties recognize and rethink their patterns of conflict management. One expert says that if a conflict has come up over the same issue three times, it's not about the issue but about the pattern of communication and resolution. In an assessment role, you're not just guiding the participants through negotiation but making suggestions for handling conflict differently. Engage the participants as stakeholders and treat the process as an exercise in problem-solving. Observe, describe, and analyze patterns of interaction in conflict management to diagnose problems and suggest solutions. Keep in mind that if this assessment does not lead to action and improvement, increased conflict may result. It's important, therefore, to get agreement on concrete, positive steps from all parties involved. ∎

Important Term

fractionation: A useful conflict management technique that consists of breaking or "chunking " large conflicts into smaller parts and dealing with the parts separately.

Suggested Reading

Cloke, *Mediating Dangerously: The Frontiers of Conflict Resolution.*

McCorkle and Reese, *Mediation Theory and Practice.*

Assignment

1. Look back at the last time you tried to help someone else with a conflict, and ask yourself these important questions:

   - How well did your intervention work out?

   - Was the appeal to you for help a case of triangulation?

   - Did you try to focus your help on coaching or mediating?

   - If you tried to mediate or facilitate, did you stay focused on the process the conflicting parties were engaged in, or did you get involved in the content?

   - If the intervention didn't work out perfectly, what might you do differently if you had the chance to do it again?

Helping Others Manage Conflict
Lecture 19—Transcript

We've talked about where to get help now, but there are some times when we're called upon to step up and actually be the helper. While triangulation is definitely a dysfunctional strategy that we need to avoid and we'll talk about how to do that, there really are times when we as a neutral party can step up as that third party and help others solve a conflict. There are times when we're called upon as a friend, a family member, or work colleague, or as a supervisor or a manager to step in and help.

In this lecture we're going to talk about when and how to help others in guiding a resolution process. We're going to offer you some important guidelines, guidelines for amateurs and point out some pitfalls to avoid.

How can third parties help? Begin by noting as we did in the last lecture that an objective third party all by itself being present for a conflict management process, understood as a neutral third party and objective, helps because the parties in the conflict tend to calm down, they tend to get more reasonable, and they tend to get more cooperative just your being there. You're already helping if you're trusted as being neutral and impartial, you're already helping just by your presence.

But there are more specific ways and the first one of those is coaching. You can help people sort through an issue, help them identify their goals, help them recognize the other party's perspective, help them decide whether and how to proceed with a resolution effort. That's a common way to help people informally in conflict resolution.

Here's an example. It's kind of a small conflict that could foul up a friendship or in this case a family, including the person, that would be you, who's being asked for help. Here we're going to look at two sisters Phyllis and Margaret and they're talking about working with their older sister Sue on a plan for their parent's 50th wedding anniversary party. Let's listen in.

[Video start.]

Phyllis: I just get the feeling Sue doesn't trust me to help with Mom and Dad's anniversary party. You know, she's not giving me any of the information I need. I may be the youngest, but we're all adults now. I figured she'd be happy to have me do this. It's not only frustrating, it hurts.

Margaret: Well, I can see you're upset, and I do understand.

Phyllis: Well, do you think you could talk to her for me?

Margaret: I think you ought to talk to her yourself. But I can help you sort things out so that you can figure out exactly what it is that you need from her. I mean, she did ask for your help.

Phyllis: Well, okay.

Margaret: Okay. So what is it that you need from Sue?

Phyllis: First of all, I need a list of people to invite …

[Video end.]

Notice what Margaret is doing here. She's beginning to help Phyllis pin down what the problem is. She's coaching; that's an appropriate role. She's not stepping in and triangulating the conflict. She's just helping. Coaching is not telling the other person how to resolve their conflict, it's helping them think it through and decide. So that's coaching.

What's a second way that you can help as an informal mediator, just helping others resolve a conflict? Second way would be serving as that mediator, guiding the parties through a constructive conversation process where you actually sit down with them and you focus on the process and keep them on track and in motion so that they can focus on the content. It's important if you do that, that you don't focus on the content. That's theirs. Let them deal with resolving the thing, but you help them stay focused on the issue themselves, keep them taking turns speaking, and help get them to listen to one another.

How might that look? Let's look at an example of that. In this one we're going to look at the three sisters meeting, Margaret serving as an informal mediator for Phyllis and Sue. Let's listen in again.

[Video start.]

> **Margaret**: Well, thanks for letting me help. I think just have a few things that we need to iron out, so let's try to stay on track. This party's just around the corner.
>
> **Phyllis**: Yeah, and we need to get our invitations out soon.
>
> **Sue**: And that's just the tip of the iceberg of all we have to do.
>
> **Margaret**: Okay. Well, let's just settle what we can get done here. Phyllis, you needed some information from Sue?
>
> **Phyllis**: That's right.
>
> **Margaret**: Sue, You on board?
>
> **Sue**: Sure.
>
> **Margaret**: Okay then, maybe Phyllis, you could just start us off and tell us what you need.
>
> **Phyllis**: Well, okay. To start with, I need a complete list of people to invite, and we need to agree on our budget.

[Video end.]

That's going pretty smoothly. They all seem to be agreeing that sharing the information and it's the purpose of this meeting and they're moving toward doing that. Notice the process guide, and it's often called facilitating, that overlaps with the meaning of mediating a lot. Facilitating means just making it easier. In this case Margaret is making it easier for Sue and Phyllis to focus on the content of what they need to decide. It's handling the process so the participants can focus on the content and sort out a satisfactory conclusion.

So that's that. There's a third way that you can informally help others deal with conflict. What this one is about is helping the parties involved assess the patterns, the general patterns, that emerge and that they're going through in their efforts to deal with conflict. This can be done, by the way, as a coach or as a facilitator, but I wanted to separate it out because you might be looking at the general patterns of interaction rather than the specific conflict that's up.

If you're going to do that kind of thing, what you want to do is check conditions before you would intervene. Intervening should not be undertaken lightly so you want to check for the conditions that would make it right for you to intervene. You could ask whether you have clear authorization to intervene, and both parties need to agree. Has one or both parties requested your assistance and has the other one consented? You really want to know that before you step in.

Or maybe you have an assigned role for instance. For instance, if you're the supervisor and the manager as we were looking at in our last lecture where Claire stepped in so excellently. Sometimes you're the minister. You might have a role where that fits. Then you've got to be concerned with whether the conflicting parties are really interested in finding a mutually-satisfactory solution.

You want to explicitly ask and in fact insist on a clear and unequivocal answer. Is that what they're after, because if they'll agree with you that that's the agenda and they both want your help in doing it, then you've really got a handle that you can use to be an effective helper in the process. If one or both parties is not willing to do that, to commit to working toward a real resolution, I want to suggest that you refrain from engaging. Don't be afraid to step back and say no I don't want to do that. You don't want to ever assume greater responsibility for this conflict being resolved than the parties themselves. You want them to take responsibility, and if they're doing that, you're willing to help them.

If they're not willing now, you can say look, at the time when you're both really willing and you want to do that, call me again and I'll really help you then. So you don't have to know right away, but don't take more responsibility than they're taking for resolving their conflict.

There are some other things to be concerned with before you step in and help. Ask yourself do I think I have the necessary communication skills. I don't have to be a professional at it, but I have to be good at some things. I have to be pretty good at listening. I have to be able to empathize with people. I have to have a reasonable ability to analyze statements and issues and ask helpful questions. I've got to be able to open and honest in my interactions. I've got to be trustworthy. I've got to be willing to honor the trust they place in me or all parties place in me, and that means keeping things confidential if they have to.

I've got to have the right motives if I'm going to help people. It's really got to be about helping them, and Kenneth Cloke that mediator whom I respect so much, lays out some important criteria for what should be the motives that are involved. He says you've got to avoid self-centered reasons for helping others. He's got a list of these that's pretty useful. Ask myself am I doing this to get help for myself. If I am, if I'm looking for something back for it later, I shouldn't be doing it.

If I'm wanting to do it in order to satisfy my own needs for gratitude and recognition, not a good reason to step in and help. It's liable to backfire if I do that. I'm probably not going to be very helpful. I'm working my agenda instead of helping them with theirs.

What if I'm trying to mend some poor self image of mine or get more self-esteem, wrong reason. If I just want to gain companionship, get friends this way, wrong reason. The only motivation should be helping them. That's pretty stringent. Ask myself these questions.

If those pass, then I can say yes to helping. However, before proceeding what I want to do is to get determined and agreed upon what my role is going to be as the helper. If they want me to help, let's ask and specify what assistance I'm going to give. Margaret remember was very careful with Phyllis to say this is what I'll do and what not, and the parties agreed to that. You've got to make it clear that you're not interested in taking sides. Remember those criteria that mediators and ombudsmen have where they need to be neutral and impartial? You want to be neutral and impartial in the same way. Those principles that the professionals follow is something you want to follow. You want to be equally on both peoples sides.

Then you want to try to determine how best you can help in that coach, mediator, or facilitator sense. How do they want the help with this? And try to sort out where it's going to be and get agreement. If you can clearly state your role and get the consent of both parties, then you can proceed. Be careful here to avoid triangulation.

Parties will come to you presenting themselves as victims and they want you to be the rescuer. That's really tempting. That victim/rescuer set up is a terrible temptation into a triangulation role. It may feel noble riding to the rescue and helping someone who feels weak, but being the victim is damaging to the victim. If they didn't have to be the victim, you don't want to help them do that. Being the rescuer, you know what happens very often, you ride in and abuse somebody else defending what you regard as the victim and later they're going to turn on you. So don't get sucked into doing that. You've got to be on both people's sides.

You also want to be very clear that this conflict is theirs. You're here to help, but it's theirs to do. So how can you do these kinds of things?

Let's look a little more deeply at these three levels of helping. Let's start again with coaching the other party. If only one party has come to you for help, you can help there by just functioning as a coach and you only need their consent. But remember when you do that, you're hearing only one side of this thing. You can validate their feelings, tell them you understand how they feel that way, but don't jump in and take sides. You're only hearing one side of it and it would be looking very different if you were hearing it from the other side.

You want to be a calming and an empowering influence. You want to encourage that person to be taking responsibility for themselves, and you want to help them work toward and think about working toward a mutually-satisfactory resolution. You can help them define the issue, you can help them sort feelings. You can help them identify goals, and you've got lots of talk in this course and ideas about how to do that. You can help them make a decision about whether and how to pursue resolution. You can help them through steps one, two, three, and four in the seven step process we talked about back in Lecture 11.

Let's look at an example here of some of that work being done. In this case let's have a character named Gary who's struggling with a relationship that's perhaps going somewhere and perhaps not, and he's just not sure how it's going. He's talking to his friend Roy looking for some advice.

[Video start.]

> **Gary**: I just get so stressed out and confused every time I think about it, man. Sarah invites me over, then when I get to her place, it's like I'm not even there. One minute she's really nice, and then she ignores me for no reason. It's been like this for 3 months.

> **Roy**: Man, that's got to be frustrating. Do you really like this girl? I mean, is it worth the stress?

> **Gary**: Well, to be honest, I do like her, but I've about had it with this hot-and-cold business.

> **Roy**: Listen, has it occurred to you that maybe how she acts has nothing to do with you?

[Video end.]

Gary is attributing Sarah's behavior to how she feels about him. Hmm, that could be that fundamental attribution error we talked about back in Lecture 4. But Roy is being a good friend here and a good coach. He's really helping Gary sort this thing out. He's helping Gary calm down and consider possibility; nice start into coaching on his part.

Let's next talk about the role of mediator and facilitator here. I'm using these terms fairly interchangeably in this informal sense. The role of the mediator, the facilitator, needs to be sorted out; what's it going to be. You need to identify what's the process that's going to be followed and you need to spell out what's going to be your role and what's going to be theirs. When you're sorting this out and it's well to set it up in front, to talk about it in front and not just try to let it evolve.

You want to let the disputants own the content of their negotiations and agreements. They're not yours. You're guiding the process. You claim the role of guiding that fair and open process. Your job is going to be to promote open communication. One thing about that is to refuse to hold secrets. Mediators have that role, the professional mediators have that thing of keeping the process informed. You might use that as a guide. You want everybody to know everything. Don't get stuck holding anybody's secrets when you're trying to be neutral.

You want to appreciate and let the parties know you appreciate their willingness to trust you in doing this. Thank them for that. That's a trust that they've give you. You can help arrange a meeting for the parties once they've agreed to all of that, and then you can help them negotiate when they do.

Let's talk about when that meeting takes place. You want to begin by thanking the parties for trusting you. Start again by thanking them, and then encourage them to seek a resolution that really serves both parties. That's setting that agenda that we talked about back when we talked about the seven steps, and you're guiding them through in this way. Then you want to remember that the example we considered a few minutes ago where Margaret was helping Phyllis and Sue. Margaret began by thanking and setting the objective of the meeting. So remember, have that picture in mind, that's what you're trying to do.

Secondly what you want to do is create a safe environment. Sometimes, not always, but sometimes that requires asking for ground rules. I've often done this with clients. I say let's set some ground rules and one of them is no personal attacks. Don't attack the person. That really helps separate the people from the problem using the Fisher and Ury guideline of separate people from the problem, and it helps keep things safe. You want to create that.

The third thing you want to do is go ahead and guide that discussion. What I always draw upon to do that is exactly what I laid out for you in Lecture 12 in steps five, six, and seven of that seven step process. I also follow Fisher and Ury's four principles when I'm guiding them through, and you can do that. You have those four principles now.

Fourth, it really helps to ask questions and check perceptions and get them to be clear with one another. You have to be careful asking questions and checking perceptions because people then will sometimes, they'll turn and talk to you and you want them to talk to each other. So you can lean in, ask a question. What did you mean by this, and when they tell you point them to the other person and say tell him or tell her. So you keep them talking to each other. You can also listen very carefully for the verbal and nonverbal messages, and when they don't seem to match, you can ask questions to double check that. You can always do that. You can really help move the communication and keep it clear as that third party, and it really isn't terribly, terribly hard to do in most conflicts.

Now let's look at an example. Let's turn to the discussion of our three sisters again and see how important it is to check for consistency between the verbal and nonverbal messages. This is one of those things that you can check.

[Video start.]

> **Sue**: Well, Mom and Dad are finishing up the invite list with everybody's addresses. I can't rush them—you know that. They

said they'd have it by Monday and I can pick it up then. I can bring it to your office on Wednesday, Phyllis. How's that?

Phyllis: Okay. I guess that'll work.

Margaret: Phyllis, I know you said okay, but the face and your voice sort of suggest that that might not work too well. Are you sure you don't need Sue to drop it by earlier, a little earlier than Wednesday?

Phyllis: Well, could I get it sooner? I could pick it up myself at Mom and Dad's on Monday.

Sue: I was going to talk to Mom and Dad about the venue when I picked it up.

Phyllis: How about this: What if we both meet at Mom and Dad's at 4 on Monday and nail down the location and get the final list?

Sue: Sure, that works for me.

Phyllis: Okay!

Margaret: Great. So what else do we need to settle?

[Video end.]

Did you notice Margaret picking up on the doubt in Phyllis's voice? It was there in her voice, it would've been there on her face. Even though Phyllis is agreeing to Sue's offer to bring the list to her, there was doubt there. It didn't look real. Margaret stepped in and checked it and that's when they move toward a really solid solution when what they were agreeing to before wouldn't have worked. That was a marvelous contribution on Margaret's part to that negotiation that was taking place.

What else can you do? You can guide the parties to stay focused on this conflict and on the issue that they're intending to resolve. It's easy for discussions to stray off of that if you don't. So that's a nice help you can provide as the facilitator. You also want to avoid that tendency to have issues multiply. You'll find this happens when people start to talk about what's bothering them, issues get added in, and you want to intervene on that and say now let's just stay with this and we can come to that one.

You can even create a list on the side. Sometimes I do that, I'll take a separate pad of paper when I'm helping people and say let's make a list of what else you want to negotiate and that's that, but that's not this negotiation so it goes somewhere. They feel safe. You don't want issues to multiply in this conversation. What you want is for this conversation to stay on this issue and move toward a resolution.

You really want to guide parties to describe their perceptions of the conflict and explain their feelings. You've got to get those things on the table. You've got to get them out. Once they're out and they've been described, you don't want a petition going. What you want to do is move them towards solving the problem. You've got to ask are you guys really willing to try to solve this now and if they are start asking for suggestions. So it really helps to move them past the complaints part and the feelings part and get them to focus on now and in the future asking for suggestions for what they're going to do to resolve it. That's a marvelous contribution that you can make.

If this conflict appears very complex and very resistant to solution, hmm then you can do one of these other things that we talked about earlier. You can suggest fractionation. You can suggest breaking the conversation into parts and working on one matter at a time and seeing if there are some that you can solve at this time. Solve part of it, build trust and then you can come back to others later. As this all goes on you want to be honoring and validating the expressions of emotion. But you don't want them to get out of hand; you want to keep them level. One way that you do this is you keep your own tone level, discourage emotional escalation, and the best way you can do that is to stay level and reasonable yourself.

You can validate emotions and check perceptions by paraphrasing back a description of the emotion that's being said to you. When you do that, you keep your emotional tone level, but supportive. This can be difficult, but it's easier for you as the helper to do that then it is for the parties in the conflict who are feeling the conflicting emotions themselves. By the way, this advice goes if you're coaching just with one person or mediating in a conflict between the two. It's the same kind of a setup. You want to keep level and not rise in emotion with them. It helps them stabilize the conversation and keep it moving toward a solution.

Let's consider an example of that. Let's look at a coaching situation that's easier for us to describe here. Remember Roy and he has just proposed that Sarah's behavior might have nothing to do with Gary, it might be more about Sarah and he's helping Gary stay level. Let's go back to Roy and Gary's conversation and see where they go.

[Video start.]

> **Gary**: Man, how could it have nothing to do with me? It has everything to do with me! I'm sure she doesn't act like this with everybody! It's like it's some kind of weird game.

> **Roy**: Okay, take it easy. Maybe it has something to do with you and maybe not. I still wonder if there's something else is going on here. Is there anything that sets her off? Money issues, family problems, stress at work?

> **Gary**: Well, come to think of it, it does seem like her mother calls a lot when I'm over there.

> **Roy**: Okay. So have you asked Sarah about that?

[Video end.]

Notice what Roy is doing here. He's a calming influence on Gary as we think about this, and Gary keeps wanting to get wound up. He's really helping Gary begin to look at a possible root of Sarah's behavior. So Roy is keeping that thing level. He's validating how Gary feels, but he's keeping the feeling of this thing nicely level. Roy is doing a good job.

Now let's go further. When an agreement is reached, when the parties get to the point where there's an agreement, what you can do is make sure that both parties clearly agree and that the content of that agreement is clear and about behavior. Remember we talked about that in the seven step process. That's step six. You can ensure that that agreement is absolutely clear by checking meaning back and forth. You can point out that it needs to be about behavior because it's got to be what they're going to hold each other responsible for, and then make sure that it's clearly agreed to on the part of both parties.

You can do that job. You can really be the facilitator guiding the process and it's not terribly difficult to do in most conflicts, especially if the parties are really willing to trust you and they're looking for a resolution and will let you know that.

The final thing you might want to do, because remember in the seven step process there was another thing to do, was follow through. If I've gotten involved in the discussion, I might need to clarify what's going to be my role in the follow-through because the parties might expect something from me in that.

Having done that let's go to the next level where you can help, and we talked about that in some other ways. You can help the parties assess the patterns that are going on. Patterns are tricky and as we see these happening it might not be one conflict, it's what's going on in general. If it's that kind of a question and I'm asked to help, then my role as a helper is to help improve an ongoing pattern of what's happening in conflict management.

The same sort of conflicts, if they keep recurring, suggests a pattern. One expert says you know what, if the conflict has come up over the same issue three times, it's not about that issue, it's about a pattern that you want to go and look at. So you can ask people to do that. If you're being asked about it and this thing is coming up over and over, you're being asked to help with a pattern really even though the person asking for help may not know that. So how do you work with this?

Once again you want to begin by clarifying your role in this assessment process. In suggesting solutions for improvement, you want to be careful because here it could be suggesting patterns of conflict response where you may be suggesting do something differently rather than just guiding a process they're going through. In our roles and organizations and also in extended families we're very, very often asked to be pulled in on the kind of thing where what's going on is really a pattern that has emerged where people are handling conflict poorly and they're not getting resolved.

We very often belong to the group, the family, the work unit, the team, the organization where this is going on and we may even be in it. It can be more tricky to handle in that case. If we're members of the group that we're being asked to help, it's especially important to define and clarify your role up front so that we can step out of being in the middle and define that role as the helper. We can help with the analytic process though of figuring out what that pattern is.

How do we do this? We can help by engaging with the participants and the stakeholders involved around in figuring out what's going on and then devising solutions. Treat this as problem solving. Here's the pattern that's happening, how are we going to get out of it? If you treat it as problem solving and call it a pattern, that would work. It's better to help the participants though with their assessment and ask the right questions than to really offer very many answers, because you want to be helping them, you don't want to be stepping in and opposing an answer on them.

There's a definition of assessment that's usually provided here if you're talking about assessing patterns, and the definition is kind of useful I think. Assessment is described as observing, describing, and analyzing an interaction pattern, a set of relationships, or a conflict management process in order to diagnose its problems and provide an understanding. With that understanding you can then suggest solutions. You and the participants are going to need to gather information. When you're doing this assessment remember that it's really important to get all of the different points of view; what's going on here will appear very different from the different perspectives. So you want to ask all the stakeholders, you want to get information from all points of view about a pattern, and you want to get as much objective information as possible.

When I say objective information, that's what you're after, but you better remember that objective truth in this kind of situation is often very elusive, sometimes it's even irrelevant, it's how people see it. But you want as much objective information you can. When you've done that, what you want to do is focus at least as much on the interactive processes by which people are dealing with issues as on the issues themselves. You can sometimes help assess patterns in that way and help people get to a solution. So there's lots you can do to help in that way.

I do want you to think though that if you participate in an assessment like that, you've got to remember that the assessment itself is an intervention. Once we start asking questions with a view to solving problems, we've generated new perceptions and new expectations; and if what we do in that assessment does not lead to action and improvement, the assessment itself will have been harmed. It will reduce credibility. It'll make people more demoralized so things will get worse.

Conflicts occur in systems as systems themselves. They occur as chain reactions. They make spirals, they become vortexes. You can think of them as dances and in these all the participants may acquire roles and labels and expectations. The opponents in these things are cooperating in a process that keeps the conflict going, and so these systems develop patterns and rules of engagement and those patterns are sustained by rewards that are provided by all the participants. They're cooperating in this. A pattern is a complex thing. Once you provide a diagnosis with that assessment, it's really important to figure out what you're going to do to resolve it.

So that one is tougher, but you can do it. You can help by facilitating a problem-solving discussion for where you go from there once the pattern has been identified.

So there are lots of ways you can help. You have to be careful about triangulating but there are lots of ways you can help. You're sometimes called upon to help and a lot of the times you can do it. You don't have to be a professional mediator or facilitator to do it. You can help people solve conflicts.

In summary, here are the essential things that I want to suggest you be careful to remember. One, you want to realize that you actually can avoid triangulation and still help as a coach, mediator, or facilitator. Two, carefully clarify your role, be it as coach, mediator, or facilitator, or some combination of those three. Three, really honor the trust that people place in you, both parties, when you step in to help with a conflict. Four, look out for the pitfalls that are here. Make sure that your only motive is to help all parties work out a resolution.

Do not be drawn into aligning yourself with one side or the other, that's a serious pitfall. Know your own limits, don't get in over your head would be another pitfall to avoid. Often people who set out to help can do more harm than good. So don't do that. Helping others deal with conflicts is a complex, challenging art. Even highly trained professionals make mistakes in their efforts, but you don't have to do a perfect job in order to be helpful. All of us can make some mistakes and still be helpful.

That's helping others. Here's an assignment for this lecture. Actually you're going to get an assignment soon enough from someone else probably that'll come up to do with it, but try this one just as a function of this lecture. The assignment from me is this. Look back at the last time you tried to help somebody else resolve a conflict. Try to remember it in detail and ask yourself some important questions. How well did that actually work out? Was it a case of triangulation? Did you try to focus your help on coaching or mediating? If you tried to mediate or facilitate, did you stay focused on the process? If it didn't work out perfectly, having heard this lecture, what do you think you might want to do differently? That's a tough assignment but try it. That's helping others.

Where are we going to go from here? There are some conflicts these days that appear to be beyond help. The resolution appears to be unreachable, the conflict appears to be intractable. These conflicts really frequently reach across cultural divides. They're conflicts that center on issues of morality, moral conflicts, they're called and they really represent the frontier in our effort to understand and deal better with conflict. We need to deal with them before we finish this course, and we're going to start doing that in Lecture 20.

Moral and Cultural Conflicts
Lecture 20

> If you can get people to see and understand each other and begin to talk in ways that they can understand, that demonizing and that kind of negativity can be broken down and you can ... begin to break through and get mutual trust and understanding.

When conflicts are framed as matters of morals, they pose particularly difficult challenges to anyone trying to resolve them, and they can even seem to justify violence. They appear to preclude win-win resolutions and render approaches to negotiation and compromise morally suspect. Are such conflicts hopeless, or can workable solutions be found?

Moral conflicts are those in which the issues are framed as matters of what is morally right and morally wrong. Note from the outset that this absolute framing is a dysfunctional conflict strategy. Moral values are inherently subjective, yet they are usually held as nonnegotiable absolutes. In a dispute about a moral question, it's difficult to reach a win-win resolution.

Barnett Pearce and Stephen Littlejohn, two well-known communication scholars, point out that our values tend to be embedded in clusters and are essential to our sense of order and function in the world, essential to holding communities and cultures together. For example, the Israelis and Palestinians each believe deeply that Jerusalem is their God-given homeland, and this belief plays a significant role in the religion and culture of each nation. A challenge to any one value in such a cluster threatens to unravel the whole.

According to Pearce and Littlejohn, opposing sides in moral conflicts tend to describe the issues using "incommensurate language"; that is, they talk about the issues in terms that just don't compute with the other side. This tendency leads to us to view our opponents on moral issues as villains or enemies. At the same time, these scholars tell us that people often oversimplify moral issues and speak about them in absolutes, which can sometimes justify a move to violence.

Abortion is a moral issue that remains controversial in the United States today. Each side of the debate over the legality of abortion frames the issue in absolute terms. Anti-abortion proponents view abortion as the killing of an unborn child. Pro-choice supporters see a government prohibition on abortion as a violation of a woman's right to control her own body. Each side views the other as advocating the violation of a moral principle; thus, compromise or negotiation doesn't seem to be an option. Further, the values of each side are embedded in wider moral clusters: One is focused on having legitimate authority to enforce clear moral standards, and one is directed toward ensuring individual rights and freedoms. Surrender on the issue of abortion would threaten these larger clusters of values.

The language used by one side on the abortion issue does not compute with the other side because each is speaking from a different moral system; they're unable to engage in a discussion that could lead to any agreement or conclusion. Beyond that, each side tends to oversimplify the issue greatly: the right to life versus the right to choose. To some extent, the opposing sides are also both guilty of the fundamental attribution error that we discussed in Lecture 4. Taking a stand on one side of the conflict or the other is attributed to basic character traits; in this case, our opponents seem fundamentally evil. It's hard to comprehend that people on the other side of the issue are basing their actions on a coherent moral code in which they sincerely believe and, therefore, are behaving ethically. The issue of whether or not same-sex couples should legally be allowed to marry presents a similar picture of a moral conflict that is seemingly intractable.

We should also note that moral conflicts tend to develop long histories, in which positions harden. Multiple and complex issues are reduced to simple moral imperatives, and the opponents' actions come to be viewed as grave moral offenses that may justify violent responses. Such conflicts can last for generations.

Today, a number of major moral conflicts, including those between Israel and Palestine and between Shiite and Sunni Muslims, seem to deny efforts at resolution. Is there any hope for peace? Scholars, diplomats, and internationally recognized mediators, including William Ury, are gaining some success in finding peaceful resolutions to international conflicts.

Among the specific tactics that may be helpful in dealing with moral conflicts is **reframing**, that is, finding a constructive new way to view a conflict through a different lens or frame. Other useful tactics include fractionating, developing empathy, and attempting to build mutual trust. Finally, note that moral conflicts don't always take place on a national or international scale; they also happen in our own lives. In our personal lives, we tend to frame moral issues in black-and-white terms and view our opponents as immoral or unethical, rendering negotiation difficult. If you fall into this pattern, try to reframe the conflict so that will be understood and accepted by all parties. ∎

Important Terms

moral conflict: A conflict between parties who are locked into opposition.

reframing: Finding a new, constructive way to look at a conflict issue through a different lens or "frame."

Suggested Reading

Cloke, *Conflict Resolution: Mediating War, Evil, Injustice, and Terrorism.*

Pearce and Littlejohn, *Moral Conflict: When Social Worlds Collide.*

Assignment

1. Consider the following questions:

   • When, if ever, might violence be justified in addressing a moral conflict?

   • When, if ever, is tolerance of others' views on serious moral issues morally wrong?

   • Might it help us to deal with moral conflicts if we got past the taboo against discussing moral issues with our friends and colleagues?

Moral and Cultural Conflicts
Lecture 20—Transcript

Israel versus Palestine, Islamic beliefs versus Western values, the battle over whether abortion should be legal in the United States, what all these conflicts have in common is that at their core each of them is an issue of what's morally right versus what's morally wrong. They also have in common that they really appear to be intractable. They really appear to defy any effort at real resolution.

It turns out that when conflicts are framed as matters of morals, they really pose particularly difficult challenges to anybody trying to resolve them, and they can even seem to justify violence. They appear to preclude those win-win resolutions that Deutsch introduced us to and render approaches to negotiation and compromise themselves, even the effort to compromise to be somehow morally suspect. So is it as hopeless of solution as it appears to be or can workable solutions be found?

In this lecture and the next we've got to talk about moral conflicts. What are called moral conflicts? What's the nature of moral conflicts? How are they different from other conflicts? We'll observe some characteristics of them that make them different, and try to better understand why they're so daunting when we try to manage them. But it's really not hopeless and we'll get to that.

Let's begin with a definition. Moral conflicts are conflicts in which the issues are framed as matters of what is morally right and what is morally wrong, or who is morally good and who is morally bad. I want you to notice that that kind of framing is black and white thinking. It's absolute framing, and way back in Lecture 9 when we talked about dysfunctional strategies we listed absolute framing as a dysfunctional strategy. One way to think of a moral conflict then is a dysfunctional strategy of absolute framing, *writ large*, only for people with strong moral values of any sort when one of those values is involves, it can really be unavoidable. No matter how dysfunctional, that's the way it's framed for that person.

Certain as we may feel about our moral values, we do on the other hand have to recognize that they're inherently subjective, values are subjective and yet they're not so negotiable. They're usually held as absolutes; they tend not to be amenable to any kind of compromise. In a dispute about a moral question, both sides really can't be right, so you can't get to a win-win in any ready or obvious way. For most people, morals are just not negotiable and they're not something that you can compromise. Moral conflicts are tough to deal with.

Barnett Pearce and Stephen Littlejohn, who are two very well known communications scholars, both of whom have focused a good deal of their research on management of conflict, really made it an effort to study and better understand and explain these moral conflicts, and they reported them in a book called *Moral Conflict.* They tried to explain and here are some of the ideas that they pointed out. They recognized that we have embedded values that are clusters. Our values are embedded in these sort of clusters of other values and they have complex histories that have developed over time.

They're not just separate things that are held and negotiable separately. They belong to clusters and whole moral orders. They're essential to our sense of order and function in the world, they're essential to holding communities and cultures together. So this business of clusters of values which develop into full moral codes is something we really need as societies and communities. They tend to constitute an integrated sort of moral order in which all the specific values are going to support one another.

For an example of that you might think about the deeply-held values that Israelis and Palestinians have regarding something like what they consider to be their God-given homeland. Each thinks of Jerusalem as a place that's central in their history and they're committed to it in their religious beliefs and their cultural beliefs at a moral level. So they really have a difference that each holds deeply that's tied to other things.

A challenge to any one of these values in such a cluster, if you let go of that value, seems to threaten to unravel the cluster, and people have a sense of this even when they're not very carefully analyzing what's going on. So you really find that people often when confronted with the idea of changing on a particular value that may not seem important, will appear to unreasonably hold on to that moral value even in the face of clearly contrary facts they want to hold to their beliefs. The problem is that letting go of that seems to threaten to unravel the cluster, and that's a larger value that they can't let go of because that value is embedded in this whole moral order. So they tend to be resistant.

That example of the Palestinians and Israelis, would you really think that the Palestinians could negotiate away possession of the place from which they believe Mohammed went into heaven, the Dome of the Rock in East Jerusalem? On the other side of that could you expect the Israelis to negotiate away their claim to Jerusalem as the center of their land. That's deep with them and it's not just a history question or a legal rights question, it's a moral question with both of them, and if they let go of that how would it threaten the wider sense of their history and who they are in the moral order that they belong to. So that's an example of the clusters of moral values that they've got to hold on to so they don't unravel.

The next thing that Pearce and Littlejohn point to, and it's a very important point, is that they say the opposing sides in moral conflicts tend to describe the issues using what they call *incommensurate language*; that is, they talk about the issues in terms that just don't compute with the other. That's connected to that cluster of moral values that they're working with and this just doesn't compute for the other side. So they tend to talk past each other and they don't understand one another at all.

In moral conflicts that we deal with in our own lives, we tend to do this. We avoid discussion of moral issues, especially in the United States, because they're uncomfortable when they come up, so we don't talk about them. Given that we don't know the different language and the way others see it we tend to see opponents on moral issues as people we don't know and can't relate to. Given that we tend to see them as villains or enemies

Beyond this Pearce and Littlejohn tells us one more thing. They tell us that people tend to oversimplify moral issues. They tend to talk in absolutes, and those absolutes can sometimes justify moving to violence, even when we're clearly wrong and we think we're the good person, we can justify violence on a clearly-held moral position in a conflict, which can get dangerous.

Let's think of some specific moral issues that we confront today and apply Pearce and Littlejohn's description of how a moral conflict works and why it's so difficult to those. Let's talk about an obvious one that's very present in the United States today, and that's the question of whether abortion should be legal or illegal. That is framed by both sides in this debate as a moral issue with each side viewing the other as wrong. One side says abortion is killing, it's killing an unborn baby. The other side views a government prohibition that would be enforced as a violation of the woman's right to control her own body and what happens in it.

Each side sees that very much in moral terms, but the language doesn't compute with the other. Each side views the other as advocating a violation of a moral principle that they hold dear. So that's not something you're going to compromise or negotiate away very well. Those values of each side are embedded in wider moral clusters that those people hold on to in wider moral orders. One is focused on having legitimate authority enforce clear, moral standards they believe the society needs to hold on to, and the other side is focused on ensuring individual freedoms and rights, which are hard won especially more recently won for women to control their own bodies. Surrender on that one issue poses a threat to the wider cluster of values that's involved.

Also the language that the two sides use in this argument is incommensurate in Pearce and Littlejohn's terms. The arguments they present, the claims that they make, simply do not compute with one another because they're talking in those two different moral systems and they talk past each other. So they don't really engage in a discussion that could lead to any agreement or conclusion.

Beyond that what they do on both sides is they tend to oversimplify greatly. Oversimplifying is very useful when we're making an adversarial case presenting to the public. Slogans are very helpful in radio and television and in news. But slogans also oversimplify, and you have a classic case of that in this conflict. On the one side you have people identified by the slogan they're in favor of the right to life and on the other side they're in favor of the right to choose. We put these out as simple statements and we reduce this deep moral conflict that's very complex and has histories on both sides to a couple of slogans that are also incommensurate language passing beyond one another without really engaging. So we oversimplify and that makes it worse.

We can go beyond what Pearce and Littlejohn tell us here because we can go back to Lecture 4 when we talked about perception. If you remember in that lecture we discussed what psychologists call a fundamental attribution error. I said at the beginning of this lecture that moral conflicts give us the fundamental attribution error *writ large*. That's the case in this conflict and we're very tempted to say about the other side. He or she advocates that or does that or does those things because that's the way he is. That's how he feels. That's just the way he is. That's his character. When we do that what we do is exaggerate and solidify that fundamental attribution error.

What happens is that's the way he is or that's his character readily morphs into that's what he does because he's evil, and now we're connecting the problem with the person, which is quite the opposite of what Fisher and Ury tell us and we get very stuck with that. It is, in fact, pretty difficult for us to comprehend that the persons on the other side of a conflict that's a moral conflict and is very important to us, it's very hard to comprehend that those people over there are basing their actions ethically on a coherent moral code in which they sincerely believe and therefore behaving morally within the subjective values that they hold and are committed to is very hard for us to do. So we tend to commit that fundamental attribution error.

Then conversely you know what happens? They're over there having the same problem when they look at us. So they tend to see us as evil ourselves. That makes moral conflict awfully, awfully difficult to deal with.

Let's go look at another example, another one that's here and present in the United States and is currently being argued as it works its way through courts. This is the moral issue that's in place in the question of whether same sex couples should be legally allowed to marry. That's framed by both sides as a moral issue. So it fits our definition. One side asserts that prohibition of gay marriage violates the moral principle of equal rights. So they're advocating that gays should be allowed to marry.

The other side asserts that sexual relationships of same sex partners are sinful and they shouldn't be condoned by society. Wow, opposite sides clearly framing as a moral conflict. Each side is viewing the other's position here as advocating a violation of a moral value that it regards as really imperative. The values in this dispute on both sides are embedded in values clusters that represent a wider moral order that people adhere to, and surrendering on the one point about whether same sex couples should be allowed to marry one way or the other has some threat value for the rest of the moral code that the two sides are attached to, the moral clusters that they hold on to. So it's very problematic that way.

Once again, the language is incommensurate in Pearce and Littlejohn's terms. They talk past each other. One side talks in terms of "marriage" as a sacred sacrament ordained by God that's for the primary purpose of creating children and raising them well. The other thinks and talks in terms of marriage as a union of two persons based on mutual love for the purpose of joy and comfort that everyone should have a right to. Incommensurate language, once again we're talking past each other.

Both sides once again oversimplify, and some, fortunately a relatively small minority, view this conflict as something that allows for justification of violence. So they could act on that in a violent way. They do that both with the issue of abortion and the issue of gay marriage. Fortunately it's a very small minority.

So there are a few examples there, moral conflicts, two right here in the United States and some other countries as well, and they appear to be utterly intractable.

Beyond that, we haven't finished complicating it yet. Beyond that we need to note that moral conflicts, once they're engaged, tend to develop histories, and long histories in which position harden because people can't get them resolved, so they're struggling with this; they're seeing each other through those fundamental attribution errors and violence is occurring. So they tend to develop histories where things get uglier and longer and more complex. Each side treats the other as the enemy, sees them as morally inferior, and sometimes they go to the extent of dehumanizing them in doing that.

The multiple and complex issues that are reduced and oversimplified get treated that way as simple moral imperatives and when people act in that way they do behaviors that multiply and make more complex the conflict that's occurring. As this goes, on the opponents' actions are viewed as being some kind of grave moral offenses that justify revenge and violent responses. When they're treated in that way and justified violent responses, someone acts in that way and then a crime is committed or some harm is done, it becomes a new moral issue and that increases the complexity. So these things develop histories.

How long do they last? Someone wisely said that resentments don't die when people do. They last for generations, and the anger and the resentment can go on and on and multiply and harden as these things happen. We can think of some examples from history.

I grew up in the state of Kentucky, so one of the great examples for me of moral conflict going on for generations is the classic feud in Kentucky and West Virginia between the Hatfields and the McCoys, two families, one in Kentucky the other in Virginia. There's dispute about it all, but that appears to have begun with the murder of a McCoy who was a Union soldier by a pro-Confederate Hatfield. It was exacerbated then apparently when a McCoy was charged with crossing a state line in order to illegally vote on the other side of the border.

Both sides framed this whole thing in the context of the Civil War which each side viewed as a moral crusade. What happened was starting from that first murder they traded killings back and forth for generations and they lost track of the original issue. They thought the other was evil and they fought them out. Hatfields and McCoys, through generations, fortunately some years ago the families got together and actually officially buried the hatchet and put an end to that one. But the conflict went on framed morally for decades.

Let's talk about another example. I live now in the southwest in Arizona where I teach, and there we have a marvelously deep history of the southwest with the missionaries coming over and the many Native American tribes, and I really enjoyed getting into that history. There's some deep moral conflict that takes place over a great deal of time there. One that's very central is that the Franciscan missionaries when they came over really looked at the Native American shamans as being in the way of converting people to Christianity, and they thought the shamans were evil. So believing that and believing they need to destroy their influence, they actually had many of those shamans publicly hanged or beaten to death.

So the shamans were killed. I don't know how the Pueblo Indians felt about that, but it certainly wasn't very good. They viewed it as a violation; they viewed it as murder. That went on and it's an interesting thing in the history of the southwest that there was a point in 1680 when the Pueblo Indians did a great revolt and they killed many of the Spaniards really focusing on the priests, and literally drove the Spanish settlers out of Texas and New Mexico. It took time for the Spanish to get back.

How long did that one last? Well you know what, a couple of centuries later in the 1890s, when the Native Americans were trying to get their sense of identity back and really beginning to recover in some good ways, they began doing more of their dances, and the local Whites thought this might be devil worship that would lead to more violence, so they enforced a ban on native dances. That was the 1890s, a couple of hundred years after that Pueblo rebellion.

Now it's three centuries later, and you know what, Native Americans in the Southwest where I live, many of them are still very secretive about their religious beliefs and practices. They really are afraid to share that with Whites and it has become a code with them that you don't tell Whites about those things, and I don't blame them for being reluctant to share that information. Moral conflict over time hardens and resentments don't die when people do. So it's there.

Today we've got these major moral conflicts that really do confound us and they seem to defy our efforts at resolution. They have these deep and complex histories that have taken place over time, very much the same as and sometimes much more complex than those two examples I just gave you from Kentucky and the southwest. For instance, this Israel/Palestine conflict, both of them have centuries-old claims to the same territory that are tied to their histories and their cultures and to their moral values and religious beliefs.

Those claims are based on their understandings of their own religious histories. That's really tricky and it's many centuries old. It's moral conflict and it's complex. There's also the very deadly moral conflict between Shiite and Sunni Muslims. That one continues to confound efforts to build a unified Iraq today, and it foments mistrust between Iran and Iran's Arab neighbors. The roots of that one date back to the 7th century into a dispute over the leadership of Islam. There's a long history that involves a lot of pain and bloodshed between those two sides, difficult for one for them to just go ahead and sort out. So we're confronted with very difficult ones as we attempt to do this today.

That would raise the question is this thing hopeless? Is there any hope for resolution of these kinds of things? There really is hope. To begin with, there are some very smart and very good people who are working very hard at it. There are a great many researchers and practitioners working hard on this challenge. There are academic institutes that exist precisely to study methods to achieve peaceful resolution, and these have multiplied in recent decades and they're producing a growing body of research. I'm not going to tell you there's a silver bullet anywhere near in site, but there are helpful insights being produced at a good rate. So good people, smart people are working at this very hard.

In addition to that, there are diplomats that have engaged successfully in this kind of thing at least in some issues. There was an interesting one not very long ago when former President Clinton of the United States flew to North Korea to negotiate the release of two U.S. women who had illegally crossed into North Korea. This was a moral issue on both sides. The North Koreans saw this as spies coming into their territory. These were bad people that needed to be dealt with. Americans saw this as two innocent women who just may've innocently strayed across the border and the brutal North Koreans were treating them badly.

Mr. Clinton was able to go over and do the conversation and get a breakthrough and get the thing resolved. So there are diplomats who are able to do this kind of thing. There are also internationally-recognized mediators who are engaged in the effort, and they're adding to the understanding and making progress. It's notable that William Ury, of Fisher and Ury who gave us the principles for negotiation, Ury was involved with helping Chechnya and Russia work out a cease fire in that terrible conflict that was taking place. He went over there and helped them work that out.

So there are good people working at it and they are gaining some success. In addition to that there are some specific processes that we've talked about in this course and specific tactics that actually have been found to be possibly helpful in dealing with moral conflicts. One of those is reframing. We've talked about that. Let's define it again for our purposes here. What you do when you frame an issue is you decide the terms in which it's to be understood. It's about this. You can reframe it and think about it differently.

If you change the way you think about and describe which requires changing the language and gets you behind that problem of incommensurate language, and if a mediator can help the parties do this, you can actually make progress in resolving a conflict that's a moral conflict. So that can help you get around that problem of incommensurate language and the intractableness of the issues that are there. If you can get people to see an issue in a different way, then they may have a chance to compromise because it's less about a moral issue and more about something else or even achieve a win-win.

The other kind of process or tactic actually that has been shown to be useful here is the tactic of fractionating. We mentioned that one in our last lecture. What you do in fractionating is when you've got a complex issue with a whole lot going on in it, you find one issue that really may be amenable to working with and you take that one and you try to solve it. You break it into its parts and you start with a part that looks like you can negotiate a resolution, and you talk about that and you try to work out a solution. That can permit a partial resolution, and then you can work later on the other parts.

Part of why moral conflicts are so intractable is because of this hostility and mistrust that's built up over time. But with fractionating if I can get people to agree on some part of the conflict and how they're going to resolve that, get that agreement into place and get it to work, the hostility can be reduced and you can begin to build trust again and you can begin to get breakthroughs in an incremental way that way. You can also develop empathy between people. That's a third kind of thing you can use.

If you can get people to see and understand each other and begin to talk in ways that they can understand, that demonizing and that kind of negativity can be broken down and you can see the other as a human being, you can begin to breakthrough and get mutual trust and understanding. We'll do some heartwarming examples of this actually in our next lecture when we talk about some successes.

Fourth I want to note that you can build mutual trust by combining that fractionating with empathy development, and with some patience you can move things in a direction that really does help get us to where we can have solutions, at least partial solutions, at least progress in dealing with moral conflicts. So it's not hopeless, there's progress taking place.

I want to note also before we leave this subject that this business of moral conflicts doesn't just happen on that large international level, or large issues of public discussion and public policy at the national level. It happens in our own lives. We also see another person's actions sometimes as unethical or dishonest or unfair. We tend often in our personal lives to see issues as moral ones. When we do that, we frame our issue in these terms, we trap ourselves into black and white thinking and we render negotiation extremely, extremely difficult.

When we do that what happens? We present it that way. We say you're not being fair. The other party reacts defensively and we've set off managing the conflict in a way that's structured as a moral conflict, and we're not going to get it solved. In our personal lives, what I strongly suggest, don't go to a moral level unless you have to. If you're thinking that way, try to reframe it, try to present your position as an I statement if you can. Instead of saying something like that's not fair to the other person, say you know that puts me at a disadvantage because and explain what the disadvantage is. If you're not talking about fair, but you are talking about disadvantage, you've reframed in a way that's going to be useful.

So all of this about moral conflict we can bring down to some of the conflicts that happen in our moral lives. That's not where we want to go. We don't want to frame as a moral conflict unless it really is that okay. Of course moral conflicts really are sometimes unavoidable, and when that happens if they're real we do have to draw a line and stand upon our morals.

So what can we conclude at this point? Obviously moral conflict is just profoundly, profoundly challenging. But we're working on understanding what makes it so difficult, we're getting better at that, and we are finding ways to break through and get help resolving at least some moral conflicts.

What's our summary then? What have we observed so far? Moral conflicts are presenting an exceptionally difficult challenge. They always do. They often appear to be and they sometimes really are absolutely intractable. Moral conflicts generate complex histories and perceived moral outrages so they harden and develop over time. When we deal with moral conflicts there are some ways that will help and sometimes these ways help. The key ones we know so far are reframing and fractionation and building empathy and trust. Those tactics actually have been shown to be helpful. These also can be applied not just to those large conflicts, but remember them when we feel like we're in a moral conflict in our own personal lives.

I can't give you an exact assignment for something to go do on a moral conflict. What I'd rather do in this case is give you three questions, important questions to consider for yourself about moral conflicts. One is consider this, when, if ever, might violence be justified in addressing a moral conflict? It's helpful to have a considered view on that point. Secondly when, if ever, can tolerance of another's view on a serious moral issue be morally wrong versus morally right? Thirdly, might it help us deal with moral conflicts if we got past the taboo against discussing moral issues with our friends and our colleagues? Maybe we can get better with dealing with them if we talked about them more often. Three questions to consider.

We've done a general discussion of moral conflict and why it's so difficult, and we've talked about some history examples of moral conflict, and we've talked about hope for doing better. We want to do one more lecture on moral conflict. What we want to do is take this to real examples and I want to give us more hope by pointing to some fairly recent, very successful stories about the handling of moral conflict. There is hope, there have been some real successes. We'll talk about them in Lecture 21.

Managing Moral Conflicts—Success Stories
Lecture 21

> If empathy and trust building and fractionating and reframing can help to achieve agreements in these moral conflicts, you know what? They can help us in our personal lives, as well.

Just because moral conflict is challenging doesn't mean that we have to accept defeat. In this lecture, we'll look at three success stories in dealing with moral conflict from recent history and see the three strategies of building empathy, fractionating, and reframing at work.

The first of these success stories occurred in 1978, with the negotiation of the Camp David Accords between Egypt and Israel. The conflict between the two nations had an extensive, ugly history. For many years, the Arab nations, including Egypt, had challenged Israel's right to exist as a nation on land taken from the Palestinians. Israel strongly asserted its claim to the region based on its ancient historical occupation and its right to freedom from persecution in the aftermath of the Holocaust. Three costly wars had been fought over the issue of Israel's nationhood, in 1948, 1967, and 1973.

In 1978, Israel occupied the Sinai Peninsula, which was historically a part of Egypt. The major players involved in trying to negotiate the conflict were President Anwar Sadat of Egypt, Premier Menachem Begin of Israel, and President Jimmy Carter of the United States. Sadat suggested fractionating the conflict—focusing only on the Sinai Peninsula—instead of trying to

The Jimmy Carter Presidential Library.

President Sadat fractioned the conlict between Israel and Egypt to get a peaceful solution.

negotiate the large-scale solution that Carter originally sought. Begin was amenable to the fractionation and asserted that Israel would be willing to return the Sinai if the nation could be guaranteed a secure peace. Carter realized that the situation presented an opportunity for progress, so he shifted his focus to this incremental approach. Carter invited Sadat and Begin to the United States; in the resulting negotiations, the parties made a conscious effort to draw on the principles of negotiation set forth by Fisher and Ury. Carter played an important role in the negotiations by building empathy, serving as a mediator in some instances, and reframing the issue as one that would affect the children and grandchildren of Egypt and Israel. Sadat and Begin shared the Nobel Peace Prize for signing the Egypt/Israel Peace Treaty of 1979, a treaty that has never been violated.

Carter played an important role in the [Camp David] negotiations by building empathy, serving as a mediator in some instances, and reframing the issue as one that would affect the children and grandchildren of Egypt and Israel.

Another excellent example of fractionation can be found in the negotiations between the United States and the Soviet Union that resulted in the first Strategic Arms Reduction Treaty (START I). Both nations had framed the global conflict of the Cold War as a moral conflict, and the two had fought proxy wars in Korea and Vietnam, the Middle East, and Africa throughout the 20th century. Unable to curb the arms race in which they were engaged, the two nations remained deeply suspicious of each other; neither could see a way to reduce the level of threat even though they acknowledged the value to be achieved in doing so.

Ultimately, Ronald Reagan proposed a negotiation to Mikhail Gorbachev for the two countries to reduce or limit the number of nuclear weapons each held. These negotiations took much longer than the Camp David Accords, but in 1991 they resulted in START I, which went into effect in 1994. Since that time, the original treaty has been renegotiated to reduce nuclear armaments even further.

Our third example is the negotiation that took place between the governors of Utah and Oregon over issues of environmental management. Note that debates about environmental issues are typically framed in moral terms: Environmentalists talk about saving the planet, while those on the other side talk about destroying jobs. In the late 1990s, at an annual meeting of the Western Governors' Association, John Kitzhaber, the liberal governor of Oregon, and Mike Leavitt, the conservative governor of Utah, were asked to draft a common statement that the association could make concerning environmental management.

In the course of struggling over their differences, the two governors reframed the discussion to come up with a list of points of agreement. This led them to focus on the principles that should be applied in making environmental policy decisions rather than on the policies themselves. At a later meeting, about 400 stakeholders were brought in from all sides of this issue to attend breakout groups with the aim of refining a shared environmental doctrine. The ultimate result was a set of guidelines called the Enlibra Principles, which steer government toward balanced environmental management.

It's interesting to note in all three of these examples that the strong stands taken by both sides of an issue may be necessary to break through to a genuine negotiation. The figures who made progress in each of the examples were not middle-of-the-road folks but people who stood firmly on their moral principles. It's also heartening that in all three cases, these leaders were willing to come together to resolve serious moral conflicts without compromising their principles. ■

Suggested Reading

Begin, "Nobel Lecture," http://nobelprize.org/nobel_prizes/peace/laureates/1978/begin-lecture.html.

Leavitt, speech to the Western Governors' Association at the Plenary Session of Shared Environmental Doctrine, http://www.westgov.org/wga/initiatives/enlibra/leavitt_speech.pdf.

Sadat, "Nobel Lecture," http://nobelprize.org/nobel_prizes/peace/laureates/1978/al-sadat-lecture.html.

1. Identify one or two moral conflicts on which you have a strong opinion. Consider whether you could agree to some reframing of the issue without compromising your values. Or, in order to seek a resolution, could some part of the conflict be carved out and negotiated on its own?

2. Thinking about other contemporary moral conflicts, can you see possibilities for more examples of success stories?

Managing Moral Conflicts—Success Stories
Lecture 21—Transcript

In our last lecture we really talked seriously about moral conflicts. Conflicts that are framed in terms of a moral issue where each side feels the other is supporting something that's actually morally wrong. These pose really special challenges because they appear utterly intractable. They seem to be what we can't compromise about or even negotiate let alone win-win. They sometimes even justify violence. So moral conflict is a particular challenge and I described it in that last lecture as the frontier of our work on managing conflict better.

But that doesn't mean we've really got to accept defeat. So what I want to do in this lecture is talk about three examples in which what happened was we got a real success in an effort to deal with a moral conflict. They're three examples from recent history. In each one of those I want you to notice that they are these three things, three strategies that we talked about, building empathy, fractionating, and reframing, some combination of them will appear in each of the strategies we discuss.

Let's get started. Let's go back to 1978. What happened in 1978 was the negotiation of what are called the Camp David Accords between Egypt and Israel, and that was done at Camp David here in Washington D.C. What was that about? There had been a longstanding conflict between Egypt and Israel. Notice that it was framed really as a moral conflict. The Arab nations including Egypt really seriously challenged Israel's right to exist as a country on land taken from the Islamic Palestinians. Conversely Israel strongly asserted its right as a moral right to exist based on its ancient historical occupation of its historic homeland and its right to live free from persecution which required a homeland after the holocaust in World War II.

Both of these sides treated this as a moral conflict. This conflict really had a lot of extensive, very ugly history to it. There were documented atrocities on both sides. There's a history of bloodshed and dispossession of people on both sides. There were three costly wars fought, 1948, 1967, and 1973. Israel had emerged victorious from all of those with a lot of help from our western allies.

At this point in 1978 Israel occupied territory captured from Arab nations, and the territory that's of concern for this example is the Sinai Peninsula, which was historically a part of Egypt. This conflict really appeared to be beyond some kind of peaceful resolution at this point. Here are the major players. There were three people involved, three key people at least. One is President Anwar Sadat of Egypt, the second one is Premier Menachem Begin of Israel, and the third is President Jimmy Carter of the United States. This effort, this peaceful solution, was actually initiated by President Sadat of Egypt.

At that point, the Carter administration had really been focused on attempting to restart the Geneva Conference, this time including a larger number and including a specific Palestinian delegation, which hadn't been included in the talks up until then. They were looking for a large scale solution to the whole thing by bringing everybody to the table. What did Sadat do? Sadat just lacked confidence in that Geneva Conference approach. He just didn't think it would work to bring all the parties together and frame a grand peace. He thought that was beyond reach.

What he did instead was he boldly announced an intention to go to Israel himself and begin discussions, and he did that. Meanwhile the Carter administration is still focused on seeking an overall solution, but what Sadat is doing in this case is he's actually going to shift to a strategy of fractionating the conflict. What he did was zero in on the Egypt/Israel issue that's specifically in play here to talk about this, and that is the matter of the Sinai Peninsula. He wanted to divide the overall conflict into its parts and focus on the Sinai Peninsula.

Now let's talk about Begin. What did Menachem Begin do? Given that narrowed focus that Sadat brought to him, Begin has a willingness to really discuss the issue of the Sinai Peninsula. What he said was you know what we might be willing to return the Sinai if we could be guaranteed a secure peace. So there was a period there where Begin was publicly favoring reconvening the Geneva Conference, but at the same time he and his Likud party were engaged in secret negotiations with Egypt. Fractionation in this instance, it turns out, served Israel's strategic interests. Strategically it really would've helped Israel a whole lot to secure a solid peace on at least one of its borders so it couldn't get invaded from all sides at once again, which had happened before. So there was a strategic interest, in this case it was big enough to bring Israel to the table beyond the problem of the moral issue.

That's Sadat's role and Begin's role. What about President Carter? Mr. Carter at this point, to his credit, was able to recognize that there's an opportunity for progress to be made here. So he shifted to this incremental approach. There's some evidence that he had read a Brookings Institution Report suggesting that an incremental approach using fractionation might be more successful at about this same time. So he turned on strategies and shifted. What he did was invite Sadat and Begin to come to the United States and he offered to host them at Camp David in order to negotiate a peace settlement.

They accepted the invitation. Mr. Carter served as host, and they came to Camp David to negotiate in September of 1978. It's interesting here that in those negotiations there was a conscious effort to draw on the principles for negotiation that Fisher and Ury had been working out because those overlapped in time. So principled negotiation was being employed at this conference.

When we talk about this I don't want to cast this as a story in which President Carter saved Israel and Egypt from each other. Carter played a very important role, but we do have to give primary credit to Sadat and Begin who represented their countries boldly in a very difficult situation and achieved a peace. But Mr. Carter did a wonderful job of keeping them at the negotiating table even when it was very difficult. He made some really interesting efforts to build empathy there that seemed to have worked. There was one that I heard him speak about once when he was being interviewed in which he talked about something that cut right to the core of the morality issue.

What he did was he told them each that he respected their faith and he invited them to pray with him. So you have this phenomenon of Mr. Carter, an evangelical Christian, and Mr. Sadat, a Muslim, and Mr. Begin a Jewish person praying together for their success in this negotiation. They did that, and it probably helped build some empathy. I'm speculating on the building of empathy, but I don't see how it could've gone otherwise.

When the negative emotions ran very high at one point and it looked like things were going to run apart, Carter engaged in shuttle diplomacy moving back and forth between the two. He was serving as a mediator, a helper to resolve things as we described in earlier lectures. There was one point when it looked like things were really not going to work out and it seemed impossible when he took them over to Gettysburg and showed them the battlefield, and they walked through it, and he said if we can solve this and come together as a country you too can work this. So Mr. Carter worked very steadily to keep them at the table, keep hope, get them to know each other, and build empathy.

One of the other wonderful things that Carter did though had to do with reframing. That story kind of works like this. The date for this one that's best documented is September 17th, and there was a point here where they almost had things together, but there was an important point that Israel needed to agree to before Sadat could sign the Accords, and Mr. Begin was just feeling unwilling to do that. Mr. Carter went to see Begin and he took with him pictures for Begin's grandchildren, had their names written on the pictures. He laid out the pictures and showed them to him. Begin became emotional with this and Carter said this is not about Sadat and you. It's not about us. It's about them. It's about the future.

So Mr. Carter succeeded in reframing the discussion to being one about the future of children and grandchildren in Egypt and Israel, and on that basis, with that reframing Begin was willing to sign and he agreed and the Camp David Accords were signed. They led them to the Egypt/Israel Peace Treaty of 1979. Sadat and Begin shared the Nobel Peace Prize for 1978 for having accomplished that. That treaty between Egypt and Israel continues in place today, and that's a treaty in the volatile Middle East that's never been violated.

Hardliners on both sides extraneously objected. Mr. Sadat went home and was assassinated in 1981 by one of his countrymen, and Begin was roundly condemned by many of his countrymen for agreeing to this, but the treaty held. Notice what happens in that story. There's empathy built, there's the fractionating that Mr. Sadat initiated, and then there's the reframing that was so helpful in finishing it and making it happen at the end. So you can do that with a very difficult moral conflict that's already got a long, complex and difficult history.

That's example number one that I wanted to share with you. Now let's talk about another one. Let's turn our attention to the START treaty, the Strategic Arms Reduction Treaty, START 1 in this instance, the first one that was negotiated. It's an excellent example of fractionation once again that can occur.

This one is between the United States and the Soviet Union. During the Cold War, the United States and the Soviet Union each framed that conflict, that global conflict as a moral conflict. Each saw the other as a mortal enemy and each saw the other as somewhat evil. The United States fielded a global defense strategy, and believing that the Soviet sought to conquer and rule the world imposing communism on it, that strategy was played on a worldwide basis.

The Soviet Union on the other hand viewed the United States as a threat to its very existence, and the two countries fought proxy wars in Korea and Vietnam and in the Middle East and in Africa. There were proxy wars being fought where we engaged in various degrees, all the time holding each other at bay with nuclear weapons. The most notable one of these that came to near world destruction was in 1962 with the Cuban Missile Crisis. Each of these countries is defining the other in morally negative terms and condemning the other on those terms. President Reagan called the USSR the evil empire. So we're viewing this as a moral conflict.

The result of all of that, given that both of these countries had nuclear arms, was called the balance of terror. That was what we called it in popular jargon. In military circles, that balance of terror which we called it and I read in the newspapers in those days was called mutually assured destruction, mutually assured destruction, MAD for short, MAD.

Where were with this? That's a serious moral conflict. Unable to unwind their arms race in any single step, these countries remained deeply suspicious of one another, each saw potential threat from the other, and they couldn't see a way of reducing the level of threat even though they could see a value that might be achieved if they can do that. So how did that get to where we could talk about it?

There was a face-to-face meeting that occurred between Ronald Reagan and Mikhail Gorbachev. The two men got along reasonably well in that meeting and it turned out to be cordial. A certain amount of empathy was established between them. They began to understand each other a bit as human beings. Not long after getting to know Mr. Gorbachev a bit, President Reagan proposed negotiating an agreement to reduce and or limit the number of nuclear weapons. It wasn't a proposal to do the whole thing; it was a proposal once again to fractionate. Could we just bite off this piece of the great arms race and see if we can bring things down a bit doing that.

Mr. Gorbachev agreed. The negotiations were scheduled and they began. These negotiations took a whole lot longer than the intense couple of weeks it took to get through the Camp David negotiations. They in fact went on for years. They addressed fixed missile sites, submarine launched missiles. This was a huge, complex issue, strategic bombers, nuclear warheads. It was very complex and it required figuring out how they were going to mutually verify what was agreed to. So they had a lot to talk about.

It took them years to work this out, but the treaty working this out was finally agreed to. It was signed in 1991, President Reagan was no longer in office; it was signed by President George H. W. Bush in 1991. It went into effect in 1994. Its provisions were really interesting. They limited the two nations to a maximum of 6,000 nuclear warheads. That's an awful lot. You can do plenty with that.

What else could they do? They had extensive, intricate provisions for verification. Some of these are interesting. There were 365 B52 bombers in the United States flown to Davis-Monthan Air Force Base which is down there in Arizona where our university is, close to where I live. They split them in five pieces and left them dismantled there on the ground for three months so that the Russians could fly their satellites over and confirm the dismantling. I've seen pictures of that. So they did that. There were similar verifications that we were able to do there.

There's a Titan Missile Museum in Arizona near Tucson where we were allowed to keep one Titan Missile base with one missile in place unloaded. It's there at the museum, you can visit it today. The Russians were able to verify that there's a concrete door over it that's locked into place, half open and half closed and it can't be moved. So they trusted, but they verified. They worked this thing out, and they achieved a START I treaty based on fractionation of their big conflict.

When that treaty ran out, its time was up, they were able to negotiate again and just recently a further extension was negotiated by President Obama and President Medvedev of Russia. So we're still going with that one and we've been able to reduce the nuclear armaments a bit further. So that's a second really strong example of reducing a moral conflict.

Now I want to give you a third example. For this one let's bring this home to the United States and talk about what two western governors were able to do on the very morally-loaded issue of taking care of the environment. The two governors I want to talk about, one was very much an obvious liberal, a strong liberal; the other is a strong staunch conservative. One was the governor of Utah, the other was the governor of Oregon. And what they did was find a way to reach agreement for governors on how governors ought to manage environmental issues. They did it by carefully reframing a question that they were addressing.

If you think about this for a moment, issues of environmental management in the United States are typically framed in moral terms. Environmentalists talk in moral terms about saving the planet. On the other side people talk about destroying jobs. Those practicing policies and activities that are condemned by the environmentalists feel really unjustly and personally attacked and they tend to respond very defensively with scorn.

Each side in this struggle feels that it's morally right and that the other is morally wrong. So this thing is very much felt and structured in most conversation, most debate, as a kind of moral conflict. Direct real communication between these two is very unlikely, it doesn't work very well.

So into this scene, into this scene, let's bring the western governors to discuss the problem. Environmental management is very much something that western governors have to deal with. They are after all in these large western states where there are huge issues of environment. In my own state of Arizona, things like water are just huge. There's nowhere near enough of it for the number of people there and the more that are coming. There are issues of an environment like that that are enormous that have to be dealt with.

So the western governors have this thing in common. They're concerned about how they're going to do things. They had discussions going about how they could reach some agreement in terms of what they ought to do, but some of them are very liberal and some of them are very conservative. So how could they reach agreement?

In the late 1990s at the Western Governors Conference, one that was held up in Alaska, they had been having one of their governors-only discussions where just the governors met and talked, and the rest of the group that were there asked two governors John Kitzhaber of Oregon, the liberal, and Mike Leavitt of Utah, the conservative, if they could come together and try to draft a common statement that the association could make about how to manage environmental issues.

These two men are so much from opposite ends of the political spectrum, especially on matters of the environment. So what did they do? Let me note as we begin to move into their reframing, I was able to have several conversations with Governor Leavitt about this. He told me that these two men knew each other and had already achieved a level of respect for one another even though they were on opposite ends of the political spectrum. So these are a couple of guys with heavy responsibility. They share this business of being a governor of a western state, and they are two men who, though their politics are different, have a lot of respect for one another.

So they sat down to work this out. What did they do? As they were struggling to work it out, arguing over things, there was some moment and it's not clear, I don't think with either of them the way they describe the story, it's not clear with them, one of them asked is there anything about this that we can agree on. So they set out to make a list of the points of agreement that they had between them. They wrote it out on a piece of paper, they sketched it out, and they looked at it and it looked pretty promising.

What they were doing to get that points of agreement thing was they reframed it. Instead of debating the issues on which they differed, they changed the question and they said let's consider, let's brainstorm what we agree on. So they reframed the discussion. What they focused on were the principles that should be applied in making the decisions about those policies rather than what the policy should be. So it was a list of eight principles that they worked out.

Then in June 1998, the Western Governors Association held a conference. They took this, Kitzhaber and Leavitt had their staffs work this up. They invested some political capital in it. They brought it back to the western governors, and what came about next with this conference that was held in June of 1998 where what they did was they held a conference on shared environmental doctrine. They did some wonderful things for conflict management. They invited about 400 identified stakeholders from all sides on this issue. They structured it into various questions arising from these principles that Governors Kitzhaber and Leavitt had identified. They structured it into breakout groups.

They had a facilitator for each breakout group. I was privileged to be one of those facilitators. It was wonderful to get to be there. They had a governor host each breakout group, and they had people from all sides discuss an issue. It was held in Phoenix, Arizona and it's close for me to get to. What those breakout sessions did among other things is first produce some human understanding. They produced empathy the way there had been empathy between Leavitt and Kitzhaber to begin with.

Environmentalists softened a lot when they heard people on the other side really talk about how that felt. One of those instances in the session that I participated in involved, you had a number of environmentalists talking about the degradation of land caused by ranching, raising cattle on the land in the west. There was this rugged old rancher on the other side who listened to a whole lot of that and then he spoke up. He said, you know what's wrong with what you're saying is that we're all going to participate in the benefits that might come from that, but only a few of us are really going to pay the costs. You're asking me to pay the cost. He said I'm the fifth generation of my family to own and operate this ranch. We've always prided ourselves on taking good care of the land and developing it, and he said I don't want to be the member of my family who loses it.

When he said that and you could see the emotion in him, there began to be real communication across those sides. Governor Leavitt was the host of that session. He sat there and listened, it was a deeply moving moment, and by the time it was finished those people were all talking to each other very, very well.

What was the overall result of that conference? What happened was that the report-outs from the groups were put together and they were refined by the staffs. What the governors did then was build a set of principles which are called the Enlibra Principles. It's a term Governor Leavitt is very well wedded to, believes in. That set of principle, the Enlibra Principles, were adopted by the western governors and used and subsequently adopted by the National Governors Association in the United States.

It's a simple set. I'll give them to you in shorthand rather quickly here. The first principle said National Standards Neighborhood Solutions. The second principle said Collaboration, not Polarization. The third principle said Reward Results, not Programs. The fourth principle said Use Good Science for Facts and Good Process for Setting Priorities. The next principle said Markets before Mandates. The next one said Recognition of both the Benefits and the Costs of Environmental Efforts. The next one said Solutions that we Arrived at need to Transcend Political Boundaries. And the final one said Change a Heart, Change a Nation. Nice set of principles to follow that were adopted and they've conducted a number of conferences since listening to people and doing the work with those policies.

I want you to notice something about all three of these examples. It's something that's paradoxical. That is that the willingness and the ability of the people on all sides to take and defend a strong stand may be essential, at least it's important in breaking through to a genuine negotiation. These characters who did these things and achieved these agreements were not the middle of the road folks who see the gray. They were people who saw things in clear black and white, and they are people who really stood on their principles.

Begin stood on his principles, Sadat stood on his. Ronald Reagan stood clearly on his and didn't compromise. Gorbachev stood on his, and Leavitt and Kitzhaber, both, all stood on their principles here. All of these men held strong convictions. They stood by their principles. There isn't any compromising here. There's gaining empathy. There's fractionating, and then there's reframing to find something that they can all really strongly agree on.

That's three good, important examples that we can see where with a serious moral conflict people were able to come together and achieve something like a resolution. So in those examples of resolving moral conflict, there's plenty of hope there.

Let's try to summarize this. We've got these three marvelous examples. There are others, but those are three that I find particularly compelling. They're examples of successful management of a complex, apparently-intractable moral conflict. I want you to remember how much is involved here with building empathy and trust, doing the fractionating, and doing the reframing because those are approaches that have already been demonstrated to work and that can be successful in a moral conflict.

Note too that these are not examples of leaders abandoning or compromising on principles. It's not about having to compromise a way, but it is about achieving a win-win on the fractionated issues the way we've reframed them. So we can do that.

If empathy and trust building and fractionating and reframing can help to achieve agreements in these moral conflicts, you know what, they can help us in our personal lives as well. We do a lot of thinking of conflicts as moral in our own personal lives. What do we do with those in our communities, in our organizations, and at home? So what we could do is when we're tempted to describe a conflict in moral terms with someone else or we're feeling it that way, what we can do is remember these examples, look for empathy, fractionate, and reframe. We can bring these down to our level of moral conflicts too.

Here's your assignment for this lecture. Remember that all of us hold beliefs on some issues that we see as moral conflicts. I want to suggest that you identify one or two moral conflicts on which you have a strong opinion, a real moral commitment. Then ask and try to answer for yourself whether without compromising you might be able to agree with some reframing of that issue. Really wrestle with that and work with it. Do that in order to seek a resolution on some part of it so that you can carve out something, fractionate, and do a negotiation. Test that out in your own mind and see if you can see the possibilities for a better solution. That's moral conflict.

Where are we going to go from here? We've spoken a great deal about conflict and conflict management and conflict resolution, getting things to where they're resolved. There's one more big issue that we really need to talk with here in terms of conflict and getting our own conflicts resolved, and that is its aftermath. Conflict management doesn't necessarily end when we get a conflict resolved. We've still got work to do in following through, in cleaning up damage, in healing broken trusts and relationships. That's what we're going to talk about in our next lecture, healing conflict's aftermath.

Managing Conflict's Aftermath
Lecture 22

> When [transgressions] happen, we don't get to go back to the way it was, but we do get to move forward toward some new kind of normal state that can be good.

Managing conflict doesn't end when you reach an agreement, yet the aftermath of conflict is the most overlooked aspect of conflict management. This aftermath is often marked by emotional residues, damaged trust, and relational distance. How do we bring those in conflict back to a healthy relationship?

Even a well-intentioned effort at conflict resolution can sometimes yield the discovery that the differences between parties can't be bridged; one person may have to lose, which results in hurt feelings. That kind of damage can cause resentments to linger and new conflicts to emerge. What we need to work toward in conflict management are acceptance, apology, amends, forgiveness, reconciliation, and healing.

In the small number of conflicts that result in win-lose resolutions, the "loser" has to choose among accepting the outcome, escalating the conflict, or exiting. If you're in this position and you accept the outcome, take full responsibility for that choice. Remember that the other party hasn't decided to keep offending you; you've decided to live with certain conditions. This decision doesn't have to be permanent, however; you may choose to negotiate again later, escalate, or leave.

Escalating the conflict involves additional costs and risks—it may mean turning to official channels—but even if the conflict is escalated, it's still possible to move on after a resolution has been reached. If the conflict can't be resolved and you don't feel you can accept the conditions, you may have to terminate the relationship. You will feel the loss associated with termination even if you're leaving a bad relationship, but don't think of termination itself as a failure; in many cases, termination is the result of finally being honest about a failure of the relationship.

As we said, even conflicts that end with good resolutions often leave behind painful emotional residues. In the heat of a conflict, you may say something that hurts the other person. Trust may be broken if you discover that the other party wasn't completely honest with you. These "relational transgressions" are defined as actions or inactions that are perceived to be sufficiently serious violations of the relationship that they require explanation. Such transgressions often result from pursuing topic goals in a conflict at the expense of relational and identity goals. Managing conflict aftermath means moving toward healing in these instances; the goal is to work toward making the relationship positive again for both parties.

Reaching this goal begins with apologies, which have five parts: (1) a specific definition of the offending behavior, (2) an acknowledgment that the behavior caused harm, (3) a statement of responsibility for the behavior and the harm, (4) a statement of regret, and (5) a commitment to avoid repeating the behavior. If you are apologizing, focus on your own actions and avoid explaining them as a response to the other party's behavior.

Forgiveness is not approval of the other party's behavior but a letting go of emotional residues, and it may take time to occur.

The next step in the healing process is making amends, that is, fixing what has been broken, which may be part of the relationship itself. Beyond that is forgiveness. It may seem backwards, but it's true that if you're the one who has been offended, you forgive to benefit yourself. Forgiveness is not approval of the other party's behavior but a letting go of emotional residues, and it may take time to occur.

Next, you move toward reconciliation. This is an interactive process between the parties in a conflict that requires cooperative effort. It does not involve denying that the transgressions occurred but acknowledging them and trying to move forward. Reconciliation requires noticing new behavior and giving positive feedback; it may also require an iterative process of renegotiation.

The last step, healing, applies to both individuals and relationships. It involves getting to a point where you can reframe the conflict in a new context of your relationship. When you reach that point, you should honor yourselves for the struggle you've undergone to work through the conflict successfully.

The aftermath of a conflict can present several pitfalls: a lingering sense of opposition and resentment, insecurity about the relationship, and the emergence of taboo subjects. In all these cases, open communication and affirmation by both parties of each other can help get the relationship back on track.

Although the work is difficult, don't put off healing valuable relationships, or you may run out of time to do so. There's a saying that pain is necessary, but misery is optional. When we don't deal with the aftermath of conflict, we're continuing to be miserable when we don't have to. Making apologies can be hard work, but it's often very much worth doing. ∎

Suggested Reading

Fisher and Brown, *Getting Together: Building Relationships as We Negotiate.*

Gottman and DeClaire, *The Relationship Cure: A Five-Step Guide to Strengthening Your Marriage, Family, and Friendships.*

Lerner, *The Dance of Anger.*

Assignment

1. The next time you have an altercation with someone with whom you have an ongoing relationship, make a good apology, being sure to include all five components that we discussed in the lecture. Identify your part in whatever went wrong, regardless of what the other party did that may have been much worse.

Managing Conflict's Aftermath
Lecture 22—Transcript

In this lecture I want to look at what I think of as the most overlooked aspect of conflict management. This is the part that takes place over time, probably after what's thought of as a resolution has been achieved, or perhaps after the parties have even parted, or maybe they've just decided to carry on. It's overlooked in our lives; it's less studied by scholars, and frankly, I'm not clear why it's less studied by scholars because it's obviously important.

What I'm talking about in this lecture is what I call the aftermath of conflict. Managing conflict doesn't end when you get an agreement. There's the after part that goes on. That aftermath includes what are called emotional residues, the feelings that linger and stick around and come up again, and the damaged trust that might've taken place, and the relational distance that's happened, the hurt feelings, that stuff that's going on. How do we bring people back to whole? How do we bring the relationship back to whole? And how does this happen over time? That's what we need to talk about in this lecture.

How come there's all this aftermath to deal with? First of all nobody's perfect in conflict management, not I, not anyone else that I know of. All of us do some dysfunctional things when we're dealing with conflict and so there tend to be some hurt feelings and there are often damages to trust that take place. Those damages don't just disappear. It's not really all gone. I may feel better in the moment, but when I remember what happened, those bad feelings and that lack of trust will come back. That's why they call it residues. They're there and we can bring them back just by remembering.

Even a well-intentioned effort at resolving a conflict can sometimes yield a discovery that the actual differences here can't be bridged and somebody is going to have to lose, and losing even with the best of intentions on everybody's part still hurts and the hurt just doesn't stop. So it doesn't have to be dysfunctional. It can hurt anyway. That damage continues to happen. There's a tendency for relationships to harden, resentments to linger, and new conflicts to grow out of that.

Here we are in this lecture talking about managing conflict's aftermath. What we want to do here is explain the concepts that are involved with managing the concept of acceptance, apology, amends, forgiveness, reconciliation, and healing. I'm going to offer you some suggestions for accomplishing each of these.

I also want to note here that in some conflicts the aftermath is just too great to overcome; the breaches of trust may be too great, the emotional harm too painful, the relationship too broken. So we do also have to discuss termination here, letting go and moving on.

So let's get started. Let's start with the problem of having to lose. Sometimes, 20 percent or so as the rule of thumb, sometimes we can't get a win-win resolution. If we assume that in that left over 20 percent maybe we can take care of half of those with a compromise. That would leave us with 10 percent or something like that where somebody has got to lose. What if I'm the loser? I'm going to have to choose between accepting, escalating the conflict, and exiting, getting out of there. Those are my three choices. We talked about them earlier. Does that sound familiar to you, because we actually talked about them when we talked about the seven step process?

How should I make this choice? Let's start with acceptance, that's the first one that I can try. How do I do acceptance? It may be the best choice because no other person, no organization, no relationship can ever really be able to meet all of our needs and wishes. So there may be some things wrong that I've got to accept. There will always be some that aren't perfect. And in important relationships it's often reasonable to decide that the risks of escalating, or the costs of separating are just not worth it. So my choice is to accept.

The key to accepting and doing that well is to fully take responsibility for this choice. I talked about taking responsibility back when we talked about the seven step process as well. If I decided not to deal with this I said I've got to take responsibility for deciding not to deal with it. It's the same decision here. If I'm choosing to accept this condition, I'm choosing that. The other party isn't deciding to go ahead and keep offending me, I'm choosing to live with this condition. It's acceptance on my part. We dealt with that in Lectures 11 and 12 on the seven step process.

I may have to work at this in aftermath over time though, it's part of managing the aftermath and in virtually all couples and friendships and work relationships there tend to be behaviors of those other persons that we don't like, at least some behaviors, and we make this choice. We've decided they're not deal breakers so we're working at accepting them. That decision though doesn't have to be permanent. I'm taking responsibility, but you know what, I can still choose to negotiate again later or escalate or leave. So acceptance for now is the choice that I can make.

I might want to articulate that clearly to the other person that that's what I'm doing. If I just can't manage to be okay with it, I can always change my mind and go back and negotiate. We can look at an example of that.

Remember Rebecca and Jane, our roommates from Lecture 1. We've visited them several times. What if they negotiated an agreement, they had it worked out, and it wasn't going to work for Jane in one instance so she's now going to approach Rebecca and try to negotiate a temporary adjustment in that agreement. How would that look?

[Video start.]

>**Jane**: Hey, Rebecca. How was class?

>**Rebecca**: This public health seminar is really rough. But, I'll get through it.

>**Jane**: I know you will. And hey, only 6 more weeks to go! Listen, I know you need to get back to studying, but I have to ask you a favor. I know Wednesdays are supposed to be quiet nights, but my book club really needs a place to meet for the next two weeks. Is there any chance we could work something out just for this week and next?

Rebecca: Sure. I guess. I can probably go to the library and study those two nights.

Jane: Great, thanks.

Rebecca: So, tell me about this new project you started …

[Video end.]

That went smoothly. It didn't seem to be very difficult. It's a pretty reasonable thing to do and if you already have a pattern of negotiating and working things out with someone, that's not that difficult to do. So you can always renegotiate and change your mind.

Let's talk about the next opportunity you might have, or the next possibility to deal with this if you're the loser. What about escalation? Escalation works this way. It's going to involve additional costs and risks, if you escalate that's going to happen, but it might be the best available option. How might I escalate? This is a case where I might need to seek an ally in order to increase my power. If might involve turning to official channels and getting a formal judgment.

Remember Ben back in Lecture 17, the custodian, who had the back problem and he didn't want to have to pick up the trashcans. He didn't get an exemption from picking up the trashcans, so he said he wanted to file a grievance. His supervisor was fine with that. That's an escalation on Ben's part, and it can involve other things like threatening the other party with consequences in order to secure more cooperation.

Frequently it involves insisting on seeking mediation or counseling or arbitration. If that escalation leads to additional costs or anger or distance, then these consequences are going to have to be managed no matter how it turns out. It'll be harder, but still necessary to get to the point where everybody can just move on if we escalated a conflict. But that's what you'll want to do if keeping that feeling and continuing to feel badly wouldn't work. So escalation is an option.

What's the third option? The third option is I can just leave. It's the worst case scenario if I value the relationship, but it really is an option and we need to know that, and sometimes we need to just step up and do that. Sometimes the conflict really can't be resolved, a condition cannot be changed or will not be changed and it should not be accepted. So the best option might be to terminate a relationship. This could be an important romantic relationship, a work relationship, or a friendship.

If you remember back to Mark Knapp's point about relational stages in that model we talked about, he pointed out that most relationships necessarily are temporary because there are too many relationships for us to fully manage on a close level all the time. But terminating involves a loss. Loss always involves grieving.

I want us to note that I'm going to feel the loss and have to grieve even if I'm getting out of a bad relationship. I might be very relieved on one part away from that job and how I was treated or away from that mate who treated me so badly. But on the other hand I'm still going to have to grieve, because when I make that choice to exit, to terminate the relationship I'm also making a choice to let go of whatever it was I hoped that relationship would be, what was my dream for it, what it was supposed to be. I'm accepting the loss of what I was trying to get in that relationship and accepting that I'm not going to get it.

I'm going to have to go ahead and feel that loss. The best way through bad feelings is to go through them, go ahead and feel them.

A very wise man once said something to me about that. He said, "Michael if you're going through hell, just don't stop." I've cherished that statement. That's what we need to do. We need to go ahead and feel it and proceed through it and proceed with life anyway, feel it and keep moving and we'll get through it.

Also if you're doing that, you want to value your own and the other person's honesty and courage in getting to that decision to terminate. We don't honor that enough. We think of the termination as a failure when a lot of the time it's getting honest about a failure of the relationship that already happened and just getting real so we can move on. Sometimes termination is the best choice. They do involve acceptance of the other party when we do them, and that acceptance can be a gift to myself and also a gift to the other party.

You want to be careful if you're going to terminate to not buttress that decision with a lot of anger so that would cause you to do unnecessary harm. Don't ruminate about it, don't charge things up, don't fill yourself with enough anger to try to say goodbye. What you want to do if you're terminating is do it with what could be called a good goodbye.

Let's look at an example of that. Remember Jack and Maria, the budding romance that didn't work out. What would it look like if these people managed to do a good goodbye?

[Video start.]

> **Jack**: Well Maria, I wish our story had a happier ending. But I did want to say good-bye face to face—see you one last time.
>
> **Maria**: Me, too.
>
> **Jack**: We tried, right? I really did enjoy our time together, and I appreciated your honesty, even when it was hard to hear.
>
> **Maria**: Thanks, Jack. Yeah, I wish things worked out for us. But we have some great memories. And you still owe me your mom's cheesecake recipe!
>
> **Jack**: Yeah, you're right, I do. Well, I should get going.
>
> **Maria**: Yeah, me too. Bye Jack.

[Video end.]

Maybe that one was a bit idealistic, but you could do that. Good goodbyes really do stay with us and so do the bad ones. So if I'm parting, breaking off a relationship, it would be nice to work at making a good ending to it with a good goodbye. That's a useful tip.

What if there's a good resolution? There are aftermath problems that can come with that. Often, yes, with the very best of intentions we're working on resolving a conflict and we don't really do the perfect job of resolving it. So even though we got through to a good resolution, we didn't have to accept, we even got what we wanted, but still in that process because we didn't handle it perfectly, we've created some painful emotional residues.

One example here is that in the heat of a conflict when we're angry we can say something that really hurts the other person. We know we've said it, the minute it gets out of our mouth, we could wish we hadn't said it, you can't take it back. That's the thing about communication, it only goes one direction, once it's said it can't be unsaid. Here's a for instance.

[Video start.]

> **Jane**: Hey, Rebecca.
>
> **Rebecca**: Hey.
>
> **Jane**: So how was class?
>
> **Rebecca**: This public health seminar is really rough. But, I'll get through it.
>
> **Jane**: I know you will. And hey, only 6 more weeks! Listen, I know you need to get back to studying, but I have to ask you a favor. I know that Wednesdays are supposed to be quiet nights, but my book club really needs a place to meet for the next two weeks. Is there any way we can figure something out just for this week and next?

Rebecca: Are you kidding me? We're barely 2 weeks into this thing and you're already asking for a change for your silly book club? We made a deal! Besides, three bottles of wine and a trashy novel are hardly a book club.

Jane: Sorry I even asked.

[Video end.]

In the heat of the moment Rebecca has done some damage here. Nobody wants to hear that their book club is silly. That hurts. That was an insult and it was taken as one. So what have we got here? There are going to be some emotional residues. Often too there's broken trust where somebody was not fully honest. That would even have greater residues and more difficult things to handle. One party behaved in a way that actually harmed the other, and the challenge to the trust offending behavior, how do we know that that's not going to recur, so how do we trust again? Rebuilding trust is very difficult after it has been broken. So there's emotional distance and there is defensiveness that's created.

One of the things we call these is relational transgressions. The definition of a relational transgression is interesting. It says that an action or inaction is perceived to be a violation of the relationship that's at least serious enough to require some sort of an explanation. That's a relational transgression and what researchers look at. Transgressions are especially subject to the fundamental attribution error that we've talked about. When I do something wrong and it offends the other person that way, that person with the attribution error is most apt to think that I did that because of how I feel about them or some aspect of my character. They will relate it to me personally and that will make it hurt more.

So transgressions are a problem that's going to have to be dealt with and they often result from pursuing our topic goals in a conflict at the expense of relational goals and identity goals including the other party's relational goals and identity goals. When these transgressions have occurred, they're going to require some healing.

Managing aftermath involves moving toward healing in these instances and it requires both parties and it works on healing both the parties in a relationship. It involves addressing the past, you can't get to the future without addressing it, but moving toward the future. It involves trying to get to where we feel better, really feel good, where the relationship can be positive again and be good for both parties and strong.

How do we do that? It begins with apologies. Each party has got to take full responsibility for their part. Real apologies have five essential parts. I even hate thinking about all these because I don't like to do apologies, but I need to do this. We all do when we have a transgression to apologize for. It requires a specific definition of the offending behavior. You've got to say what you did. Then you've got to acknowledge that it was harmful, that the behavior caused harm. Third you've got to take responsibility for the behavior and for the harm. Then fourth you've got to say that you regret that, and fifth, very important, you really have to make a commitment to avoid repeating it.

Here's a good example of a good apology. Remember Barney's kids trampled on Dan's flowers in the example and Dan had the payback when we were talking about dysfunctional strategies, so Dan went and ruined Barney's vegetable garden and Dan's wife was mortified. What if Dan does a good apology for that action?

[Video start.]

> **Dan**: Barney!
>
> **Barney**: Yeah?
>
> **Dan**: Listen. I owe you an apology. I just lost it when your kids ran onto my flowers, and I went and stomped on your vegetable garden. That was way out of line. I know you and your family are upset, and I'm really sorry that I did it. It was childish on my part and I promise it won't happen again.

Barney: Thanks, Dan. I appreciate that. And I'll tell the kids to be more careful from now on.

[Video end.]

If I'm Barney I don't think I'm really ready to forgive Dan yet about that, but that was a good apology. Dan has taken responsibility for his own action. You notice he didn't justify it at all by complaining about what Barney's kids did. He just apologized for the action, and he went through those five steps I just laid out.

In apologizing we've got to focus on my own behavior and really avoid explaining it as a response to the other party's behavior. You don't want to do what I call a finger pointing apology like I'm sorry for what I did, but you did blah, blah, blah. That's not what you want to do. You want to take responsibility for your own, apologize for it, and leave the other person's apology to him or her if there's one to be had.

Here's an example. Let's revisit the scene we just looked at, but note the different language and tone on Dan's part this time.

[Video start.]

Dan: Listen, Barney.

Barney: Yeah?

Dan: I know I overreacted to your kids' running over my flower beds, and then I went and ruined your vegetable garden. I'm sorry about that. I know I upset everyone. But, you know, I was upset, too. I worked hard on those flowers and then your kids come along and trampled on them!

Barney: Okay, okay, Dan. Let's just say it's over. I'll tell the kids to be more careful next time.

[Video end.]

Isn't that what we would feel like doing often making an apology? But you notice the trouble that makes. Once you've justified it on the part as responding to someone else, you're going to lose the whole purpose of the apology. So stick to the first example. Don't go to the second one. Take responsibility for your own behavior. Apologize for that and you're okay.

Now let's turn to going beyond the apology because apology is just step one in moving toward healing. The next thing we have to do is what is called making amends. An amend is a fix. It's mending, it's making it better. Apologizing is just saying we're sorry. Amends is fixing what we broke. Sometimes I can't directly fix what I've broken, but I can make an indirect amends and restore the party of the relationship in some other way, but I want to move toward doing that.

I want to note here that apology and amends are both done to help the other party. I want to go ahead and try to fix what I've broken and I've got to be willing to do that. It's not done when I apologize. But if I'm doing that, then we move to the other party's part. If the other person is making amends and apologizing to me, what moves for me to do then in terms of the steps toward healing? That brings to what we want to talk about forgiveness.

Forgiveness is thought of as benefitting the other party, but unlike apology and amends forgiveness is done to benefit myself if I'm the one who has been offended. It seems backwards, but it's true. Pay attention to what I'm saying here. It doesn't mean I'm approving of the other party's behavior, what it does mean is that forgiving them is letting go of those emotional residues, letting go of feeling bad about it. It does preserve and enhance the relationship. I want you to note also when we're talking about forgiveness that this is not entirely a voluntary thing that we do. It may take time to occur. I can be trying, it may take time.

Forgiveness involves letting go of feelings that feel bad and we've already explained that we don't have automatic direct control of our feelings, so I just can turn off the feeling to let go. But I really do want to be moving in that direction. Counselors working with couples and families have a wonderful way to help us do this thing that many of them use. They have one person ask for forgiveness for a transgression, and then you've got three possible responses if you're the person offended by the transgression. If you're asked if you are willing to forgive or are you ready to forgive you can answer yes, no, or I'll work on it.

In that case if you're really ready to let go and it's not forced you say yes. You might not be willing to think about it if you're still angry. You can honestly say no although you want to move in that direction. But if you're in that somewhere in between working through this managing the aftermath, I'll work on it is a pretty darn good answer. So your response is that.

If we've got forgiveness going where do we go from there? The next step would be moving toward reconciliation. When we talk about reconciliation we're really talking about an interactive process between the parties. It's an interactive thing and it requires both of them to act to move together. Reconciliation is a cooperative effort that two people make working together. It takes place over time and it typically involves doing things like taking the risk of trusting somebody again when trust has been broken. You don't want to be too quick and easy with that, but you want to move in that direction.

It does not involve denying that the transgressions occurred or that the harms occurred. It does not mean that, but it does mean moving forward. We acknowledge what happened that wasn't okay and how it hurt, and now we move forward from there. It does not mean getting back to some previous state. When things happen we don't get to go back to the way it was, but we do get to move forward towards some new kind of normal state that can be good.

This is going to require noticing a new behavior. It's going to require, as I talked about in step seven of the seven step process, giving positive feedback. It's very, very often going to require renegotiating and it is what is called an iterative process, you're going to want iteration as you put something forward and you try that. If that doesn't work you renegotiate, you think about that again, and you put another thing forward. It moves in that direction, and it's real only if it's voluntary and mutual between the two parties. That's reconciliation.

That moves us toward healing. What do I mean healing here? Healing applies to both the individual and the relationship. People heal and relationships heal. Healing involves getting to a point where you can sort of reframe the conflict or the transgression itself and the new context of this relationship. People really do do this, they move beyond and things get different, they don't get the same as they were. So we reframe and think about it. It includes recognizing the struggle that you went through with the hurt and recognizing that you're getting through together, making an effort to a successful new place. You can celebrate and honor that between yourselves. Healing moves in that kind of direction.

What happens then is our identities really adjust and grow with it. We feel different from the way we were and the relationship does, what we're doing is building new experience together over that old experience. The old experience doesn't go away. The old experience doesn't go away, but we build new experience together over it. Healing the relationship requires accepting that the other party really is as he or she is. I want to remind you here that you don't want the other party to be, especially in any close relationship, like a project where you're trying to fix them or make them better. That never actually works. I've got to accept them and appreciate them as they are barnacles and all.

So healing involves all of those pieces. It takes time and effort, so be patient with yourselves, and there can be missteps on the way, but we have to give time time to really work to make the healing happen. Those are important steps in the aftermath and they can't be skipped.

I also want to talk about just several pitfalls that you want to avoid that are common in the aftermath period after a conflict. They can become very serious unless we communicate back and forth about them and try to work through them. One of them is that there's this lingering sense of opposition and resentment that can set it and harden. When that's going on, you're going to need to talk about it. Don't hide it, you've got to bring it out in the open, put it on the table, and begin to talk about it in order to move on toward reconciliation.

A second one is, and this one's very dangerous, the parties can feel insecure in that relationship, the one who has done the transgressions as well as the other one, and it's very important to use open communication and affirming of one another, getting things right, and recognizing that when you do so there's a sense of security in the relationship can be really developed, because you're going to need that.

A third one is that taboo subjects emerge. We just don't talk about that thing that that clash was about. What happens then is people get silent about it. Silence is not agreement, and silence isn't that it's settled. Silence makes us hold on to secrets, and secrets create distance and damage trust themselves. So I've got to trust one another enough to be open and get those taboo subjects on the table and try to talk them through. It's worth it if we make the effort.

Finally on this subject, I want us to think briefly about the kind of attention to aftermath that we have to give and that working at forgiveness and healing is really worth the effort. It seems like it's a soft subject; it sounds like it isn't this tender and sweet. Let me give you a true story about me on this one.

Back in the era when I was engaged very much in an adversarial processes myself, I once went through a process of advocating a grievance procedure for a faculty colleague. I won the case for my colleague, but in the process I had to cross examine a man who was the head of the department in which I taught, and this was a very kind man who had always been kind to me. In my argumentative intensity as I cross examined him I did it in a way that I really made the people judging this thing laugh at him. I made him out to be a fool and he wasn't a fool, he had just made a wrong decision.

I did that and I knew that it hurt him. This guy continued to be kind to me after that. He never complained about it. He never said anything, but I went on for several years feeling that I shouldn't have done that and feeling bad. Then one day several years later as I was much more into working with conflict management I got to thinking back about that and I thought you know I need to talk to him and apologize. The day that I decided I was going to go see him and apologize I got to the university and he wasn't there that day. It turns out that while on his morning walk that morning he had had a heart attack, sat down under a tree, and just quietly passed away and I never got to apologize.

You know what, that's a worst case scenario for me, but there are people who didn't get around to healing relationships, doing the apologies, building things back together with important loved ones all over. And people die, that's the worst case scenario. They don't get it resolved. In the meantime even if people don't die, and they don't, they're living with that misery. If we're not doing the healing, we're living with discomfort and so it reduces communication, limits rapport, reduces joy, and we have pains and things that we didn't have to have.

There's a saying too that pain is necessary, but misery is optional. When we don't deal with the aftermath, we're just continuing to be miserable when we didn't have to. So it's not the domain of soft people; it's not for the faint-hearted. Getting out and doing those apologies can be hard work, but I want to suggest to you that it's very, very much worth doing.

Let's summarize then. I hope you see now why aftermath is a part of conflict management that even though we don't like to focus on it we really need to do it. I hope you see why you need to give it careful attention and to do that over time. If we can't resolve a conflict, our choices are to accept the condition as it is, escalate, or go ahead and leave. I want us to recognize that even when we get good resolutions you can still have aftermath problems that you're going to have to deal with. We can manage the conflict aftermath and heal ourselves and we can heal the relationship in doing it.

The steps we talked about here, and they tend to come in an order are acceptance, apology, making those amends, moving to forgiveness, working toward reconciliation. All of this requires some courage and requires lots of communication between the people that are involved. They also require time and patience to get done.

I've got an assignment for you from this lecture. I want you to remember that apologizing is only the beginning of making amends and moving toward healing a relationship, but it sure is the right place to start. So here's a tough assignment. The next time, the very next time you have an altercation with someone in an ongoing relationship where you've done any part of it that could've been hurtful even if the other person did much worse to you, I want you to do a good apology. It won't hurt, I promise.

I want you to carefully consider and identify your own part in what went wrong. Identify your part regardless, get together with the other person, do it face to face, and go through those steps of apologizing that we talked about, all five steps. That's your assignment.

Where are we going to go from here? We've talked about conflict's aftermath now, there's just one more thing we really need to talk about before we can move toward wrapping this course up. And that's the future. How are we going to teach our children about this stuff so that conflict management can continue to be better and they can have a better time with it than we do. That's Lecture 23.

Teaching Our Children about Conflict
Lecture 23

Kids can learn early the principle of win-win because it's real, and they can experience win-win resolutions and carry that into their adult life.

Today's children learn a mixed set of lessons about managing conflict, some of which are helpful and some genuinely harmful. That learning begins and continues at home and takes place in neighborhoods, at school, and through the media. At home, children learn about handling conflict primarily from watching their parents and older siblings, and they may draw painful and frightening lessons from our poor handling of conflict. For example, to a child, any comment about one parent by the other, either negative or positive, is taken as a judgment about that parent and about the child. In other words, a criticism of the other parent can go right to the child's heart. Research has shown that children in high-conflict families have greater problems with psychological adjustment, conduct, and self-concept. The way parents communicate during a conflict—not whether they have a conflict—has a significant effect on the child's well-being.

The way parents communicate during a conflict—not whether they have a conflict—has a significant effect on the child's well-being.

As parents, we must model good conflict management for our children. Don't fall into the trap of avoidance, but do try to minimize children's exposure to ongoing strife. Even if you're going through a divorce, model civility and constructive communication. In addition to modeling, we can also use direct instruction. Consciously explain to children how to manage conflict and the consequences of good and bad conflict management. Provide positive feedback when children practice good conflict management strategies, and don't reinforce bad strategies, such as throwing temper tantrums.

Make sure the family structure includes power for everybody. Children don't have equal power with parents, but they shouldn't be powerless, because

Conflict learning begins at home as toddlers (if not before) and continues throughout their lives in their neighborhood, at school, and in the media.

that traps them into thinking that they're not responsible for anything. If the conflict is between you and your child, listen to the child and negotiate when appropriate. The family meetings that we talked about in Lecture 15 can be used to give children a voice.

The lessons we teach children about managing conflict are quite similar to those for adults that we've discussed throughout this course. Teach children to express their feelings using "I" statements, to listen to the other person and avoid snap judgments, to consider the other person's point of view and feelings, to take responsibility for their own behavior and apologize, to invite the other person to work toward a resolution together, to manage their emotions, and not to hold grudges.

Children also learn a great deal about managing conflict outside the home, and lessons learned while playing with other children may sometimes contradict or overshadow what is taught at home. My own experience with a neighborhood bully illustrates the fact that parents don't have complete control over what their children learn.

The research of Calvin Morrill, a sociologist at the University of California, has shown that as they move through adolescence, young people apply roughly the same set of conflict management strategies that their parents use. Further, conflict management itself seems to be a development process; as teenagers become more rational and more attuned to moral questions, they also become less impulsive. For parents, this means they should avoid being either over- or underprotective. Children must go out into the world, take some risks, and solve some problems on their own. Even at the college level, children should be able to rely on their parents for support, but we need to avoid the temptation to become "helicopter parents," hovering over our children, ready to swoop in and rescue them at a moment's notice.

Many schools now offer direct instruction in conflict management, along with peer mediation programs. In these programs, student volunteers learn conflict management strategies and help their fellow students in resolving conflicts.

Of course, children also learn a great deal about conflict from the media. Happily, violence on television does not cause the vast majority of children to become more violent, but it does result in increased aggression for some. Violence in video games seems to have an even greater affect on these same children. Researchers have also studied the influence of narratives in entertainment on children. As we know, most television shows and movies are centered on a main character who encounters an obstacle, and the narrative focuses on how that character chooses to deal with the obstacle. Seldom do we see the character pursuing a win-win resolution; instead, the plot usually involves some kind of clash or deception. As parents, we should be aware that these are the lessons children are taking in. One way to find "teachable moments" is to watch what your children are watching and talk about how conflicts are handled. ∎

Fitzell, *Free the Children! Conflict Education for Strong, Peaceful Minds*.

Gottman, DeClaire, and Goleman, *Raising an Emotionally Intelligent Child: The Heart of Parenting*.

Neuman and Bashe, *Helping Your Kids Cope with Divorce the Sandcastles Way*.

Segrin and Flora, *Family Communication*.

The following is a list of resources that feature good conflict management skills and outcomes, including children's books and books for teens.

Classics: The plots of some classics of enduring interest resolve conflicts in constructive ways. Two examples are:

- Maurice Sendak's *Where the Wild Things Are*, which illustrates the potential damage of anger and revenge and the better results of forgiveness and working together.

- Harper Lee's *To Kill a Mocking Bird*, in which Atticus Finch employs the adversary system with skill, passion, and integrity to achieve a just outcome.

For young children: TeachersFirst.com lists good books for children by age range. Examples include:

- *Curious George* by Hans Augusto Ray (for ages 4 to 8).

- *A Light in the Attic* by Shel Silverstein (for ages 9 to 12).

For teens: The Young Adult Library Services Association (YALSA) lists current books for teens in which constructive resolution strategies are effectively employed (www.ala.org/yalsa). The 2010 winner of YALSA's Michael L. Prinz Award, *Going Bovine* by Libba Bray, is an excellent example.

Assignments

1. Ask yourself what you learned about conflict from your family. Consider how your early experience affects the way you manage conflict today.

2. How can you demonstrate constructive conflict management to your children? How can you help them manage conflict constructively?

Teaching Our Children about Conflict
Lecture 23—Transcript

The problem of how to manage conflicts is not just a challenge for today, it's also a challenge for the future because we really want to prepare our children to have better lives than ours. That's every parent's wish. So we need to talk about here in this lecture how to teach our children about conflict. We know a lot about conflict that our parents didn't know. So we have an advantage there. Our challenge is to pass this knowledge on to our children to help them build skills for using it so that they can do better with it than we do.

That's our subject in this lecture. What we want to do here is look at what our children are learning about conflict and how it's managed, where they're learning it, what we're learning about how to teach children about what we're learning about what they're learning, and we want to look at ways to improve what they're learning. We're going to conclude that there's good reason to hope that our children really do have a better shot at managing conflict than we do, just as we had a better shot than our parents had.

So let's get started. What do our children learn about conflict now and where do they learn it? What they learn is a very mixed set of lessons about managing conflict. Some of those are helpful and some of them are not so helpful, and some are genuinely harmful. That learning begins and continues at home just like ours did, at least when they're toddlers if not before, but then it continues in their neighborhoods, it continues at school, and it's ongoing in the media as all of that takes place.

So how do they learn? Let's start at home with how we teach our children there. The way children learn mostly at home from their parents is by watching us and watching their siblings especially if they have older siblings, watching how we handle conflict and deal with it, and then they try things out for themselves. From the actions and words of parents, children gain a great deal and they get hurt a great deal when those don't work. They really learn what they regard as normal behavior from us watching us. We do so much more teaching of our children when we're not intending to teach them then when we're actually intending to teach them.

One of the ways we do that is whenever we handle a conflict poorly and the children know about it, that's painful and it's frightening for them and they draw lessons from it. Those lessons can be detrimental over the long run, it can be detrimental over their lives. We teach them about love and how that works. We teach them about relationships by relating, and we also teach them about who they are and how they're valued when we deal with conflict including when we deal with conflict with them.

We know some things about this. For instance we know that to a child any comment about one parent by the other parent either negative or positive is taken as a judgment about that parent, but the child takes it in also as a judgment about him or her. So criticism of the other parent can go right to the child's heart. So when we're being negative and not handling the conflict well, we're hurting the child and the child is learning something that we didn't want them to pick up.

We know from research that children in high-conflict families, where conflict is going on and it's not being handled well so that it's oppositional and hostile, those children certainly have greater problems with psychological adjustment, with their conduct, and with their self concept. The evidence suggests that the way parents communicate during a conflict, not whether they have a conflict, but the way they communicate, the way they interact with each other in a conflict, that's the thing that's going to affect the child's wellbeing most and that's what's going to give the child the lessons for how to deal with their own conflicts as they move along.

So how can we teach them, how can we do a better job of teaching them? One is we know we have to model good conflict management for our children. That can be awfully difficult. I don't like being on the spot where I've got to handle my conflicts well, not just for me, but if the kids are watching what's going on is going to have an effect on their lives. That's an enormous load for a parent to carry, but it's our load as a parent. Anybody who's a parent knows we're in over our heads, but we have to do our best.

So what I want to do is model the best conflict management I can do. That doesn't mean we ought to do avoidance of conflict or to try to guarantee that no conflict occurs. If we're avoiding, resolution is not going to occur and what the children will pick up is the resentment that that breeds and they'll see things that don't really make sense to them. They need to see good conflict management in place, not conflict avoidance.

When there's strife in the parents' relationship children really tune into that. They observe us much more closely when that's going on. So when it's strife and it's ugly, minimize their exposure to ongoing strife. If things are going to be handled, they need to be gotten on the table, you don't put it all in front of the kids, but you don't hide it from them and you don't want an ongoing struggle taking place that the kids are watching and worrying about. This is especially important in what happens when parents separate or divorce.

Getting kids through that is extremely difficult and they're watching us more closely then so they're picking up lessons and they're being more strongly imprinted. So you don't want to unnecessarily expose them to the ugly side of the conflict that happens that way. Even in those difficult times, we've got to pay attention to modeling civility for the kids, we've got to try to handle the conflicts constructively and get through that and move toward the kind of good goodbye that I was talking about in the aftermath lecture last time.

We want to help the children cope with this ongoing conflict as it takes place. If you think about it, that conflict that's occurring if it's going to a divorce or a separation, that's the ultimate for children in that critical communication context that we talked about when we talked about close personal relationships awhile ago. So we really have to do a lot more communicating and get the kids through that.

What else can we do? It's not just modeling. What else is there? There's direct instruction. We can teach children consciously describing and explaining how to manage conflict and about the consequences of good conflict management and bad conflict management. That kind of verbal instruction requires a lot of repetition. One of the things we know in communication research is that repetition is not a bad thing. Repetition is a necessary thing for any of us to get it. We need redundancy of messages for them to stick, especially when we're trying to teach kids.

So we need to explain a lot and we need to do it repeatedly. We need to watch for teachable moments when we have an opportunity to explain and take advantage of those. We also need to ensure that when the kids do good conflict management strategies they at least get some positive feedback for that, and you know they will get their share of good results, but there will be no guarantees. You don't always get good results when you do a good job, but you get your share of good results.

We also want to avoid paying off poor conflict management strategies. There should be no payoffs for kids for bad behavior, and they do that. When I think about this I think a lot of times in work situations that we can go to work and sometimes we can identify the person in the workplace who learned as a toddler that behavior of temper tantrums is going to work. I tried that with a parent and it worked and that little kid learned to do temper tantrums and got skilled at it, and some of those people are our work colleagues today still using temper tantrums to get what they want. So don't pay off bad conflict management behavior. Try to make the good conflict management behavior pay off.

It's also true in the family in terms of teaching kids that you want the family power and interaction struggle to include power for everybody. Children surely don't have equal power with parents, but they've got to have influence. They shouldn't be powerless people because that traps them into that thing where they're not responsible for anything. In families where power feels shared, where all members feel like they have at least some influence and they count in that sense, conflicts are going to be handled better. So we want that to happen for our children in conflicts.

If the conflict is between us and the children, the parent/child conflicts, we need to listen and negotiate when that's appropriate and possible, but then exercise parental authority when it's needed. These things are so easy for me to stand here and say and in the heat of the moment with the kid who has been acting up out in some way, that can be very difficult. But that's what we need to try to do as a parent.

A useful tool for doing this is practicing and teaching the kids to practice the perspective taking that we talked about way back in Lecture 4 and using those regular family meetings that we recommended in Lecture 15. Those elements, especially those family meetings, can be used to give children a voice, but in an appropriate amount and to let them speak their turn, have their say, and be heard. Those things really help children learn. We can teach them at home. We can teach them in a family how to better resolve conflicts.

What exactly should we teach them? These are the lessons that they really ought to get about managing conflict. They're the same things we talked about in the lectures throughout this course. One, we need to teach them to express feelings and talk about how they feel using I statements, not acting out, and not using you statements, the accusations of the other party. We can teach children to phrase things that way, and this is much easier to learn early if you're a child then it is to learn for us as adults.

Secondly, we can teach them to listen to the other person and to try not to judge the other person when we're doing it. As kids we want to easily snap to judgments, and we can help them refrain from doing that. Thirdly, we can teach them to consider the other person's point of view and their feelings as they move forward. It's an important thing to remind them and to teach them and we can do this talking to them and working with them when they're in conflict.

Fourth, we want to teach them to take responsibility for their own part in a conflict, their own behavior, and to apologize when it's important. It's not just tell Johnny you're sorry, but help them learn those five steps of an apology that we talked about, and teach them to take responsibility for their own behavior. Fifth, we can teach them to invite the other person in a conflict to work together with them to resolve a conflict. Kids can learn early the principle of win-win because it's real and they can experience win-win resolutions and carry that into their adult life.

Sixth, we need to teach them to work with their emotions, to manage those emotions. I don't mean to teach them to turn emotions off or turn emotions on because we can't really do that as adults and kids certainly can't. But we can teach them not to behave in ways where they're acting out on negative emotions. We can teach them to take a time out and calm down and not focus on the thing that's upsetting them. We can teach them to manage their behavior when they're having emotions so that they can report those emotions appropriately and get on with working through the conflict.

Seventh, we can teach them not to hold grudges, to move toward healing and getting past things. We can teach kids that we can talk to them about it. We can show them and we can suggest ways that they can do it. And eighth, we can teach them to practice these skills. We can work with them to practice these skills in conflicts with us as we move along. So we've got a lot of teaching that we can do. We have great opportunities as parents to work with our kids and teach them directly about managing conflict.

That's managing conflict in the home. What about what they learn from managing conflict, what about their learning outside the home because we don't get to keep them under our care all the time? Children learn an awful lot about how they're going to manage conflict outside the home, and we can think of this as beginning in the neighborhood. The lessons that happen on the street and with kids when they're playing in the yard and a lot of these lessons can contradict what they learned at home and they can be more potent.

When I think of this I always go back to an event that happened in my life when I think I was seven, I might've been only six. It was the point where I was beginning to go out and play beyond the yard and move up and down the street on the block where we lived. Wen I got out there beyond our own front porch a thing that happened on several occasions would be that I would get out there and this one other boy in the neighborhood would come bounding out from behind a bush or a tree and come running up and hit me, knock me down, and actually stomped on me. It was pretty ugly, and I who was a skinny, little kid in terror would jump up and run home screaming and run in the house crying.

This happened several times. My mother was very upset by this and she immediately went down the street to the boy's house and complained to his mother, which in turn got him in trouble, so the next time I went out he hit me even harder. So this wasn't working out for little Michael. Intervening on this was my dad and our next door neighbor, a wonderful guy, Mr. Benton our neighbor. They decided that little Michael needs to learn to defend himself, these two men did.

So they went out and got two pairs of boxing gloves and my dad got down on his knees with me in the living room and he taught me how to block a punch and how to throw a punch straight from the shoulder, and he explained to me carefully you never attack another person without being attacked, but this is how you defend yourself if the other person attacks you, block a punch, throw a punch. We practiced in the living room.

Then when they thought that I had learned this lesson we took the gloves off and I went out the front door and went out to play, and sure enough that fellow from down the street came out from behind a bush, came running up and went to take a swing at me, and just as I was taught, blocked that punch, threw a punch straight into his face, right into his nose, which obligingly began to bleed profusely. He burst into tears and ran home crying.

My dad and Mr. Benton had seen this through the living room window. They came out onto the front porch and cheered, and a got a ride on my dad's shoulders up the street to the neighborhood drugstore and I had the first chocolate milkshake I'd ever had in my life, and it was the most wonderful thing I'd ever tasted. That was a marvelous lesson in conflict management.

Notice my dad was teaching me in the house how to do this right, careful instruction, but I learned some things on the street. I didn't just learn how to block a punch and throw a punch when I was attacked. I had also learned that ambush and terrifying the other person is a really potent and powerful thing to do. I became a bit of a neighborhood bully after that, and I ambushed a few people myself. So which lessons did I learn? In part I learned them both, but the parent doesn't have full control of what the child is learning. We learn things on the street.

Then we go test our learnings themselves and we experiment with independence. Most research on how young people handle conflict has really been focused on whether they're going to learn violence, especially when they get into gang violence. That's where so much research has been done. But there's also research that's broader going on. Calvin Morrill, a sociologist at UC Berkeley, and some of his colleagues have been taking a much wider view, a much wider contextual view of this.

They've been looking at how young people really learn to apply strategies for conflict and how they handle conflict in general. What they're finding is these kids, as they move up through adolescence, are applying roughly the same set of conflict management strategies that their parents are applying. They're finding that this is a developmental process; that the kids tend to get more rational and more attuned to moral questions as they do that, what's the right thing to do as they move along, and they get less impulsive as they progress through adolescence. Pretty good news in terms of how people handle conflicts in general.

How do we want to deal with any of this as parents? We're going to want to avoid being either overprotective or underprotective. The kids have to get out there in the world and learn and develop as they go along. But we have a lot of teaching still to do. They are going to have to learn to take some risks and solve some problems on their own. That's really an essential part of their development.

One of the things we have as a term at universities these days that's pretty widespread is we talk about what we call helicopter parents. The helicopter parent is a parent where hovering in a helicopter over their kid as they move through campus and to our classes ready to descend and rescue the kid whenever the kid gets into a problem, and in this age where the kids can talk to their parents on cell phones day in and day out as they move about the campus, that's a strong temptation.

So kids are going to need to feel, all the way up through college level and into adulthood, that they can rely on their parents for support and backup, but they don't want to be jumping to mom and dad help me as soon as they get into a conflict. So parents do need to and they usually do know what their children are encountering, but not in detail. They need to be able to help them process what happens, but we don't want them to jump in and just resolve every conflict for the kids. They've got to learn some conflict management themselves. So that's when they hit the streets and where they go from there.

What about learning conflict management at school? Schools are interesting places for learning this these days. Kids of course get modeling form their teachers and their peers at school, and the same things they learn in the neighborhood they learn on playgrounds and in the halls. Those lessons are continuing. They're continuing to learn from peers the same way they would there, but at schools these lessons and influences seem to be significantly magnified.

What does happen at school is teachers serve as models, children observe how they handle it, and observe how teachers deal with each other and with the staff. But beyond there's direct instruction that takes place at schools these days. It's uneven, some schools have excellent programs, some have none at all. It's uneven, but many schools these days do some very good instruction of children in terms of conflict management.

One of the best things for doing this, one of the best programs for doing this is called peer mediation. There are peer mediation programs in many schools in the United States and in Canada. In these programs what happens is the students are invited to volunteer, they learn about it and they're invited to volunteer, and then the students that volunteer receive instruction in how to help others resolve conflicts. It's the helping others material that I gave you in that lecture. They learn those things and are only taught at a children's level in grade schools and some in high schools.

These programs have an excellent track record. Then what happens is when other kids in the school have a conflict going, they have the opportunity to have a peer mediator, one of these children that has been trained, and they have an excellent track record helping each other work through conflicts. In that process, all the kids learn to better manage conflicts. So these things work very, very well. There are other structured programs that are called peace circles and there are programs at schools these days for managing bully behavior on the playgrounds, a whole lot of different programs, but I'm very impressed with those peer mediation programs that take place.

There's actually a section of the Association for Conflict Resolution called the Education Section, which is actively supporting development of those programs. All kinds of schools, colleges very often have these. Many colleges and universities have courses in conflict management these days that the kids can take. I'm always delighted to teach a course of that. I do at least one a year.

The NCAA actually also has a program called Step Up that works with athletes. It's not directly a conflict management program, but it has a lot of training in it that focuses on how to help others manage conflicts because young athletes are looked up to and they're often looked to to step in when an altercation occurs. It's a very good program supported by the NCAA that's on many campuses throughout the United States these days. So there's lots of help in schools that's taking place.

We need also to talk a bit about television and video and film because children just don't learn at home, in the neighborhood, and at school. They get a lot of that through the media. It can be frightening how many hours children spend looking at a screen on any given day. The average appears to be somewhere between three and four hours a day, and that can pose a difficult challenge. One of the things that has been looked at a lot is violence in television and film and what is the affect of that and does it incite kids, does it cause them to get more violent.

One of the things we can take heart from that's emerging from the research on this is that the vast majority of kids do not respond to those things by becoming more violent. However that same research shows us that a significant number of kids, it's a minority, but it's a significant number, and it includes girls just about equally as boys, will be induced to become more aggressive and some violent as a function of the violence they see in film and on television. Moreover in the research on video games, video games, normal kids they don't affect as much, but that minority those video games have an even greater effect on. So there's learning about how to handle conflict in a violence realm that's a little bit frightening. So those children are more susceptible.

The leading researchers on this argue that this evidence is very, very strong. There are some others that argue that it's not all that conclusive, but it certainly leans in that direction. Can we predict which kids are going to be more susceptible to those really harmful influences? We can't exactly, not very well. That's still a little murky, but it is very clear that kids who grow up in a family where the family itself, that environment includes violence or who associate with peers who are violent, will hook more into the violence they encounter in the media, especially those video games and they're going to be more affected, so that's the danger area to look at.

Researchers are learning all of that, but that's focused on violence. Researchers are also learning more about how the narratives in entertainment influence children, and that's an important area we ought to think about because it's wider than just a question of whether a kid is going to become violent or not. This research may be able to inform various policies on media and parents in terms of what they expose kids to. The broader significance here is the narratives about how issues are dealt with in the various fictional episodes that occur, television, film, especially. What are kids seeing here and how does that affect them?

Children learn about life and they act out some vicariously and that includes their interaction with the media that they're so exposed to. What they're constantly hearing are lessons through narrative stories that reinforce lessons that they learn and attend to. So early in life, what do they listen to in the media, this could be fairytales and books read to them by their parents, easy to get the good, positive lessons in those.

But early on most children are exposed to lots of television, videos, and movies and it's not just the violence or not violence, these narratives engage kids' imagination and every story involves the kind of situation where you have a main character who encounters some sort of an obstacle, something in the way, some sort of a conflict and the narrative moves on how that main character chooses to deal with that and what works out, how it gets to a good conclusion. It's very seldom in those narratives that what happens is the main character decides to pursue a win-win resolution and negotiates that and it works out.

You know why? That's really what we want to do, but it's kind of boring TV and movies. So the narratives don't go that way, there's more clash and there are devious means and there's manipulation and there are all kinds of other things that happen, and that's what the kids see and take in as lessons.

Then they see how that works out they're exposed to that and they draw conclusions from that.

So we really want to look at what the kids are learning. We want to reduce although we shouldn't even try to eliminate those things where conflict isn't resolved in a positive way. But we want to try to watch what the kids are watching and move it in a direction so they at least see some things where the conflict management strategy is more constructive. It's nice to watch shows along with the kids when we can, and talk with the kids about how conflict was handled and when it wasn't handled in a good way talk about that.

We want to try to expose our children to good stories, exciting stories if possible, in which conflict is handled in a constructive way and resolved with some kind of good will and negotiation. There's a list of these, a beginning list at least in the guidebook that you can turn to for this course. That's teaching children about conflict.

Let's move to a summary here. Whether and how much conflict management will improve in the future depends a whole lot on what we teach our children about conflict. Whether it improves in their individual lives depends a whole lot on what we teach them. That's really going to affect the quality of their lives as they move through. So if you're parents, what I hope you'll most take from this lecture is that there are basic actions and steps that we can take in terms of teaching our children about conflict.

The first one is this. We really need to be careful to model the interaction in general and the conflict management behaviors that we want our children to learn, and that's especially hard to do given that it may not be what we learned as little kids. We're trying to overcome our early learning and pass the better way onto our kids about modeling, an enormous challenge, but we can do it and the better we do it the better lessons the kids will learn.

The second thing is we need to spend some time teaching our kids about good conflict management skills. We need to teach them to express their feelings in terms of how they feel with I statements, not accusations, you statements about the other person. We need to teach them to listen to the other person without judging, to consider the other person's point of view, and the other person's feelings. We need to teach them to take responsibility for their part in the conflict and apologize when it's appropriate, hard to do, but we need to do it.

We need to teach them to invite the other person to work together with them for a win-win resolution, and if we can get them to do that and have some success, that'll be a lesson they'll hold on to and continue. We need to teach them to manage their emotions by not acting out but rather expressing them appropriately by talking about them as I statements and teach them too not to hold grudges. Those are all lessons we should teach our children.

The third thing we ought to do is make sure they get positive feedback at home when they handle conflict well. We need to honor that. Fourth thing is we need to pay attention to what they're learning about conflict in the neighborhood and at school, and try to help them understand those lessons and discriminate. We can work with them on that. Fifth, we need to monitor what the kids read, what they see on TV. We can't do a perfect job with this, but we've got to look and try and try to get some of it to be positive.

Sixth, we can also work with the children's school to establish some conflict management programs, those peer mediation programs could be in a lot more places than they are. This is a pretty daunting challenge I know that I'm asking you to do, but we really do have the opportunity because we know more about conflict management than our parents knew, and if we pass these gains along to the kids, they're going to have a better future, they're going to have a better life, and you know what, they may learn more than we were able to teach them and pass those lessons beyond onto their kids. So this is really about the future. We've got a job teaching our kids. That's the future of conflict management.

I've got an assignment for you, especially if you're a parent. Ask yourself what you learned about conflict from your family when you were little. Try to consider how early you learned that and how those lessons have affected your life and your conflict management as you've gone along. Then I want you to consider how you can demonstrate more constructive conflict management to the children. Try to come up with some specific things you can do, and act on those and do them and then how you can manage to help them manage conflict constructively. That's what I want you to do.

Let's talk about what's going to happen in our final lecture. We've been through the whole thing from start to finish and ended up in this lecture with teaching our children in the future. What I want to do now in Lecture 24 is to go back and kind of review the lessons we've learned. I want to compare what we knew back in 1950 and how things would've gone to what we know now and how we can do it better and how we need to do it better now. I also want to end by focusing on what it is we still need to learn, what the challenge is going forward from here with conflict.

Conflict Management—A Success in Progress
Lecture 24

Despite all that we can learn from the research and all the practices we have for better conflict management, I want to say this: Conflict remains a delicate art, and it's a major challenge.

In this lecture, we'll consider what knowledge and skills in conflict management we have today that were not available to us in 1950 when Morton Deutsch first gave us the idea of the win-win resolution. We'll then conclude the course by exploring some topics in conflict management that offer promise for future study.

Recall the three typical conflicts we looked at in Lecture 1: two roommates in conflict over noise in their apartment, the married couple who reached an impasse over whether the husband should take a job offer in another city, and the battles in a company over where to set the boundaries of sales districts. Back in 1950, the two roommates would probably have viewed their conflict through a lens of the other's character, and each might have concluded that she needed to endure the problem or work out a compromise. Today, the roommates would be more likely to view the problem as a matter of behavior to be negotiated.

The conflict between the married couple, Kate and Ken, is a little more complex. In 1950, Ken probably would have made his career choice, and the two would have moved. On one level, that's simpler, but it doesn't give Kate an equal part in the decision. Today, there's a much better chance that Ken and Kate would negotiate with more equality and try to take into account each other's perspectives. If needed, they might get professional help from a couples counselor. Even though the situation would be more complicated today, the couple would have a better shot at a win-win resolution.

In the third conflict, it's likely that back in 1950, Don, the salesman, would have made an appointment with his boss, Dale, to discuss a change in sales territories. It's also likely that Don would have had to cheerfully accept whatever decision Dale made or find another job. In our time, that issue would probably be addressed in a meeting with all the salespeople, and the group would work together to create territories everyone could agree on.

These examples show that we now have concepts and strategies we can use to negotiate better resolutions. Throughout my professional life, I've seen many instances where even incremental changes in the way conflicts are handled have made for happier employees and greater productivity. On one assignment at a state agency, I learned of the sincere apology made by the deputy director to a group of mailroom employees after she learned that she had badly misjudged their work ethic. On another occasion, I was asked to participate in working out a resolution between the state of California and the Environmental Protection Agency over verifying reductions in auto emissions. I worked with focus groups of stakeholders to brainstorm solutions that were later approved by both the state and the federal government.

As we become more willing to speak up for our individual interests, we bring more conflicts to the surface and make the process of handling conflict more complex.

Despite the extensive research conducted in conflict management since the 1950s, we still have much to learn. For example, dissemination of the knowledge we've gained is still limited. Further, as we become more willing to speak up for our individual interests, we bring more conflicts to the surface and make the process of handling conflict more complex. Thus, we need to better balance our needs for belonging and affection with our pursuit of individual interests and freedom. In our personal relationships, we need to learn to accept and become comfortable with the things that we can't change about others. We also need to learn more about how our children deal with conflict and how we can do a better job of teaching them. Finally, in looking at moral conflicts, we need to learn toleration and appreciation for the differences of others.

Let's close with 10 fundamental lessons you should take from this course: (1) Conflict is inherent in human interaction, but we can learn to manage it better; (2) we can achieve a win-win solution most of the time; (3) we need to report and take into account one another's perspectives; (4) we need to be aware of our multiple goals; (5) we have a better shot of achieving a win-win solution if the power between the parties is close to equal; (6) we need to work with a broad repertoire of conflict strategies; (7) we have useful processes and steps to follow in conflict negotiation; (8) our personal and professional relationships have important dynamics of their own; (9) we have to manage the aftermath of conflict; and (10) professional help is available if we need it.

Conflict points us to problems we need to solve and challenges us to fully encounter ourselves and others with whom we have relationships. We can't avoid conflict, and life would be less interesting without it. ∎

Assignment

1. How can you continue to improve your conflict management skills in your personal, professional, and community relationships?

Conflict Management—A Success in Progress
Lecture 24—Transcript

Today's world is radically different from the world of the mid-20th century when Morton Deutsch gave us the great breakthrough on the idea of win-win. Today what are we? We're globally connected; we have transcontinental communication that's absolutely instant; we have Internet access to almost any information we seek; we have immediate cell phone access to one another; we travel across continents in hours; our cars have computers in them to manage much of their operation. Our physical and material lives in many ways are quite beyond what we would have imagined back in 1950.

But our personal and relational lives are radically different too, they've changed in a great many important ways, some of which have to do with the managing of conflict, and those changes are harder to see. We don't have a picture of how our parents dealt with conflict the way we might have pictures of our father's cars. Relationships, the way we relate are more like the air we breathe; they're just there and we don't think about them.

Since Deutsch reported that most conflicts are not competitive, and they can be resolved with a win-win, I want us to note here they we've made major gains in the way couples and friends, and families, and work colleagues, and communities actually work through conflicts. What I want to do in this last lecture in the course is go back to those three examples that were typical conflicts that we talked about back in Lecture 1. I want to consider what knowledge and skills and what help we would have access to today that were not available back in 1950.

I want to observe that we actually need to be more skilled and have more help today in the managing of conflict because there are more voices at the table. There is more equality; there's more awareness of our individual interests and more permission to pursue them. The truth is that life is more complex today than it was back in 1950 and we need better conflict skills and more help. I'm going to conclude with a look at where we need to go from here, what we still need to learn.

So let's get started here. Let's go to those three examples. Remember what they were. Recall the example that we had. We started with two roommates sharing an apartment, one in graduate school, the other a working young professional, and the problem was the noise in the apartment bothering the graduate student. The second one was the married couple whose impasse of whether the husband should take a job offer in another city. And the third we took it to work and the battles in a company over where to set the boundaries of sales districts.

So let's look at those examples and see how they'd be different today from the way they were back then. Let's start with our roommates. How would they have viewed one another back in 1950 had this conflict arisen? As we begin to think about this some interesting observations arise. You know what Jane, the young working professional, would've probably just been a secretary and wouldn't have had a budding career of much back then and it's not very likely that Rebecca, our graduate student, would've been in graduate school. There were very few women in graduate school then whereas the majority of graduate students in the United States today are actually women. So things are very different.

But back in 1950 and some years after that, these two would probably have viewed each other as wrong, maybe even morally wrong or unreasonable in their positions. Each would view the conflict through a lens of the other's character or personality, that would've been much more likely back then unless they were just prescient and wise beyond their years. Having never heard of win-win, which they hardly would've heard of back in 1950, they'd have thought they needed to endure the problem with one another or at best work out a compromise.

Now how would that be different? Well some, but not all of course, would view the problem as a matter of behavior that could be negotiated. Where might they have learned this? They might've learned it at home today, young professionals. They might've learned it through participating in something like mediation programs in grade school or high school. They might've learned it in one of several college courses they might have taken. They might've listened to this course, you have. So there were a lot of places they might have learned it. So they might know today they'd be much more likely to know today how to deal with that conflict and be able to resolve it.

Let's tune in on our roommates Rebecca and Jane and see where they are with that now.

[Video start.]

> **Jane**: I'm really bad with noise. I grew up with four brothers and sisters, so it kind of came with the package. It didn't bother me in the dorms either—I could study almost anywhere.
>
> **Rebecca**: And I'm distracted by almost anything. Having Monday and Wednesday as quiet nights should work, but I may still have to ask you to turn down the TV sometimes.
>
> **Jane**: I'm okay with that. Anything else?
>
> **Rebecca**: Well, on weekends, I'll still need to study, but I guess I can do that at the library. Let's stick with it for a month and see how it goes. And then we can talk again and see if anything needs adjusting.
>
> **Jane**: Great. That was easier than I expected.

[Video end.]

It's better now. This is an example really that's a common student conflict that I hear from students at the university, especially from my students taking my conflict management course. They are people who are learning to live with one another as young adults and the problem of noise in the apartment is one of the most common things that they struggle over. There's lots of emotion involved. Somebody needs to study for a test. Somebody wants to have a good time. So it's there; one is frustrated and angry, the other wants to be able to relax.

You know what most of my college students do with this today? Of course they're in my conflict management course, but what they tend to do is take their cue from the course. They set out to negotiate it as a matter of behavior and look for a win-win. It's marvelous. I have them write papers applying what they're learning and I get this back in papers. What I get back is a success story very regularly and they come to me and talk to me and they tell me how easy it was. Success story, it works in most cases. Of course there actually are a few cases where what happens is they don't work it out, the other student won't cooperate and they part company at the end of that semester. But by and large this is a success story that tends to happen.

Let's go to our second example. That second example is a little more complex. Here we've got the married couple Kate and Ken in Chicago. That would've been far less likely to even happen back in 1950. If we think about then versus now in this conflict, he would probably have made his career choice, he might've consulted his wife a bit, but it would've been his choice about his career, and she would've gone along with him to Colorado. On one level that's more simple and on another level they're not both getting an equal part in that. It's simpler, but it's less likely to really get resolved.

Each would've worked to fulfill the roles that have been assigned to them that they thought were theirs. Each would've been a little less than fully satisfied. They might've even been resentful. There probably wouldn't have been anything like a marriage counselor who understood this kind of thing, who could've helped them work through it. Of course Kate probably wouldn't have had a career to work with so there wouldn't have been that equality. These two would probably have loved each other, lots of couples did back in the 1950s, many a wife moved with her husband to wherever his career took him and tried to so in good humor and many made that work. But there would've been distance and there would've been a challenge to that.

How would this work now if the two had this conflict? There's a much better chance now that each would explain to the other what their wishes and needs were. They would negotiate now with much more equality and try to take into account each other's perspectives. They'd be trying to find a solution now much more likely, at least, that would work for both. Thousands and thousands and thousands of married couples do this now every year. If needed they might very well know that they could get help from a couples or a marriage counselor or a mediator, someone with professional skills to help them through this and look for a win-win, and they might go and seek that help.

There's a whole lot less chance that Ken in this case would insist on moving to Colorado to take a job. It would be much more negotiable and a situation with much more equal power. That's the way it would come out today.

Remember in the example we had for today, Kate's personal power was greater because she had the career and the career edge taking place at this particular time. Today there's a much better chance that these two people will find a resolution that really is going to work well for both of them; even though it's more complicated today, they've got a better shot.

Let's think about an example of this. Let's go back now and check in on Ken and Kate and see how that works out.

[Video start.]

> **Ken**: Honey, take a look at this. It's with a company in Denver. You know how much I want to get out west.

> **Kate**: You know I can't leave Chicago right now. Not this year, maybe not next.

> **Ken**: I know. You need to stay put right now; I can't ask you to damage your career.

> **Kate**: But I don't want to keep you stuck in Chicago for life. What if you don't apply for this job, but we work on a long-term plan that lets us both get to where we want to go.

> **Ken**: Really? That'd be great. It won't be easy, but I think we can work it out.

Kate: Me too. And if not, I'm sure we can get some help.

[Video end.]

Ken and Kate, that example is kind of like what really did happen. I took this example from a couple that I happen to know. Their names are not really Ken and Kate and they didn't really live in Chicago, but the fundamentals of the story are taken right from the lives of my friends.

In the real world case that happened, the husband agreed that it would be harmful to interrupt his spouse's career at this time and that there would be more opportunities for him. She agreed that this situation with her career wasn't permanent and that she would be very willing to move with him at a time when it could be done without damaging her career.

So they worked that out, they got the help of a counselor to do it, and they set about doing it. They worked that out. It took four years to get around to where a move could be made, and during some of those years the Ken guy actually did chafe some. It wasn't all easy, but they stayed with it, worked it through and then what happened is four years later they actually did move out west. They moved to Colorado, nobody lives happily ever after exactly, but you know what, these two persons are happily married, they're happy with each other, they moved at a time when it was good for both of their careers and they both love where they live today. So that couple worked its thing out and it works very well today beyond what could've happened then.

Let's go to our third example. Example three here if you remember, we have Dale the sales manager and the salespersons Don and Pat. What their problem is is what should be the boundaries of the sales territories. How would this have looked back in 1950? Back then, the Don character, the salesman, who certainly would likely have been a man, and Pat, of course, would've been a man too in that instance back then, but having gotten his sales territory, if he was uncomfortable with it he would make a dutiful appointment with the boss and make his pitch for an adjustment, and if the boss agreed the boundaries would be reset. And if not, the Don character would've been required to cheerfully accept the assignment as it was or else go look for another job.

422

Pat of course wouldn't have been consulted, and Pat would probably have been a man. So that's another wrinkle for this thing back then. Finally, in the organization where they would've been working, there would not have been someone like a ombuds-person or anyone who could facilitate in an informal way to help them resolve the problem, no one really available to help them with the process.

Here in the 21st century, that issue is going to be a lot different. This issue today would much more likely be addressed in a meeting with all the salespersons present with the boss. Ideally that would be Dale's, the boss', first response when there was a question to convene a meeting of the sales staff. So let's check in on these people now and see how that conference is going.

[Video start.]

> **Dale**: All right. As the two of you know, I've been trying to rework the sales territory in a way that's efficient and relatively equitable. And that's proving to be a bit of a challenge. I'm figure we've got the best chance of getting it right if the three of us work together. Now, the final decision's mine, but I want input from the two of you. I want to see what we can work out.

> **Pat**: Okay. Sure.

> **Don**: All right.

> **Dale**: Okay, so here's what we've got so far …

[Video end.]

That's what would happen today more likely, not in every case, but if you've got a team leader who's really on top of this issue and knows what he's doing, that's more likely what would've happened. So things would be different today in all three of these examples than they would've been back in 1950. That's radically different; it's very different. Power here in this latest case is not equal, but it's much closer, and the power differences are much less extreme than they would be in 1950.

So this group would've met, they'd have created territories that they all agreed on. In some cases the boss would have to arbitrate and make the decision, but they would know that at the time. If the conflict proved intractable or difficult in many, many organizations there would be available an ombudsman or a mediator who could steer them toward a win-win resolution. So it's a better world in these ways today.

All of these folks in these examples, and you and I, have concepts that we can use to negotiate better resolutions. They are there in the concept of principle negotiation and the seven step process that I laid out for you in a great many of the examples that we've laid out. So these comparisons really illustrate that we have come a long way. At least the term win-win has spread all over the world. Remember the Russian president Medvedev after working the new treaty with President Obama declared that it was a win-win conversation. So we're beyond now where we were then in very significant ways.

My experience has documented this for me in a great many instances. I've been in positions where I could see this happen, both in my professional and my personal life. I've been able to work with dozens of organizations public and private, and profit and nonprofit, from bookstores to churches, to banks to government agencies. I've seen lots and lots of instances where these gains have taken place, where even incremental changes in the way conflicts are handled make for happier employees and greater productivity.

There are specific conflicts that occur and most of them really are very human, very immediate, some of them are small and personal, but all of them matter. I have some favorite instances among those things. One of my all time favorites is the conflict that I call the mailroom conflict that occurred.

In this instance I was actually working with a state agency and that agency, which was a very large one, I was working on building a new strategic plan and I was the facilitator for that process. We were doing stakeholder engagement and of course when you're engaging stakeholders, among the

424

most stakeholders are employees. So I was doing focus groups with various groups of employees. On the day this came to my attention I was doing a focus group with the mailroom staff, the group of folks, the very blue collar folks who worked in the mailroom who got the mail in and distributed and got stuff collected and sent out.

They filed into the room where I was supposed to meet with them and I was prepared to get their input, and all of them sat there stone faced and they were not going to talk. I couldn't get a response from them and I didn't know what was wrong. They just didn't want to talk to me, and they all looked grim. So I sat with them for a bit and finally I said you know what we've got two hours to sit here and this is going to get awfully long if nobody talks.

Then it came to me to say you know perhaps I can help you. What is the trouble here? Finally one of them broke the silence. It was a woman in her mid 50s, and she was a very strong blue collar woman who'd obviously done a lot of work outside of her time. She spoke up with a great emotional intensity and she told me a story of what had happened to several weeks earlier. What happened on that day several weeks earlier was that this crew came to work early because there was a big mailing that had to be gotten on a mail truck that left at 3:00. They showed up for work early by agreement. They worked straight through, they skipped their morning break, they skipped their lunch hour, they worked steadily and they hustled and they got everything together and they got everything on that truck just in time to have it go away.

They were thrilled with their own performance. They were successful. Do you know what happened after that? Just as they sat down then to have their lunch and laugh and talk about it, through the room came the newly appointed deputy director on her inspection of the place. The new deputy director saw these people all sitting around laughing and talking after 3:00 in the afternoon, this was not break time, this was not lunch time, they were sitting around eating. Her conclusion was these people are loafing on the job.

She chewed them all royally, told them they were all getting a letter of reprimand, went back to her office and drafted that letter of reprimand. They all got a letter and it went in their file. They were deeply wounded and nobody talked. When they finished telling me that story and the others had chimed in, I then went upstairs and went to see that deputy director and told them what they told me. She looked concerned, but I wasn't sure what she was going to do.

I found out later what she did do. What she did was have those letters taken out of their files, replaced them with a letter of commendation for what they had accomplished, made copies for them, had her own appointments canceled for the next day, showed up for work the next morning at 7:30 in the morning wearing blue jeans and said I need to apologize to you. I was wrong, I didn't understand what you had done. Here's a letter of commendation for each of you. I've had the letter or reprimand removed, and I want to stay here and work with you in this room all day today so I understand your work, and I'll never make that mistake again. A beautiful resolution that she made and a beautiful act of apology and a healing, the kind of thing that I've talked about all the way through, and she certainly had a loyal mailroom staff from then on.

There are some other examples I could point to, one that comes to mind is an example about the people working in a research laboratory. They were having terrible problems getting along and it was a pattern of behavior. I suspected that one member was a bully who was deliberately targeting people because that person seemed to be offending lots of folks. When we got the issues on the table, that person saw what she was doing and the effect on them, and we just negotiated ways for the others to signal her when she was being a problem. She copped to it, apologized, explained it, and those people got to working nicely together for a time after that, and they're still working well together.

There was a very large conflict that I got to deal with on one occasion back in 1990 when the federal Environmental Protection Agency had discovered that California was not reducing its pollution levels quite enough. The EPA, the Environmental Protection Agency was looking at how they might go about reducing the smog and was talking about requiring California to change the smog check system that the state had. In that state what happened is the smog check is not centralized, you can go to 900 and some odd different auto repair stations, get the check, and get your auto repaired if you need it at the same place.

The state had worked out these arrangements with all these private companies to do this, and now there was the possibility that they might be required to renege on that arrangement, and these private auto repair people who had invested money and had a business going to this might be cut out. There was a great deal of conflict about that. There was hostility. There was argument back and forth, what were we going to do. The state agency involved in dealing with them said you know what we've got to talk to these people and listen and see what can be worked out.

I got to go along with that and help facilitate the meetings with them to do it. We held discussion sessions in five different cities. We held a total of 128 different focus groups to listen to those people. And you know what happened? When we asked them to brainstorm together, to come up with potential solutions that might work, what emerged from those sessions across all those groups was a real consensus about what might work. It focused not so much on changing where you do them, the inspections for smog, but it focused on identifying the cars that are the biggest polluters and getting them off the road.

That information was taken to the governor's office, the governor's office took it to the legislature, and California argued successfully with the federal government, stuck by its guns, and a solution was found in what really had looked like it was going to be an intractable conflict. It was very nice to be present and witness that as it took place.

There're big organizations. I'm a small player in that. I've gotten to see little bits. I'm not one of the major ones, enormous important organizations, the Harvard Negotiation Project is one I've sort of tracked over the years because of just noticing that early work of Fisher and Ury, and they do a marvelous amount of work. They do it on a worldwide basis. They deal with disputes, large, small, everywhere from individuals to organizations, to communities, to governments. They work at this in a number of ways.

Most of the time when you've got mediators and organizations helping to resolve conflicts, those things are kept confidential so they don't make the news, especially they don't make the news when they work out well. But there are marvelous examples. There was one the Harvard Negotiation Project did that had to do with how they were going to deal with sewage and who was going to pay for it in New York, a huge problem. That one worked out very, very nicely.

Another one that they did had to do with cleaning up New York Harbor. They got multiple players in the game and they helped that work out. So in addition to the Harvard people there are other people. William Wilmot travels worldwide, I already told you that Ken Cloke travels worldwide. So there are a lot of people doing this, there's lots of help available, and there's lots of breakthroughs taking place with all that help. In the majority of those cases, the negotiations are confidential. So the gains are visible only to the people involved. But we do know they take place.

What I want to suggest with that is that I've told you a success story here in these 24 lectures. It's a lot better now than it was back in 1950. It's better in several ways, one is we know a lot more than we did and another is we have more help available, and it's because a lot of us are better at solving conflict and we'd better be because a lot of is more complex today than it might've been back in the 1950s.

So that's a real success story, but we're nowhere near finished. We're way out in the middle of this. We have a long way to go. There are some limitations that are huge that strike me when I think about this.

What are those limitations? One is that the dissemination of this knowledge is still really very, very limited. It has been a long time. It has been more than six decades since Deutsch made that initial discovery, but there are still people that don't know about it, lots of them. You're already helping. I hope you share what you learned in this course with friends and family and colleagues. But the information needs to get out and I'm very much interested in getting the information out as best we can.

Secondly, as we become more aware of willing to speak up for our individual interests, we actually surface more conflicts and we make it more complex. So we really need to get better at figuring out how we're going to balance the needs of the individual, for belonging and affection with our pursuit of our individual interests and freedom on the other. That's a tough one to balance. We've still got that tension and we've got a ways to go on figuring out how to just get that balancing right.

A third thing is that in our major longstanding relationships there are these perennial conflicts that surface periodically. We can get a lot better at learning to accept what it is about the other person that we're not going to change and how to handle that and be comfortable with it in the relationships that we have, more work to do on that one.

We also need to learn a whole lot more about how our children learn to deal with conflict, where they learn about it, and how we can do a better job of teaching them. We need to pass on what we've learned to them, and that's difficult. There are still some conflicts, especially those moral conflicts that we talked about, that seem to remain beyond the reach of our best efforts and beyond the methods of resolution. What do we do with those? We need to learn better how to know whether and when to stand up for a principle battle for a cause and when to go look for a win-win.

That's still a tough one. I've got great examples of success for you, but there's still a lot that faces us that we don't seem to know how to handle. So we really need to learn more and better ways to tolerate and appreciate the differences. We're still working on that. So there's a lot still to do relative to conflict. Finally though, despite all that we can learn from the research and all the practices we have for better conflict management, I want to say this. Conflict remains a delicate art and it's a major challenge.

Back at the beginning of this course, I said this is not going to be a gee whiz course where I can just give you a cookie cutter solution that you can always apply and be guaranteed to get the solution you want. We're more complicated than that and the other persons involved with us are more complicated than that. We can't always predict what they're going to do. This is a challenge for individuals. What we have to do is we've got to tailor how we do it to our individual personalities, take what we know and tailor it to that.

While we're wanting and needing to negotiate better together, we need to understand that we're going to keep creating conflicts as we work on it, and there are still going to be some that continue to confound us. So we're going to struggle with this stuff. We are going to keep struggling with it. So I want to strongly suggest—we've got a long way to go, we've come a long way, but we have a long way to go—as you struggle with it personally I want you to be patient with yourself and patient with the other persons.

I want to celebrate the progress we've made, but be humble about where we are. Perfection in conflict management is certainly beyond my capacity. I suspect it's beyond human capacity. So don't ask more of yourself than you can do.

Let's summarize. We know a whole lot more about the nature of conflict and about how to manage it now than we did all those decades ago. I want to bring this down to something like ten fundamental lessons from this course that I hope you're going to take with you and hold on to. They start from this understanding that conflict is inherent in human interaction. We can't avoid it, but we can do these things. One, we can learn to manage conflict better. You work at it, keep working at it, I do, but we can learn to manage conflict better.

Two, we can achieve a true win-win solution most of the time. That was Deutsch's great breakthrough, and he really helped us with that. Three, emotions and perspective are important internal facts. Emotions are mixed, they're complex, they're difficult. We need to report and take into account and we need to see them from each other's perspective. That's really important. Fourth, we're going to have a much better shot at achieving a win-win resolution if we're aware of our multiple goals. If we can ID those four types of goals that Wilmot and Hocker told us about, the Topic, the Relational, the Identity, and the Process goals, we've each got a much better shot at a win-win.

Fifth, we also have a better shot of achieving a win-win if the power between the parties is close to equal, the more equal it is, the better chance we've got and if we focus on our interests rather than taking positions and defending them and arguing. So work to equalize the power when you're in a conflict and you've got a better chance.

Six, we need a broad repertoire of conflict strategies. We don't want to be stuck with a few default styles. Remember what we said about conflict styles, avoidance, competition, compromise, accommodation, and collaboration. We need them all in your repertoire and we need to choose based on the situation. Seventh, we have these useful processes and ideas that we can follow, chief among those here would be Fisher and Ury's four principles and the suggestions that I gathered together for you in that seven step process that I laid out.

Eighth, I want you to notice here that close personal relationships and our professional relationships have dynamics of their own. They're important, they have a lot of conflict, and we've got to pay special attention to them. Ninth, often we're going to have to do clean-up and rebuilding and manage the aftermath. So we've got to do that forgiving and healing work that's necessary. And tenth, there's good professional help available for working through conflicts, counselors, mediators, ombudsmen, those kinds of people. So get help when you need it.

Ten really important lessons, and you know what about all these lessons, you don't have to get them all right. Any one or two of them you apply will help the odds. And these things apply in everyday life. That's what's so important to me about this course. So where are we? I can't wish that you would have no conflicts at all, conflicts are inherent in human interaction. Conflict does point at problems we need to solve. It challenges us to really fully encounter ourselves and fully encounter the other person to break through to deeper relationships, at least it makes life interesting.

But my goal for you in this course is that you'll work with the lessons that I've shared with you here. It's been my goal that the lessons that I've learned over the last 35 years, I've tried to share those. What I want you to do is keep working with these lessons, keep trying and keep learning. That's what I have to do.

Here's your last assignment in this course and it's also my greatest wish for you. What I want you to do is keep coming back to these lessons. Keep relearning them, keep getting better and better at managing conflict in your personal life, your professional life, and in your community life.

Glossary

adversary system: System of dispute resolution originating in ancient Greece, in which each disputant presents his or her claims and supporting evidence to a neutral third party, who then judges how the dispute should be settled.

arbitrator: A person with designated authority to hear and evaluate cases and render a binding or nonbinding decision on an issue between parties engaged in a dispute.

argumentation: The study and practice of how people reach conclusions through logical reasoning, that is, making claims based on premises. Argumentation includes debate and negotiation, which are concerned with reaching mutually acceptable conclusions.

BATNA: In principled negotiation, this term stands for "best alternative to a negotiated agreement." Each negotiator decides ahead of time what solution he or she will opt for if a negotiated agreement is unsatisfactory or fails.

conflict: An actual or perceived difference of some significance between two parties, each of whom perceives that the other party is interfering with his or her needs or desires. The instructor's short definition is "a discomforting difference."

conflict climate: The combination of organizational culture, organizational climate, and organizational policies and procedures that affects the way members manage conflict.

conflict goal: A desired outcome in a given conflict. Major types include topic, relational, identity, and process goals.

conflict management: Any and all actions people use in dealing (or not dealing) with a conflict, including resolution.

conflict resolution: A process leading to a recognized outcome of a conflict—a negotiated agreement or a unilaterally imposed solution.

conflict styles: Default strategies for managing conflicts that people tend to employ across different situations.

contract: A concrete, stated agreement between conflicting parties on what each party will do to solve a conflict and for which each party can be held responsible.

critical communication context: A situation in which a distressing, destabilizing event creates a "critical context" among relational partners; in this context, effective communication becomes simultaneously much more important and much more difficult.

dysfunctional conflict strategy: A conflict strategy that yields unwanted side effects that may exceed its benefits.

empathy: The skill of being able to understand what another person is experiencing from his or her perspective; the ability to put oneself in another's shoes.

family meeting: A scheduled time set aside with a structured agenda and ground rules to promote meaningful communication, encouragement, cooperation, joint decision-making, and problem-solving among all family members.

field theory: Theory developed by Kurt Lewin, which holds that human behavior is a function of both an individual's psychological field, or "lifespace," and the social environment at the time the behavior occurs.

forensic reasoning: Observing and documenting the facts in a given case and deciding how the facts relate to an established standard or rule.

fractionation: A useful conflict management technique that consists of breaking or "chunking " large conflicts into smaller parts and dealing with the parts separately.

fundamental attribution error: The common tendency to assume that the behavior of others stems primarily from personal character traits rather than the situation at hand. The "actor-observer bias" includes the opposite tendency, that is, to explain our own behavior as primarily the result of the current situation rather than our character.

game theory: A mathematical method for analyzing how people make decisions in situations involving competition and conflict. Involves choices in which each party may gain or lose, depending on the others' choices.

interests: Reasons underlying a participant's stance or position in a negotiation.

issue: A matter of concern that is unsettled or in dispute between two parties.

lens model of conflict interaction: A model illustrating that each party in a conflict has a particular view of himself or herself, the other person, and the relationship; all of these combine to form one's perception of the conflict. These views filter reality and are always distorted to some degree.

mediator: A person who is trained to act as a neutral third party and who helps disputants, with their consent, negotiate a mutual agreement among themselves, seeking win-win solutions whenever possible.

moral conflict: A conflict between parties who are locked into opposition because they are deeply committed to different moral orders and beliefs and do not share a common standard by which to settle their differences.

negotiation: A process of achieving agreement or resolving disputes through discussion.

ombudsman: A person appointed to act as an informal, neutral, independent, and confidential intermediary to help solve problems or manage conflicts.

organizational climate: Members' collective perception of how it feels to work and live in a particular organization.

organizational culture: Deep, pervasive, usually unspoken code that governs the way things are done in an organization and its overall atmosphere and determines what ideas and behavior are considered right or wrong, important or unimportant, and acceptable or unacceptable.

perception: The process of observing and assigning meaning to the things we see.

perspective-taking: Adopting a viewpoint that considers how events might look and feel to the other person.

position: A statement of what a negotiator wants or needs.

power currencies: Various sources of power that may be used to influence outcomes of social interactions, originally introduced by French and Raven in 1959.

principle of noncontradiction: Aristotle's law stating that two contradictory statements cannot both be true at the same time; one of the two must be false.

punctuation: The way each party perceives and defines the chain of events in a conflict. Each party tends to punctuate events in such a way that he or she appears to be reacting to the behavior of the other party. Disagreement about how to punctuate the sequence of events is at the heart of many conflicts. For example, I nag because you withdraw; I withdraw because you nag.

reframing: Finding a new, constructive way to look at a conflict issue through a different lens or "frame," with the goal of changing perceptions and positions from fixed and negative to more flexible and positive.

relational dialectics: Opposing tensions that result from conflicting emotional needs of relational partners; such tensions are constantly in flux and affect couples' communication patterns.

rhetoric: The art of using language to communicate effectively. Aristotle defined rhetoric as the art of finding all the means of persuasion in any given situation.

rule or norm of reciprocity: The universal social expectation that people will respond to each other in kind—responding to a positive action with another positive action and responding to a negative action with another negative action. This norm can be a powerful factor in conflict escalation and de-escalation.

Sophist: In ancient Greece, a member of a class of roving teachers of philosophy and rhetoric who taught their students to persuade or convince others.

triangulation: Drawing a third party into a conflict instead of directly addressing the other conflict party.

win-win solution: A conflict solution in which the outcome is favorable for both parties.

workplace bullying: Repeated mistreatment of a targeted individual characterized by disruptive acts that threaten the individual's emotional and/or physical health and career.

XYZ formula: John Gottman's useful formula for using "I" statements and avoiding criticism of the other person when communicating during a conflict. Usually stated as: "In situation X, when you do Y, I feel Z."

Biographical Notes

Cloke, Kenneth: An internationally recognized mediator, facilitator, arbitrator, attorney, teacher, speaker, and author. He is director of the Center of Dispute Resolution, which is a multidisciplinary, multicultural association of professionals. Cloke specializes in helping parties resolve complex conflicts in community and workplace settings.

Deutsch, Morton: Considered the founder of modern conflict management theory and practice. Deutsch received his M.A. from the University of Pennsylvania (1940) and his Ph.D. (1948) in social psychology from the Massachusetts Institute of Technology. Studying under Kurt Lewin, he focused in his Ph.D. dissertation on the question of whether conflicts were necessarily competitive situations and found that they were not. To the contrary, he discovered that most conflicts could be resolved in a way that enabled both parties to "win." Deutsch is a professor emeritus at Columbia University, where he founded the International Center for Cooperation and Conflict Resolution. He has authored many articles and several books on conflict management, including the *Handbook of Conflict Resolution: Theory and Practice* (2000), and has received numerous awards for his research.

Fisher, Roger: Professor of law emeritus at Harvard Law School and former director of the Harvard Negotiation Project. Fisher served in World War II and, after the war, helped to administer the Marshall Plan in Paris and Washington, DC. He practiced law in Washington and served as a consultant to the Department of Defense. In addition to *Getting to Yes*, Fisher has authored seven other books on conflict management. He originated the award-winning television series *The Advocates* and consults with individuals, organizations, and governments on conflict management.

Gottman, John: Well known for his groundbreaking research on marital stability, Gottman is a professor of psychology emeritus at the University of Washington and currently heads the nonprofit Relationship Research Institute. He has translated much of his research into readable, practical guides for married couples. Two of his most interesting books are *The Seven Principles of Making a Marriage Work* and *The Relationship Cure.*

Kilmann, Ralph: A consultant and author of 15 fifteen books and more than 100 articles on organizational design and conflict management. Kilmann taught for some 30 years in the Graduate School of Business at the University of Pittsburgh. He is perhaps best known for his work, along with Kenneth Thomas, on the Kilmann-Thomas instrument for assessing five conflict styles.

Lewin, Kurt (1890–1947): One of the pioneers of modern social psychology and applied psychology. After growing up and being educated in Germany, Lewin emigrated to the United States in 1933 and became a citizen in 1940. In his work at Duke University and the Center for Group Dynamics at MIT, he developed foundations for the study of group dynamics and human motivation and influenced Fritz Perls and Abraham Maslow, as well as Morton Deutsch.

Thomas, Kenneth W.: Has taught as a professor of management at UCLA, Temple University, and the University of Pittsburgh. He focuses on building tools to improve motivation and work performance. Along with Ralph Kilmann, Thomas developed the concept of five conflict styles and the instrument for assessing an individual's conflict styles.

Ury, William: A former professor at Harvard Business School and a founder of the Harvard Negotiation Project. Working with the Carter Center of Emory University, Ury continues to serve as a mediator and advisor to governments and organizations around the world. He served as consultant to the White House on establishing nuclear risk reduction centers in Washington and Moscow. Ury is the author of five books other than *Getting to Yes*, the most recent of which is *Getting Past No: Negotiating with Difficult People.*

Wilmot, William: Author of *Artful Mediation* and co-author of *Interpersonal Conflict* and *Innovation: The Five Disciplines for Creating What Customers Want*. Wilmot serves as a teacher, consultant, facilitator, and coach. In his worldwide consulting practice, he works with organizations of all sizes on innovation, team development, conflict management, and mediation.

Bibliography

Amador, X. F. *I'm Right, You're Wrong, Now What? Break the Impasse and Get What You Need.* New York: Hyperion Books, 2008. Offers sound strategies for overcoming an impasse to reach a solution.

Baxter, L. A., and B. Montgomery. *Relating: Dialogues and Dialectics.* New York: Guilford Press, 1996. Provides a full explanation of the theory of relational dialectics and its applications.

Begin, Menachem. "Nobel Lecture." December 10, 1978. Nobelprize.org. http://nobelprize.org/nobel_prizes/peace/laureates/1978/begin-lecture.html. Informative and deeply moving.

Bercovitch, J., V. A. Kremen, and I. W. Zartman. *The Sage Handbook of Conflict Resolution.* Los Angeles; London: SAGE, 2009. A comprehensive anthology describing recent research and theory in the field of conflict resolution.

Blake, R., and J. S. Mouton. *The Managerial Grid.* Houston, TX: Gulf Publishing, 1994. A recent printing of the classic work on management styles from which Kilmann and Thomas drew for their work.

———. *Overcoming Group Warfare.* Boston: Harvard Business Review Case Services, 1984. An excellent book about resolving intergroup conflicts.

Cloke, K. *Conflict Revolution: Mediating War, Evil, Injustice, and Terrorism.* Santa Ana, CA: Janis Publications USA, 2008. A strong argument for having skilled mediators help in addressing major moral conflicts and a detailed explanation of the assistance provided by mediators.

———. *Mediating Dangerously: The Frontiers of Conflict Resolution.* San Francisco: Jossey-Bass, 2001. A great book for helping us think more boldly about conflict management.

Cloke, K., J. Goldsmith, and W. Bennis. *Resolving Conflicts at Work: Eight Strategies for Everyone on the Job*. Rev. ed. San Francisco, CA: Jossey-Bass, 2005. The best overall book I know for managing conflict in organizations.

Cupach, W. R., D. J. Canary, and B. H. Spitzberg. *Competence in Interpersonal Conflict*. 2nd ed. Prospect Heights, IL: Waveland Press, 2009. A superior text emphasizing the importance of communication competence in conflicts.

Damasio, A. R. *Descartes' Error: Emotion, Reason, and the Human Brain*. New York: Putnam, 1994. An important, thoughtful book that helps us understand how emotion relates to reason.

——. *Looking for Spinoza: Joy, Sorrow, and the Feeling Brain*. Orlando, FL: Harcourt, 2003. A followup to *Descartes' Error* on the nature of feelings.

Deal, T. E., and A. A. Kennedy. *The New Corporate Cultures: Revitalizing the Workplace after Downsizing, Mergers, and Reengineering.* New York: Perseus Publishing, 1999. A book that had significant impact during the 1980s, bringing attention to the nature and influence of organizations' cultures.

Deming, W. E. *Out of the Crisis.* Cambridge, MA: MIT Center for Advanced Engineering, 1986. Describes and argues cogently for the author's systems theory of management.

Deutsch, M. *The Resolution of Conflict: Constructive and Destructive Processes*. New Haven, CT: Yale University Press, 1973. A classic work summarizing Deutsch's research and theory.

Deutsch, M., P. T. Coleman, and E. C. Marcus. *The Handbook of Conflict Resolution: Theory and Practice*. 2nd ed. San Francisco, CA: Jossey-Bass, 2006. A comprehensive advanced introduction to social psychology theory about conflict at all levels, from interpersonal to international.

DeVito, J. *The Interpersonal Communication Book*. 10th ed. Boston: Allyn and Bacon, 2003. A clear basic text on interpersonal communication.

Particularly recommended for this course are Parts 1 and 2, especially chap. 5, "Listening."

Dues, M. "Managing Conflict." In M. Dues and M. Brown, *The Practice of Organizational Communication.* Boston: McGraw-Hill Primus, 2001. Describes principles and processes, as well as the manager's role, in effective organizational conflict management.

————. *The Pursuit of Probable Truth: A Primer on Argument.* New York: Pearson Custom Publishing, 2008. A brief, accessible guide to sound argument.

Dues, M., and M. Brown. *Boxing Plato's Shadow: An Introduction to the Study of Human Communication.* New York: McGraw-Hill, 2004. Introduces the reader to the history, research methods, and value of the academic discipline of communication.

Dues, M., M. Brown, and M. Peters. "Critical Communication Contexts Following Trauma." *Psychiatric Times*, 16(6), 1999, pp. 48–51.

Fisher, R., and S. Brown. *Getting Together: Building Relationships as We Negotiate.* New York: Penguin Books, 1989. An accessible guide to building and maintaining the kinds of relationships in which conflict is handled constructively.

Fisher, R., and D. Shapiro. *Beyond Reason: Using Emotions as You Negotiate.* New York: Viking, 2005. An important followup to *Getting to Yes* that focuses on how to manage emotions in the negotiation process.

Fisher, R., W. Ury, and B. Patton. *Getting to Yes: Negotiating an Agreement without Giving In.* 2nd ed. London: Arrow Business Books, 1997. A newer version of the seminal book about reaching mutually acceptable agreements in personal and professional disputes.

Fitzell, S. G. *Free the Children! Conflict Education for Strong, Peaceful Minds.* Gabriola Island, BC, Canada; Stony Creek, CT: New Society

Publishers, 1997. Offers an effective conflict education curriculum for teaching nonviolence and peacemaking to children in grades K–12.

Folger, J. P., M. S. Poole, and R. K. Stutman. *Working through Conflict: Strategies for Relationships, Groups, and Organizations*. 6th ed. Boston: Pearson Education, 2009. An excellent general text on conflict management.

French, J., and B. Raven. "The Basis of Social Power." In D. Cartwright and A. Sander, eds., *Group Dynamics*, 2nd ed. New York: Harper and Row, 1960. A clear description and explanation of the five "power bases" identified by French and Raven.

Gerth, H. H., and C. W. Mills, trans. and eds. *From Max Weber: Essays in Sociology*. New York: Oxford University Press, 1946 and 1973. Presents Weber's classic theory of "bureaucracy," which became the centerpiece of classical management theory.

Goleman, D. *Emotional Intelligence: 10th Anniversary Edition; Why It Can Matter More Than IQ.* New York: Bantam Books, 2006. A newer edition of the first book on the importance of understanding and mastering emotions in social interactions.

Gottman, J. M., and J. DeClaire. *The Relationship Cure: A Five-Step Guide to Strengthening Your Marriage, Family, and Friendships*. New York: Three Rivers Press, 2001. An excellent practical, research-based communication guide for couples.

Gottman, J. M., J. DeClaire, and D. Goleman. *Raising an Emotionally Intelligent Child: The Heart of Parenting*. New York: Simon and Schuster, 1998. An important guide for parents to teach children how to recognize and manage their emotions.

Hall, L., ed. *Negotiation: Strategies for Mutual Gain. The Basic Seminar on the Program of Negotiation at Harvard Law School*. Newbury Park, CA: Sage, 1993. An excellent collection of readings by leading thinkers in the fields of conflict resolution and negotiation.

Harvard Business School Press. *Harvard Business Review on Negotiation and Conflict Resolution.* Boston: Harvard Business School Press, 2000. A selection of valuable writings about negotiation and managing conflict in business organizations.

Jacoby, S. *The Age of American Unreason.* New York: Pantheon Books, 1994. Makes a strong case for the need for individual effectiveness in making and evaluating rational arguments.

Kellett, P. M., and D. G. Dalton. *Managing Conflict in a Negotiated World: A Narrative Approach to Achieving Dialogue and Change.* Thousand Oaks, CA: Sage Publications, 2001. An interpretive approach to understanding and improving conflict experiences in different contexts.

Kipnis, D. *The Power Holders.* Chicago: University of Chicago Press, 1976. Presents a straightforward description of the sources of power.

Knapp, M. L., and A. L. Vangelisti. *Interpersonal Communication and Human Relationships.* 6th ed. Boston: Allyn and Bacon, 2008. An excellent general text on interpersonal communication, this recent work contains a full description of Knapp's model of relational stages.

Lakoff, G., and M. Johnson. *Metaphors We Live By.* Chicago: University of Chicago Press, 2003. A recent edition of a valuable book about the influence of metaphors on our thoughts and actions.

Leavitt, Michael. Speech to the Western Governors' Association at the Plenary Session of Shared Environmental Doctrine. June 29, 1988. http://www.westgov.org/wga/initiatives/enlibra/leavitt_speech.PDF. Leavitt explains the challenges involved in making decisions about environmental conflicts and describes the basic outlines of what became the Enlibra Principles.

Lerner, H. *The Dance of Anger.* New York: HarperCollins, 1997. A sound and readable self-help book on sustaining strong relationships by using anger constructively to work through conflicts.

Bibliography

Levine, S. *Getting to Resolution: Turning Conflict into Collaboration*. 2nd ed. San Francisco: Berrett-Koehler Publishers, 2009. A very readable book about how to resolve conflicts collaboratively for lasting solutions.

Lewin, K. *Resolving Social Conflicts*. New York: Harper and Row, 1948. An early work on conflict management, connecting the discipline with field theory.

Mayo, G. E. *The Human Problems of an Industrialized Civilization*. Chicago: Scott, Foresman, 1933; paperback edition, 2007. Presents the results of Mayo's classic Hawthorne studies and offers the first explanation of his human relations theory of management.McCorkle, S., and M. J. Reese. *Mediation Theory and Practice*. Boston: Pearson, 2005. Provides a sound guide to mediating, including explanations of underlying theories and research, as well as practical guidelines and suggestions.

Mnookin, R. H. *Bargaining with the Devil: When to Negotiate, When to Fight*. New York: Simon and Schuster, 2010. A thoughtful book on how to confront those we consider to be harmful adversaries.

Morrill, C. *The Executive Way: Conflict Management in Corporations*. Chicago: University of Chicago Press, 1996. An exceptionally well researched study, shedding considerable light on the conflict management styles of top executives.

Neuman, M. G., and P. R. Bashe. *Helping Your Kids Cope with Divorce the Sandcastles Way*. New York: Times Books, 1998. A compassionate, practical book for divorcing parents about communicating with children and helping them cope.

Notarius, C., and H. Markman. *We Can Work It Out: How to Solve Conflicts, Save Your Marriage, and Strengthen Your Love for Each Other*. New York: Berkley Publishing Group, 1994. An outstanding book about effective argument in close personal relationships.

Patterson, K., J. Grenny, R. McMillan, and A. Switzler. *Crucial Confrontations: Tools for Resolving Broken Promises, Violated Expectations, and Bad Behavior*. New York: McGraw-Hill, 2005. An excellent resource with practical strategies for handling complicated conflicts at home and at work.

————. *Crucial Conversation Tools for Talking When Stakes Are High*. New York: McGraw-Hill, 2002. A valuable guide for communicating well when the outcomes are important.

Pearce, W. B., and S. W. Littlejohn. *Moral Conflict: When Social Worlds Collide*. Thousand Oaks, CA: Sage Publications, 1997. An important text about the challenges of dealing with moral conflict.

Peters, T., and R. Waterman. *In Search of Excellence*. New York: Random House, 1982. A bestselling book for managers and leaders that is still a valuable read for anyone with management responsibilities.

Richards, I. A. "Communicating between Men: The Meaning of Language." In Heinz von Foerster, ed., *Cybernetics: Circular, Causal, and Feedback Mechanisms in Biological and Social Systems*. New York: Josiah Macy, Jr., Foundation, 1952. Describes Richards's theory of the "four critical points of view" from which each communication is heard and interpreted. Dues translates this concept as "four messages" that are sent and received in every communication.

Sadat, Anwar. "Nobel Lecture." December 10, 1978. Nobelprize.org. http://nobelprize.org/nobel_prizes/peace/laureates/1978/al-sadat-lecture.html Informative and deeply moving.

Satir, V. *The New Peoplemaking*. Palo Alto, CA: Science and Behavior Books, 1988. An early classic about how communication affects family members and processes.

Segrin, C., and J. Flora. *Family Communication*. Lea's Communication Series. Mahwah, NJ: Lawrence Erlbaum Associates, 2005. A comprehensive text describing family communication research and theory.

Bibliography

Senge, P. *The Fifth Discipline: The Art and Practice of the Learning Organization.* New York: Doubleday, 2006. A clear and useful guide for applying a systems approach to management and leadership.

Tannen, D. *You Just Don't Understand: Women and Men in Conversation.* New York: Harper, 2007. A practical, research-based book about gender differences in communication and perception.

Thomas, K. W., and R. Kilmann. "Developing a Forced-Choice Measure for Conflict Handling Behavior: The MODE Instrument." *Educational and Psychological Measurement*, 37, 1997: pp. 390–395. This article explains the research methods involved in identifying the five conflict styles and in creating the questionnaire used to assess the conflict styles of individuals.

Ury, W. *Getting Past No: Negotiating in Difficult Situations.* New York: Bantam Books, 1993. A helpful followup to *Getting to Yes*, offering practical strategies for overcoming barriers.

———. *The Power of a Positive No: Save the Deal, Save the Relationship and Still Say No.* Bantam Dell Publishing Group, 2007. A worthwhile book about saying no gracefully and constructively.

———. *The Third Side: Why We Fight and How We Can Stop.* New York: Penguin Books, 2000. A practical book about acting as a third party between people and groups.

———, ed. *Must We Fight? From the Battlefield to the Schoolyard: A New Perspective on Violent Conflict and Its Prevention.* San Francisco, CA: Jossey-Bass, 2002. Presents important research and recommendations for mobilizing communities to stop or prevent individual and group violence.

Vangelisti, A. "Messages That Hurt." In W. Cupach and B. Spitzberg, eds., *The Dark Side of Communication.* Hillsdale, NJ: Erlbaum, 1994. Documents and explains the harm we can do with words.

Watzlawick, P., J. B. Bavelas, and D. D. Jackson. *Pragmatics of Human Communication: A Study of Interactional Patterns, Pathologies, and*

Paradoxes. New York,: Norton, 1967. A classic, groundbreaking text on unhealthy interaction patterns and cycles in close personal relationships.

Wilmot, W. W., and J. L. Hocker. *Interpersonal Conflict*. 8th ed. Boston: McGraw-Hill, 2010. The best overall text I know of on interpersonal conflict. Clear and easy to read.